RUN ON YOUR NEW LEGS 3

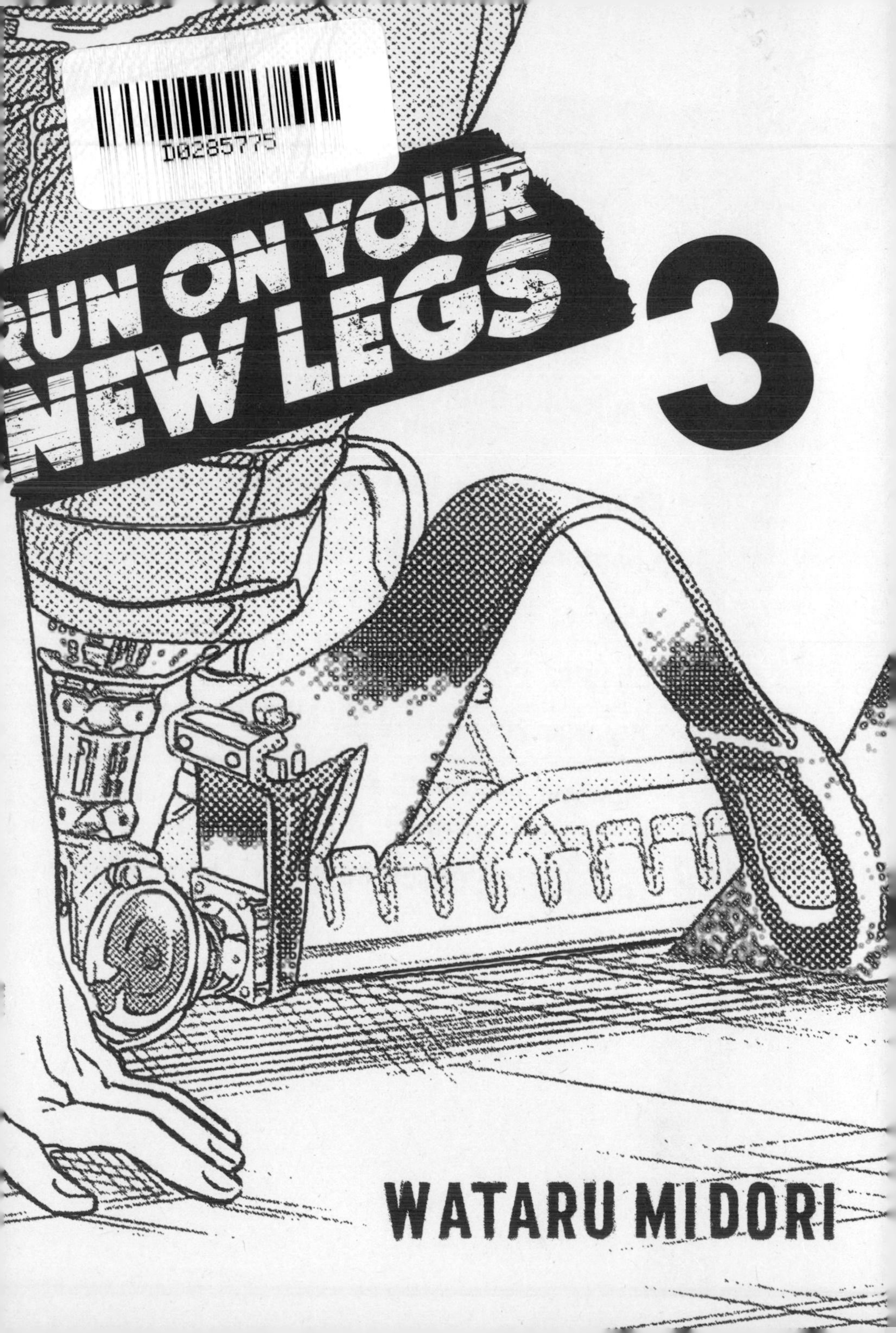

WATARU MIDORI

TABLE OF CONTENTS

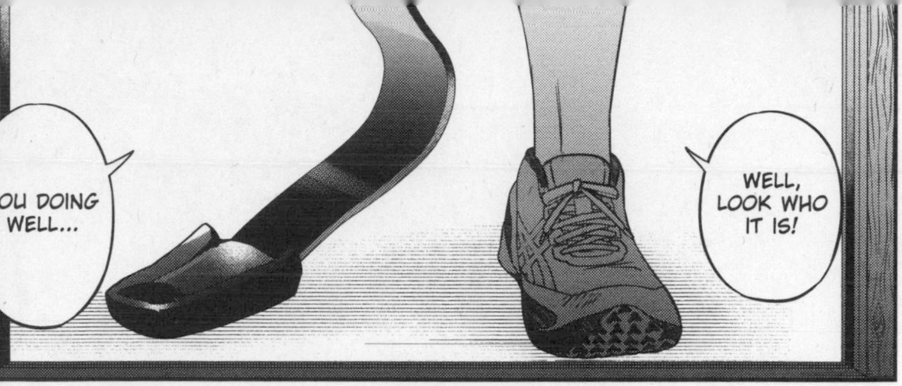
WELL, LOOK WHO IT IS!
YOU DOING WELL...

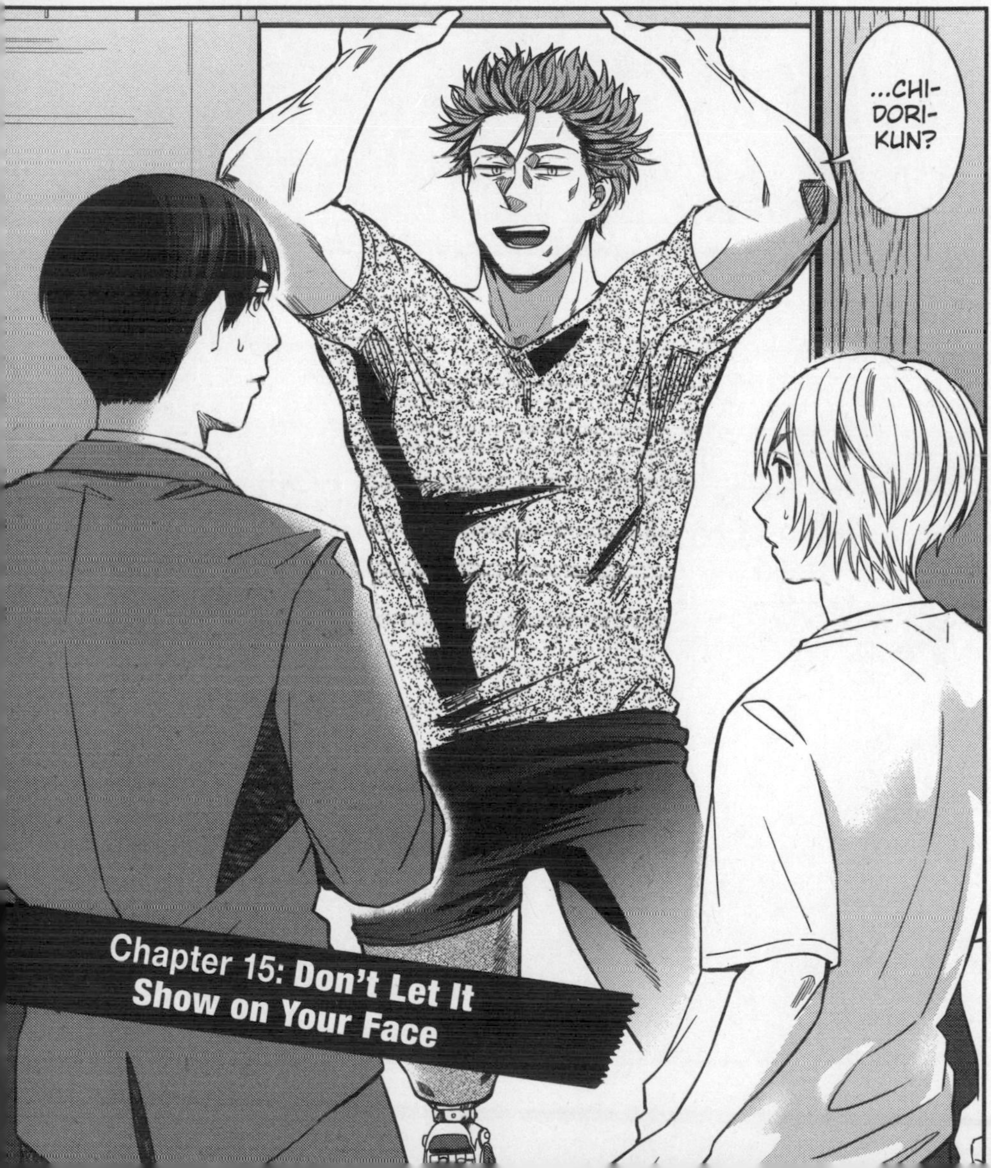
...CHI-DORI-KUN?
Chapter 15: Don't Let It Show on Your Face

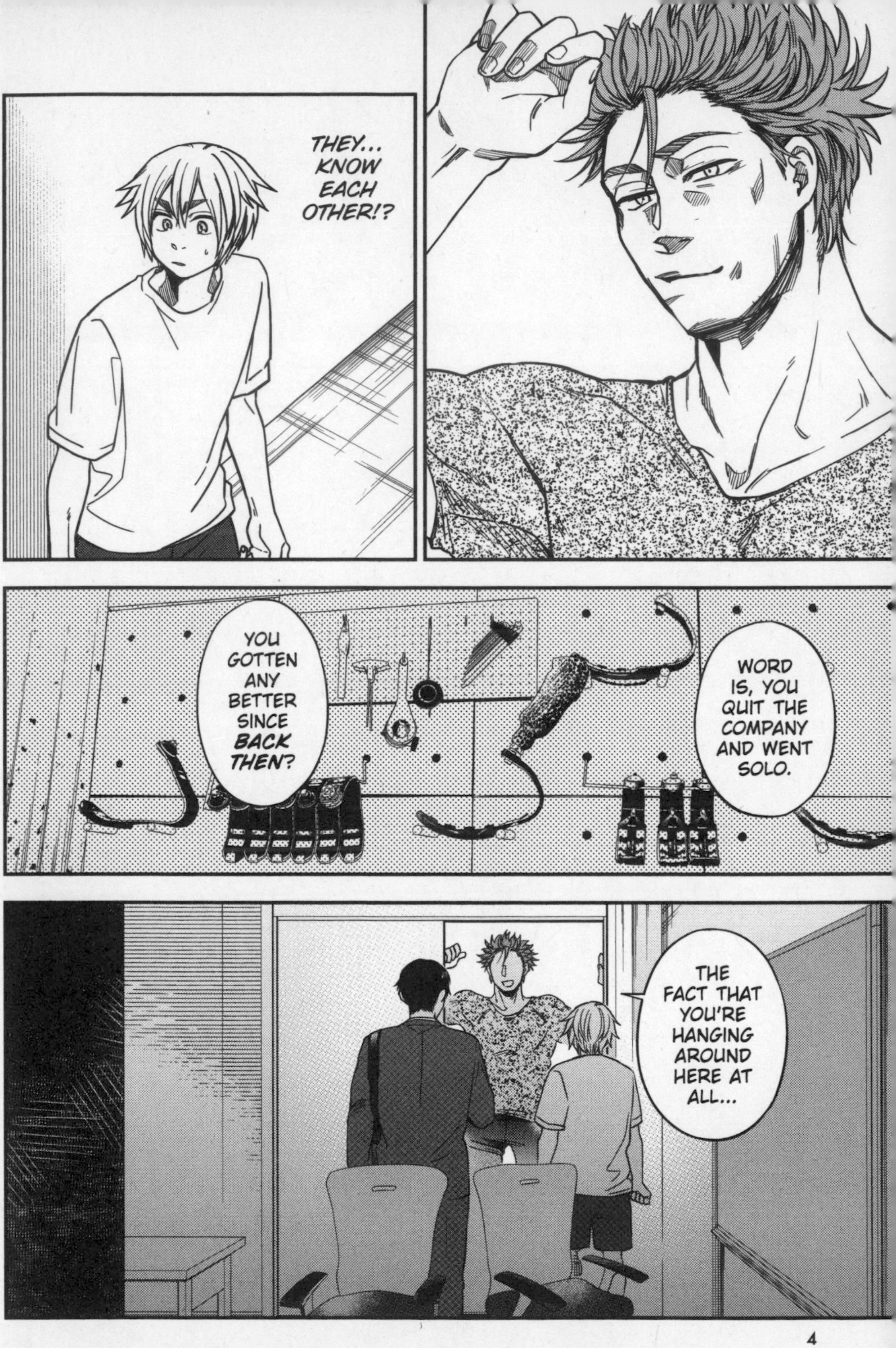
THEY... KNOW EACH OTHER!?
WORD IS, YOU QUIT THE COMPANY AND WENT SOLO.
YOU GOTTEN ANY BETTER SINCE *BACK THEN*?
THE FACT THAT YOU'RE HANGING AROUND HERE AT ALL...

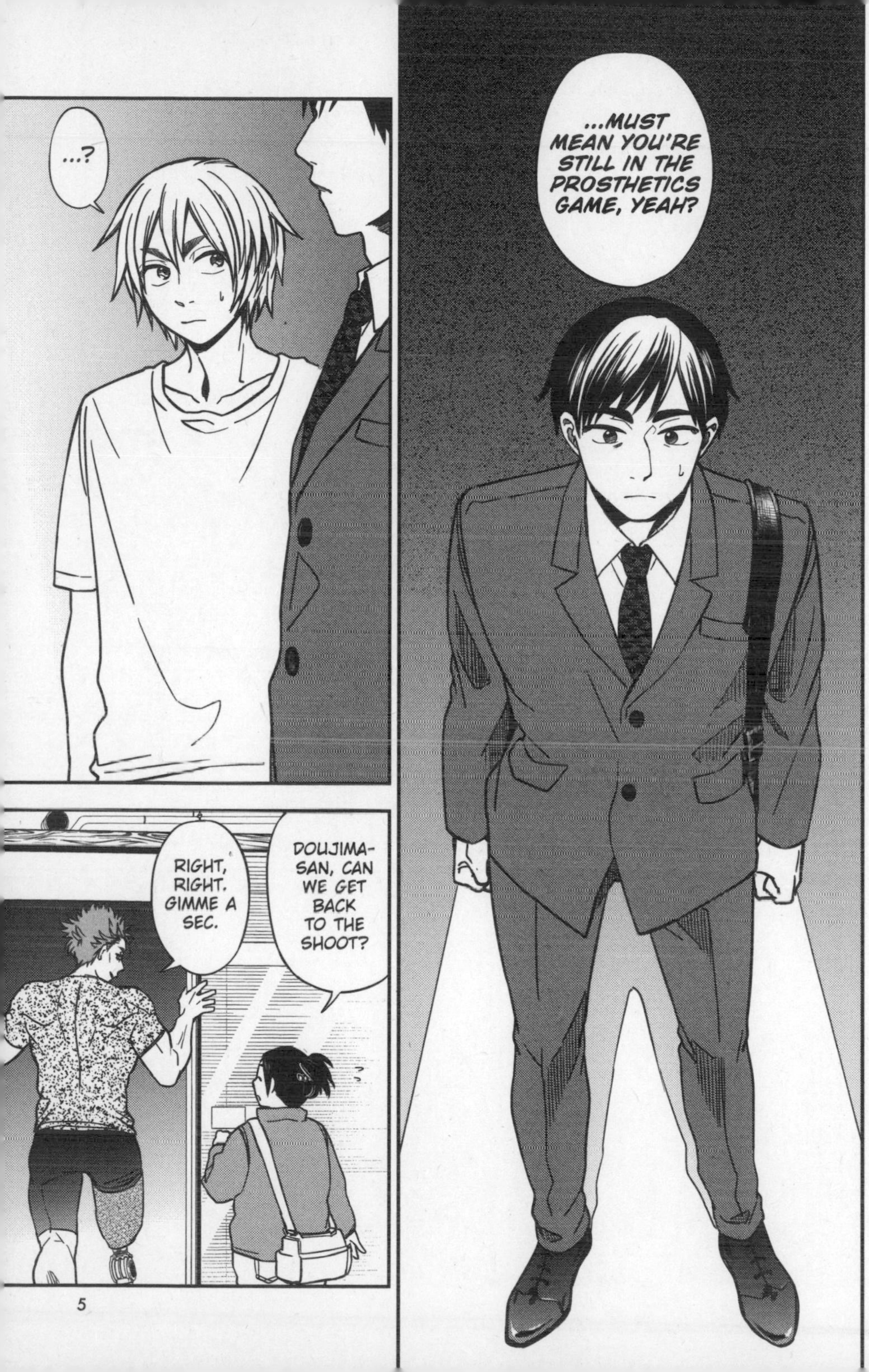
...MUST MEAN YOU'RE STILL IN THE PROSTHETICS GAME, YEAH?
...?
DOUJIMA-SAN, CAN WE GET BACK TO THE SHOOT?
RIGHT, RIGHT. GIMME A SEC.

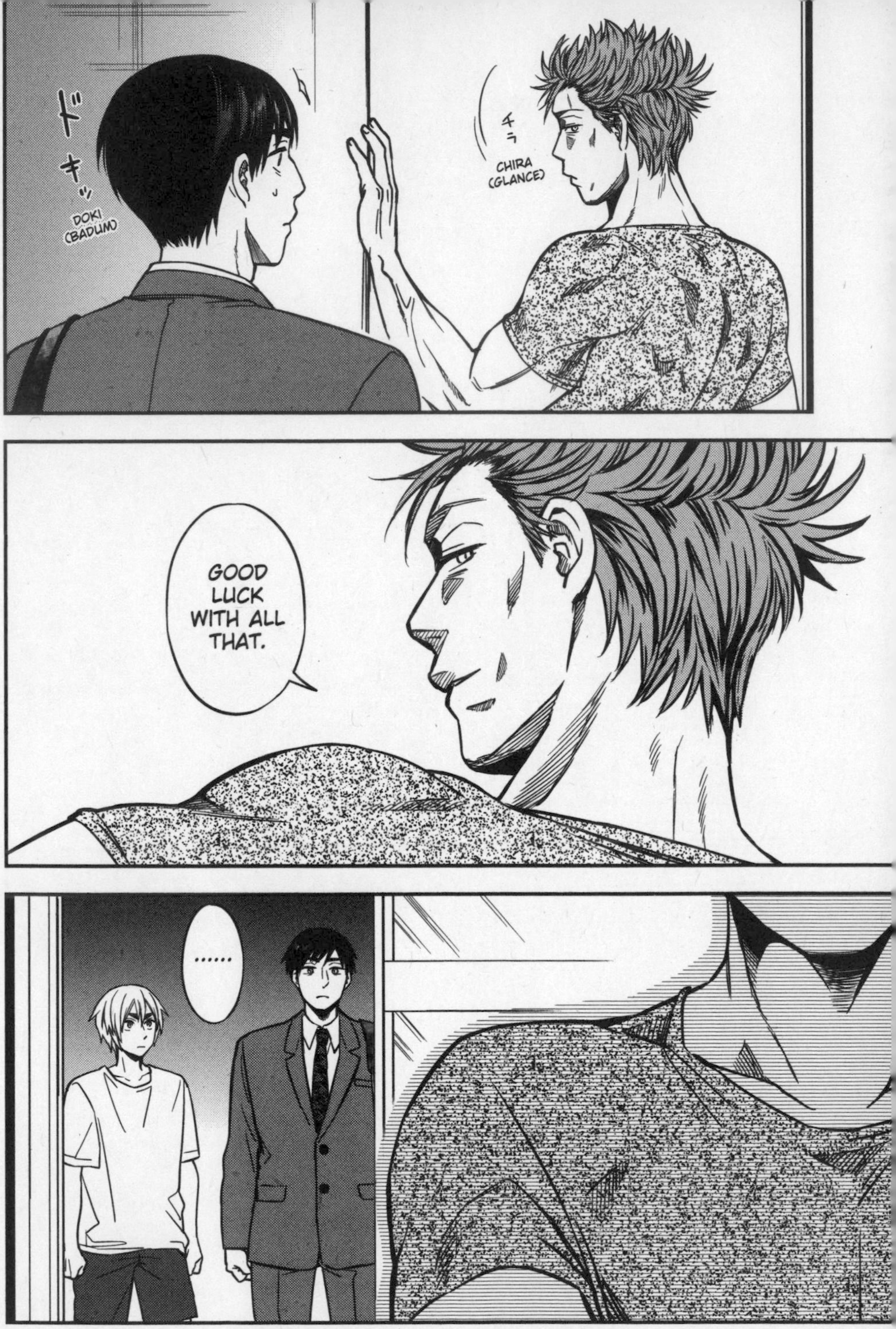
チラ
CHIRA (GLANCE)
ドキッ
DOKI (BADUM)
GOOD LUCK WITH ALL THAT.
......

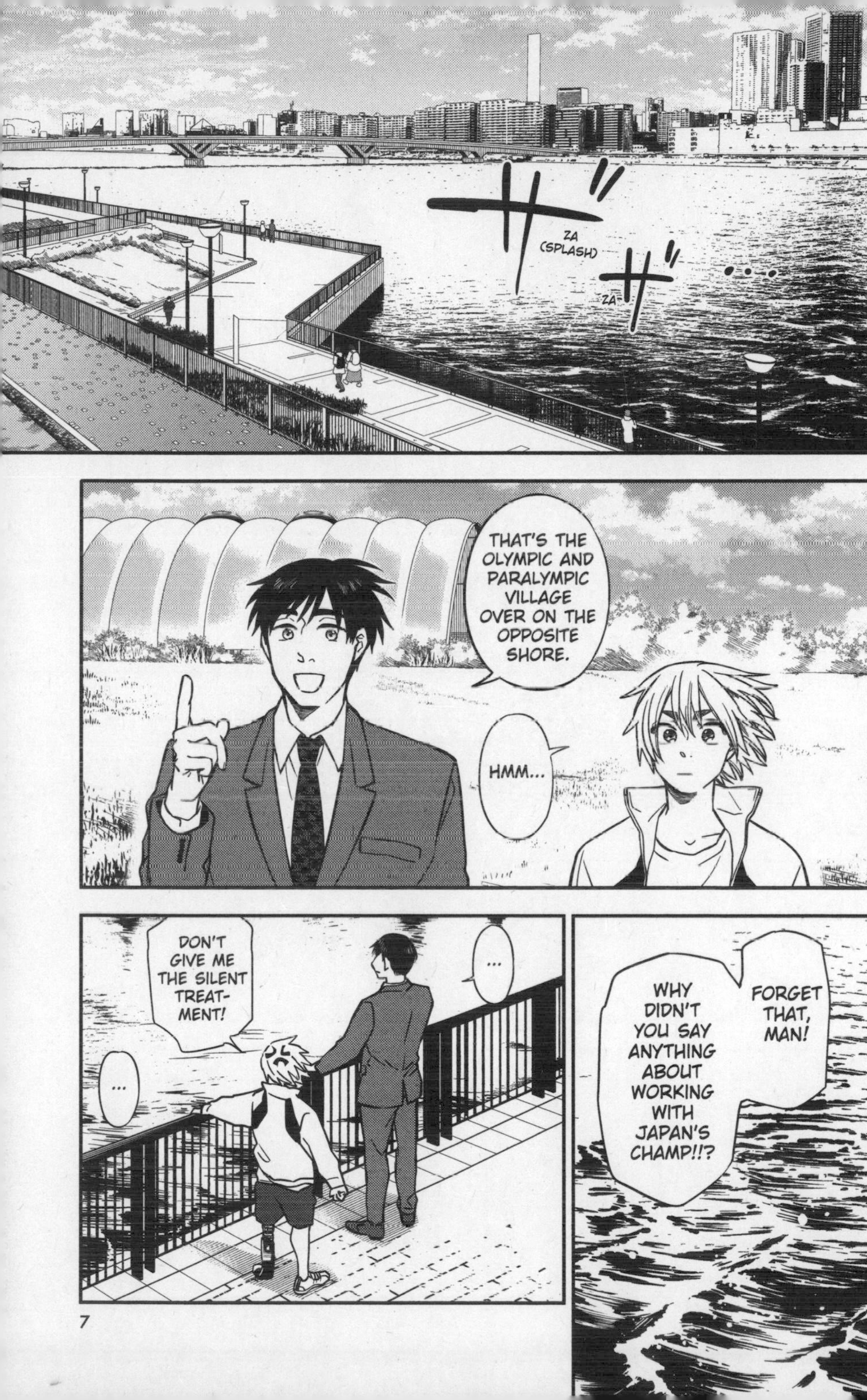
ZA
(SPLASH)
ZA
...
THAT'S THE OLYMPIC AND PARALYMPIC VILLAGE OVER ON THE OPPOSITE SHORE.
HMM...
FORGET THAT, MAN!
WHY DIDN'T YOU SAY ANYTHING ABOUT WORKING WITH JAPAN'S CHAMP!!?
...
DON'T GIVE ME THE SILENT TREAT-MENT!
...

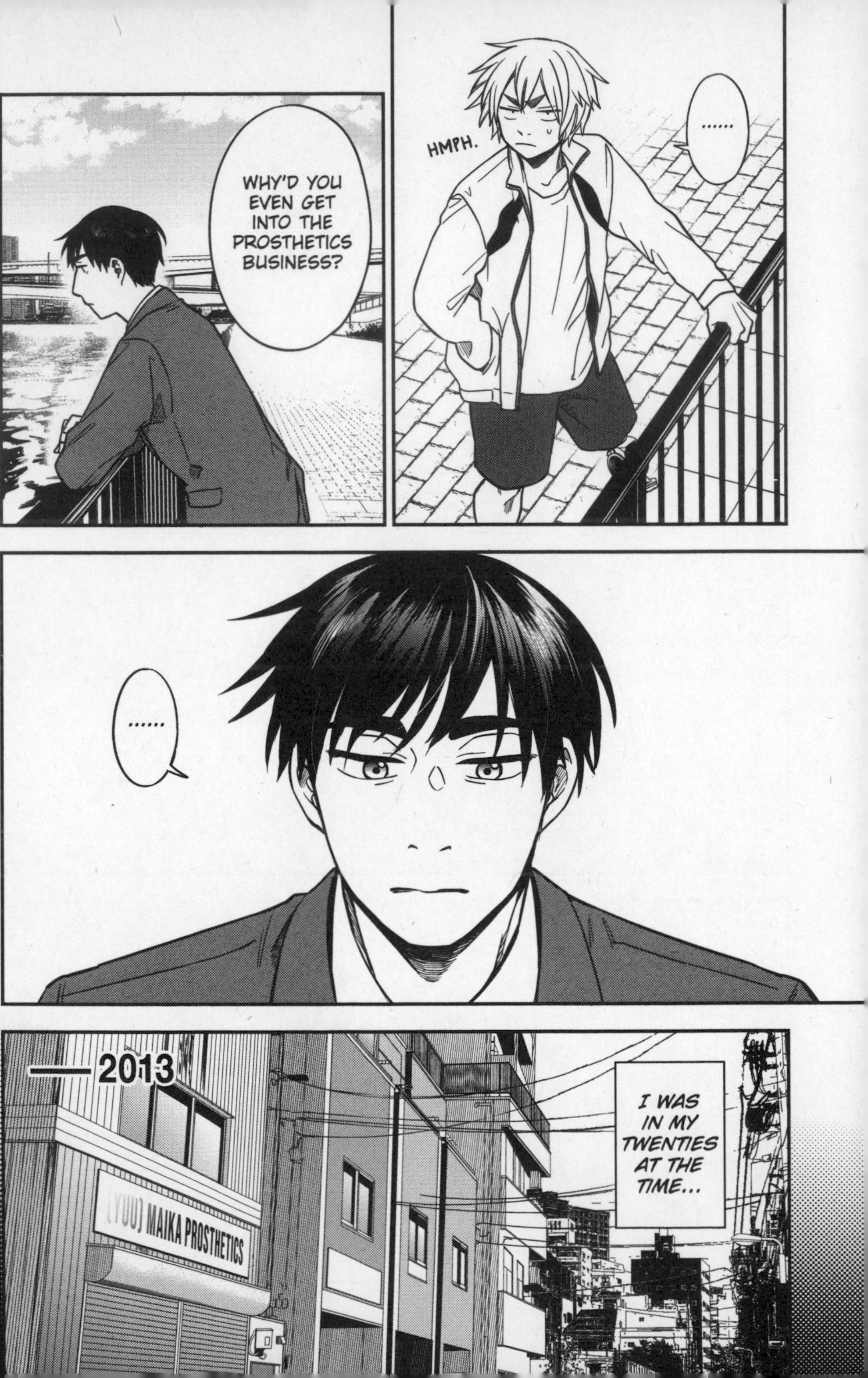
HMPH.
......
WHY'D YOU EVEN GET INTO THE PROSTHETICS BUSINESS?
......
—2013
I WAS IN MY TWENTIES AT THE TIME...
(YUU) MAIKA PROSTHETICS

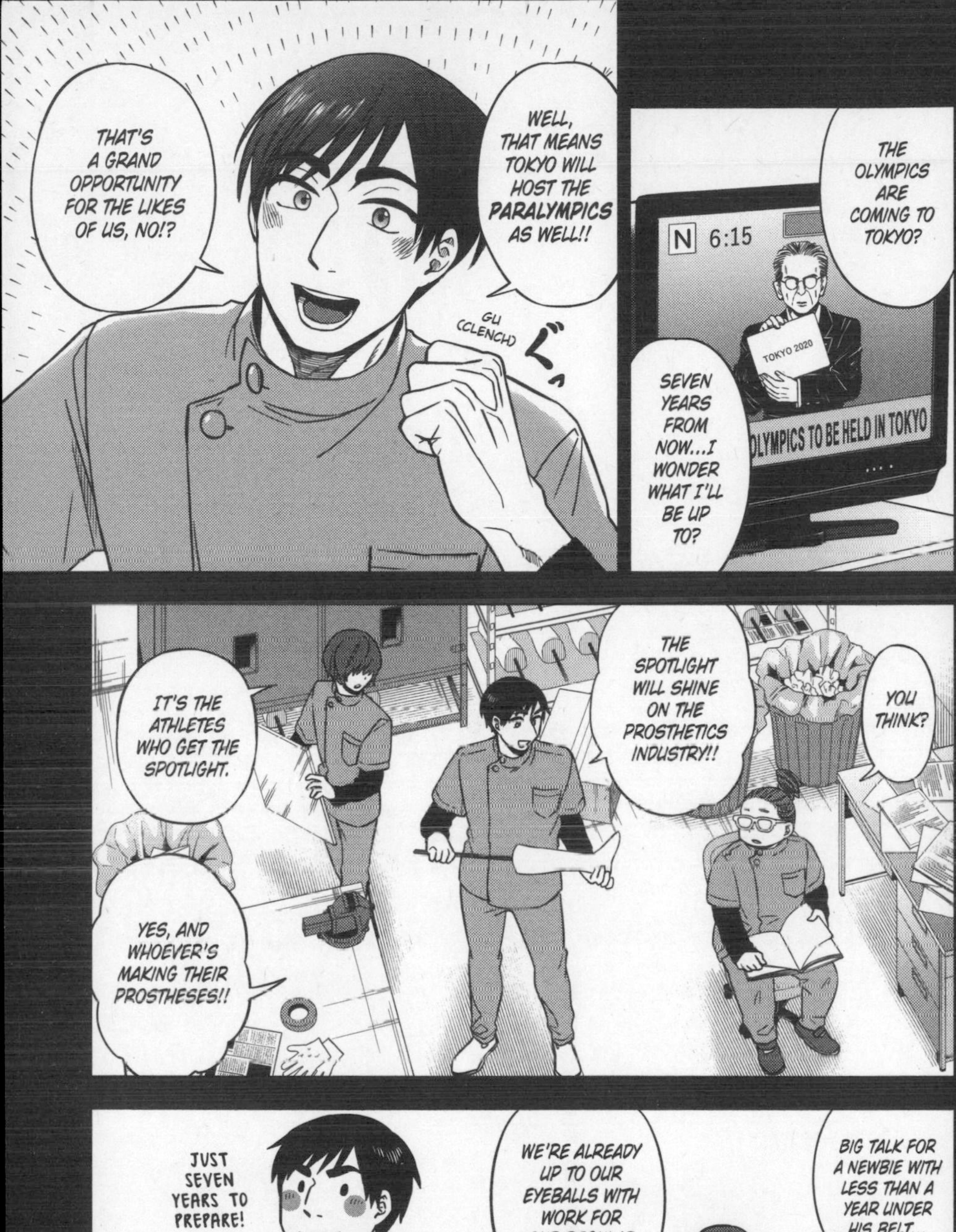

THE OLYMPICS ARE COMING TO TOKYO?
N 6:15
TOKYO 2020
OLYMPICS TO BE HELD IN TOKYO
SEVEN YEARS FROM NOW...I WONDER WHAT I'LL BE UP TO?
WELL, THAT MEANS TOKYO WILL HOST THE **PARALYMPICS** AS WELL!!
GU (CLENCH)
THAT'S A GRAND OPPORTUNITY FOR THE LIKES OF US, NO!?
YOU THINK?
THE SPOTLIGHT WILL SHINE ON THE PROSTHETICS INDUSTRY!!
IT'S THE ATHLETES WHO GET THE SPOTLIGHT.
YES, AND WHOEVER'S MAKING THEIR PROSTHESES!!
BIG TALK FOR A NEWBIE WITH LESS THAN A YEAR UNDER HIS BELT...
WE'RE ALREADY UP TO OUR EYEBALLS WITH WORK FOR OUR REGULAR CLIENTS.
JUST SEVEN YEARS TO PREPARE!

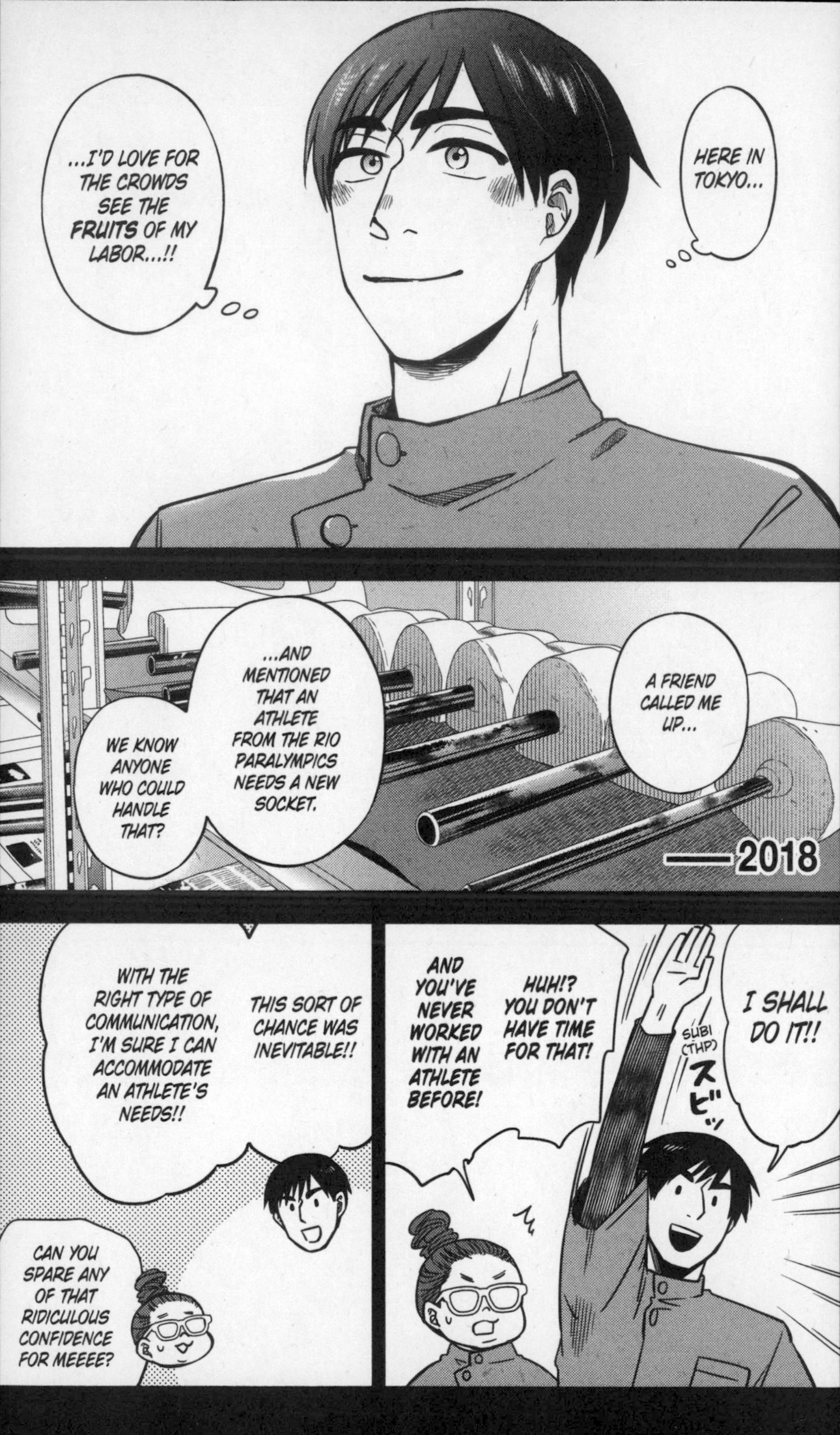
HERE IN TOKYO...
...I'D LOVE FOR THE CROWDS SEE THE **FRUITS** OF MY LABOR...!!
—2018
A FRIEND CALLED ME UP...
...AND MENTIONED THAT AN ATHLETE FROM THE RIO PARALYMPICS NEEDS A NEW SOCKET.
WE KNOW ANYONE WHO COULD HANDLE THAT?
I SHALL DO IT!!
SUBI (THP)
スビッ
HUH!? YOU DON'T HAVE TIME FOR THAT!
AND YOU'VE NEVER WORKED WITH AN ATHLETE BEFORE!
THIS SORT OF CHANCE WAS INEVITABLE!!
WITH THE RIGHT TYPE OF COMMUNICATION, I'M SURE I CAN ACCOMMODATE AN ATHLETE'S NEEDS!!
CAN YOU SPARE ANY OF THAT RIDICULOUS CONFIDENCE FOR MEEEE?

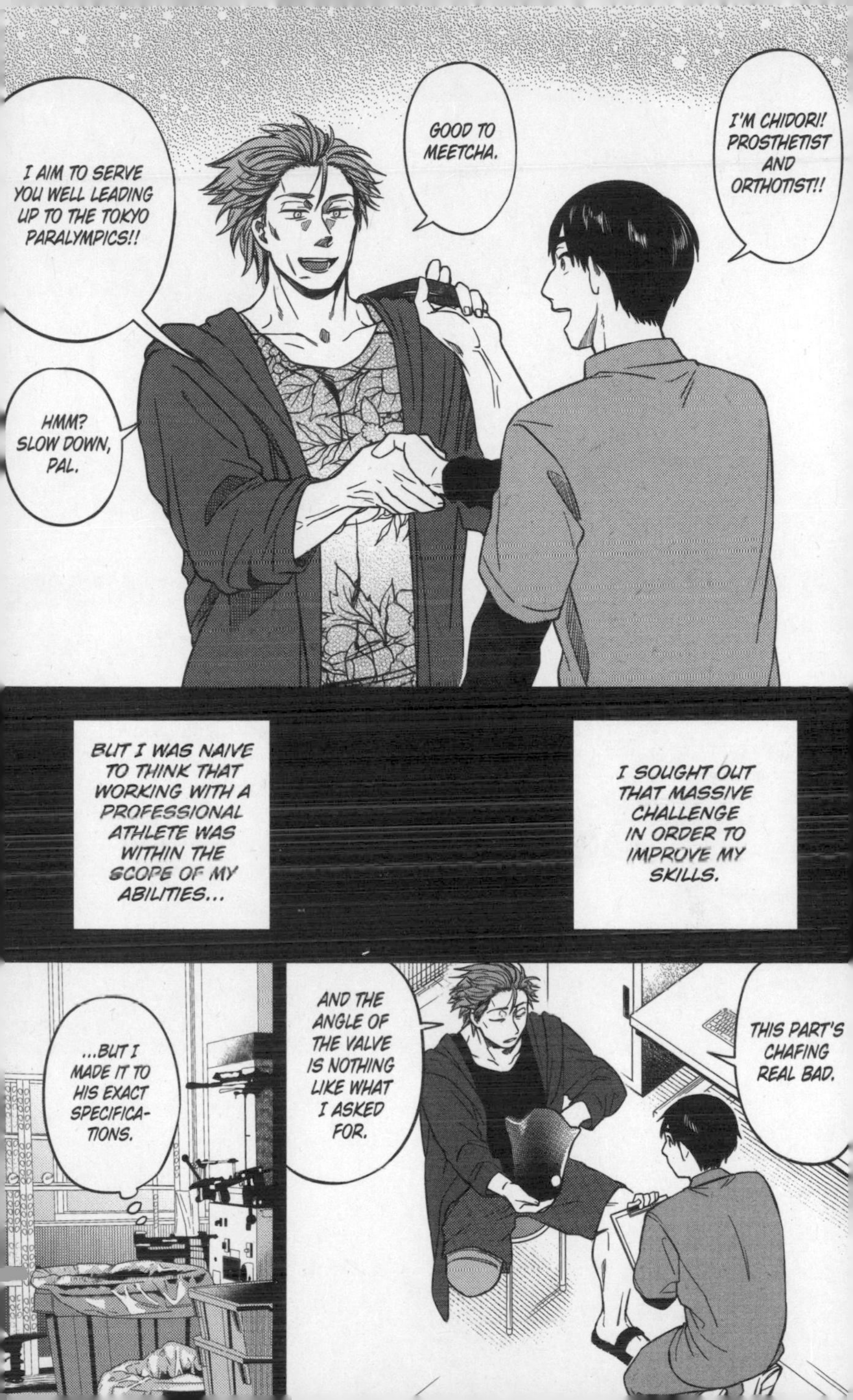
I'M CHIDORI! PROSTHETIST AND ORTHOTIST!!
GOOD TO MEETCHA.
I AIM TO SERVE YOU WELL LEADING UP TO THE TOKYO PARALYMPICS!!
HMM? SLOW DOWN, PAL.
I SOUGHT OUT THAT MASSIVE CHALLENGE IN ORDER TO IMPROVE MY SKILLS.
BUT I WAS NAIVE TO THINK THAT WORKING WITH A PROFESSIONAL ATHLETE WAS WITHIN THE SCOPE OF MY ABILITIES...
THIS PART'S CHAFING REAL BAD.
AND THE ANGLE OF THE VALVE IS NOTHING LIKE WHAT I ASKED FOR.
...BUT I MADE IT TO HIS EXACT SPECIFICA-TIONS.

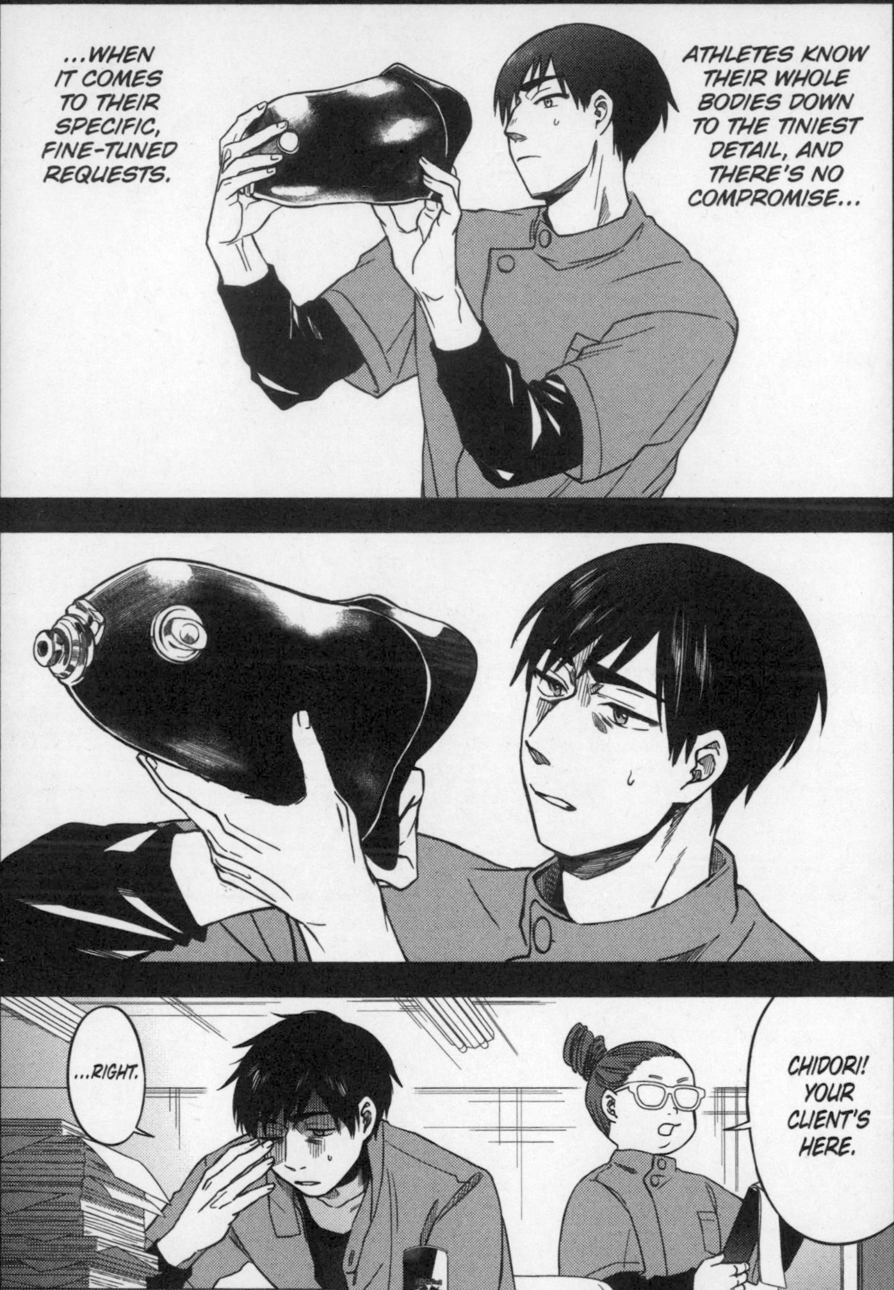
ATHLETES KNOW THEIR WHOLE BODIES DOWN TO THE TINIEST DETAIL, AND THERE'S NO COMPROMISE...
...WHEN IT COMES TO THEIR SPECIFIC, FINE-TUNED REQUESTS.
CHIDORI! YOUR CLIENT'S HERE.
...RIGHT.

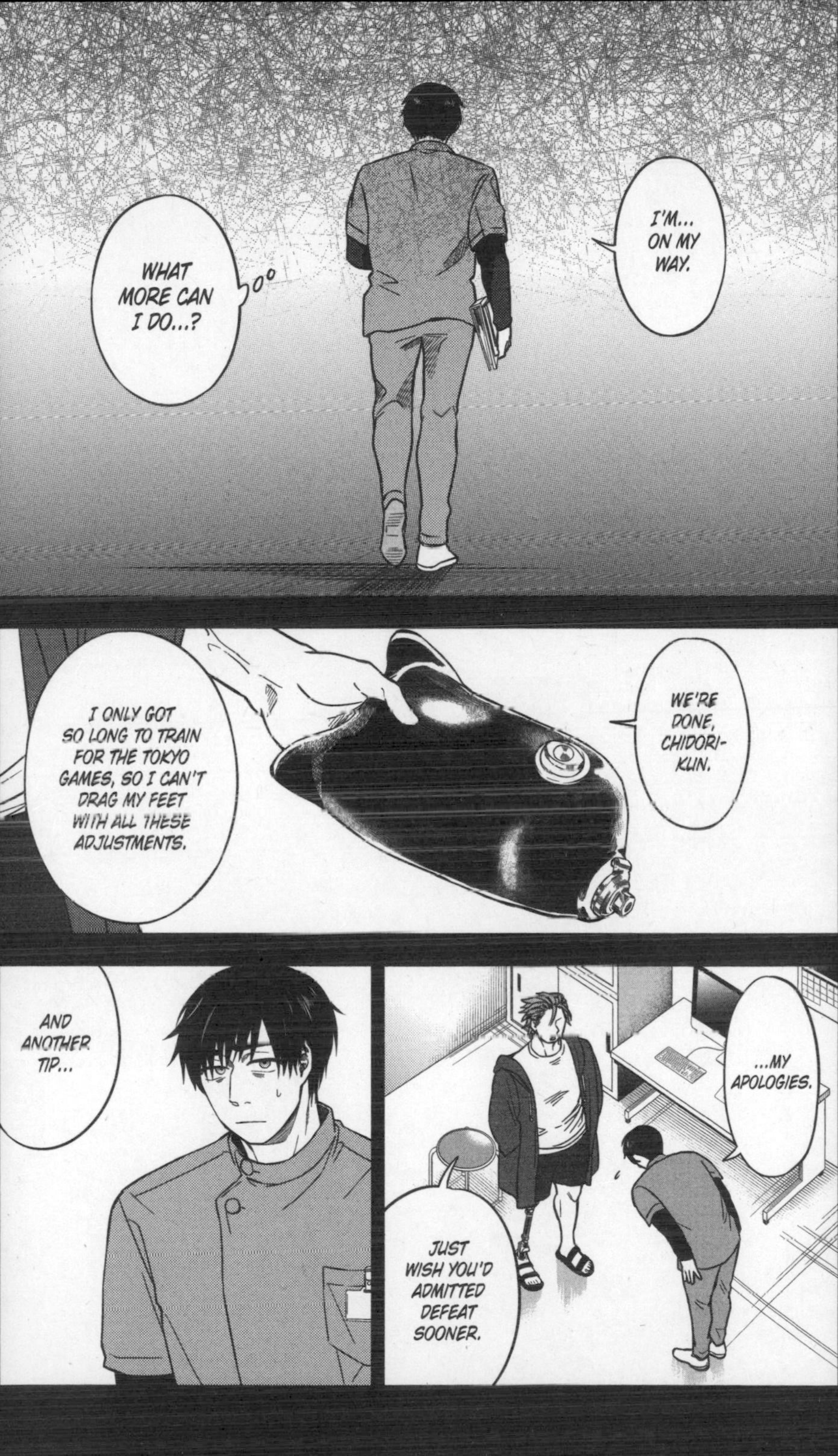
I'M... ON MY WAY.
WHAT MORE CAN I DO...?
WE'RE DONE, CHIDORI-KUN.
I ONLY GOT SO LONG TO TRAIN FOR THE TOKYO GAMES, SO I CAN'T DRAG MY FEET WITH ALL THESE ADJUSTMENTS.
...MY APOLOGIES.
JUST WISH YOU'D ADMITTED DEFEAT SOONER.
AND ANOTHER TIP...

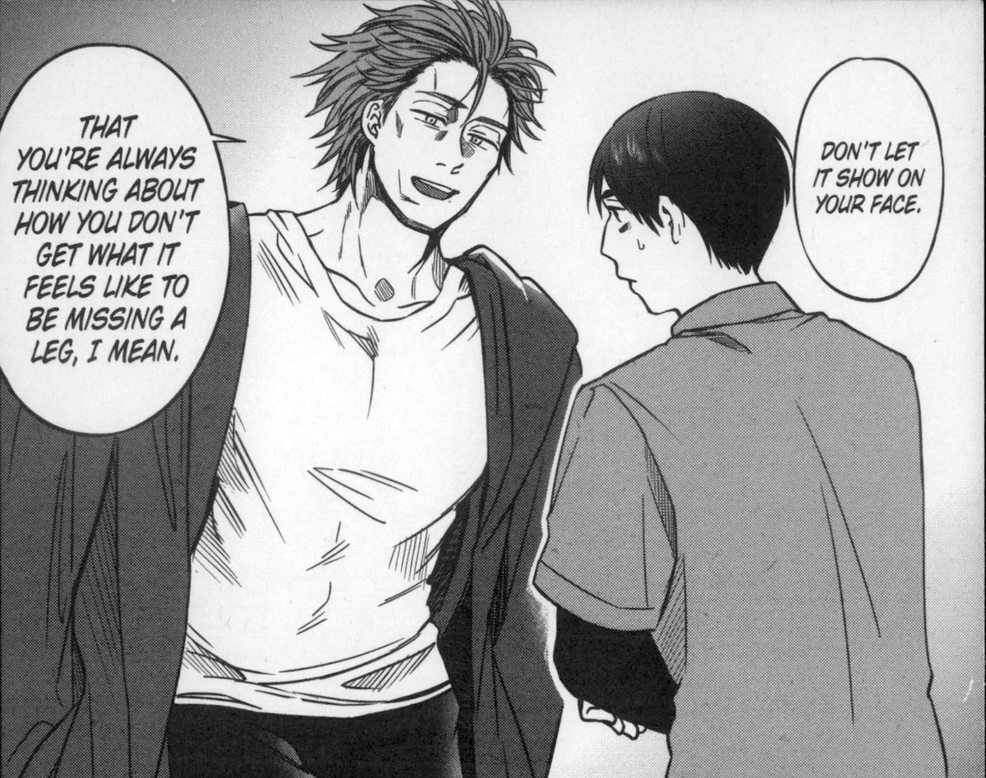
DON'T LET IT SHOW ON YOUR FACE.
THAT YOU'RE ALWAYS THINKING ABOUT HOW YOU DON'T GET WHAT IT FEELS LIKE TO BE MISSING A LEG, I MEAN.

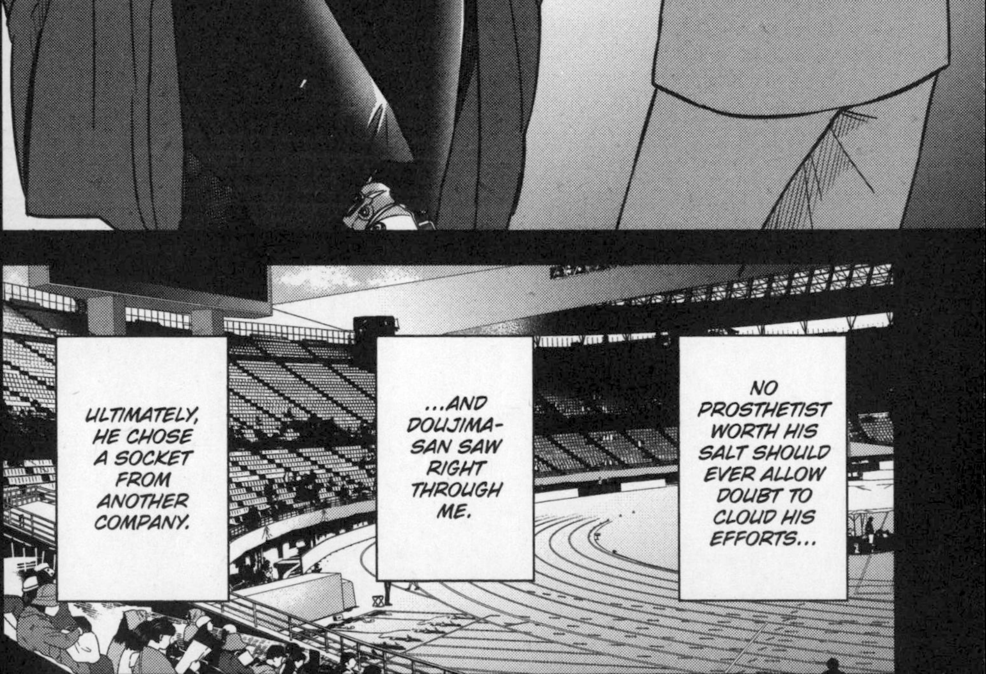
NO PROSTHETIST WORTH HIS SALT SHOULD EVER ALLOW DOUBT TO CLOUD HIS EFFORTS...
...AND DOUJIMA-SAN SAW RIGHT THROUGH ME.
ULTIMATELY, HE CHOSE A SOCKET FROM ANOTHER COMPANY.

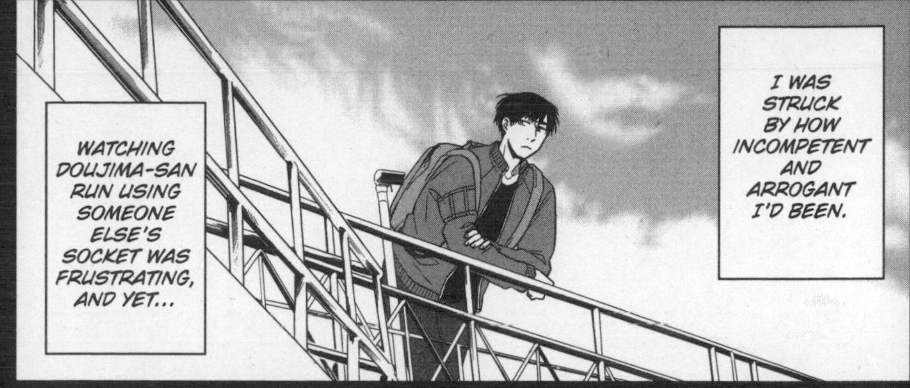
I WAS STRUCK BY HOW INCOMPETENT AND ARROGANT I'D BEEN.
WATCHING DOUJIMA-SAN RUN USING SOMEONE ELSE'S SOCKET WAS FRUSTRATING, AND YET...
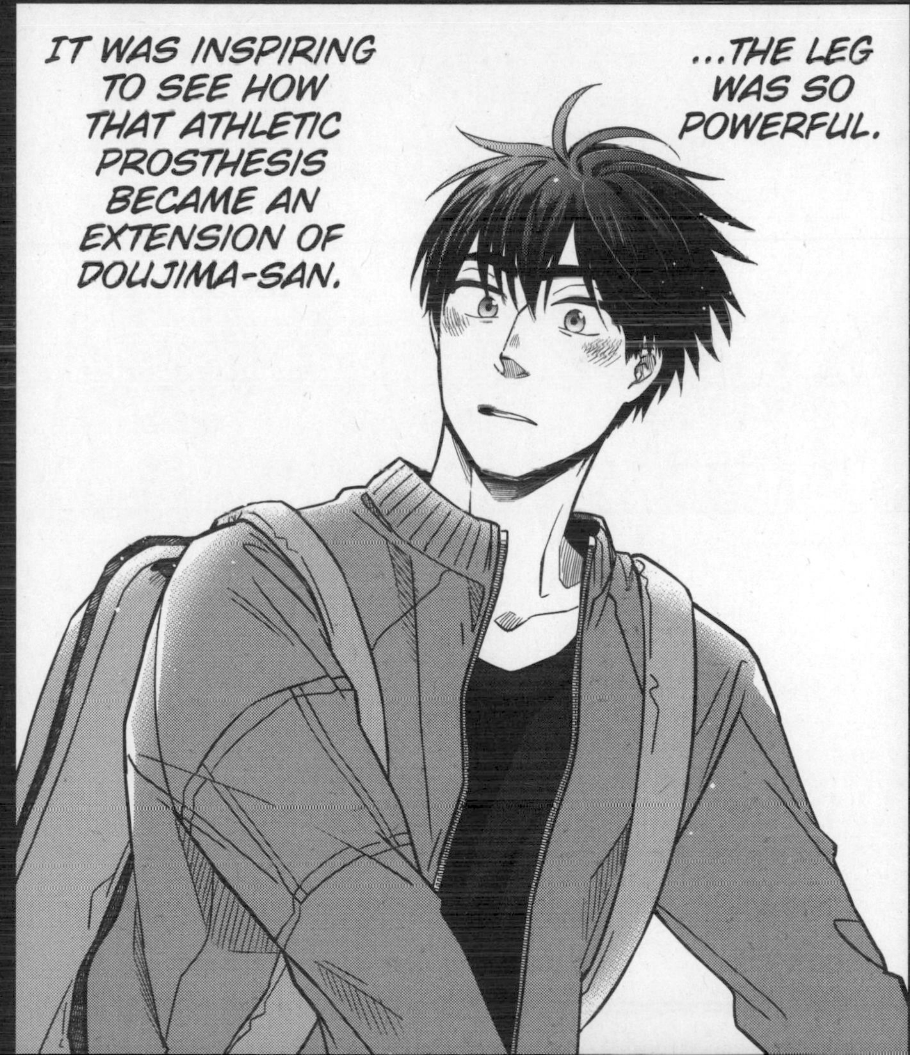
...THE LEG WAS SO POWERFUL.
IT WAS INSPIRING TO SEE HOW THAT ATHLETIC PROSTHESIS BECAME AN EXTENSION OF DOUJIMA-SAN.

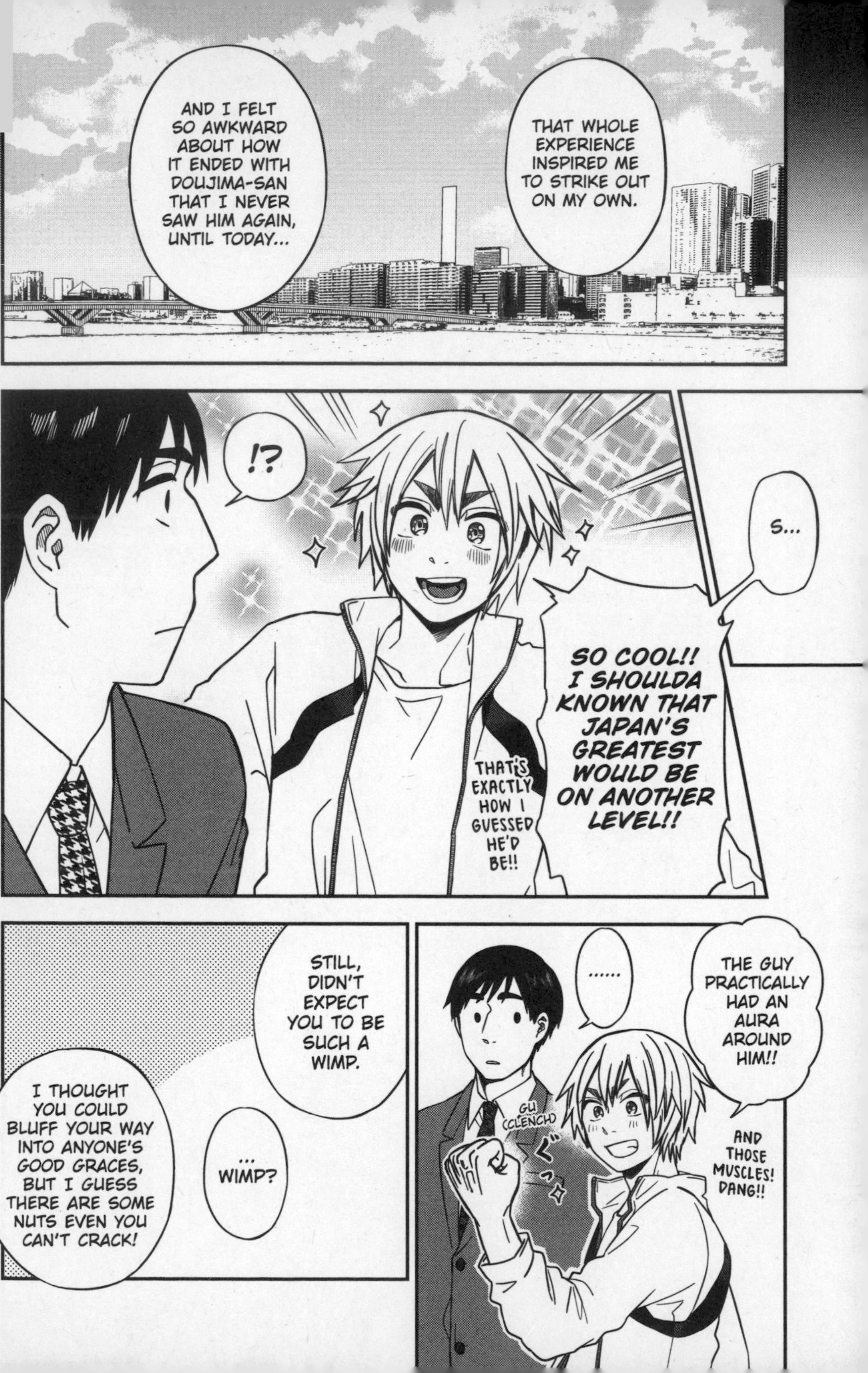
THAT WHOLE EXPERIENCE INSPIRED ME TO STRIKE OUT ON MY OWN.
AND I FELT SO AWKWARD ABOUT HOW IT ENDED WITH DOUJIMA-SAN THAT I NEVER SAW HIM AGAIN, UNTIL TODAY...
S...
SO COOL!! I SHOULDA KNOWN THAT JAPAN'S GREATEST WOULD BE ON ANOTHER LEVEL!!
THAT'S EXACTLY HOW I GUESSED HE'D BE!!
!?
THE GUY PRACTICALLY HAD AN AURA AROUND HIM!!
......
AND THOSE MUSCLES! DANG!!
GU (CLENCH)
STILL, DIDN'T EXPECT YOU TO BE SUCH A WIMP.
...WIMP?
I THOUGHT YOU COULD BLUFF YOUR WAY INTO ANYONE'S GOOD GRACES, BUT I GUESS THERE ARE SOME NUTS EVEN YOU CAN'T CRACK!

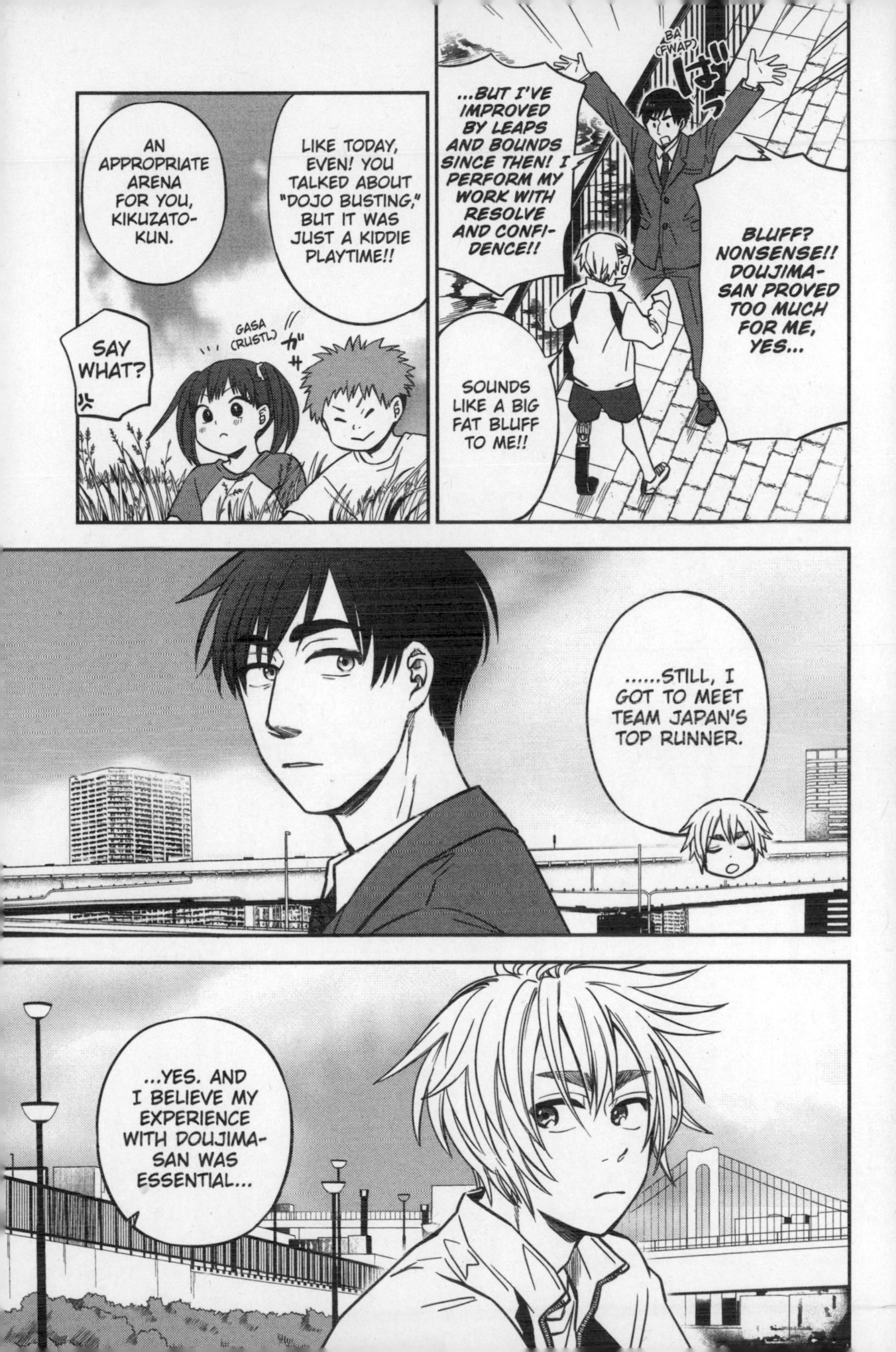
BA (FWAP)
ばっ
...BUT I'VE IMPROVED BY LEAPS AND BOUNDS SINCE THEN! I PERFORM MY WORK WITH RESOLVE AND CONFIDENCE!!
BLUFF? NONSENSE!! DOUJIMA-SAN PROVED TOO MUCH FOR ME, YES...
SOUNDS LIKE A BIG FAT BLUFF TO ME!!
LIKE TODAY, EVEN! YOU TALKED ABOUT "DOJO BUSTING," BUT IT WAS JUST A KIDDIE PLAYTIME!!
AN APPROPRIATE ARENA FOR YOU, KIKUZATO-KUN.
GASA (RUSTL)
ガサ
SAY WHAT?
......STILL, I GOT TO MEET TEAM JAPAN'S TOP RUNNER.
...YES. AND I BELIEVE MY EXPERIENCE WITH DOUJIMA-SAN WAS ESSENTIAL...

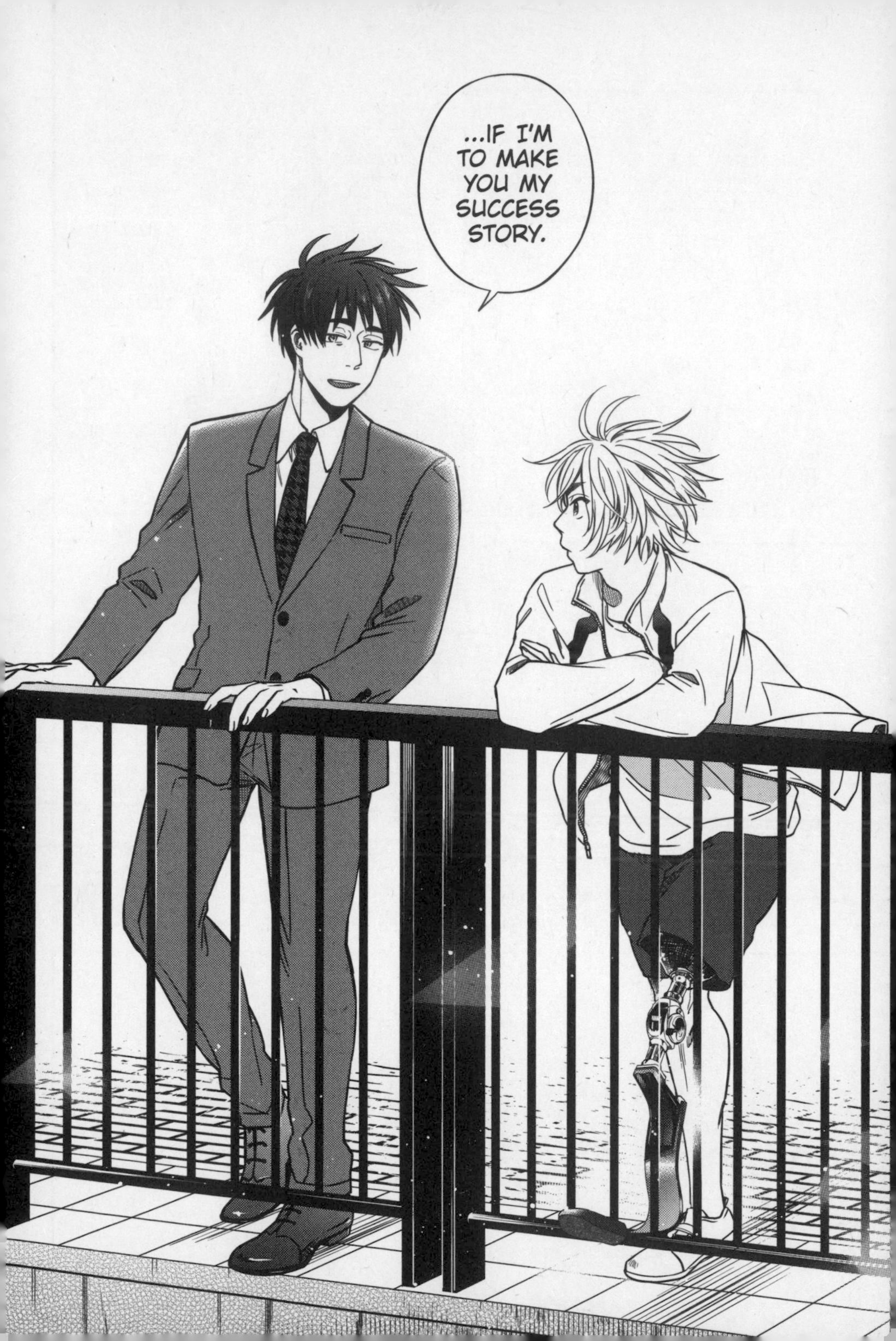
...IF I'M TO MAKE YOU MY SUCCESS STORY.

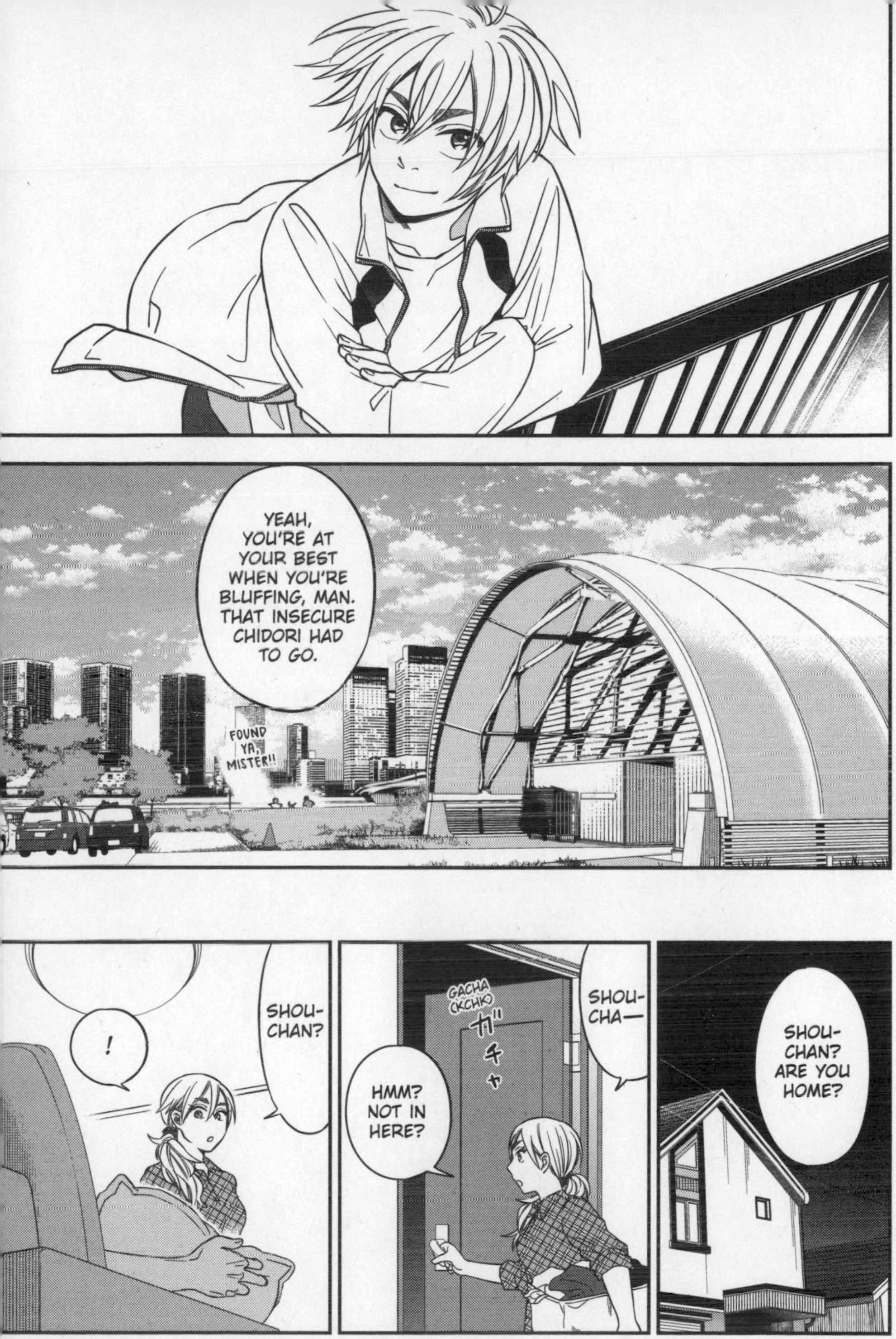
YEAH, YOU'RE AT YOUR BEST WHEN YOU'RE BLUFFING, MAN. THAT INSECURE CHIDORI HAD TO GO.
FOUND YA, MISTER!!
SHOU-CHAN? ARE YOU HOME?
SHOU-CHA—
GACHA (KCHK)
ガチャ
HMM? NOT IN HERE?
SHOU-CHAN?
!

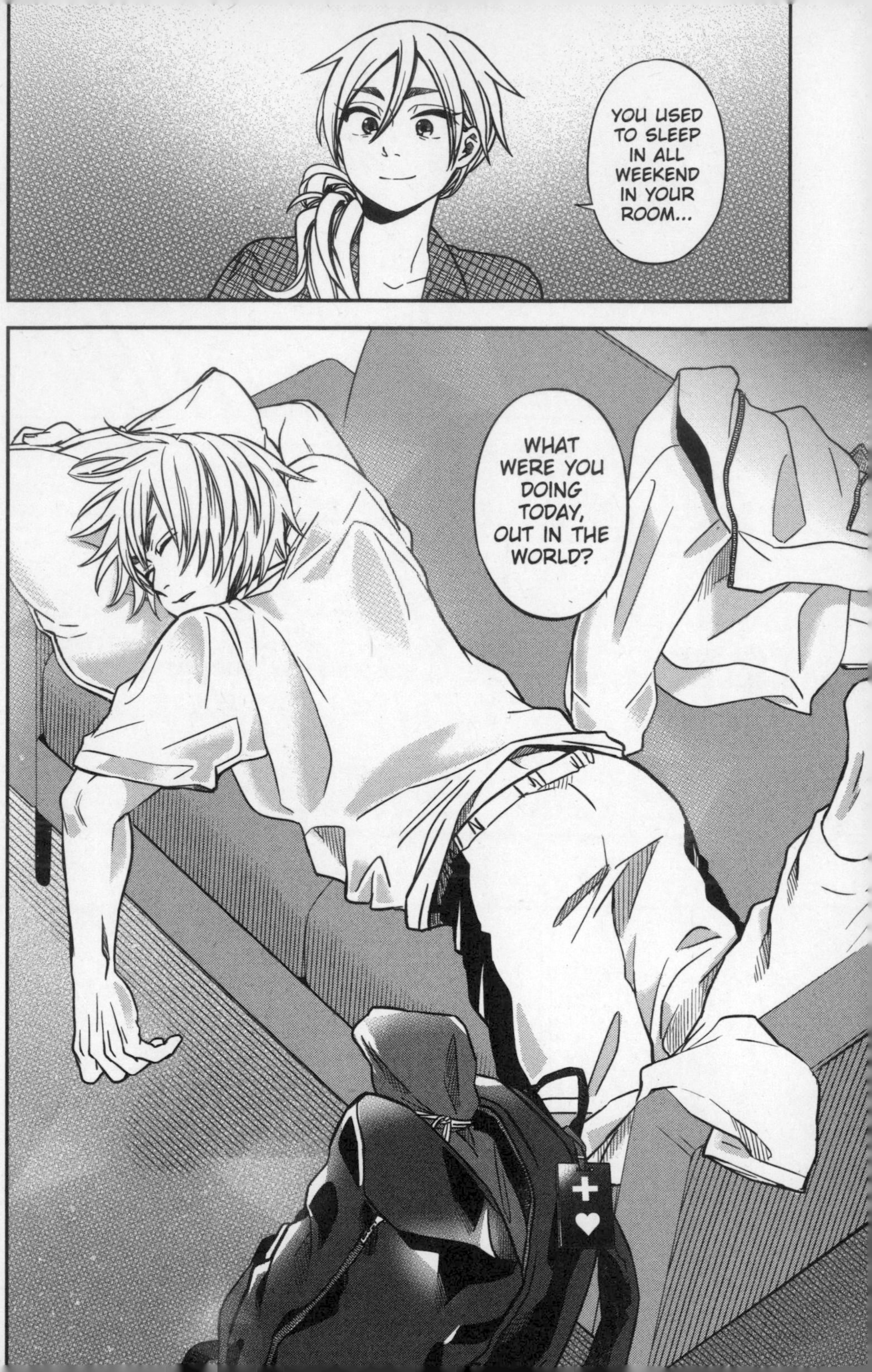
YOU USED TO SLEEP IN ALL WEEKEND IN YOUR ROOM...
WHAT WERE YOU DOING TODAY, OUT IN THE WORLD?

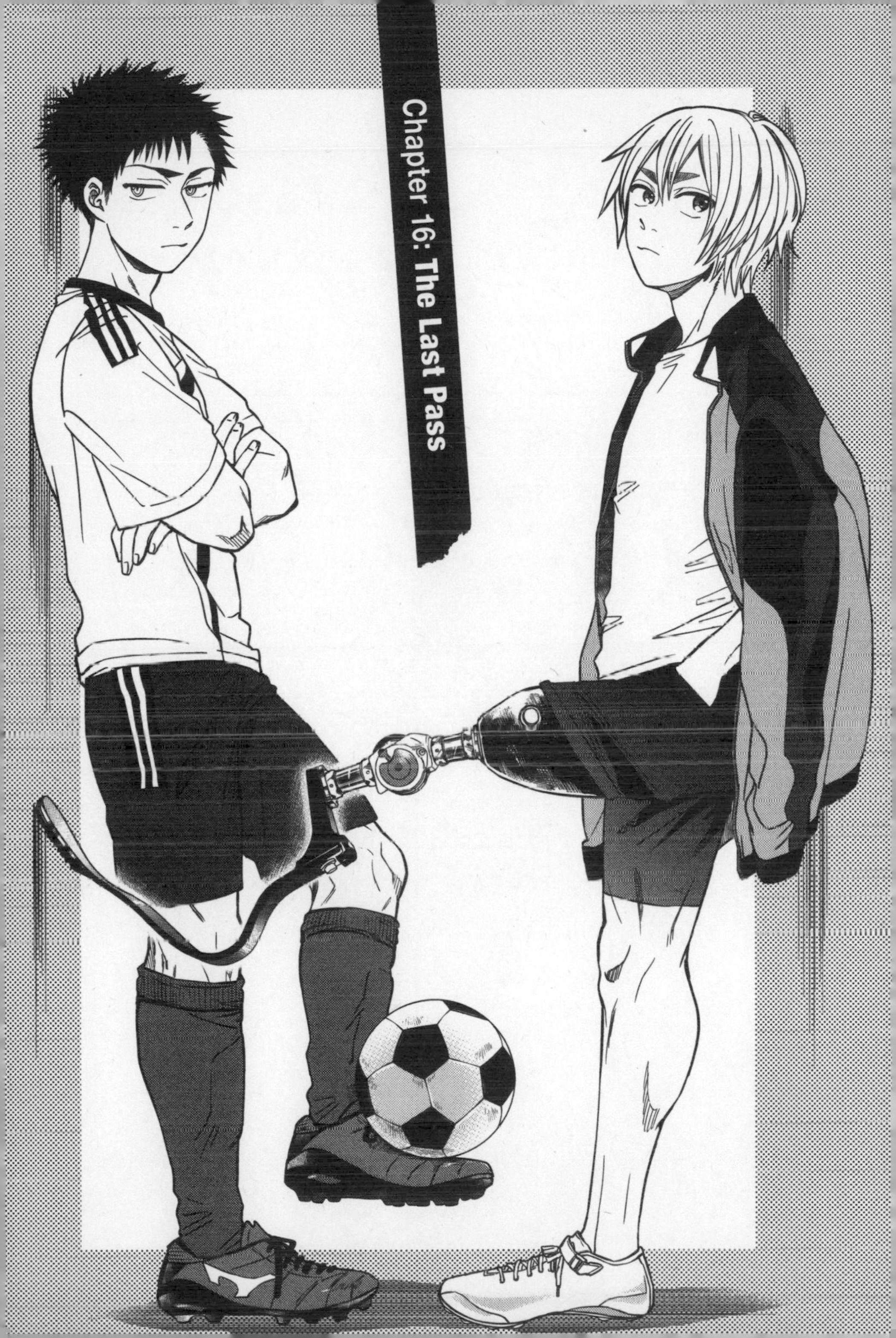
Chapter 16: The Last Pass

PAKOOON
(THWOK)

RAAAH!

RAAAH!

RAAAH!

WITH THE CROUCH START, YOUR DOMINANT LEG GOES IN BACK, WITH YOUR OTHER LEG IN FRONT.

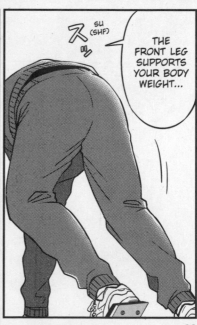

SU
(SHF)

THE FRONT LEG SUPPORTS YOUR BODY WEIGHT...

...SO WHEN YOU STRAIGHTEN THAT LEG TO KICK OFF THE GROUND, YOU UTILIZE YOUR FULL POWER!

BA
(LUNGE)

22

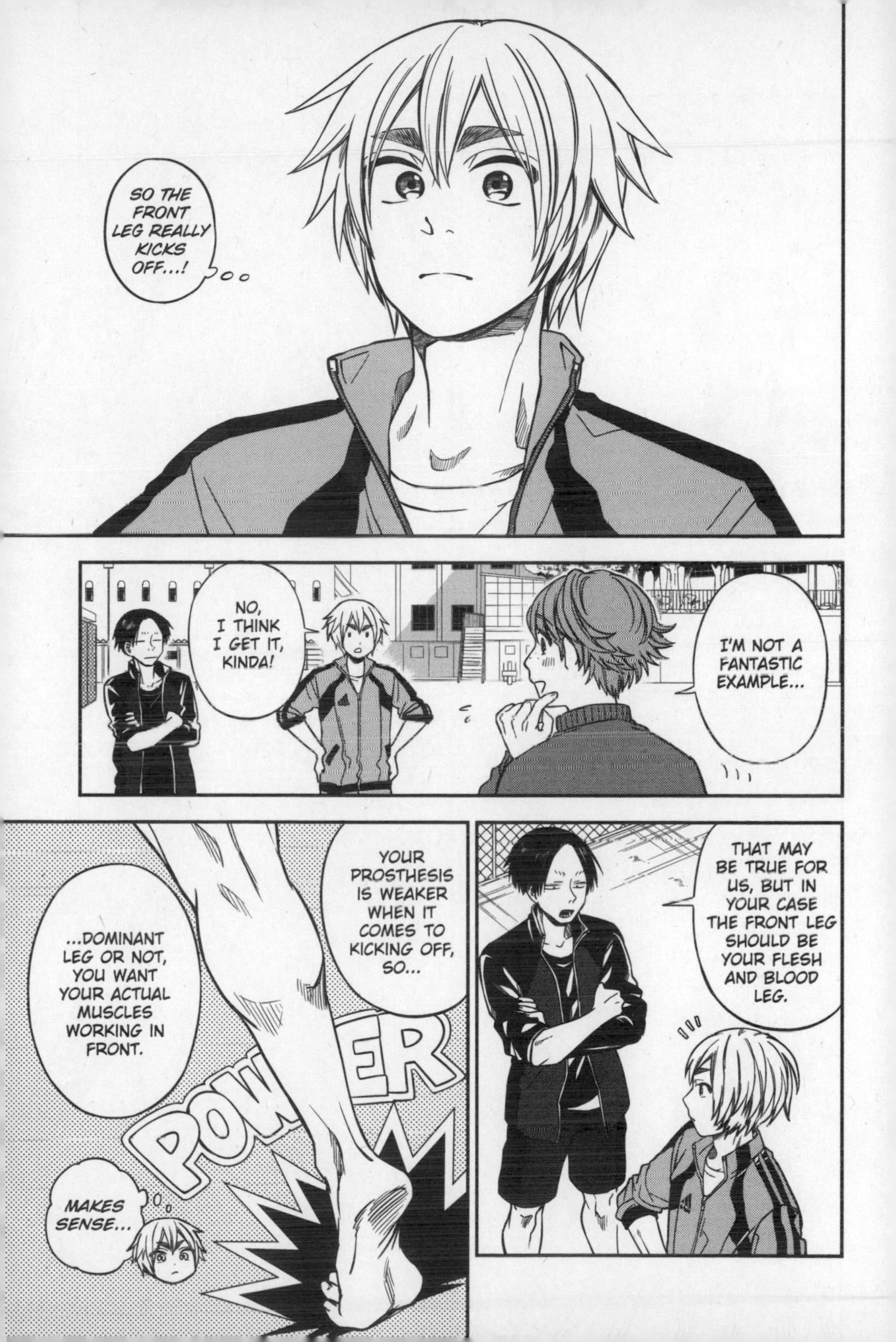
SO THE FRONT LEG REALLY KICKS OFF...!
I'M NOT A FANTASTIC EXAMPLE...
NO, I THINK I GET IT, KINDA!
THAT MAY BE TRUE FOR US, BUT IN YOUR CASE THE FRONT LEG SHOULD BE YOUR FLESH AND BLOOD LEG.
YOUR PROSTHESIS IS WEAKER WHEN IT COMES TO KICKING OFF, SO...
...DOMINANT LEG OR NOT, YOU WANT YOUR ACTUAL MUSCLES WORKING IN FRONT.
POW ER
MAKES SENSE...

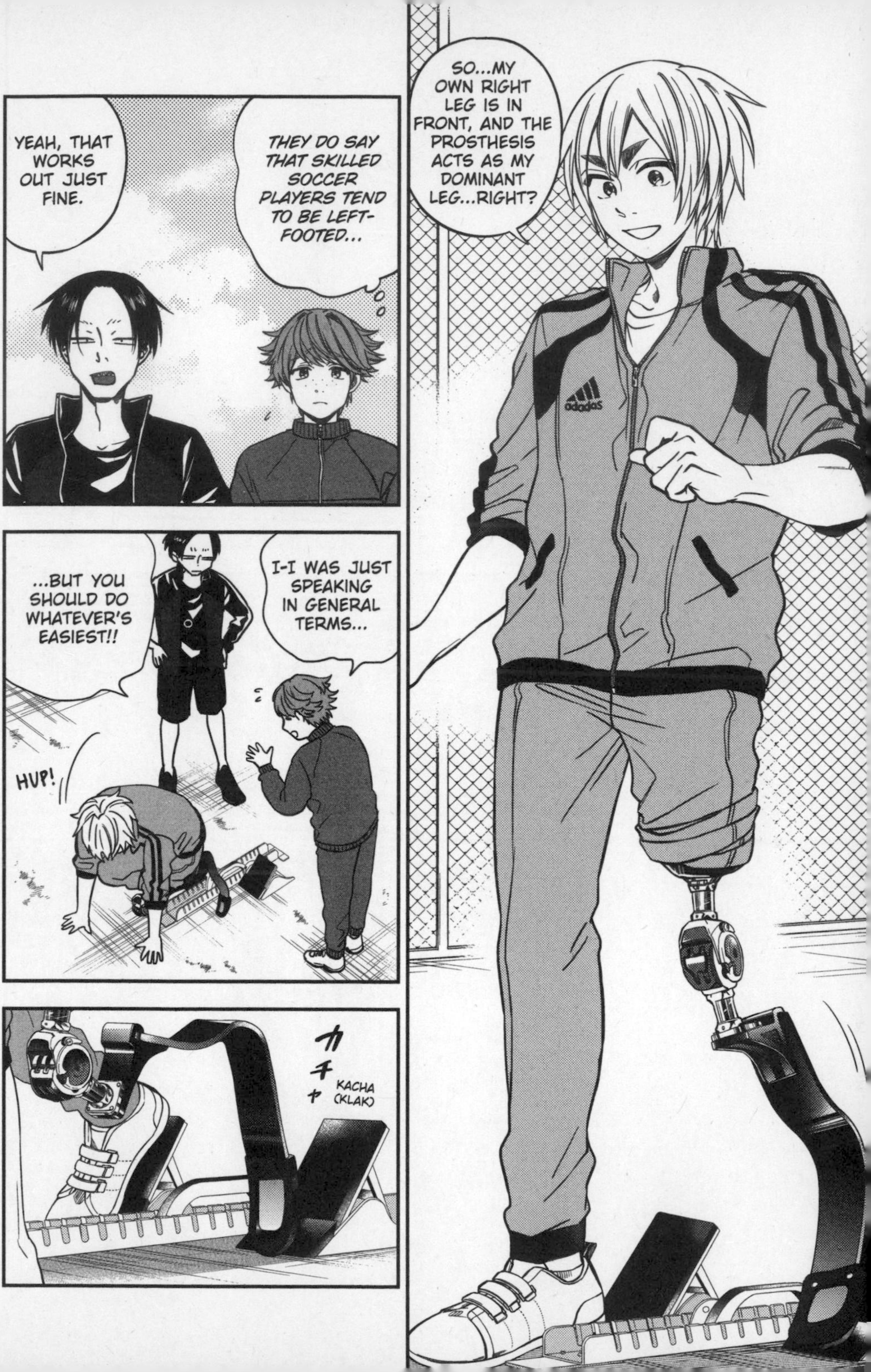
SO...MY OWN RIGHT LEG IS IN FRONT, AND THE PROSTHESIS ACTS AS MY DOMINANT LEG...RIGHT?
adidas
THEY DO SAY THAT SKILLED SOCCER PLAYERS TEND TO BE LEFT-FOOTED...
YEAH, THAT WORKS OUT JUST FINE.
I-I WAS JUST SPEAKING IN GENERAL TERMS...
...BUT YOU SHOULD DO WHATEVER'S EASIEST!!
HUP!
カチャ
KACHA (KLAK)

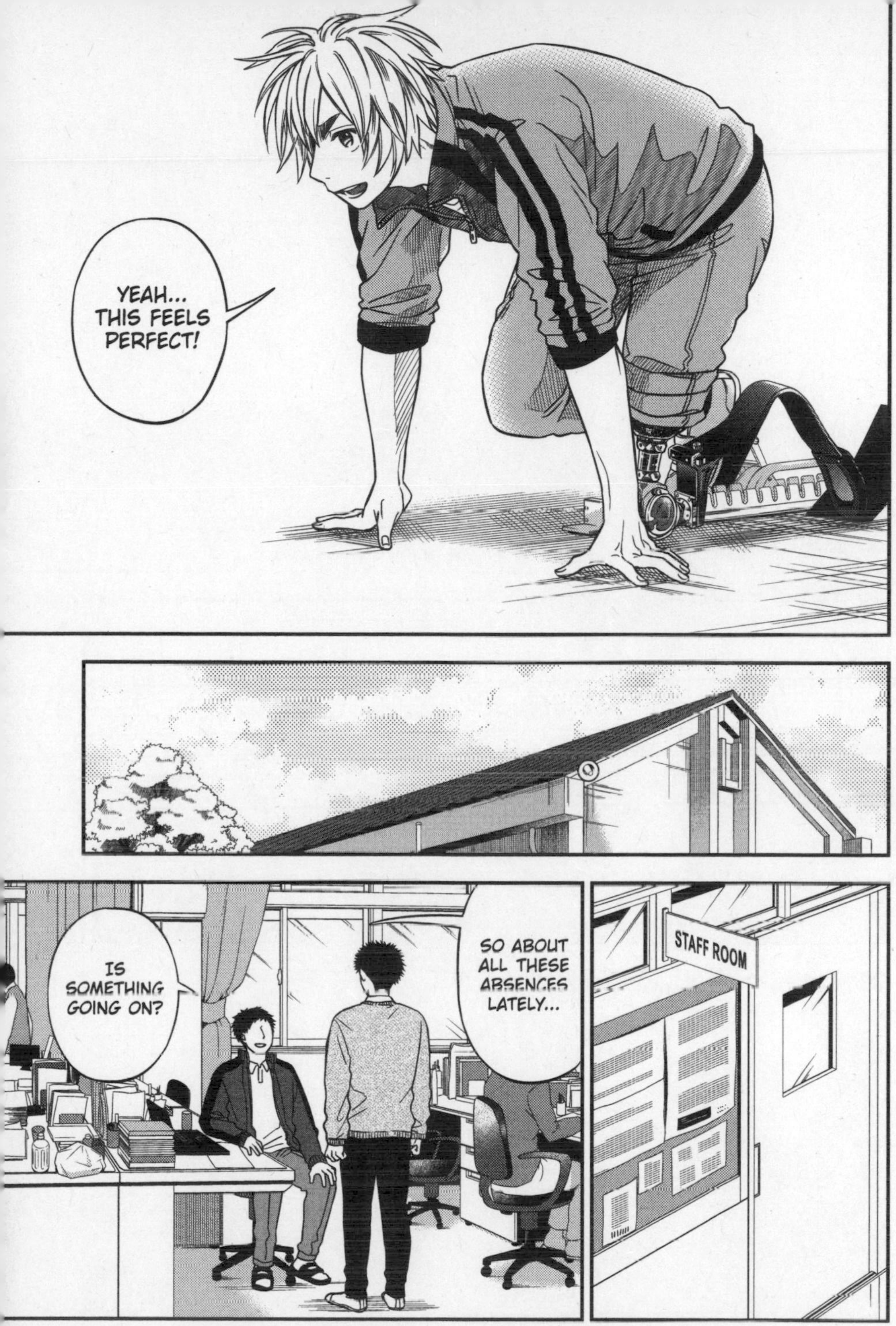
YEAH... THIS FEELS PERFECT!
STAFF ROOM
SO ABOUT ALL THESE ABSENCES LATELY...
IS SOMETHING GOING ON?

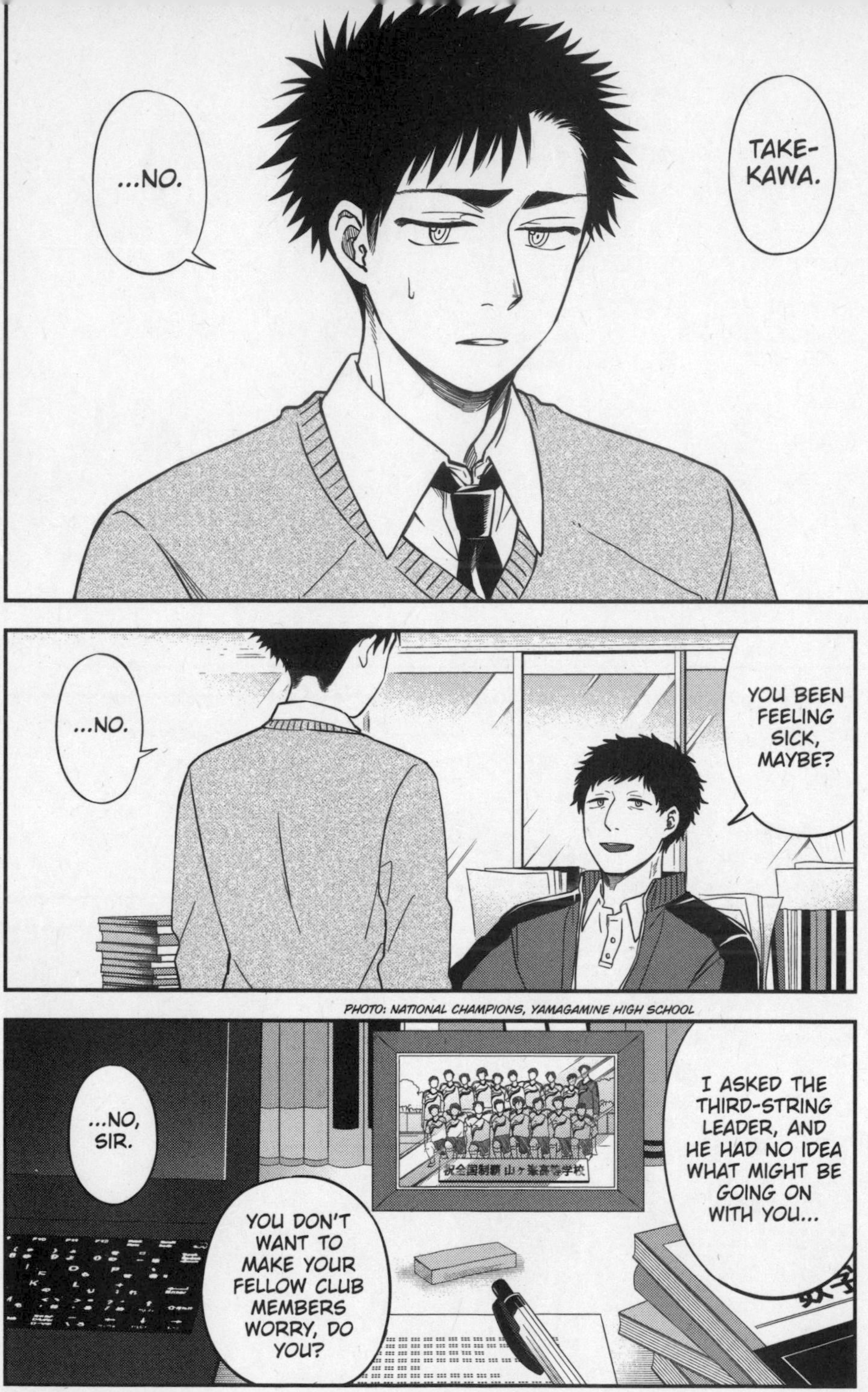
TAKE-KAWA.
...NO.
YOU BEEN FEELING SICK, MAYBE?
...NO.
PHOTO: NATIONAL CHAMPIONS, YAMAGAMINE HIGH SCHOOL
I ASKED THE THIRD-STRING LEADER, AND HE HAD NO IDEA WHAT MIGHT BE GOING ON WITH YOU...
YOU DON'T WANT TO MAKE YOUR FELLOW CLUB MEMBERS WORRY, DO YOU?
...NO, SIR.

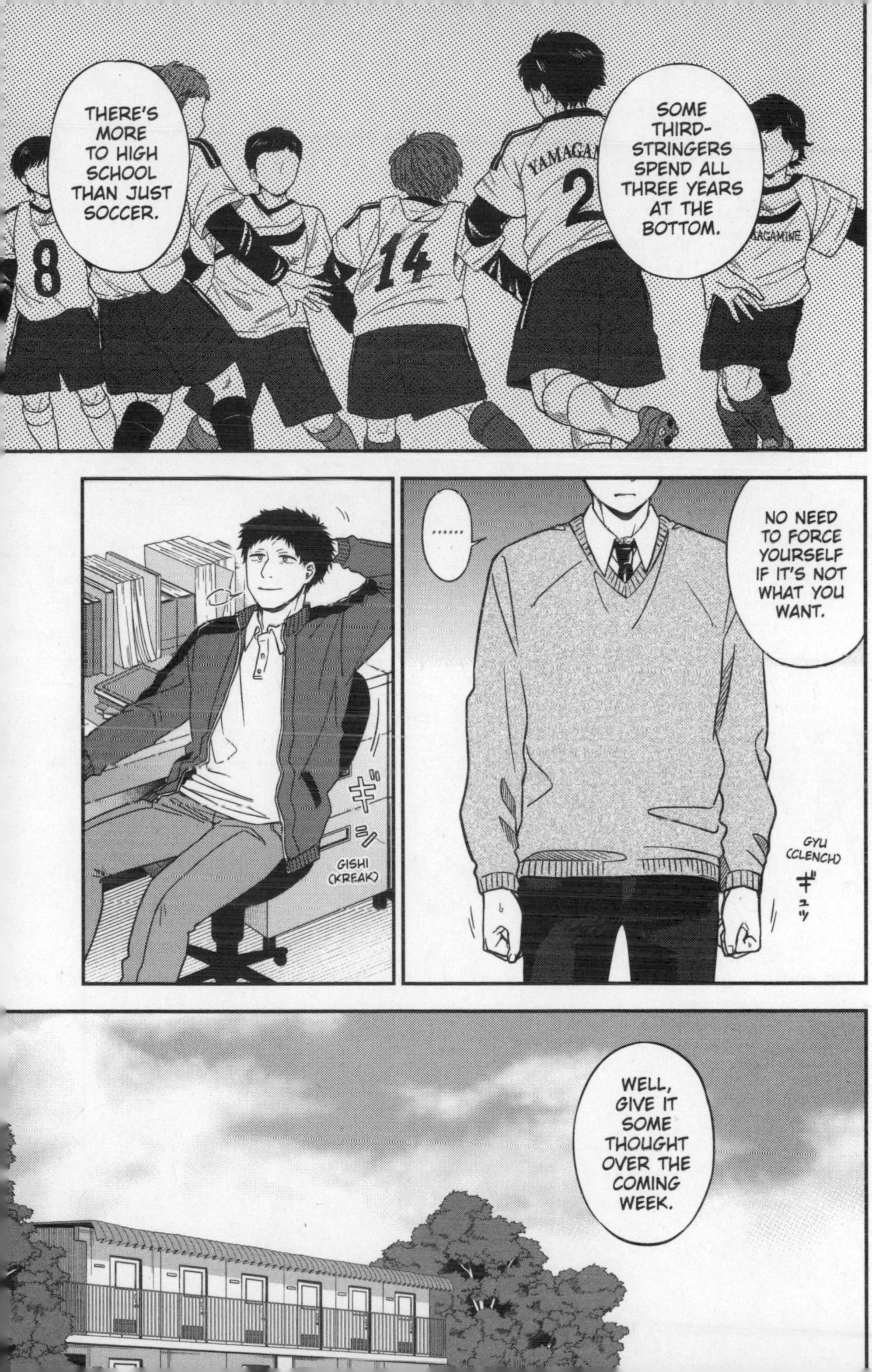
SOME THIRD-STRINGERS SPEND ALL THREE YEARS AT THE BOTTOM.
THERE'S MORE TO HIGH SCHOOL THAN JUST SOCCER.
NO NEED TO FORCE YOURSELF IF IT'S NOT WHAT YOU WANT.
......
ギュッ
GYU (CLENCH)
ギシ
GISHI (KREAK)
WELL, GIVE IT SOME THOUGHT OVER THE COMING WEEK.

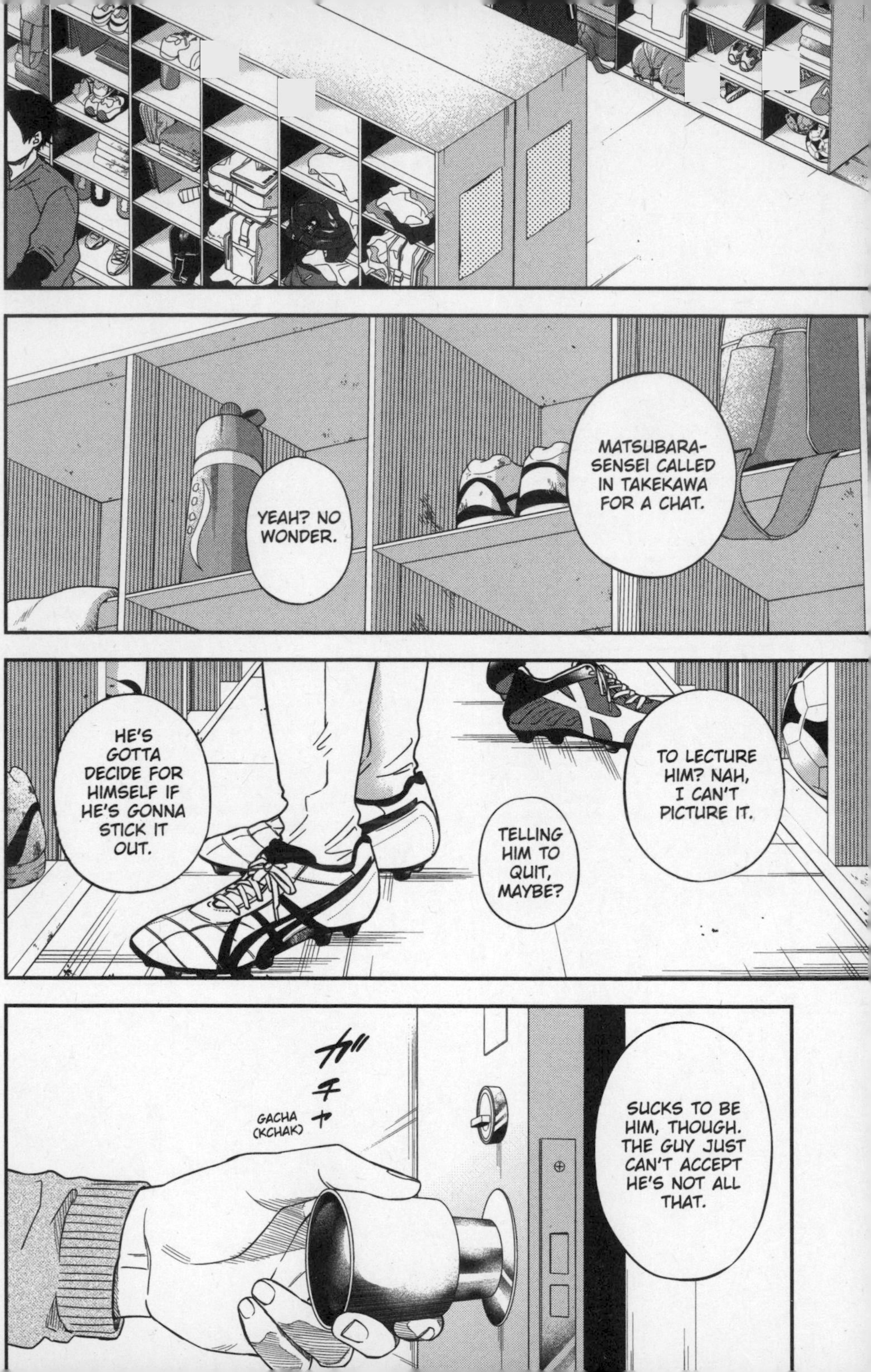
MATSUBARA-SENSEI CALLED IN TAKEKAWA FOR A CHAT.
YEAH? NO WONDER.
TO LECTURE HIM? NAH, I CAN'T PICTURE IT.
TELLING HIM TO QUIT, MAYBE?
HE'S GOTTA DECIDE FOR HIMSELF IF HE'S GONNA STICK IT OUT.
SUCKS TO BE HIM, THOUGH. THE GUY JUST CAN'T ACCEPT HE'S NOT ALL THAT.
ガチャ
GACHA (KCHAK)

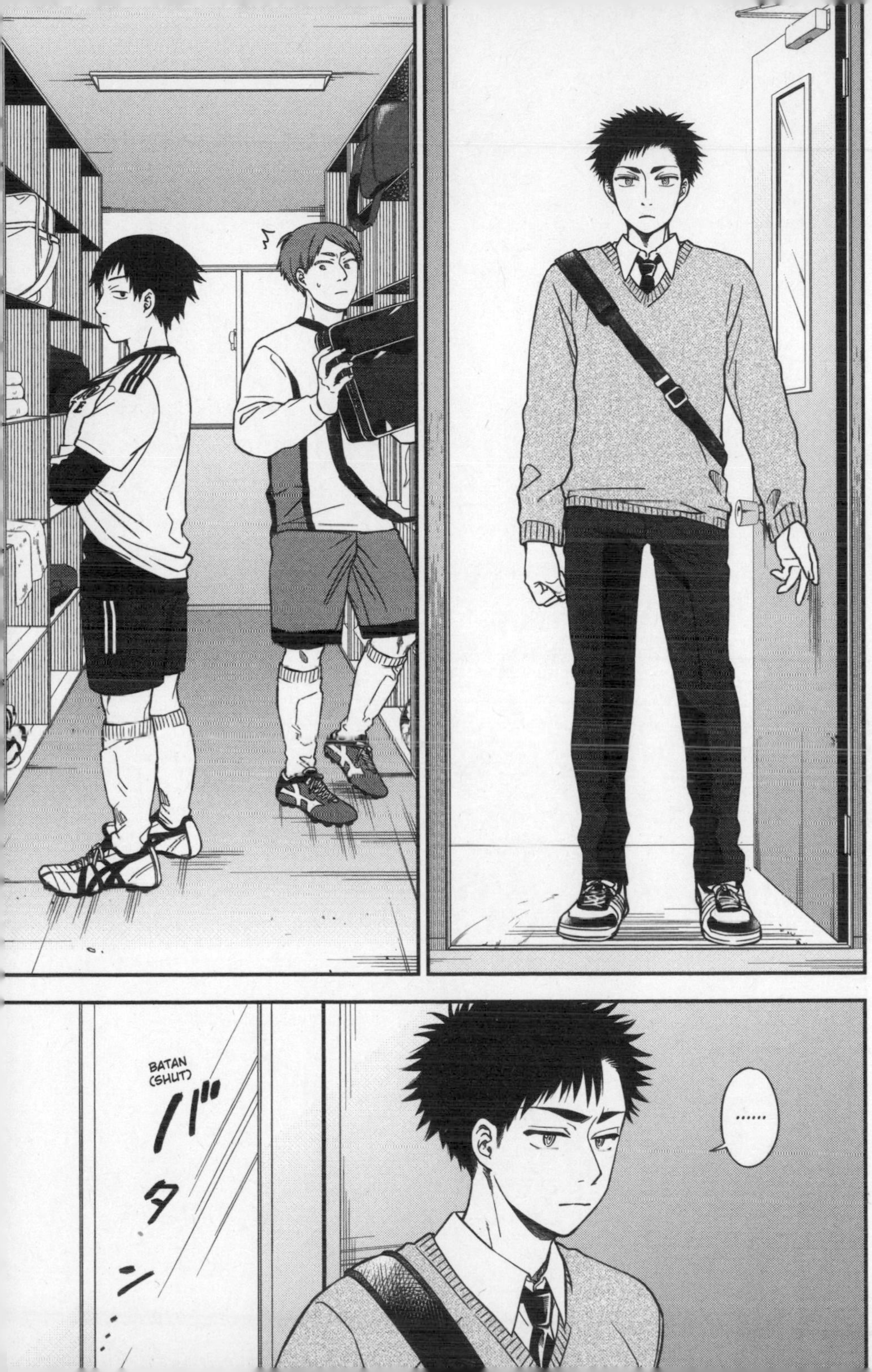
BATAN (SHUT)
バタン
......

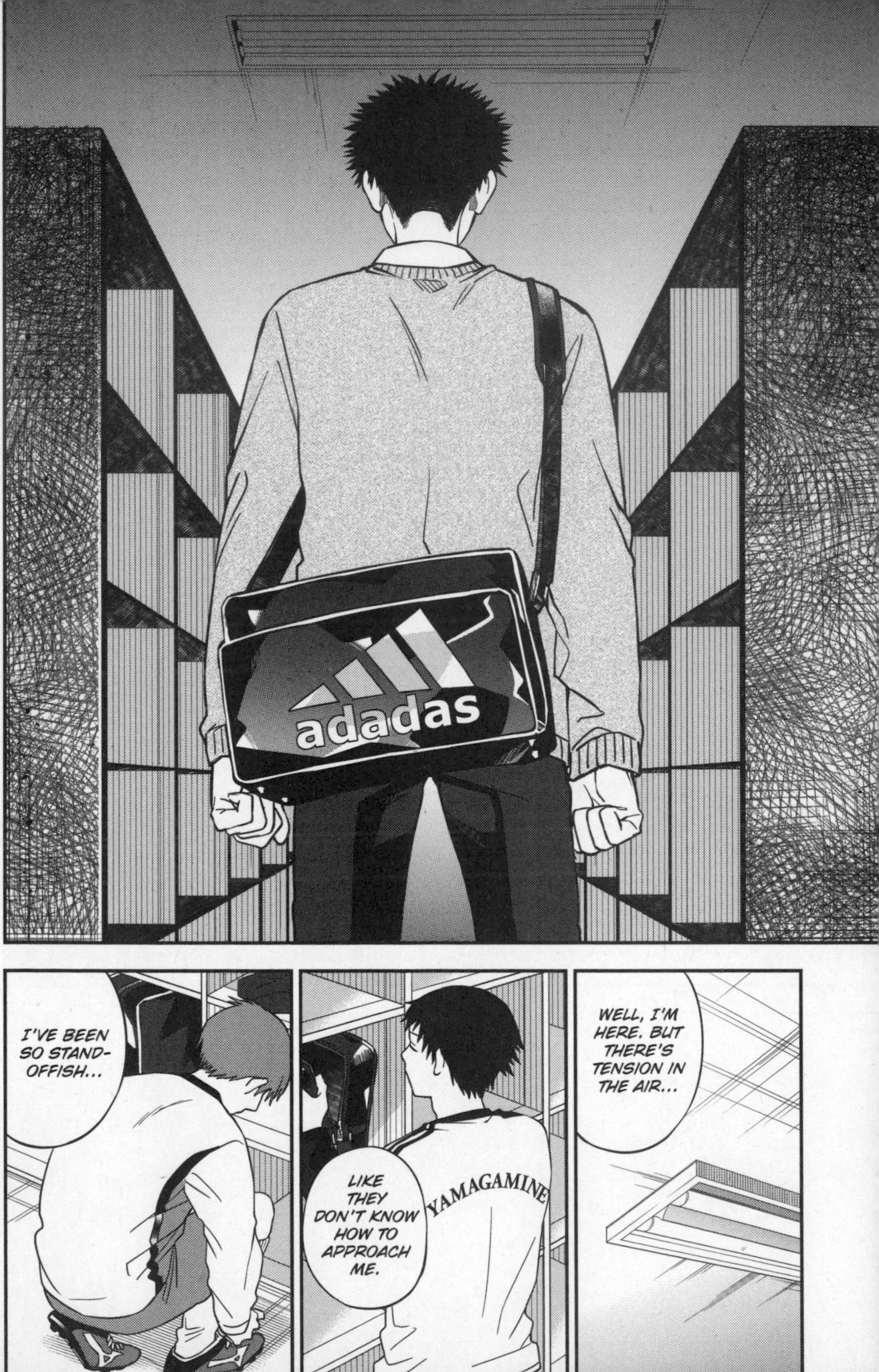
adadas
WELL, I'M HERE. BUT THERE'S TENSION IN THE AIR...
YAMAGAMINE
LIKE THEY DON'T KNOW HOW TO APPROACH ME.
I'VE BEEN SO STAND-OFFISH...

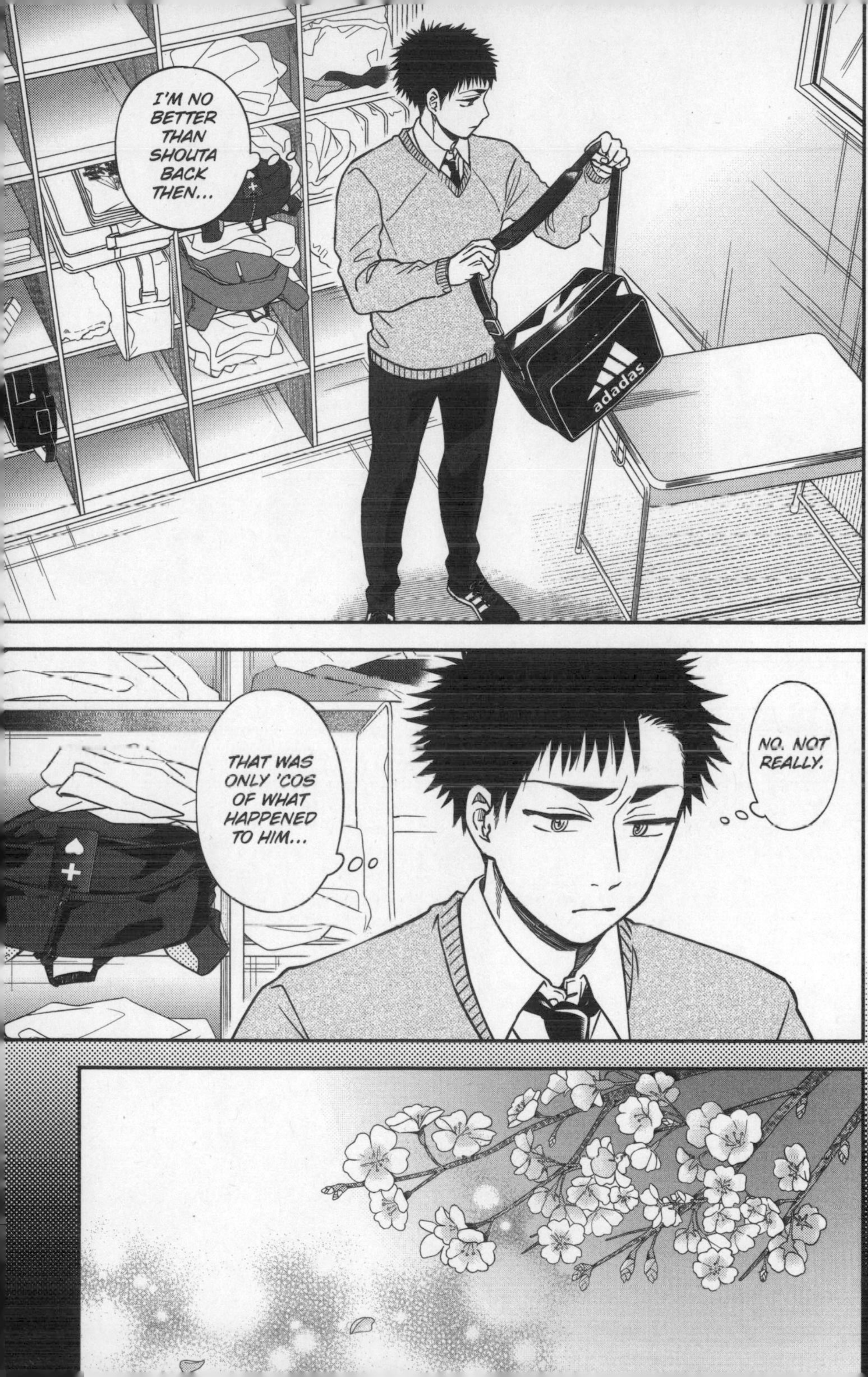
I'M NO BETTER THAN SHOUTA BACK THEN...
adadas
NO. NOT REALLY.
THAT WAS ONLY 'COS OF WHAT HAPPENED TO HIM...

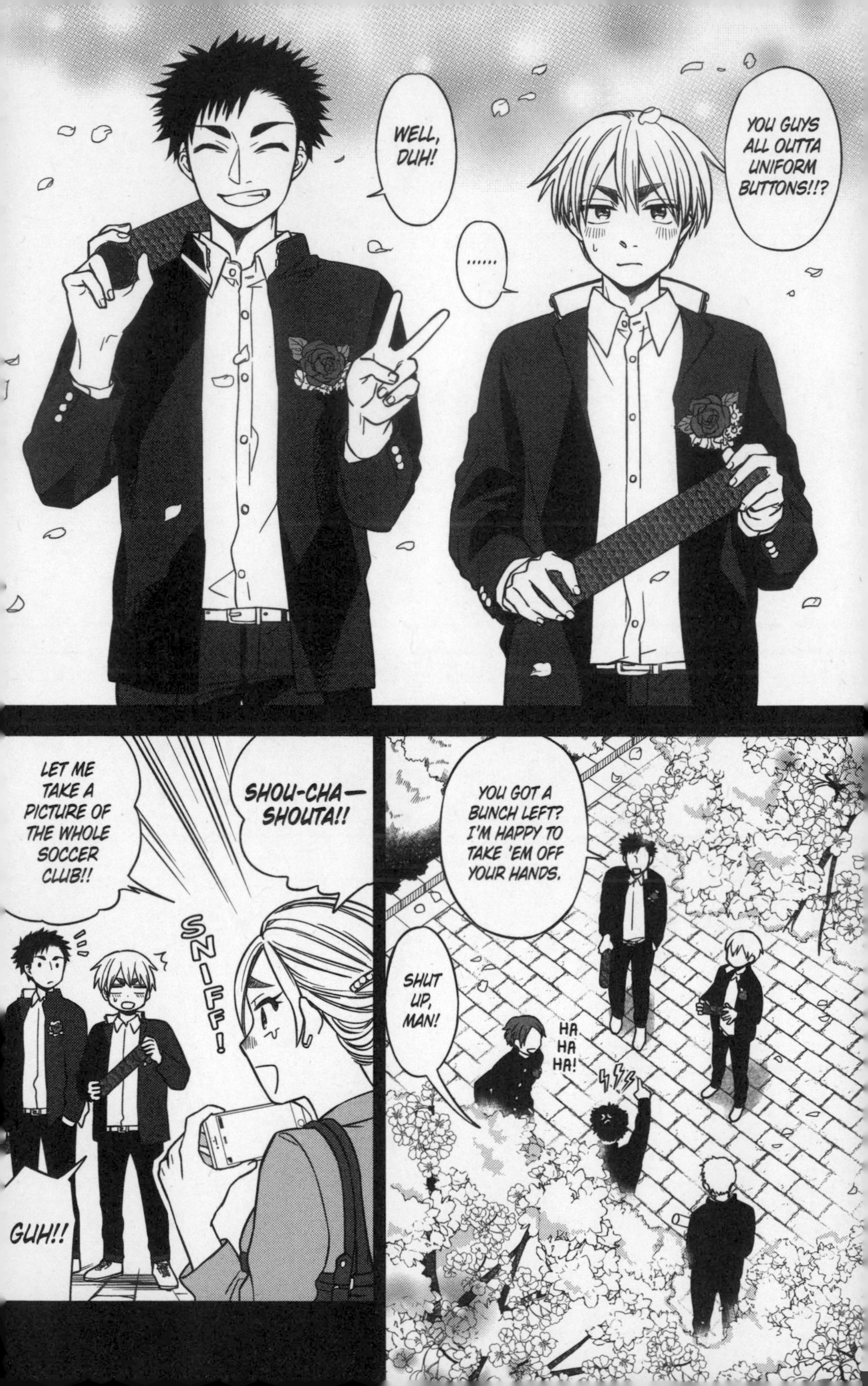
YOU GUYS ALL OUTTA UNIFORM BUTTONS!!?
WELL, DUH!
......
YOU GOT A BUNCH LEFT? I'M HAPPY TO TAKE 'EM OFF YOUR HANDS.
SHUT UP, MAN!
HA HA HA!
SHOU-CHA— SHOUTA!!
LET ME TAKE A PICTURE OF THE WHOLE SOCCER CLUB!!
SNIFF!
GUH!!

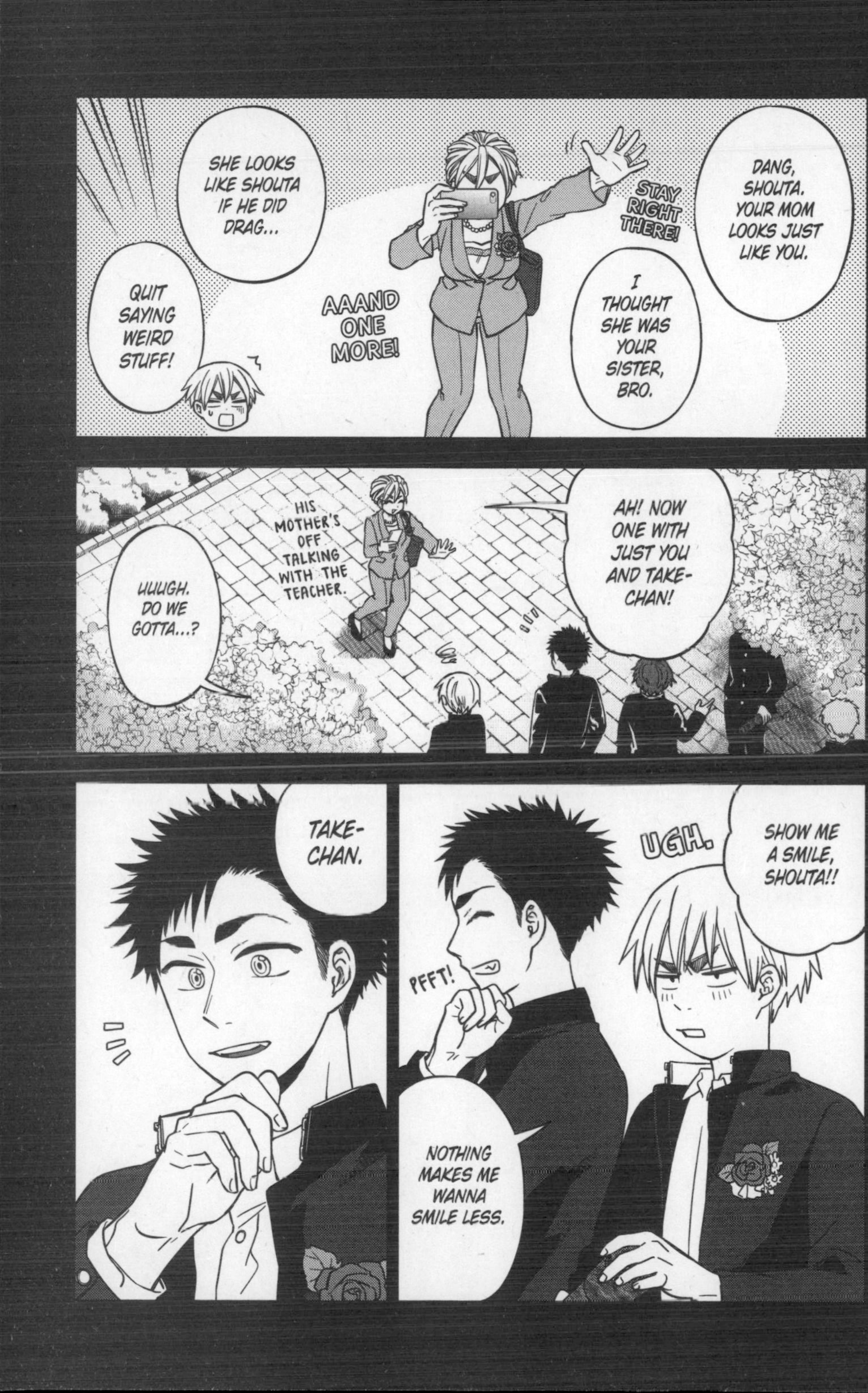
DANG, SHOUTA. YOUR MOM LOOKS JUST LIKE YOU.
STAY RIGHT THERE!
I THOUGHT SHE WAS YOUR SISTER, BRO.
AAAND ONE MORE!
SHE LOOKS LIKE SHOUTA IF HE DID DRAG...
QUIT SAYING WEIRD STUFF!
AH! NOW ONE WITH JUST YOU AND TAKE-CHAN!
HIS MOTHER'S OFF TALKING WITH THE TEACHER.
UUUGH. DO WE GOTTA...?
SHOW ME A SMILE, SHOUTA!!
UGH.
PFFT!
NOTHING MAKES ME WANNA SMILE LESS.
TAKE-CHAN.

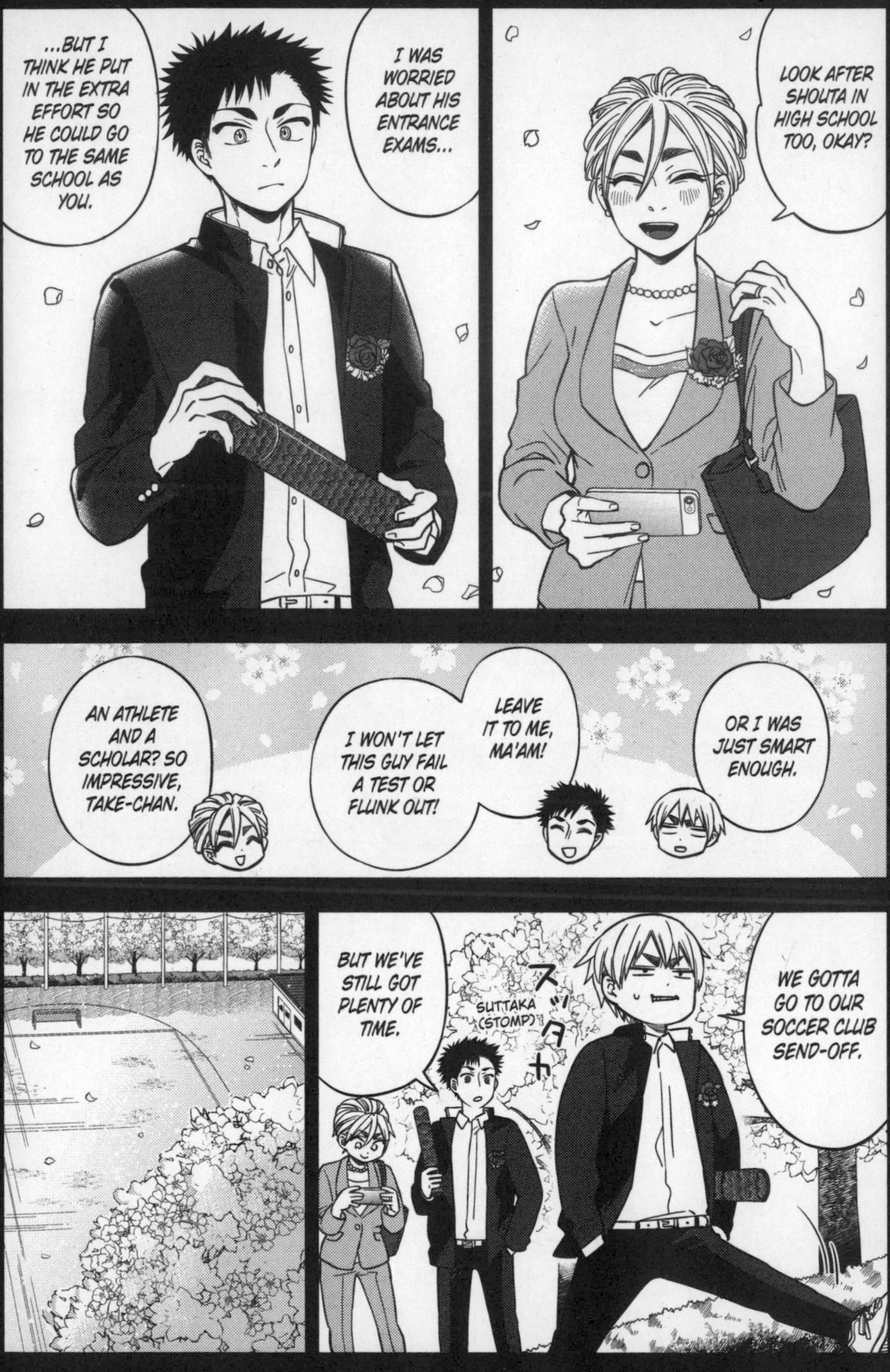
LOOK AFTER SHOUTA IN HIGH SCHOOL TOO, OKAY?
I WAS WORRIED ABOUT HIS ENTRANCE EXAMS...
...BUT I THINK HE PUT IN THE EXTRA EFFORT SO HE COULD GO TO THE SAME SCHOOL AS YOU.
OR I WAS JUST SMART ENOUGH.
LEAVE IT TO ME, MA'AM!
I WON'T LET THIS GUY FAIL A TEST OR FLUNK OUT!
AN ATHLETE AND A SCHOLAR? SO IMPRESSIVE, TAKE-CHAN.
WE GOTTA GO TO OUR SOCCER CLUB SEND-OFF.
SUTTAKA (STOMP)
BUT WE'VE STILL GOT PLENTY OF TIME.

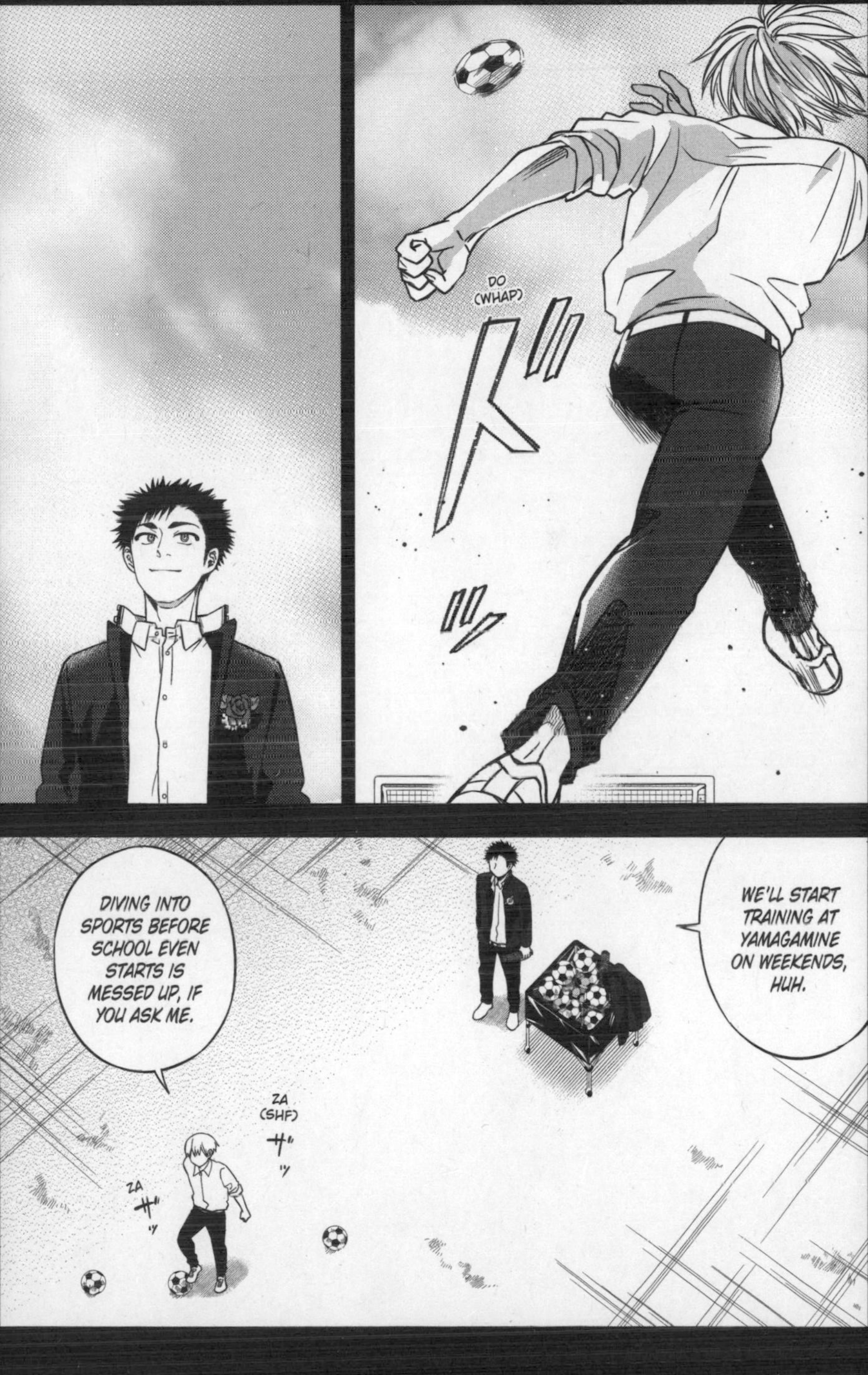
DO (WHAP)
WE'LL START TRAINING AT YAMAGAMINE ON WEEKENDS, HUH.
DIVING INTO SPORTS BEFORE SCHOOL EVEN STARTS IS MESSED UP, IF YOU ASK ME.
ZA (SHF)
ZA

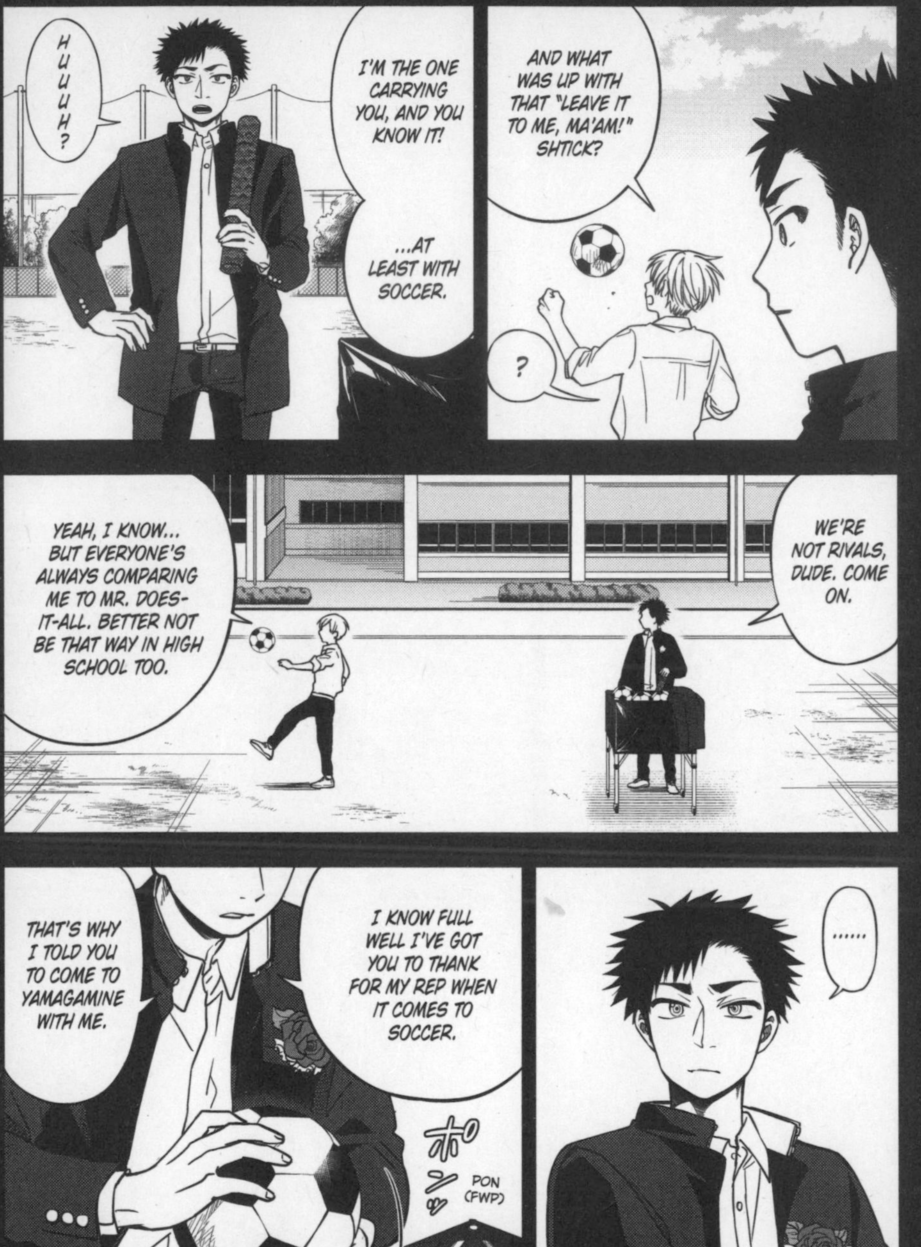
AND WHAT WAS UP WITH THAT "LEAVE IT TO ME, MA'AM!" SHTICK?
?
I'M THE ONE CARRYING YOU, AND YOU KNOW IT!
...AT LEAST WITH SOCCER.
HUUUH?
WE'RE NOT RIVALS, DUDE. COME ON.
YEAH, I KNOW... BUT EVERYONE'S ALWAYS COMPARING ME TO MR. DOES-IT-ALL. BETTER NOT BE THAT WAY IN HIGH SCHOOL TOO.
......
I KNOW FULL WELL I'VE GOT YOU TO THANK FOR MY REP WHEN IT COMES TO SOCCER.
ポン
PON (FWP)
THAT'S WHY I TOLD YOU TO COME TO YAMAGAMINE WITH ME.

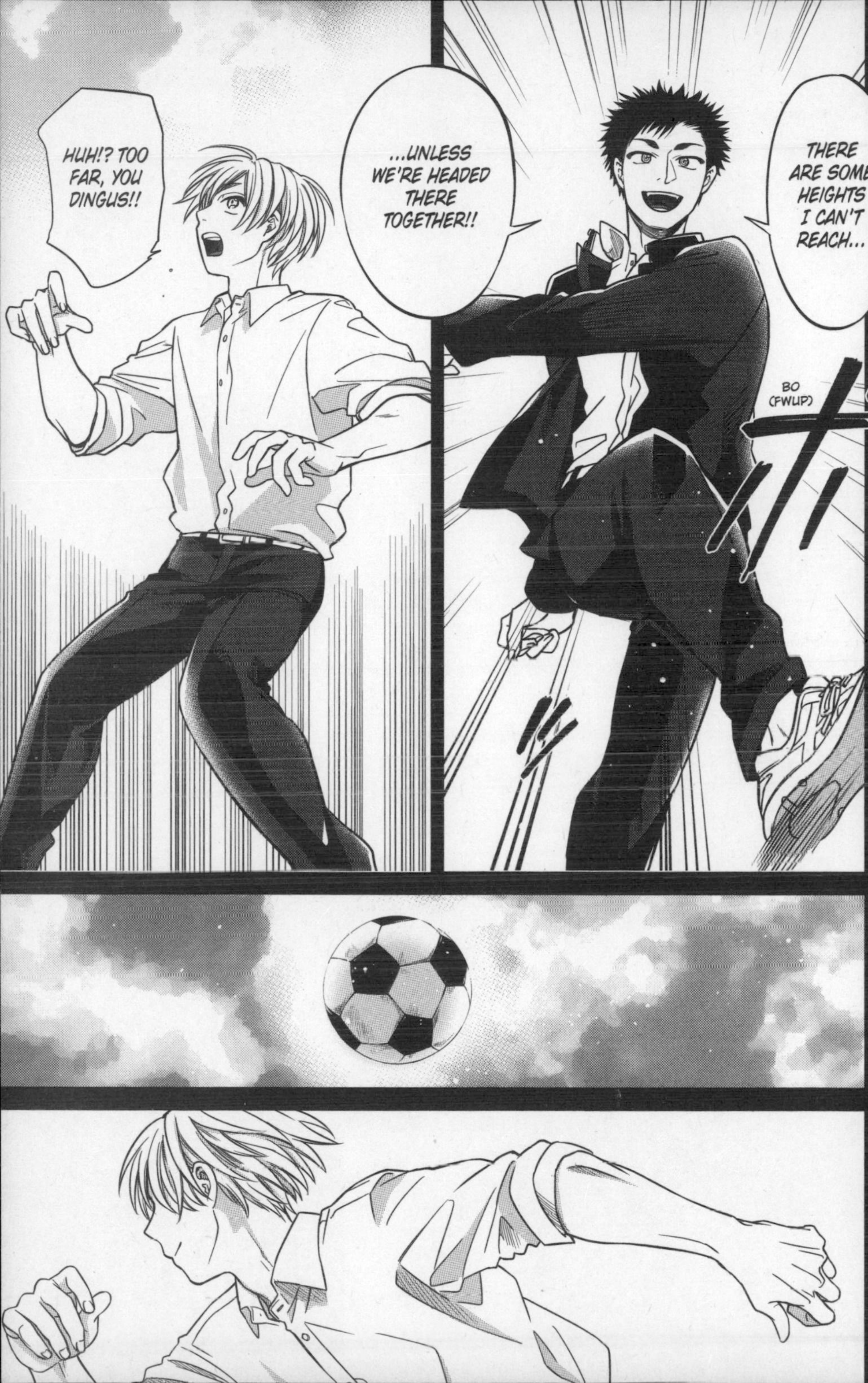
THERE ARE SOME HEIGHTS I CAN'T REACH...
...UNLESS WE'RE HEADED THERE TOGETHER!!
BO (FWUP)
HUH!? TOO FAR, YOU DINGUS!!

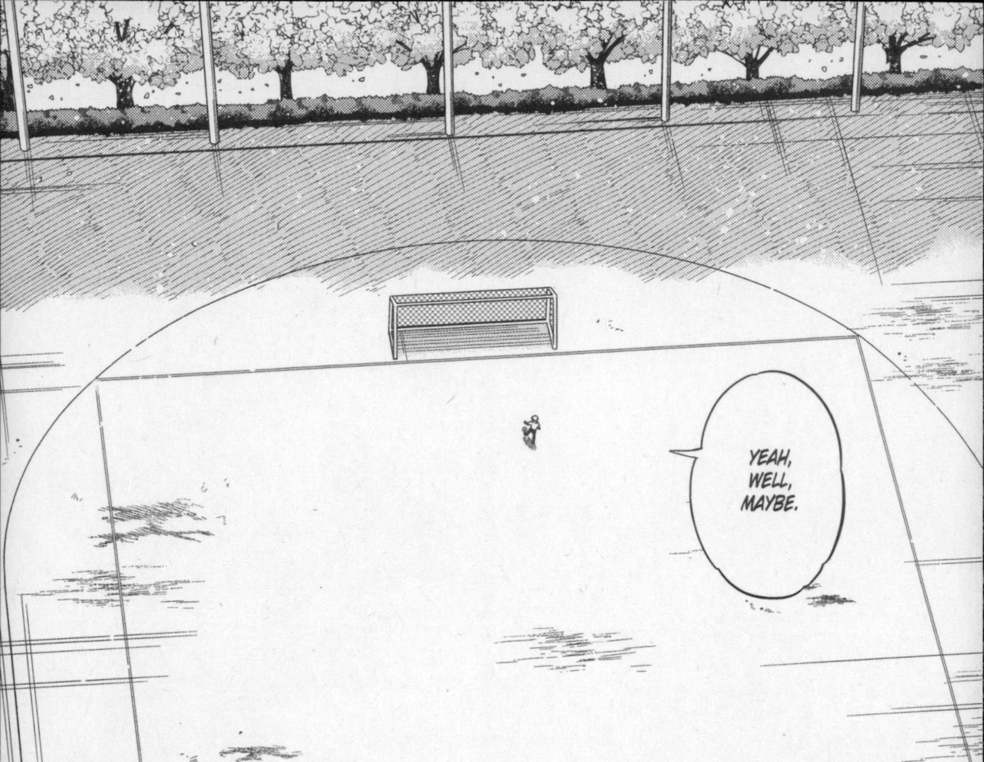
YEAH, WELL, MAYBE.
HEH, YOU'RE SUCH A PUSHOVER...

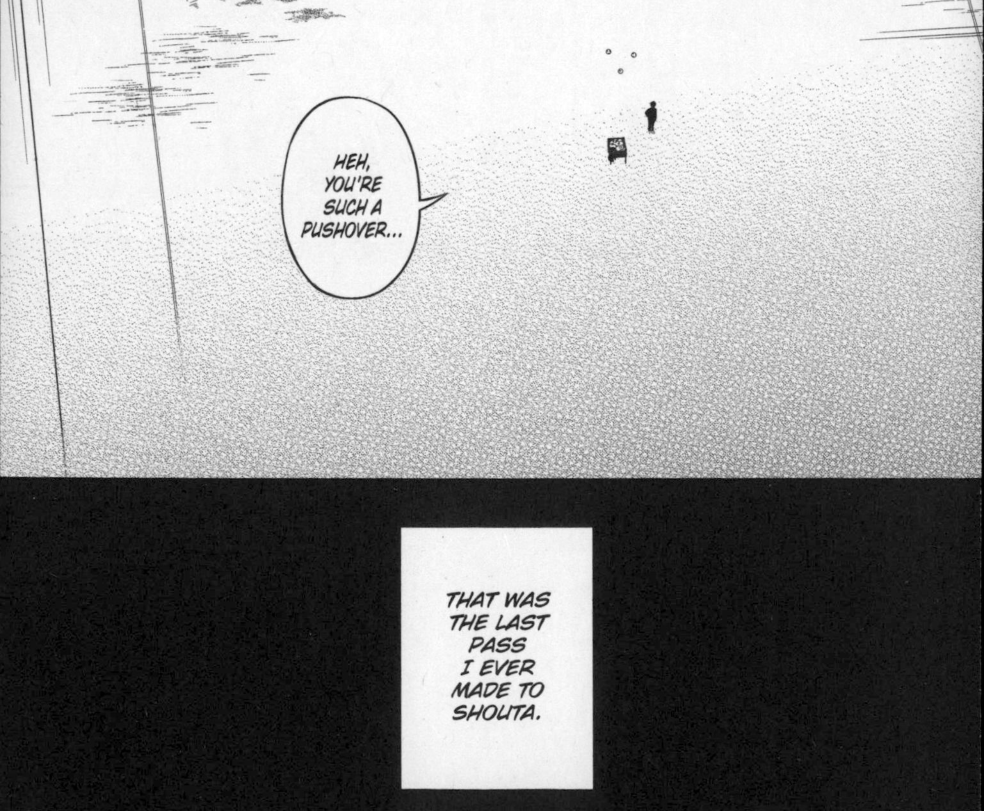
THAT WAS THE LAST PASS I EVER MADE TO SHOUTA.

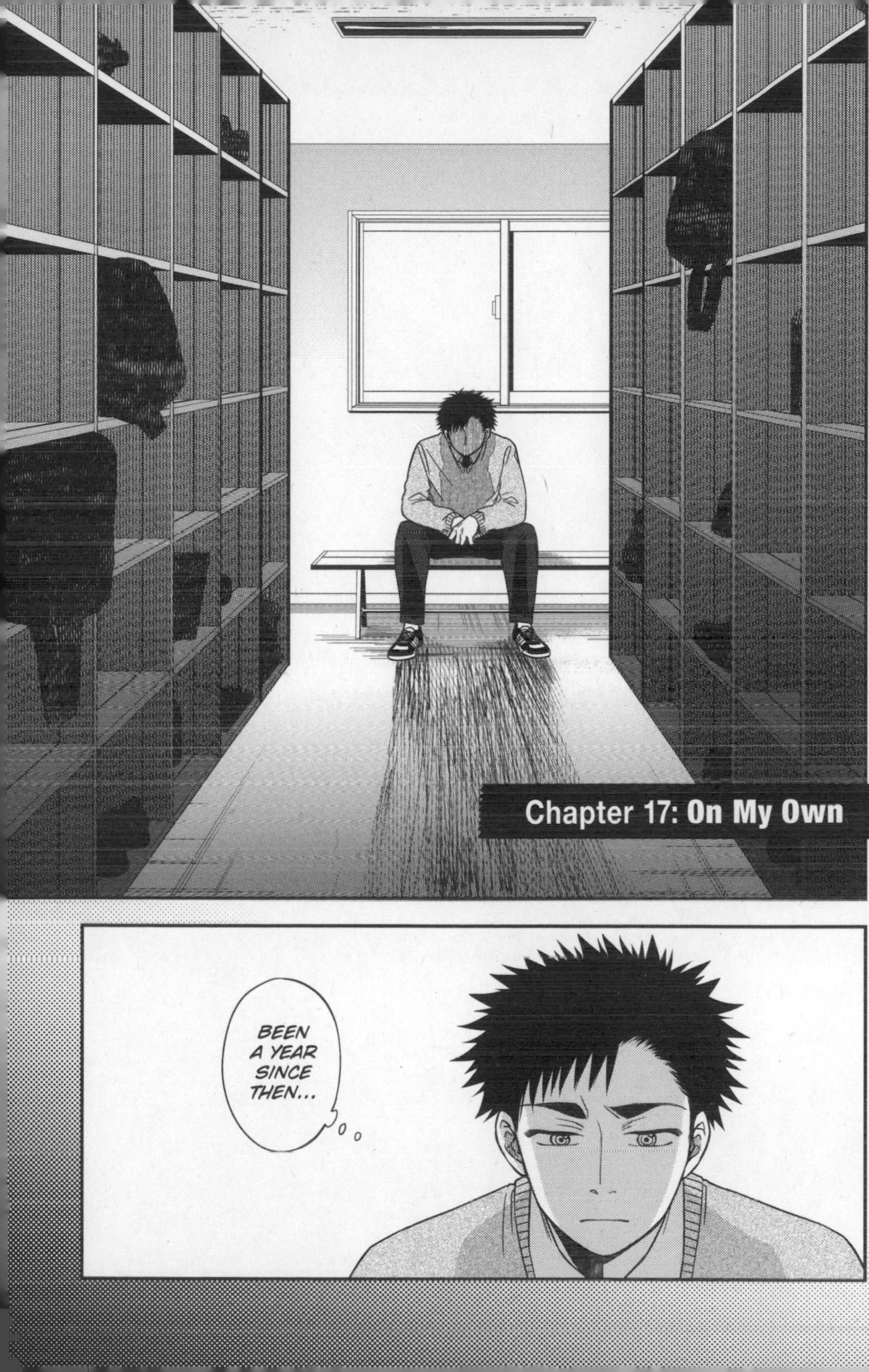
Chapter 17: On My Own
BEEN A YEAR SINCE THEN...

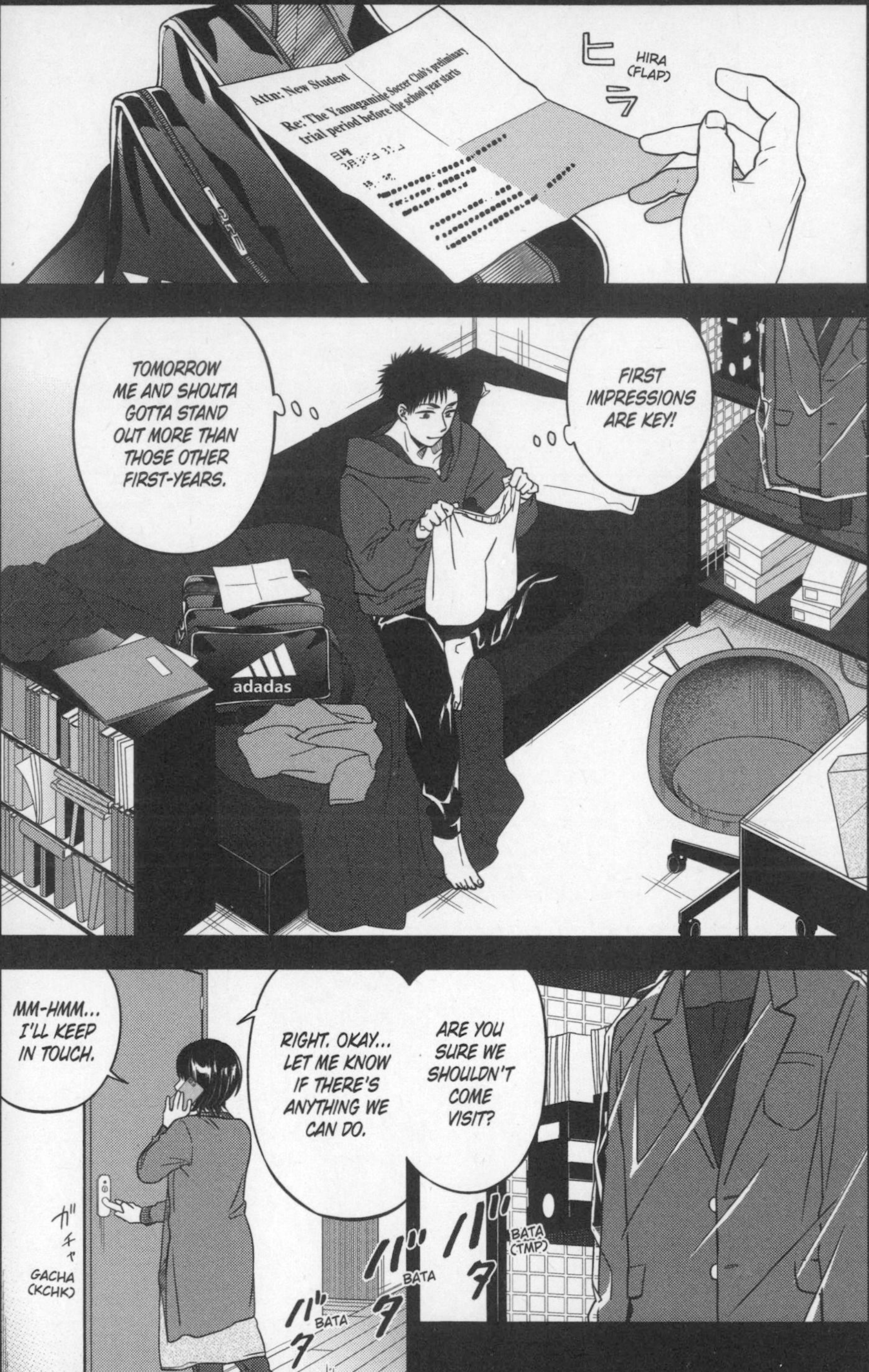
Attn: New Student
Re: The Yamagamine Soccer Club's preliminary trial period before the school year starts
ヒラ
HIRA (FLAP)
FIRST IMPRESSIONS ARE KEY!
TOMORROW ME AND SHOUTA GOTTA STAND OUT MORE THAN THOSE OTHER FIRST-YEARS.
adadas
ARE YOU SURE WE SHOULDN'T COME VISIT?
RIGHT. OKAY... LET ME KNOW IF THERE'S ANYTHING WE CAN DO.
MM-HMM... I'LL KEEP IN TOUCH.
バタ
BATA (TMP)
バタ
BATA
バタ
BATA
ガチャ
GACHA (KCHK)

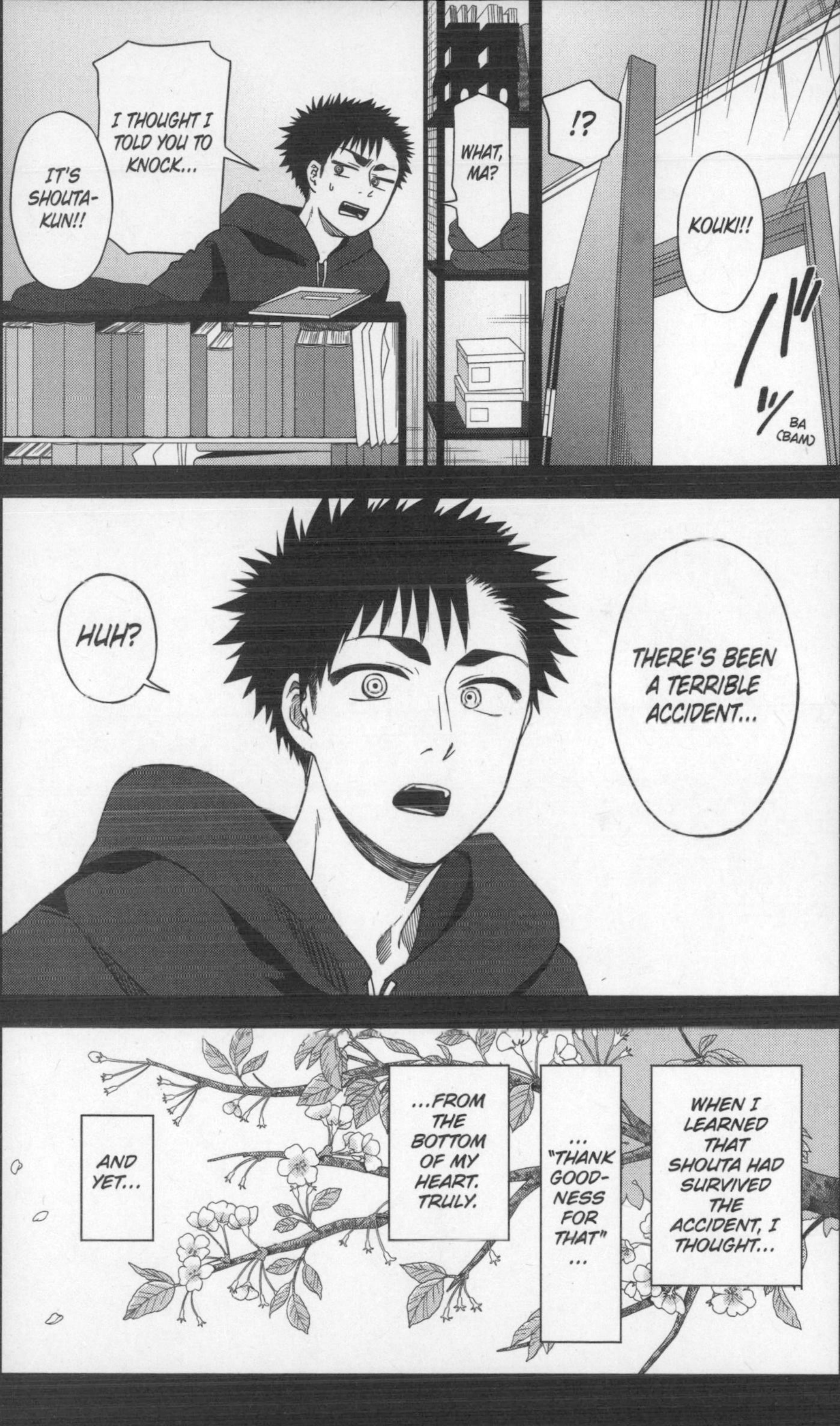
BA (BAM)
KOUKI!!
!?
WHAT, MA?
I THOUGHT I TOLD YOU TO KNOCK...
IT'S SHOUTA-KUN!!
THERE'S BEEN A TERRIBLE ACCIDENT...
HUH?
WHEN I LEARNED THAT SHOUTA HAD SURVIVED THE ACCIDENT, I THOUGHT...
..."THANK GOODNESS FOR THAT"...
...FROM THE BOTTOM OF MY HEART. TRULY.
AND YET...

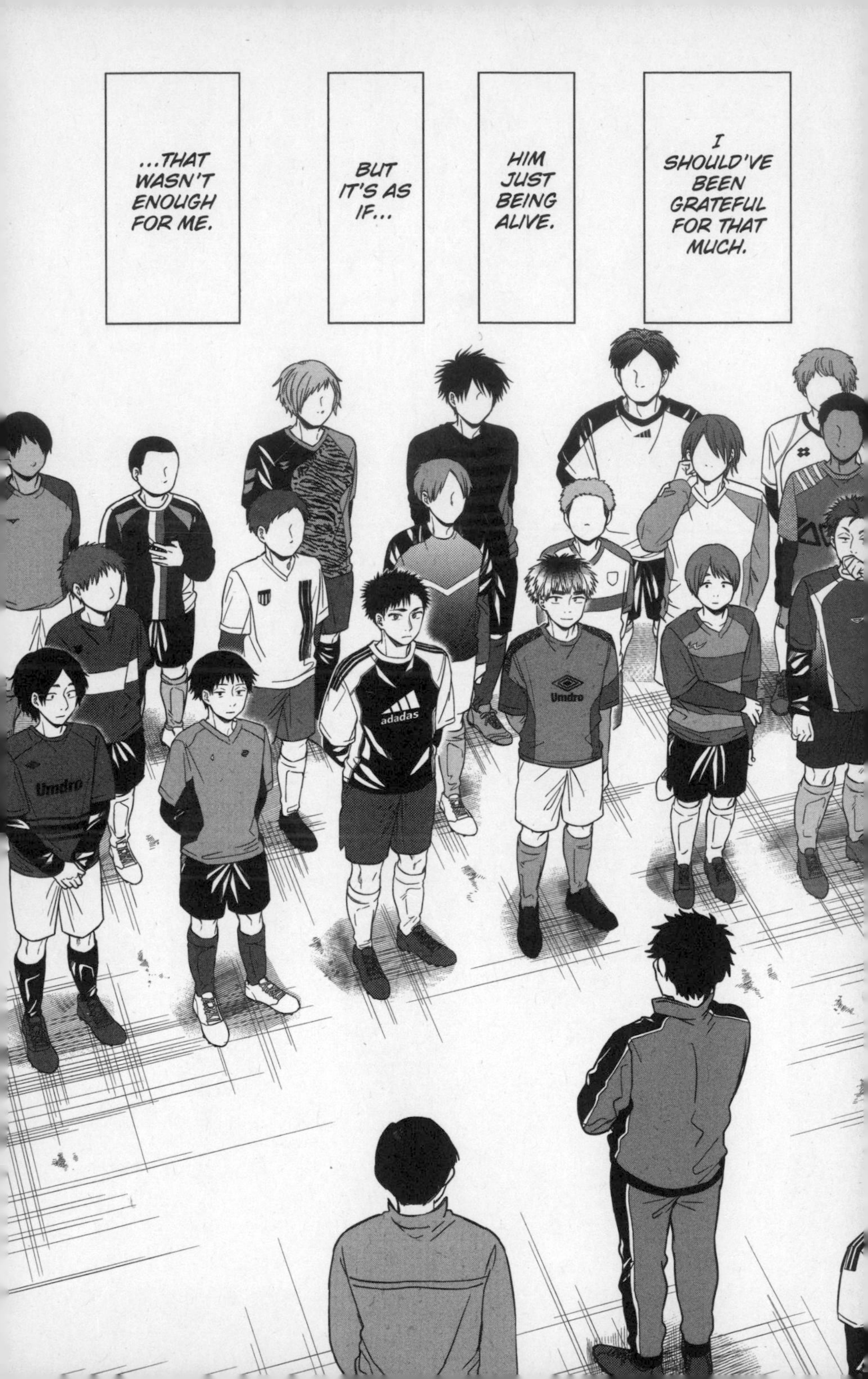
I SHOULD'VE BEEN GRATEFUL FOR THAT MUCH.
HIM JUST BEING ALIVE.
BUT IT'S AS IF...
...THAT WASN'T ENOUGH FOR ME.
Umdro
adadas
Umdro

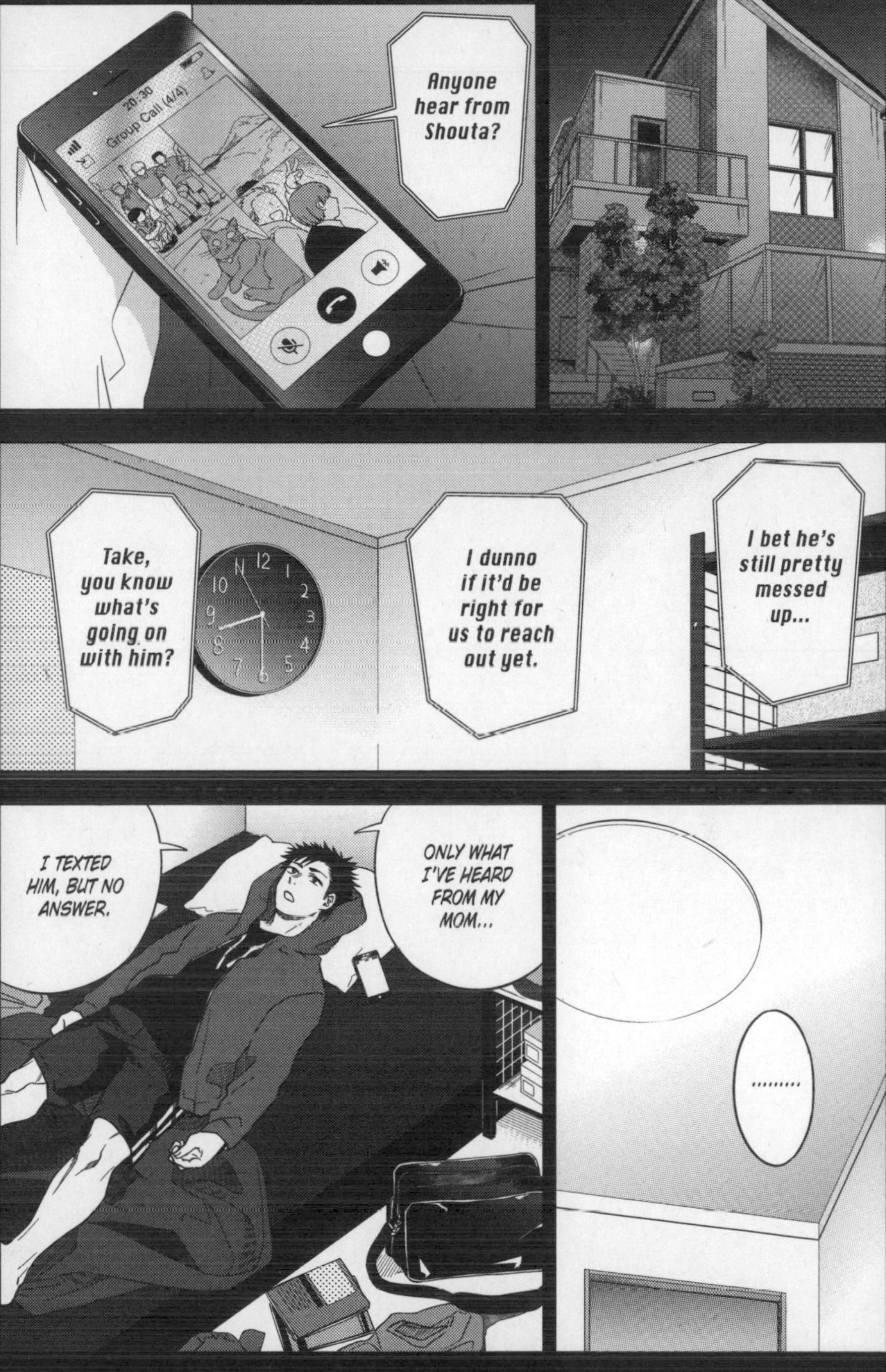
20:30
Group Call (4/4)
Anyone hear from Shouta?
I bet he's still pretty messed up...
I dunno if it'd be right for us to reach out yet.
Take, you know what's going on with him?
....
ONLY WHAT I'VE HEARD FROM MY MOM...
I TEXTED HIM, BUT NO ANSWER.

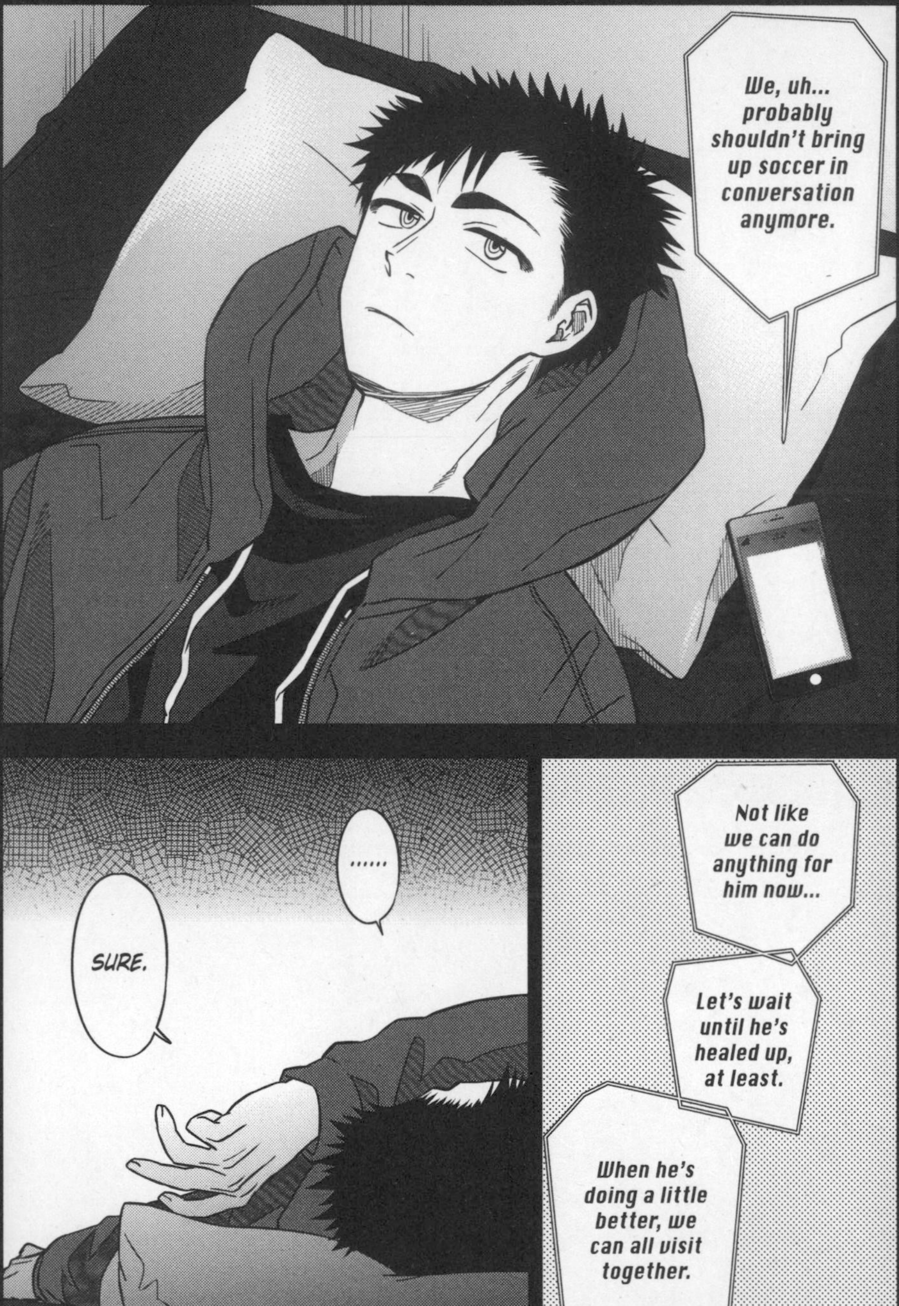

We, uh... probably shouldn't bring up soccer in conversation anymore.
Not like we can do anything for him now...
Let's wait until he's healed up, at least.
When he's doing a little better, we can all visit together.
......
SURE.

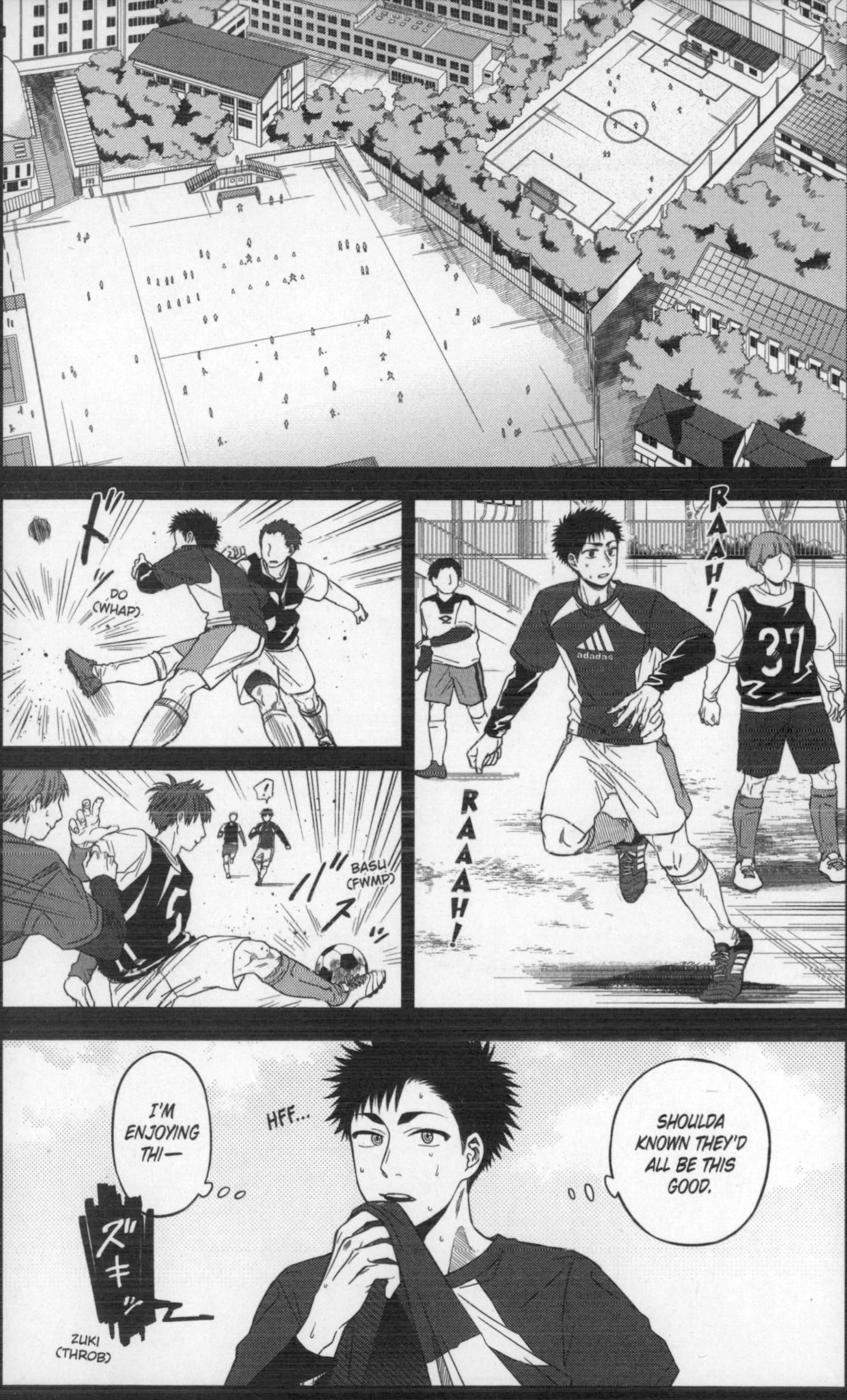

RAAH!
RAAAH!
DO (WHAP)
!
BASU (FWMP)
SHOULDA KNOWN THEY'D ALL BE THIS GOOD.
HFF...
I'M ENJOYING THI—
ZUKI (THROB)

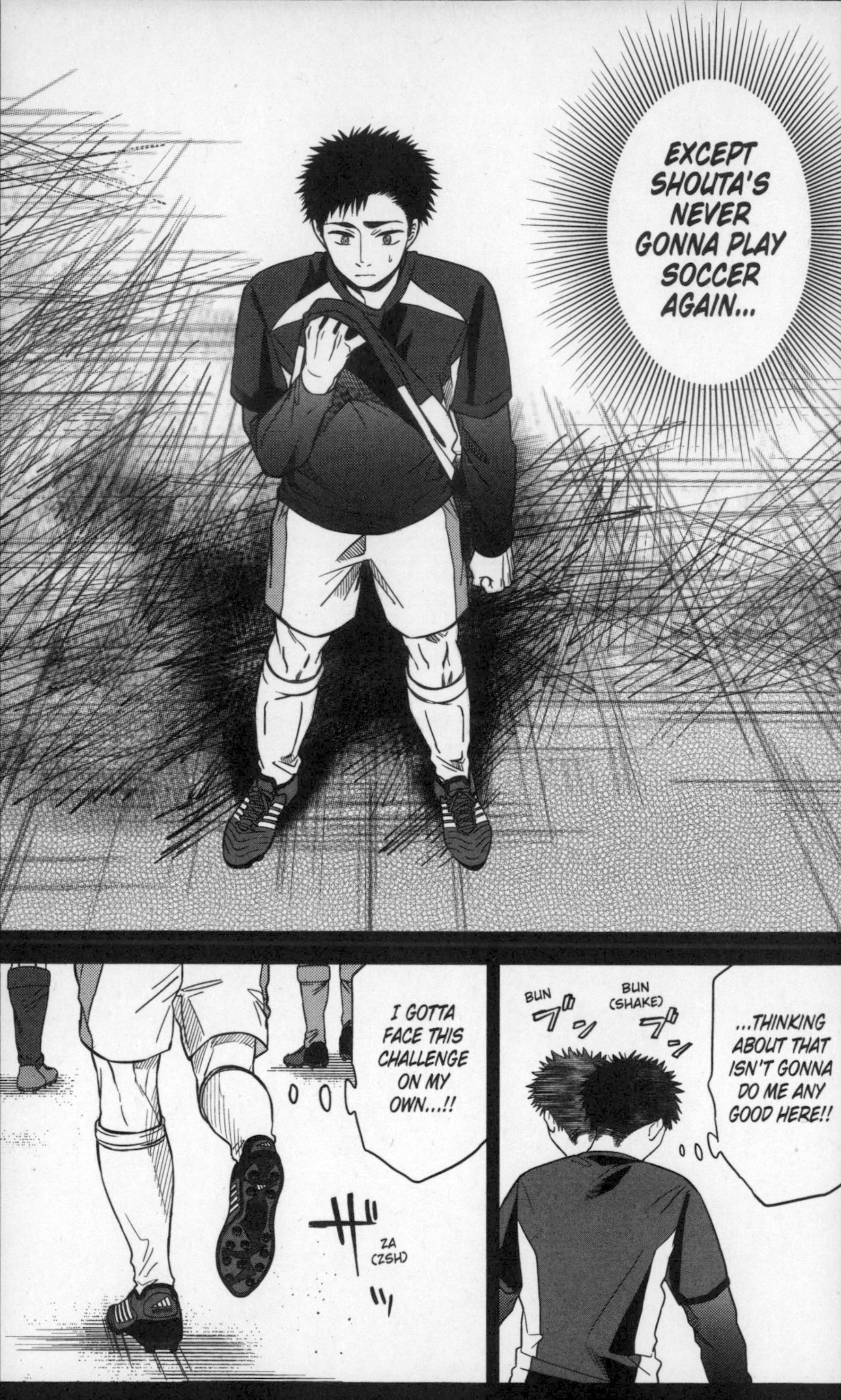
EXCEPT SHOUTA'S NEVER GONNA PLAY SOCCER AGAIN...
BUN
BUN (SHAKE)
...THINKING ABOUT THAT ISN'T GONNA DO ME ANY GOOD HERE!!
I GOTTA FACE THIS CHALLENGE ON MY OWN...!!
ZA (ZSH)

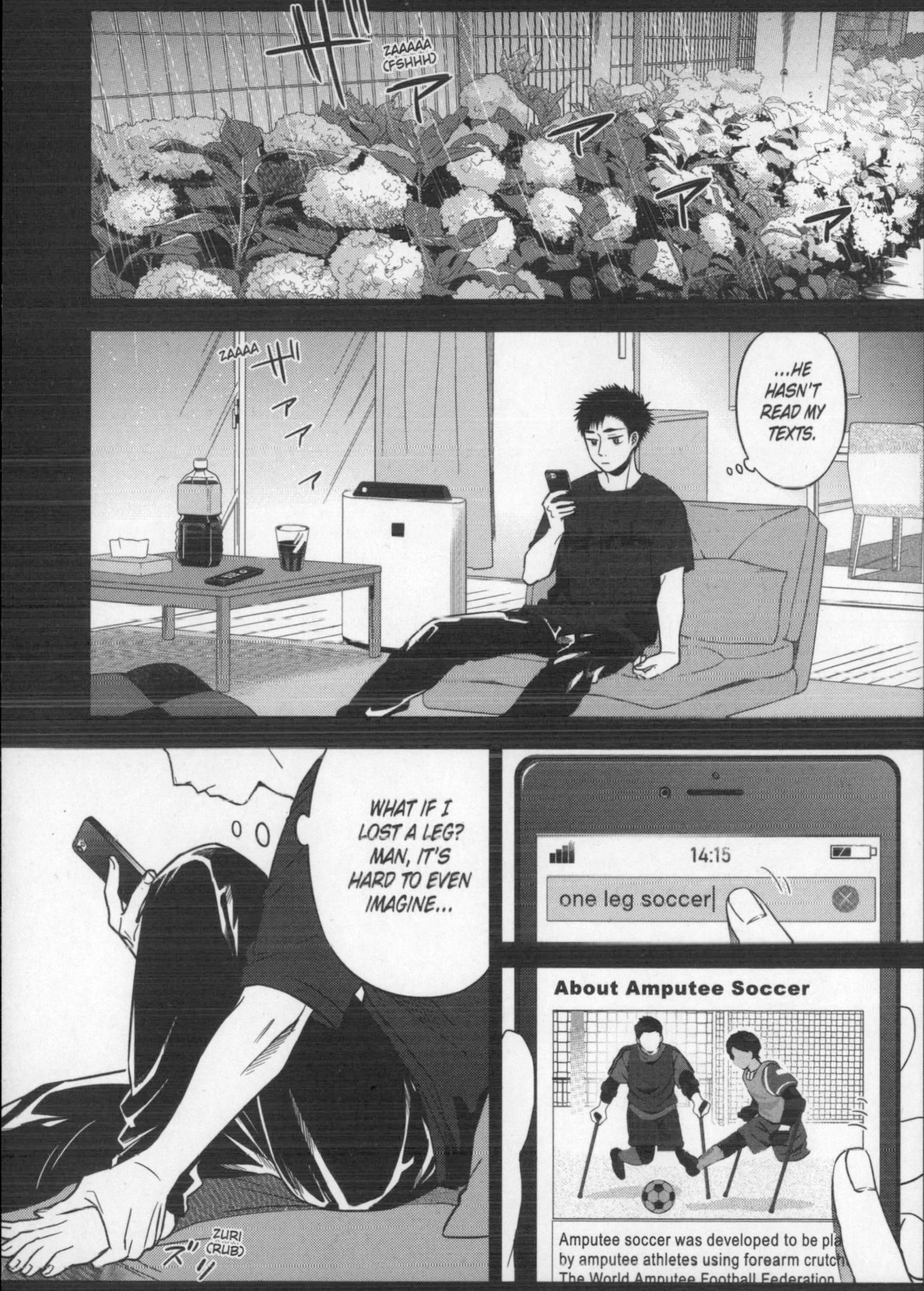

ZAAAAA (FSHHH)
ZAAAA
...HE HASN'T READ MY TEXTS.
14:15
one leg soccer
About Amputee Soccer
Amputee soccer was developed to be pla
by amputee athletes using forearm crutch
The World Amputee Football Federation
WHAT IF I LOST A LEG? MAN, IT'S HARD TO EVEN IMAGINE...
ZURI (RUB)

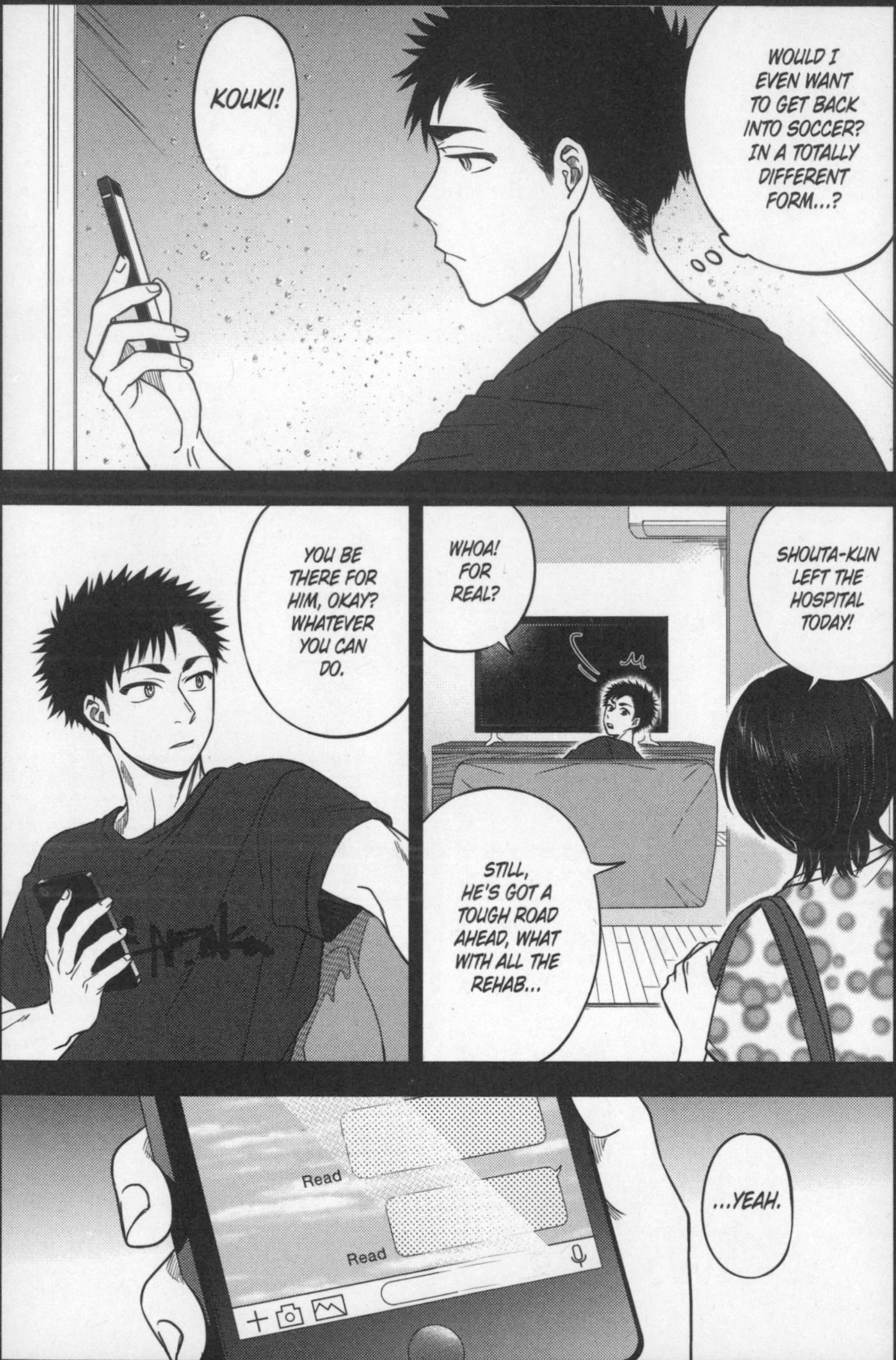
WOULD I EVEN WANT TO GET BACK INTO SOCCER? IN A TOTALLY DIFFERENT FORM...?
KOUKI!
SHOUTA-KUN LEFT THE HOSPITAL TODAY!
WHOA! FOR REAL?
STILL, HE'S GOT A TOUGH ROAD AHEAD, WHAT WITH ALL THE REHAB...
YOU BE THERE FOR HIM, OKAY? WHATEVER YOU CAN DO.
Read
Read
...YEAH.

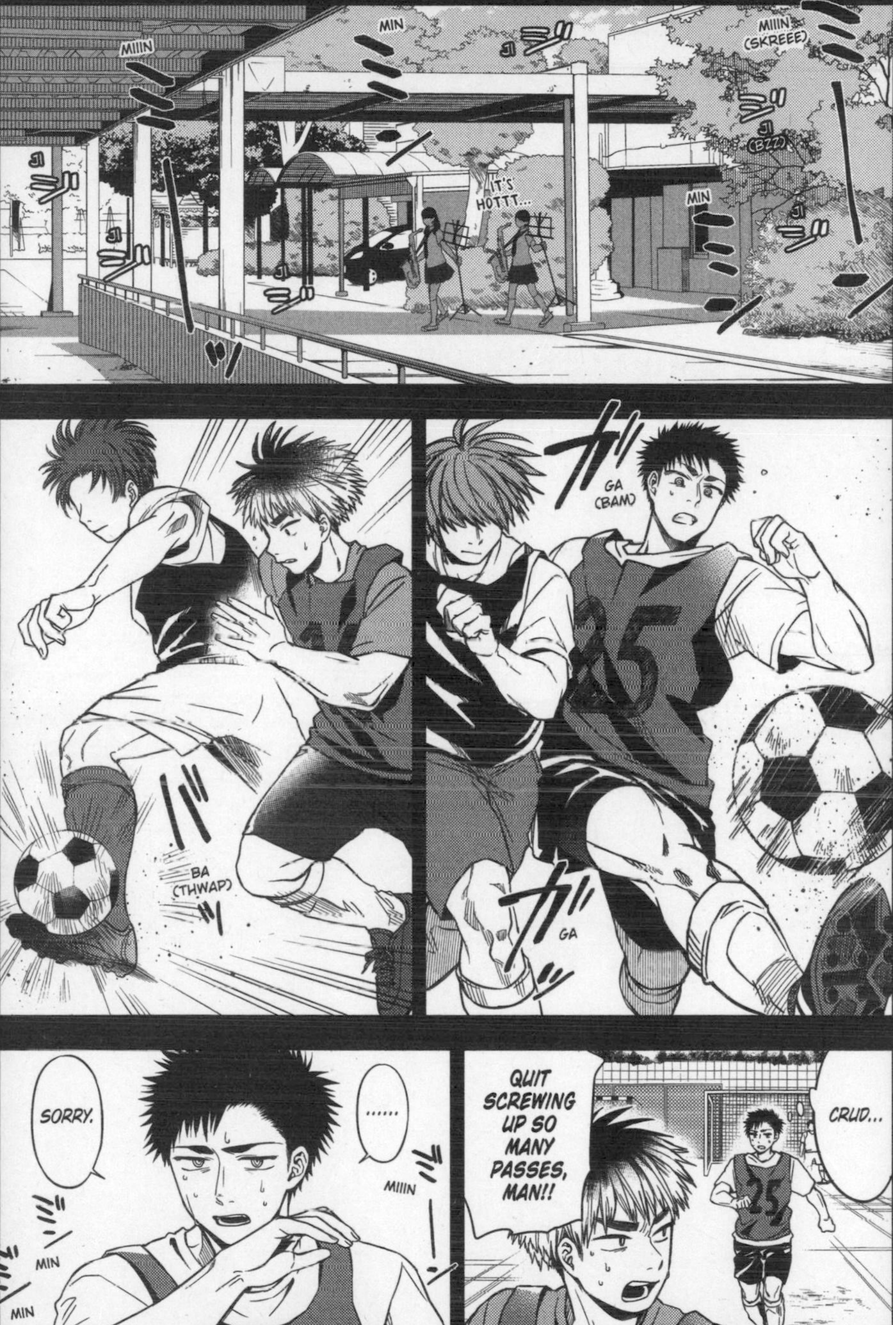
MIIIN
(SKREEE)
MIN
MIIIN
JI
(BZZ)
JI
IT'S HOTTT...
MIN
JI
JI
JI
GA
(BAM)
GA
BA
(THWAP)
CRUD...
QUIT SCREWING UP SO MANY PASSES, MAN!!
......
MIIIN
SORRY.
MIN
MIN

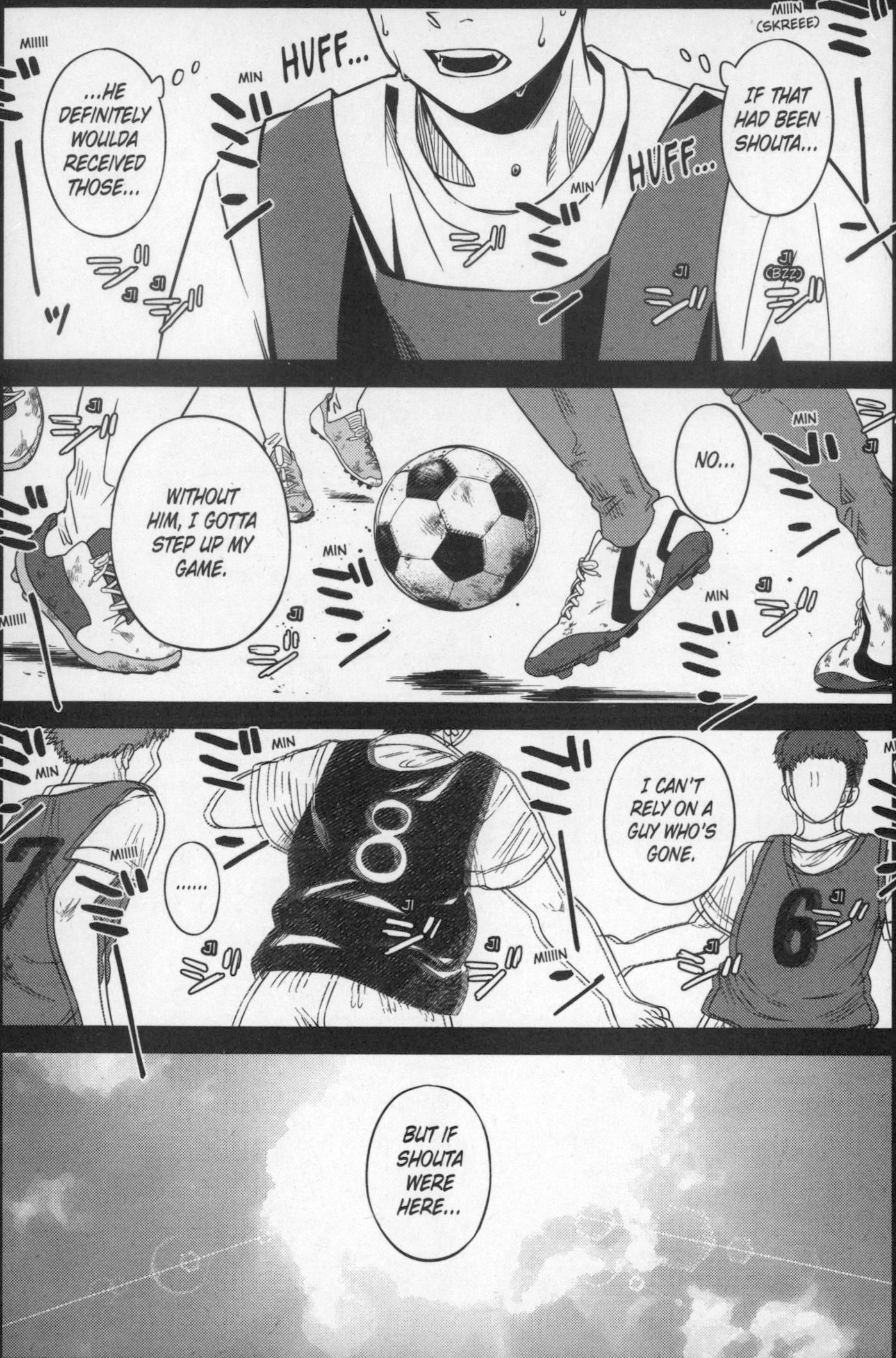
MIIIN (SKREEE)
IF THAT HAD BEEN SHOUTA...
HUFF...
MIN
HUFF...
MIN
...HE DEFINITELY WOULDA RECEIVED THOSE...
MIIIII
JI (BZZ)
JI
JI
MIN
NO...
JI
MIN
JI
MIN
WITHOUT HIM, I GOTTA STEP UP MY GAME.
JI
JI
MIIIII
MIN
I CAN'T RELY ON A GUY WHO'S GONE.
JI
JI
MIIIIN
JI
JI
......
MIIIII
MIN
MIN
BUT IF SHOUTA WERE HERE...

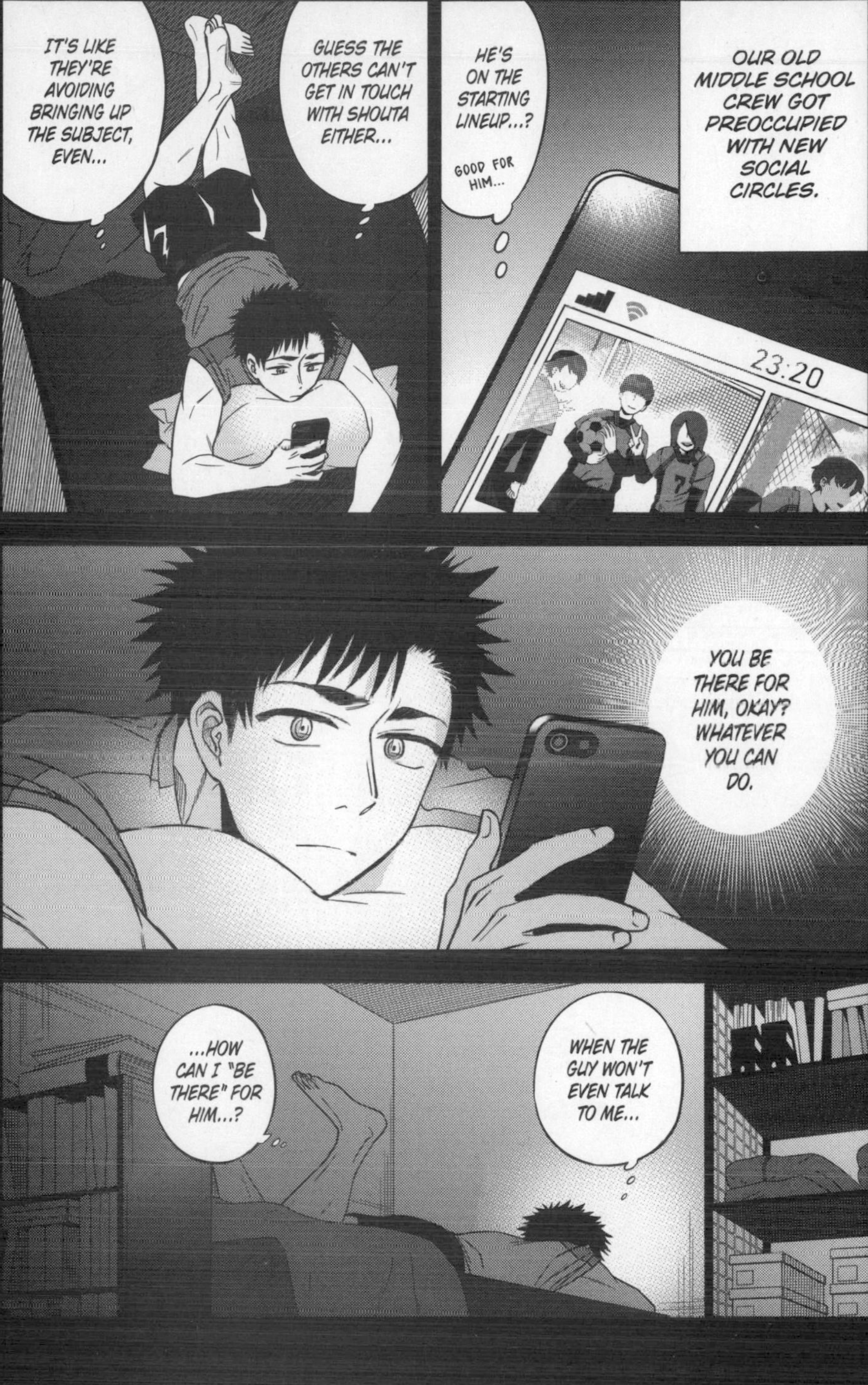
OUR OLD MIDDLE SCHOOL CREW GOT PREOCCUPIED WITH NEW SOCIAL CIRCLES.
HE'S ON THE STARTING LINEUP...?
GOOD FOR HIM...
23:20
GUESS THE OTHERS CAN'T GET IN TOUCH WITH SHOUTA EITHER...
IT'S LIKE THEY'RE AVOIDING BRINGING UP THE SUBJECT, EVEN...
YOU BE THERE FOR HIM, OKAY? WHATEVER YOU CAN DO.
WHEN THE GUY WON'T EVEN TALK TO ME...
...HOW CAN I "BE THERE" FOR HIM...?

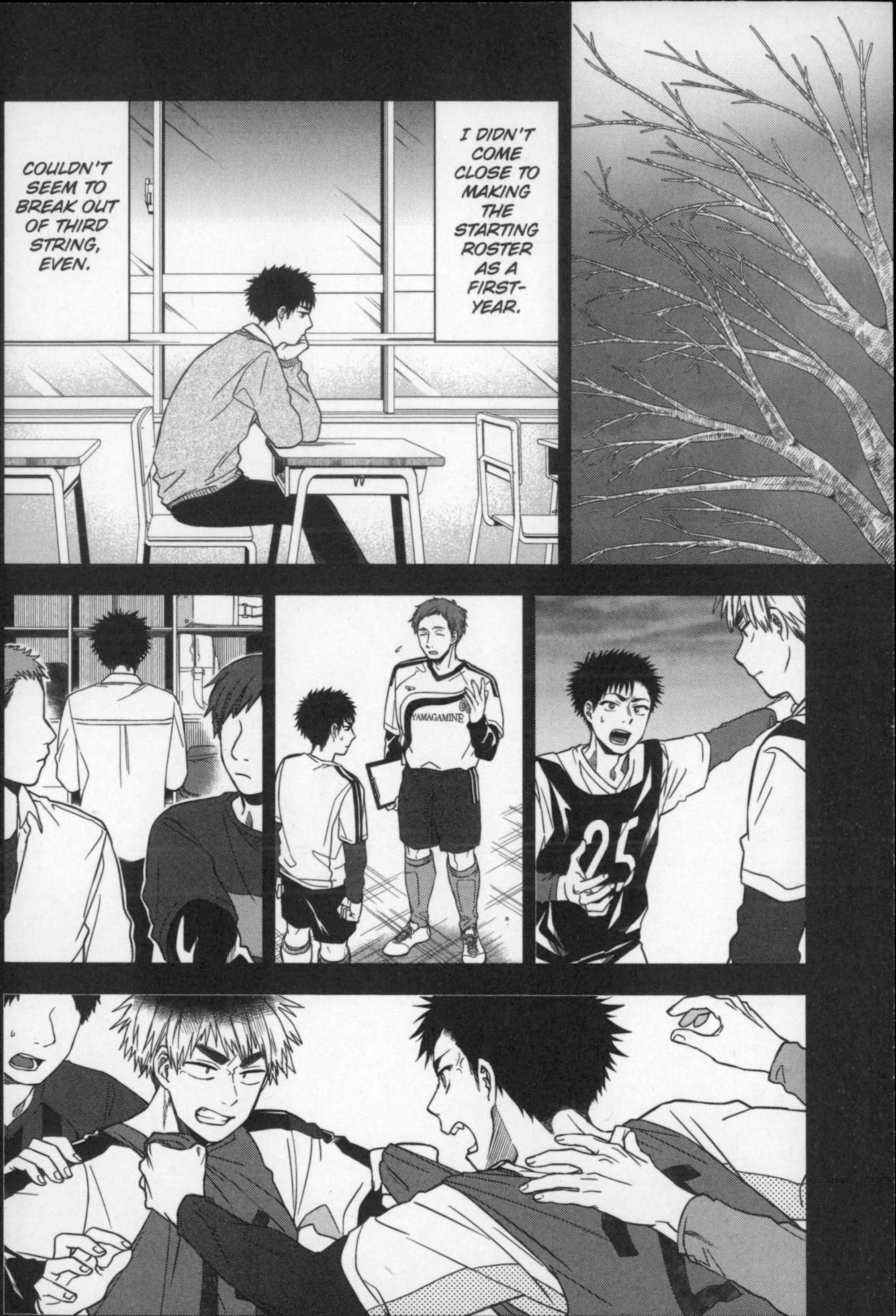
I DIDN'T COME CLOSE TO MAKING THE STARTING ROSTER AS A FIRST-YEAR.
COULDN'T SEEM TO BREAK OUT OF THIRD STRING, EVEN.
25
YAMAGAMINE

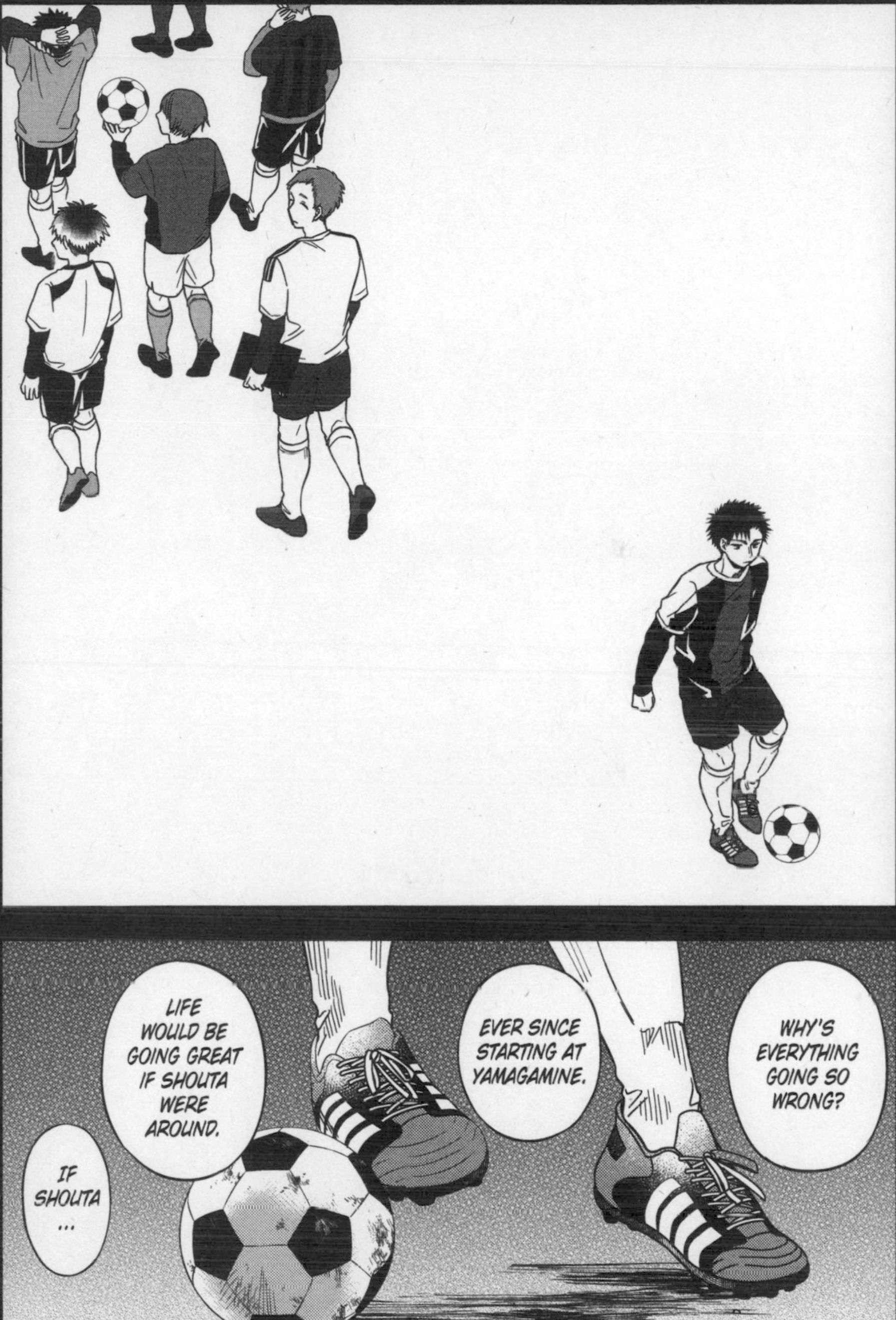
WHY'S EVERYTHING GOING SO WRONG?
EVER SINCE STARTING AT YAMAGAMINE.
LIFE WOULD BE GOING GREAT IF SHOUTA WERE AROUND.
IF SHOUTA ...

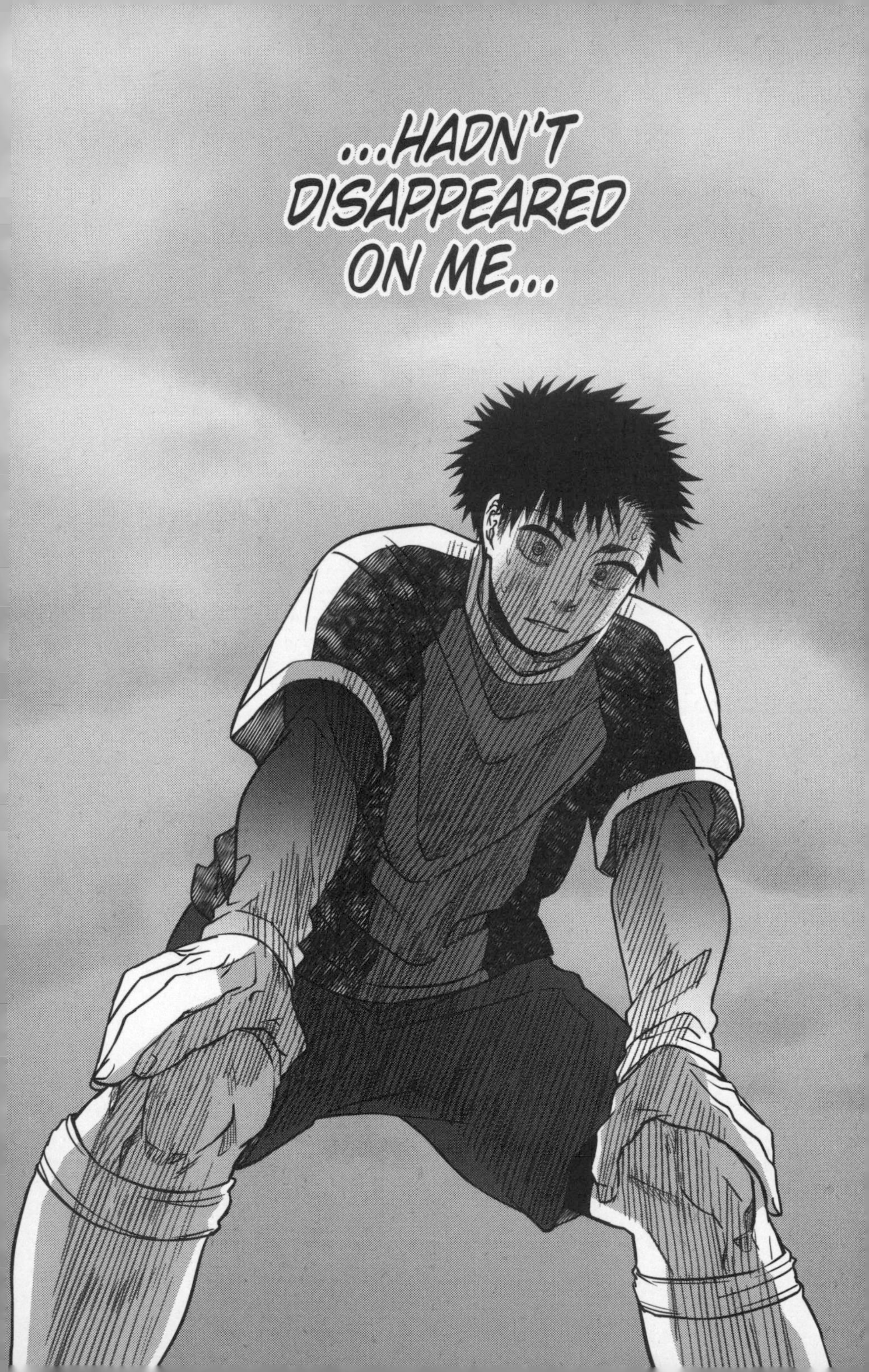
...HADN'T DISAPPEARED ON ME...

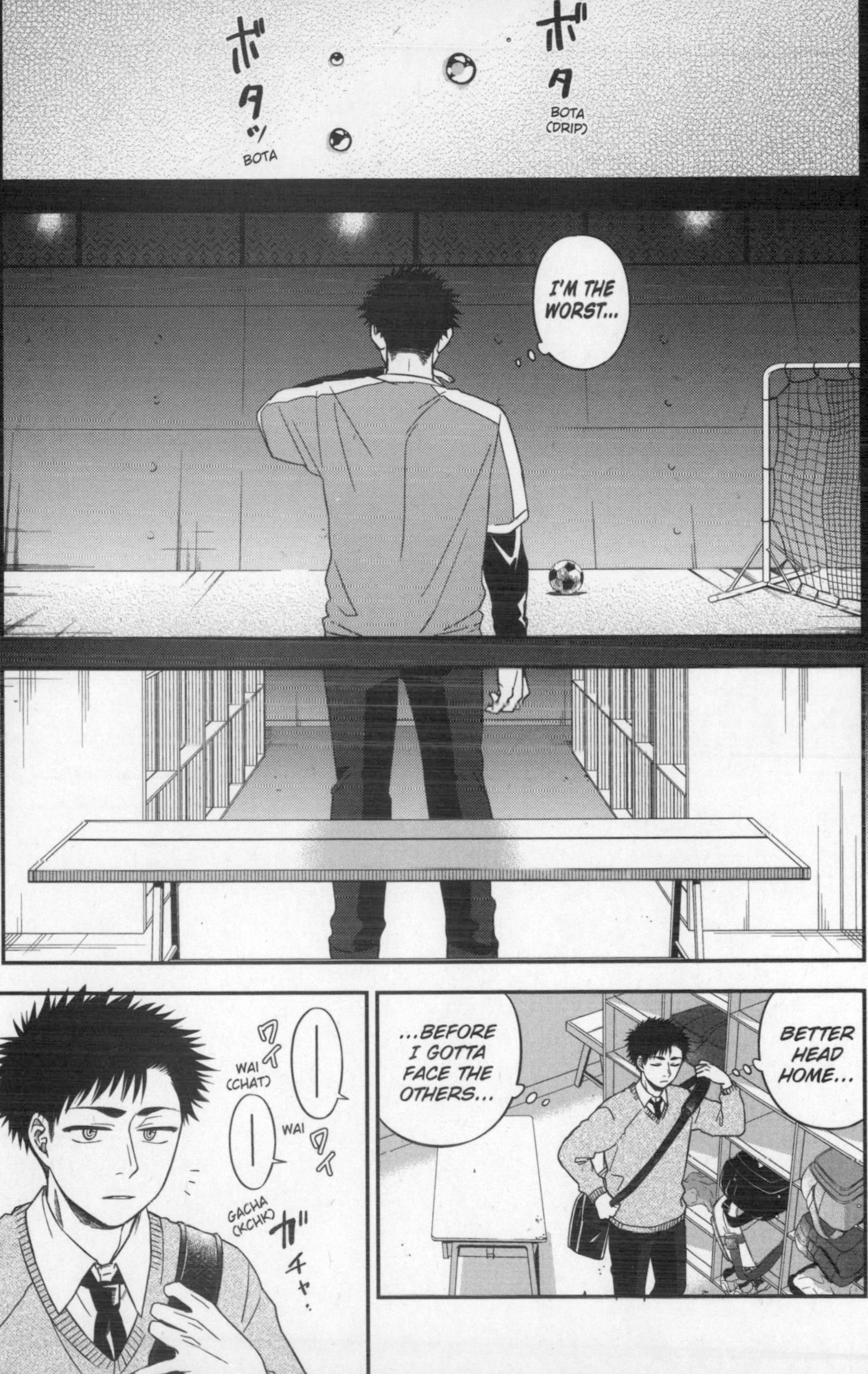
ボタ
BOTA (DRIP)
ボタッ
BOTA
I'M THE WORST...
BETTER HEAD HOME...
...BEFORE I GOTTA FACE THE OTHERS...
ワイ
WAI (CHAT)
ワイ
WAI
ガチャ
GACHA (KCHK)

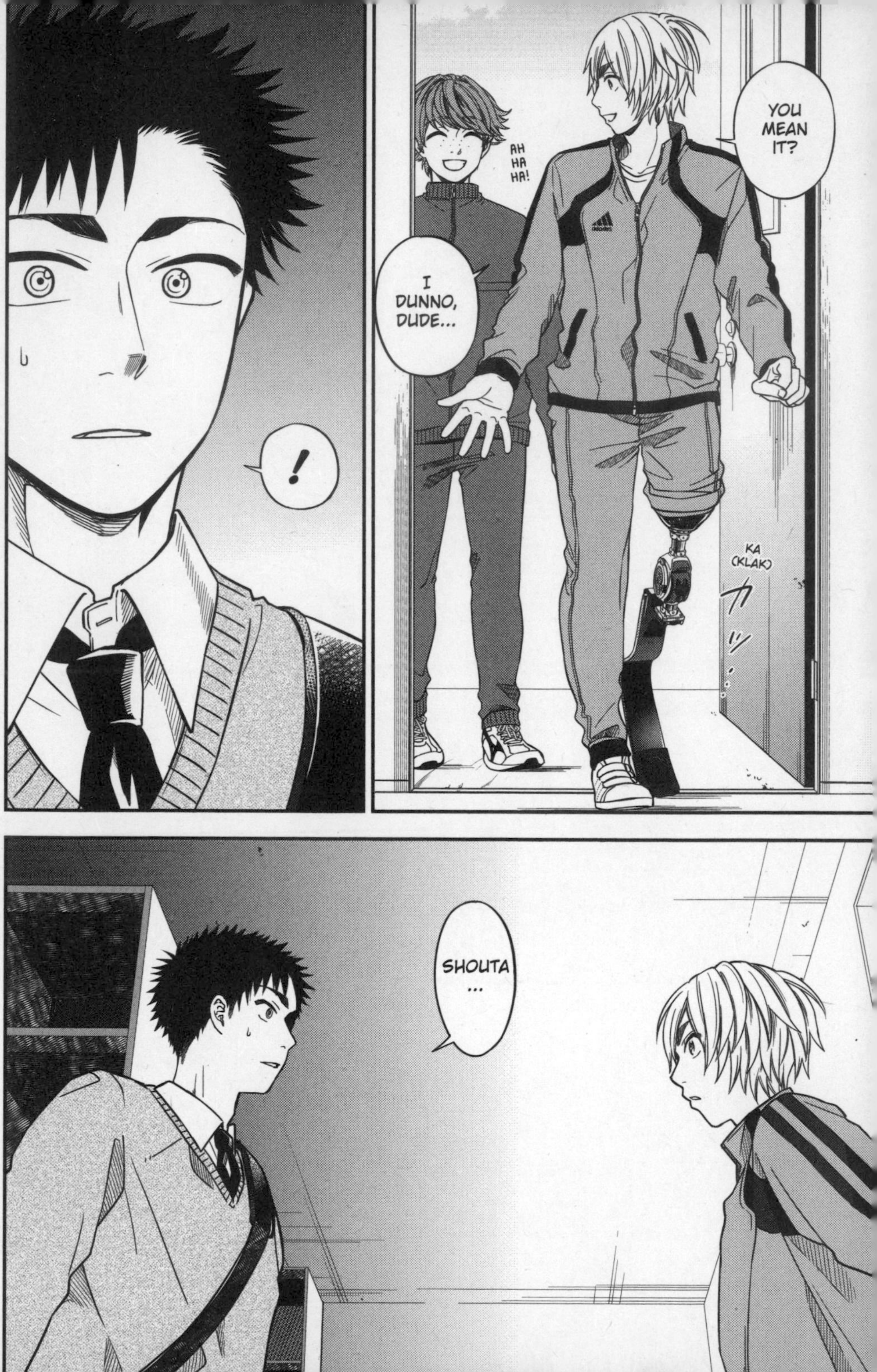

YOU MEAN IT?
AH HA HA!
I DUNNO, DUDE...
KA (KLAK)
!
SHOUTA ...

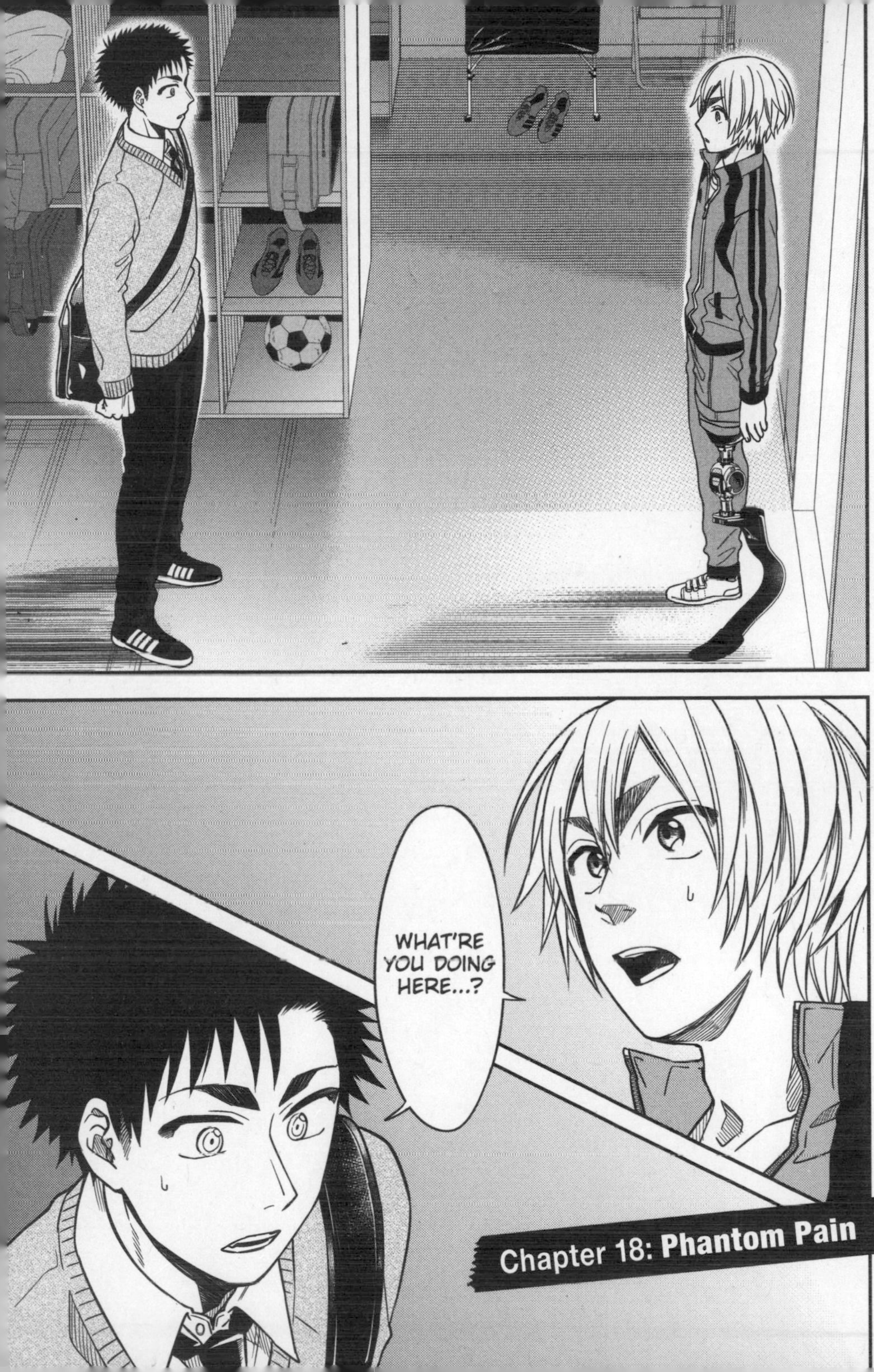
WHAT'RE YOU DOING HERE...?
Chapter 18: Phantom Pain

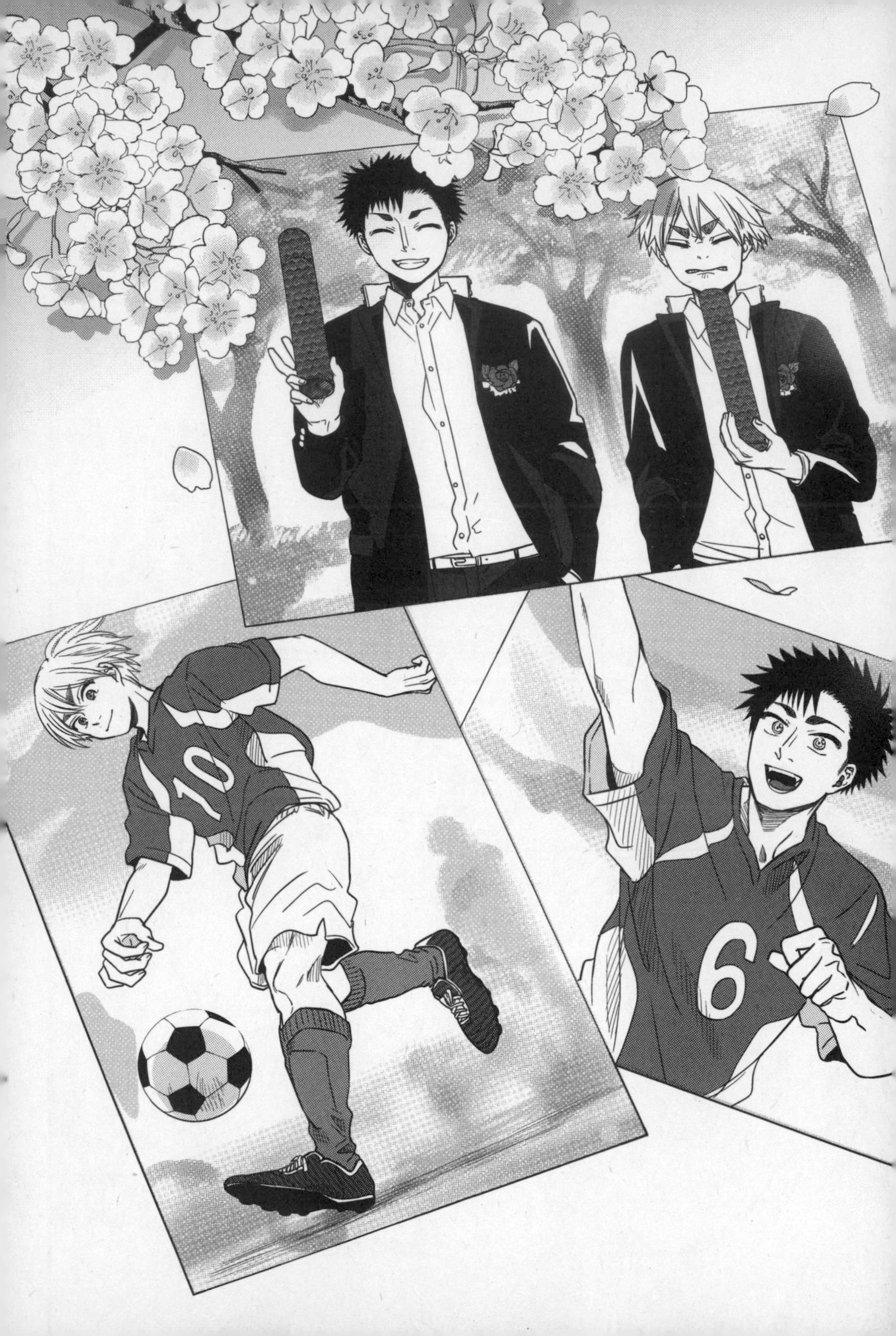
10
6

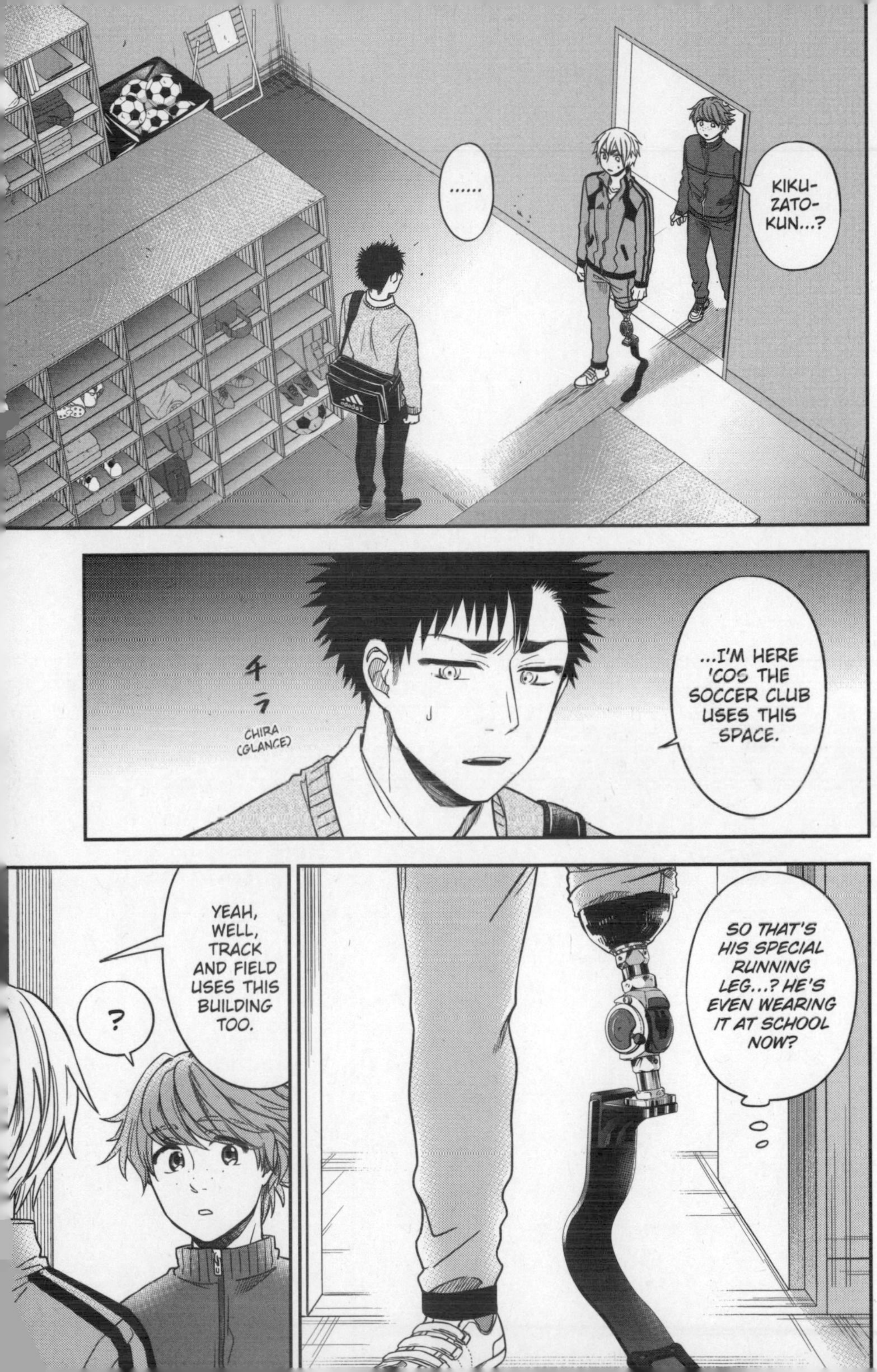
KIKU-ZATO-KUN...?
......
...I'M HERE 'COS THE SOCCER CLUB USES THIS SPACE.
チラ
CHIRA (GLANCE)
SO THAT'S HIS SPECIAL RUNNING LEG...? HE'S EVEN WEARING IT AT SCHOOL NOW?
YEAH, WELL, TRACK AND FIELD USES THIS BUILDING TOO.
?

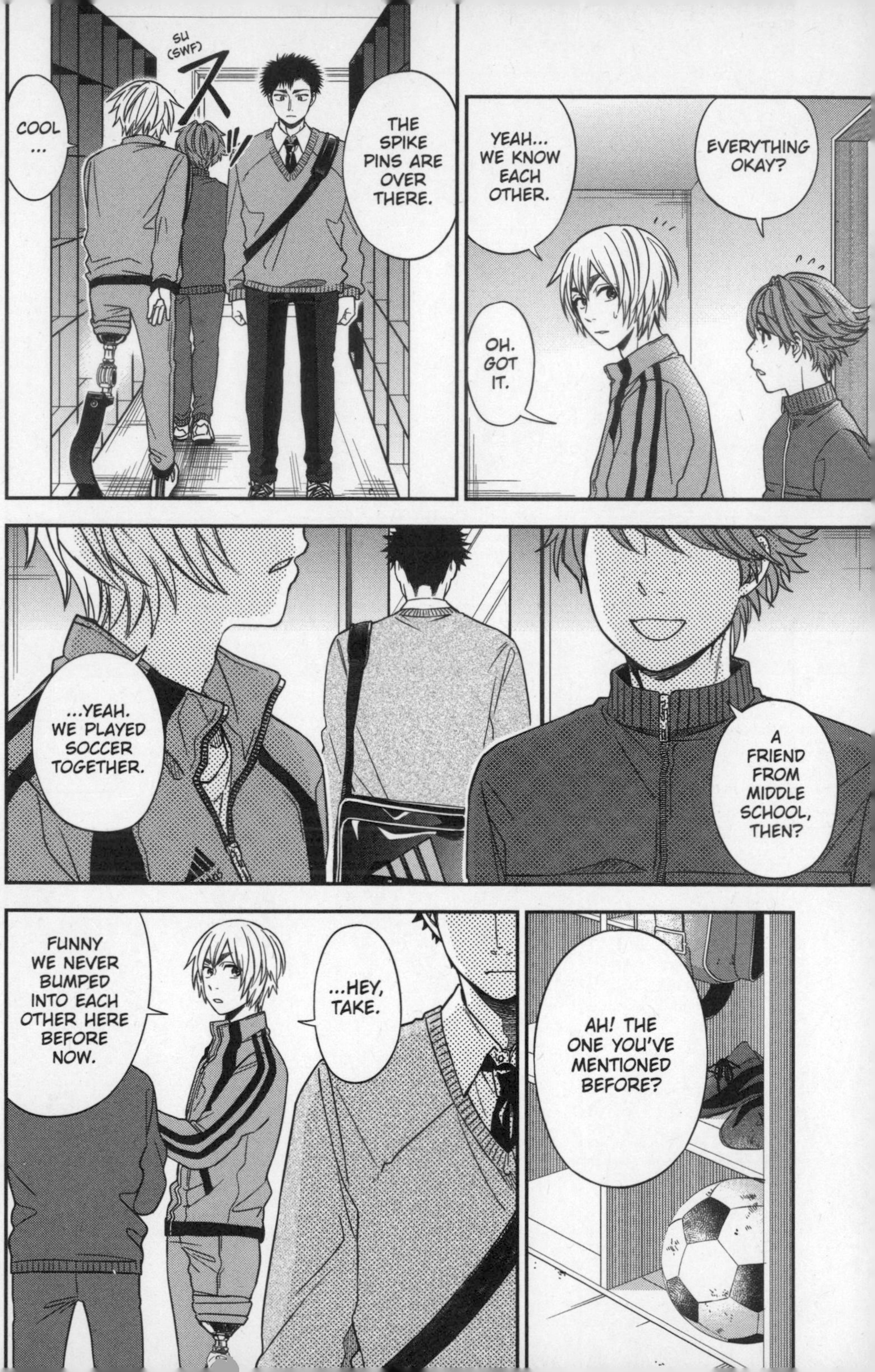
EVERYTHING OKAY?
YEAH... WE KNOW EACH OTHER.
OH. GOT IT.
THE SPIKE PINS ARE OVER THERE.
SU (SWF)
COOL ...
A FRIEND FROM MIDDLE SCHOOL, THEN?
...YEAH. WE PLAYED SOCCER TOGETHER.
AH! THE ONE YOU'VE MENTIONED BEFORE?
...HEY, TAKE.
FUNNY WE NEVER BUMPED INTO EACH OTHER HERE BEFORE NOW.

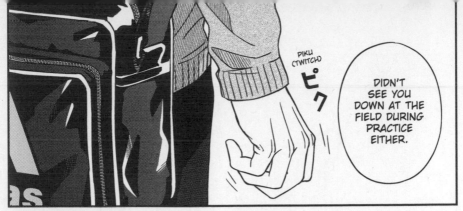

PIKU (TWITCH)

ピク

DIDN'T SEE YOU DOWN AT THE FIELD DURING PRACTICE EITHER.

I HEARD THE SOCCER THIRD-STRINGERS USE THIS CLUBHOUSE, SO...

....I ASSUMED YOU'D MOVED UP THE RANKS ALREADY.

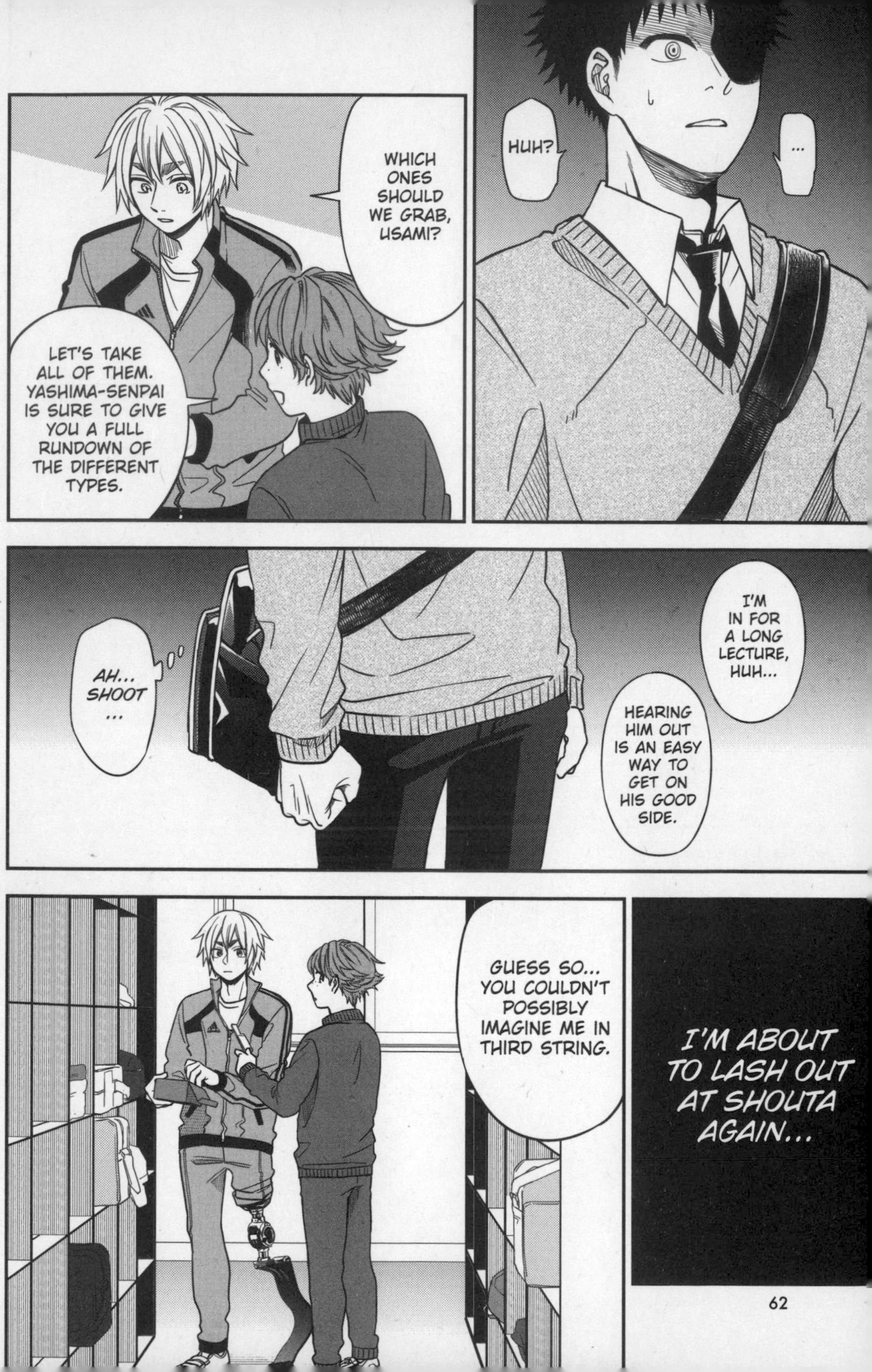
...
HUH?
WHICH ONES SHOULD WE GRAB, USAMI?
LET'S TAKE ALL OF THEM. YASHIMA-SENPAI IS SURE TO GIVE YOU A FULL RUNDOWN OF THE DIFFERENT TYPES.
I'M IN FOR A LONG LECTURE, HUH...
HEARING HIM OUT IS AN EASY WAY TO GET ON HIS GOOD SIDE.
AH... SHOOT...
I'M ABOUT TO LASH OUT AT SHOUTA AGAIN...
GUESS SO... YOU COULDN'T POSSIBLY IMAGINE ME IN THIRD STRING.

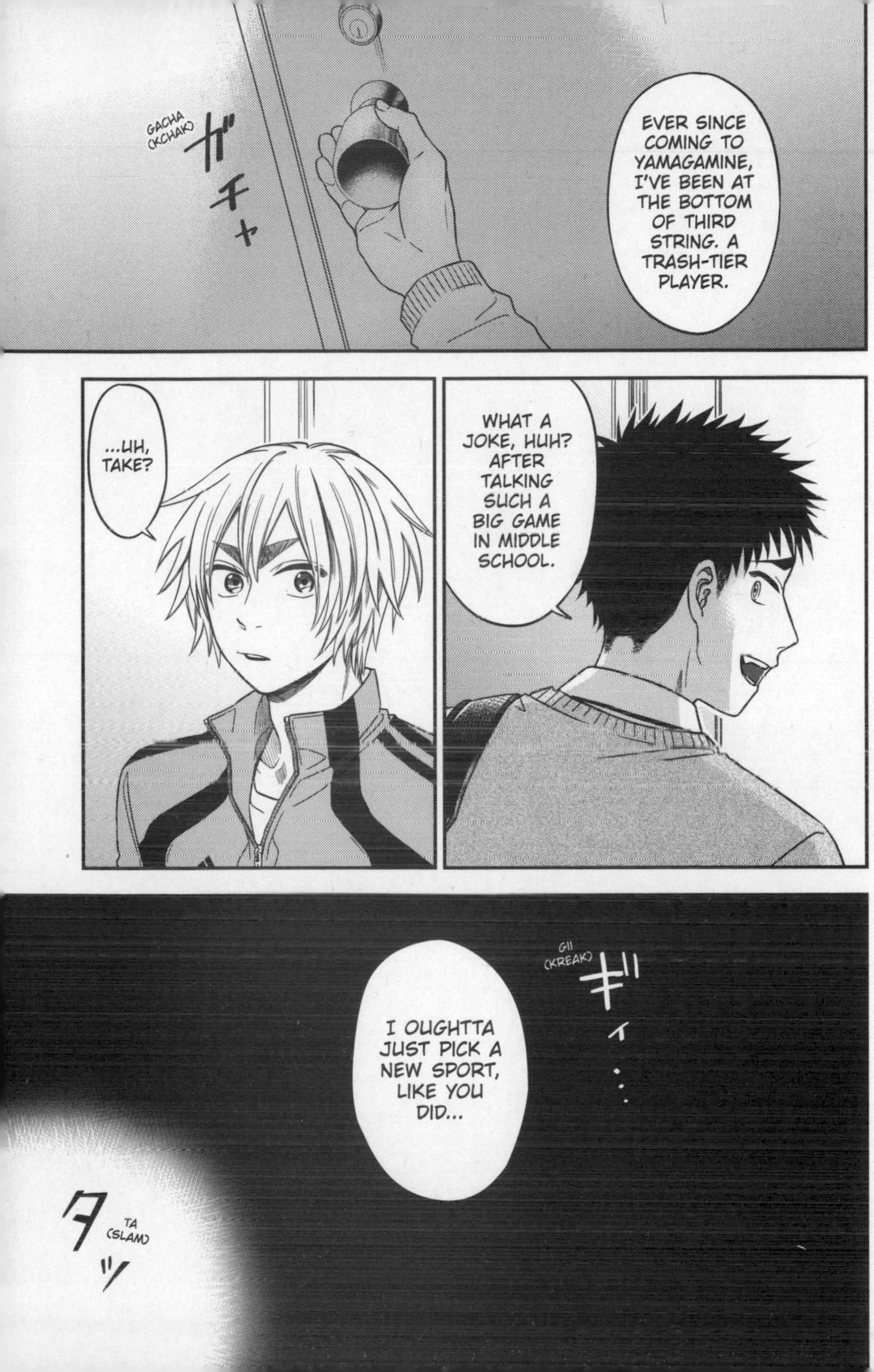
EVER SINCE COMING TO YAMAGAMINE, I'VE BEEN AT THE BOTTOM OF THIRD STRING. A TRASH-TIER PLAYER.
GACHA (KCHAK)
ガチャ
WHAT A JOKE, HUH? AFTER TALKING SUCH A BIG GAME IN MIDDLE SCHOOL.
...UH, TAKE?
GII (KREAK)
ギィ…
I OUGHTTA JUST PICK A NEW SPORT, LIKE YOU DID...
TA (SLAM)
タッ

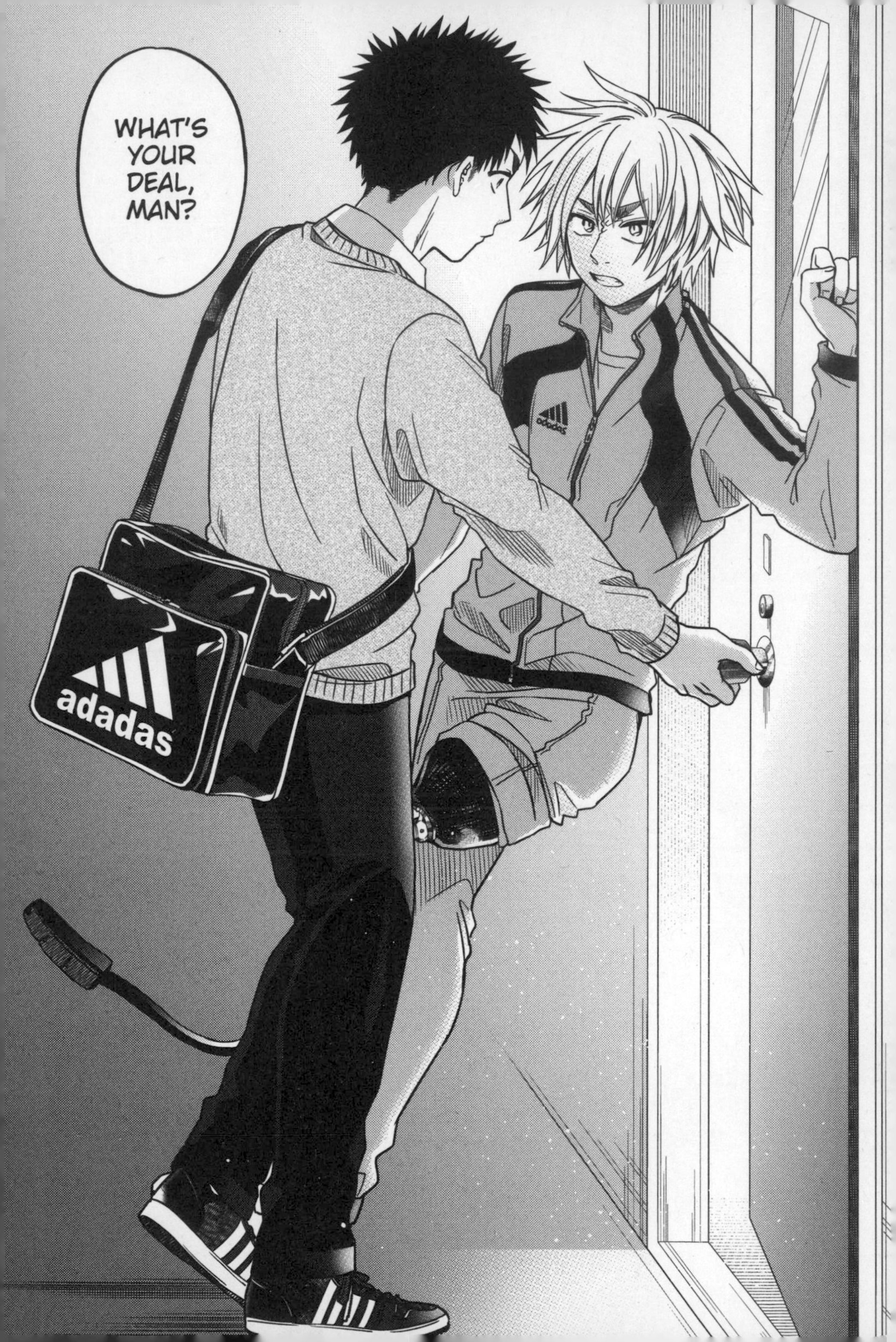
WHAT'S YOUR DEAL, MAN?
adadas
adadas

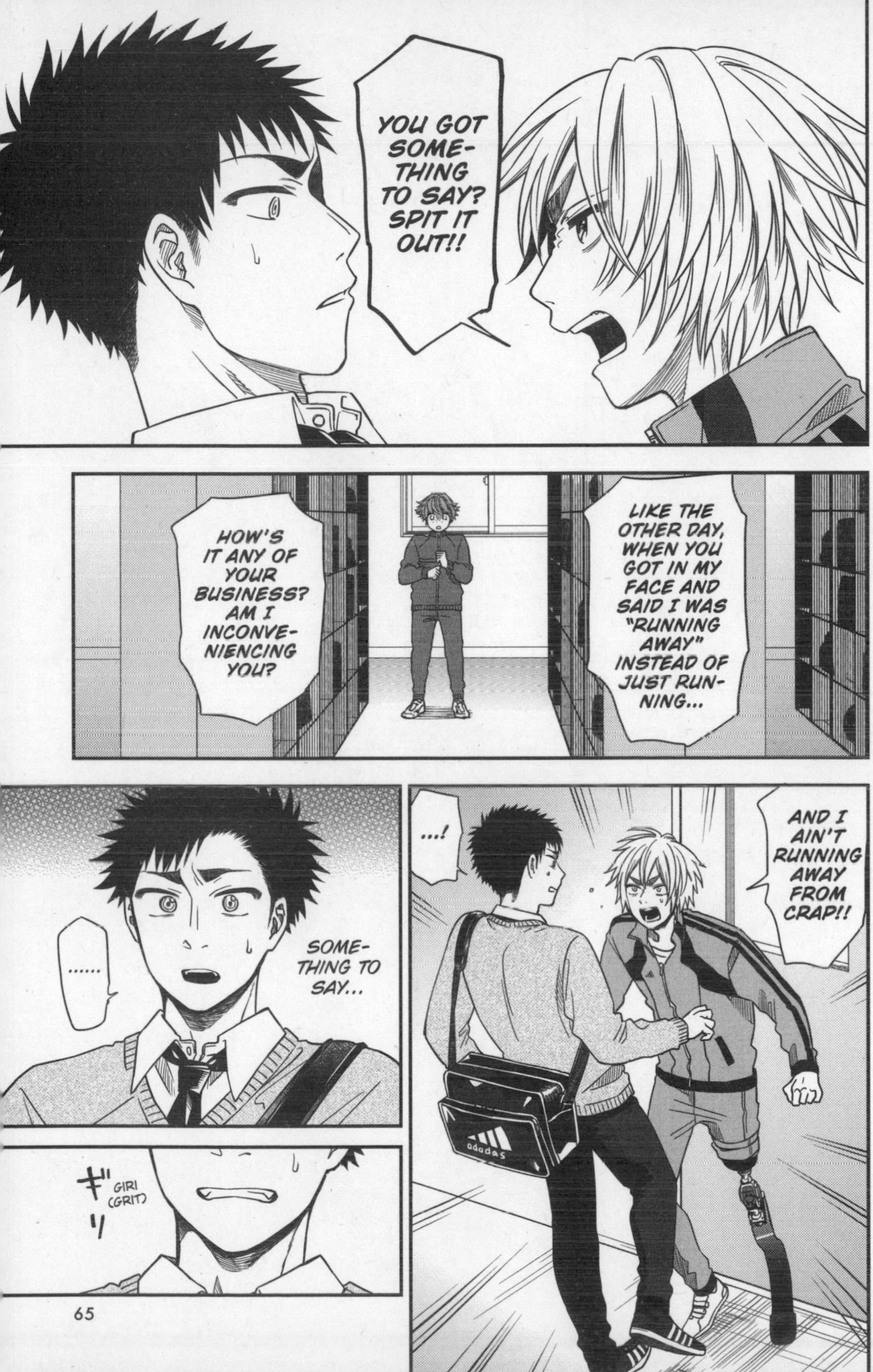
YOU GOT SOME-THING TO SAY? SPIT IT OUT!!
LIKE THE OTHER DAY, WHEN YOU GOT IN MY FACE AND SAID I WAS "RUNNING AWAY" INSTEAD OF JUST RUN-NING...
HOW'S IT ANY OF YOUR BUSINESS? AM I INCONVE-NIENCING YOU?
AND I AIN'T RUNNING AWAY FROM CRAP!!
...!
SOME-THING TO SAY...
......
ギリ
GIRI (GRIT)

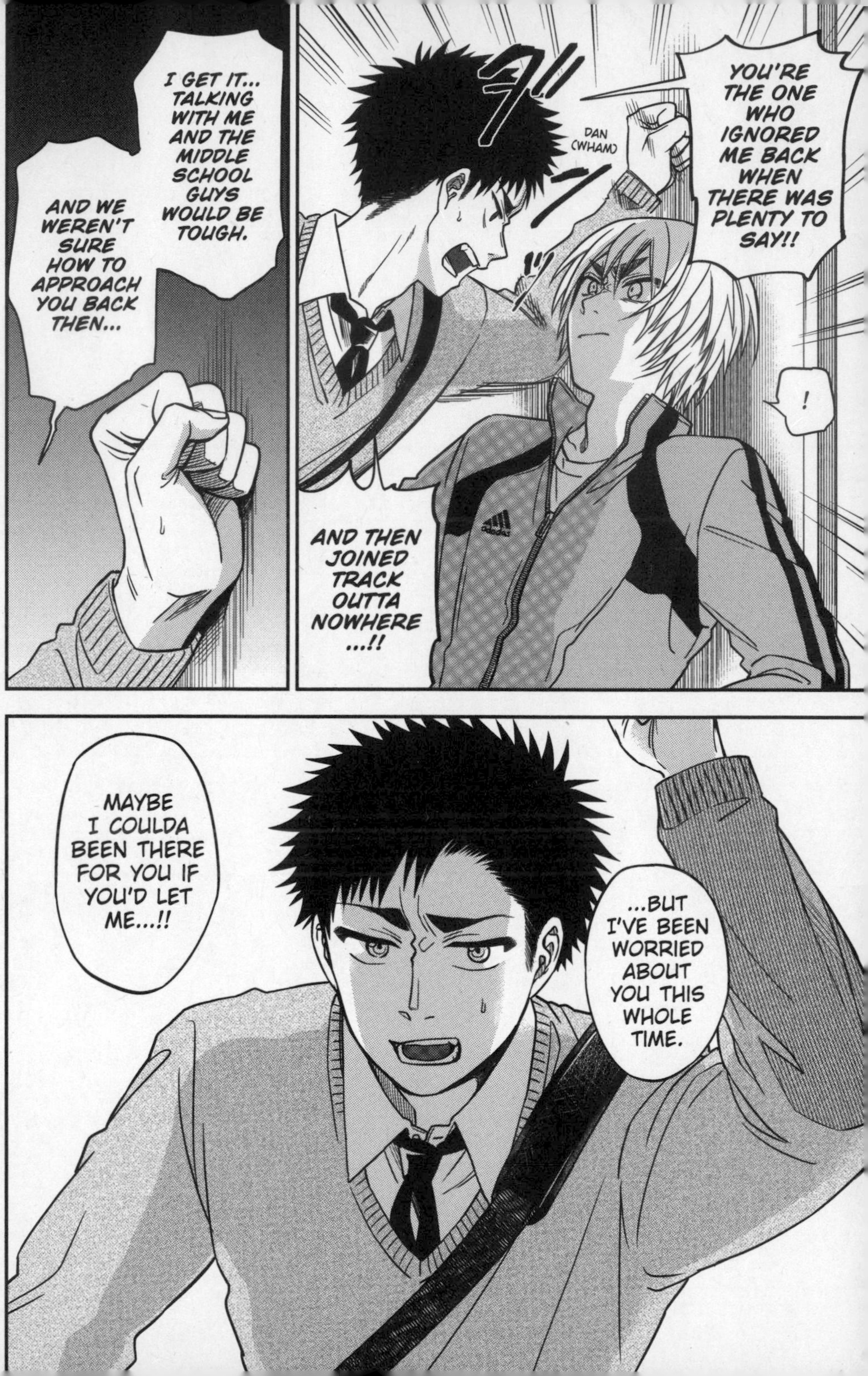
YOU'RE THE ONE WHO IGNORED ME BACK WHEN THERE WAS PLENTY TO SAY!!
DAN (WHAM)
!
AND THEN JOINED TRACK OUTTA NOWHERE ...!!
I GET IT... TALKING WITH ME AND THE MIDDLE SCHOOL GUYS WOULD BE TOUGH.
AND WE WEREN'T SURE HOW TO APPROACH YOU BACK THEN...
...BUT I'VE BEEN WORRIED ABOUT YOU THIS WHOLE TIME.
MAYBE I COULDA BEEN THERE FOR YOU IF YOU'D LET ME...!!

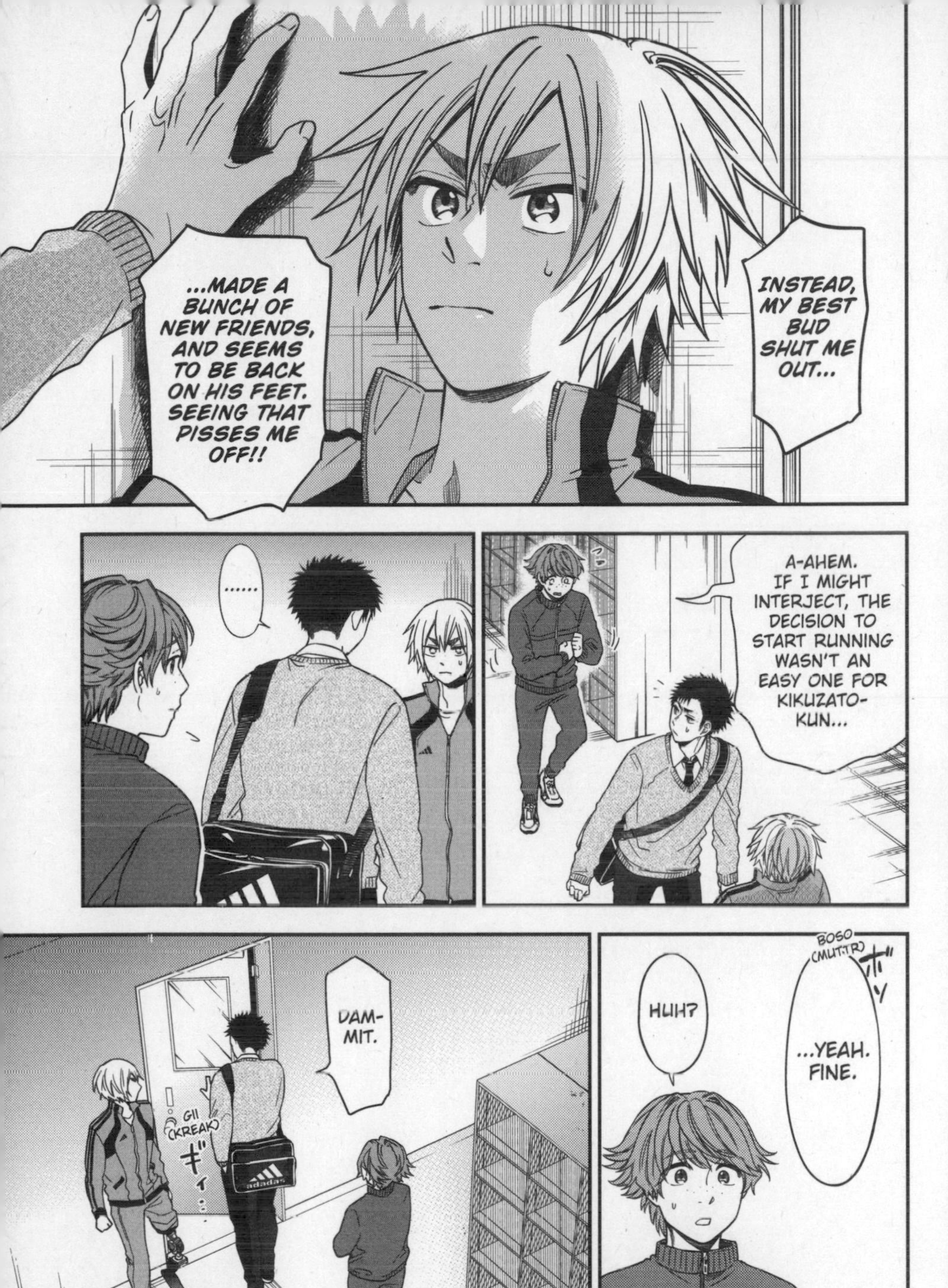
INSTEAD, MY BEST BUD SHUT ME OUT...
...MADE A BUNCH OF NEW FRIENDS, AND SEEMS TO BE BACK ON HIS FEET. SEEING THAT PISSES ME OFF!!
A-AHEM. IF I MIGHT INTERJECT, THE DECISION TO START RUNNING WASN'T AN EASY ONE FOR KIKUZATO-KUN...
......
BOSO (MUTTR)
...YEAH. FINE.
HUH?
DAM-MIT.
GII (KREAK)

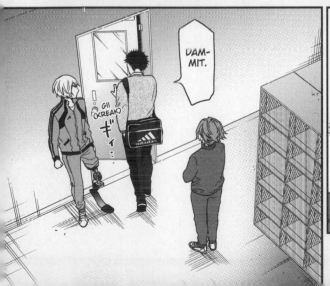

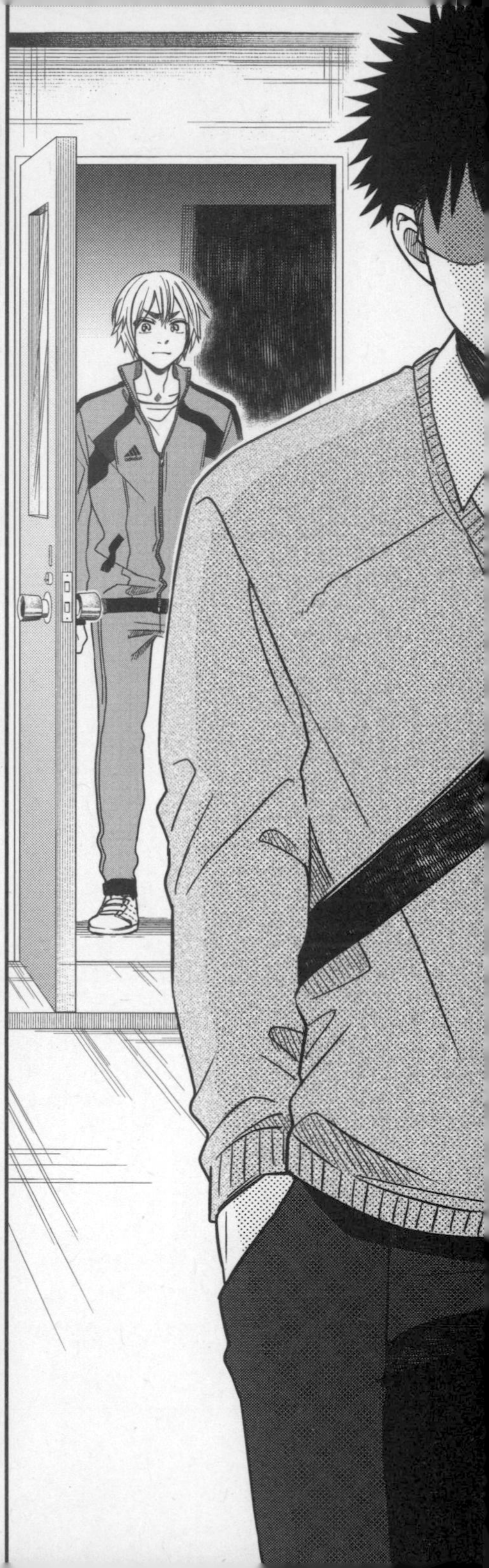

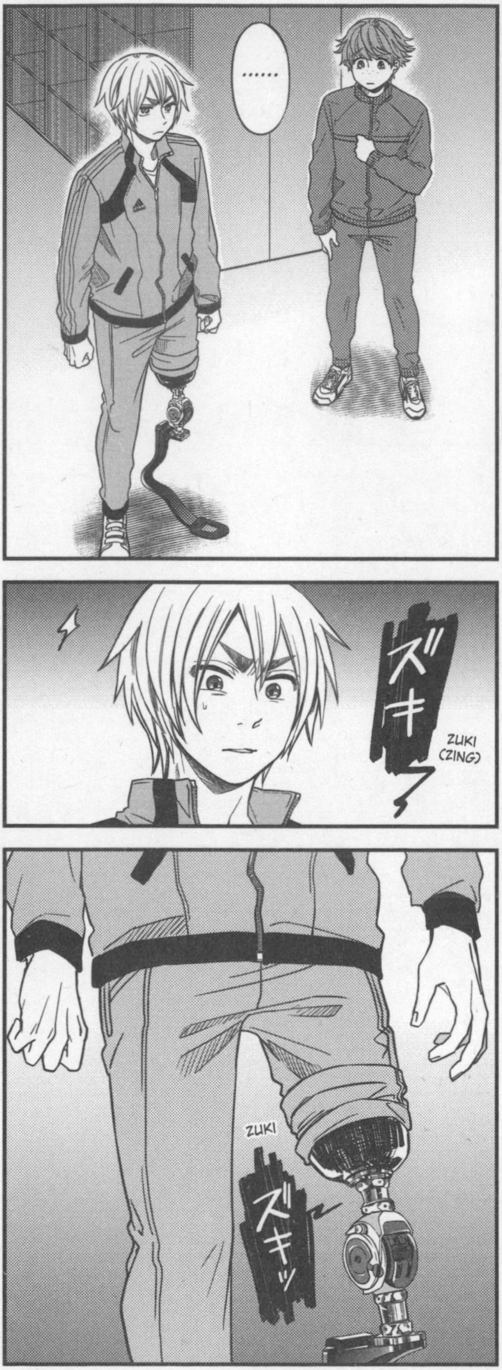
......
ズキ
ZUKI (ZING)
ZUKI
ズキッ

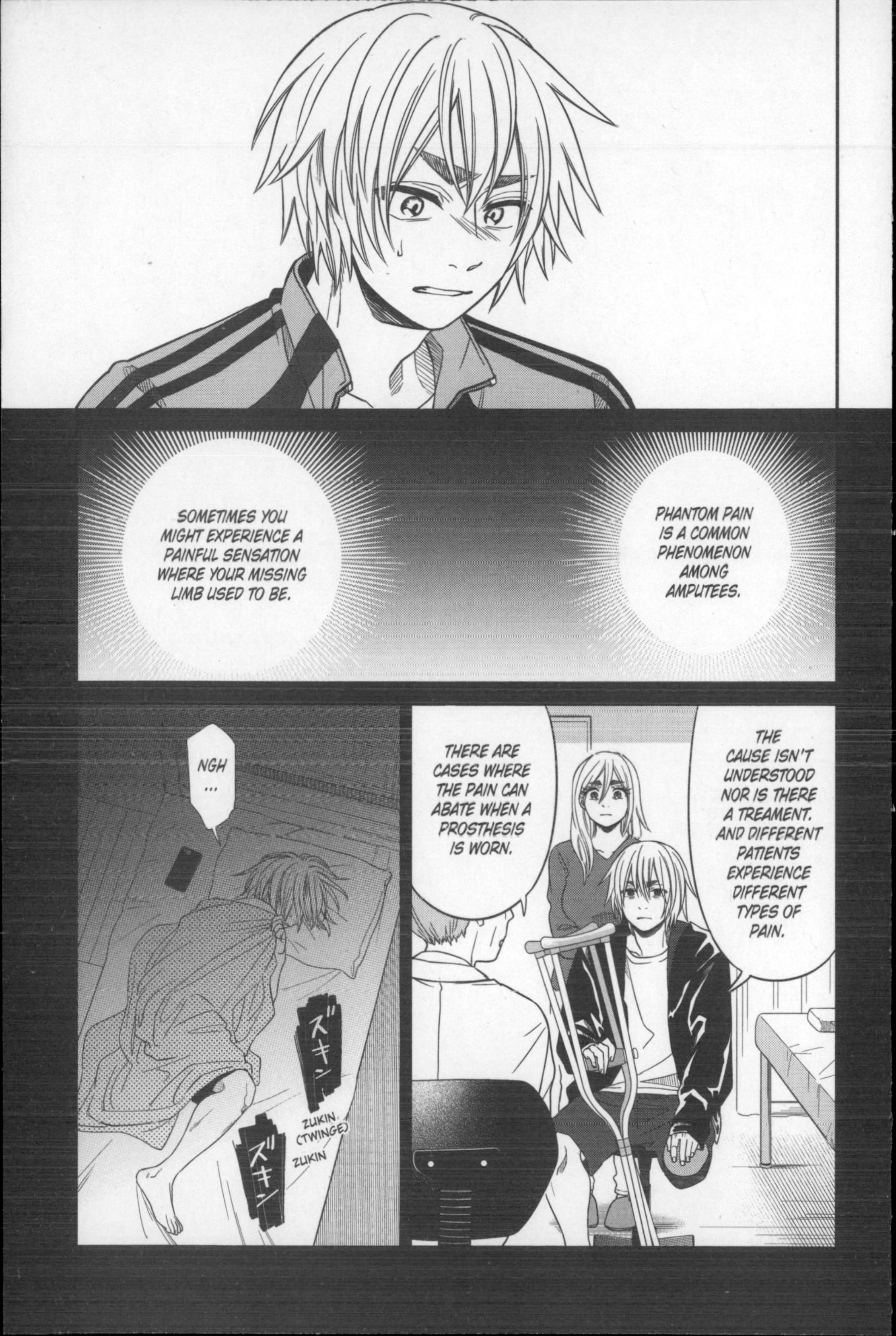
PHANTOM PAIN IS A COMMON PHENOMENON AMONG AMPUTEES.
SOMETIMES YOU MIGHT EXPERIENCE A PAINFUL SENSATION WHERE YOUR MISSING LIMB USED TO BE.
THE CAUSE ISN'T UNDERSTOOD NOR IS THERE A TREAMENT. AND DIFFERENT PATIENTS EXPERIENCE DIFFERENT TYPES OF PAIN.
THERE ARE CASES WHERE THE PAIN CAN ABATE WHEN A PROSTHESIS IS WORN.
NGH ...
ズキン
ZUKIN (TWINGE)
ズキン
ZUKIN

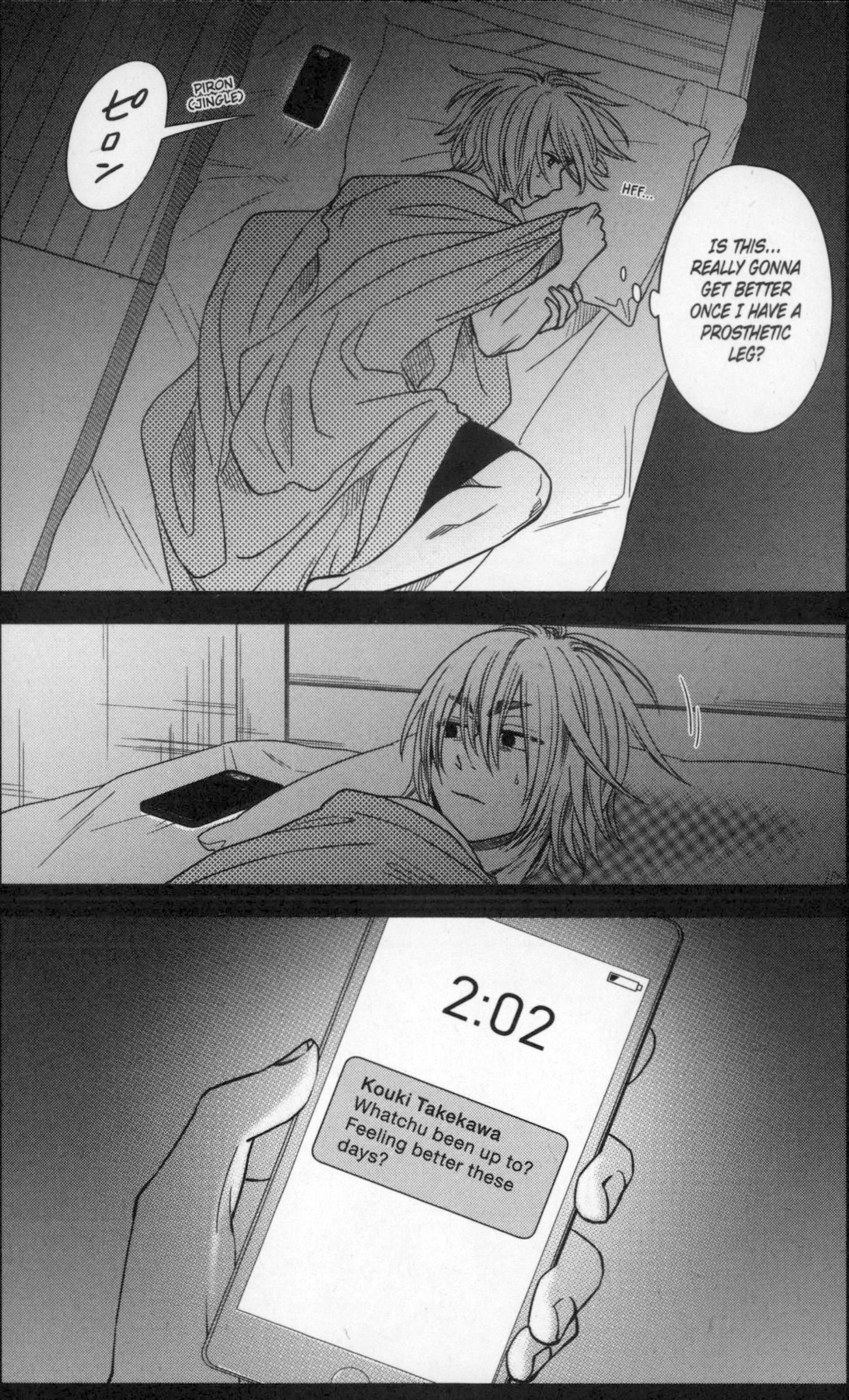
IS THIS... REALLY GONNA GET BETTER ONCE I HAVE A PROSTHETIC LEG?
HFF...
ピロン
PIRON (JINGLE)
2:02
Kouki Takekawa
Whatchu been up to? Feeling better these days?

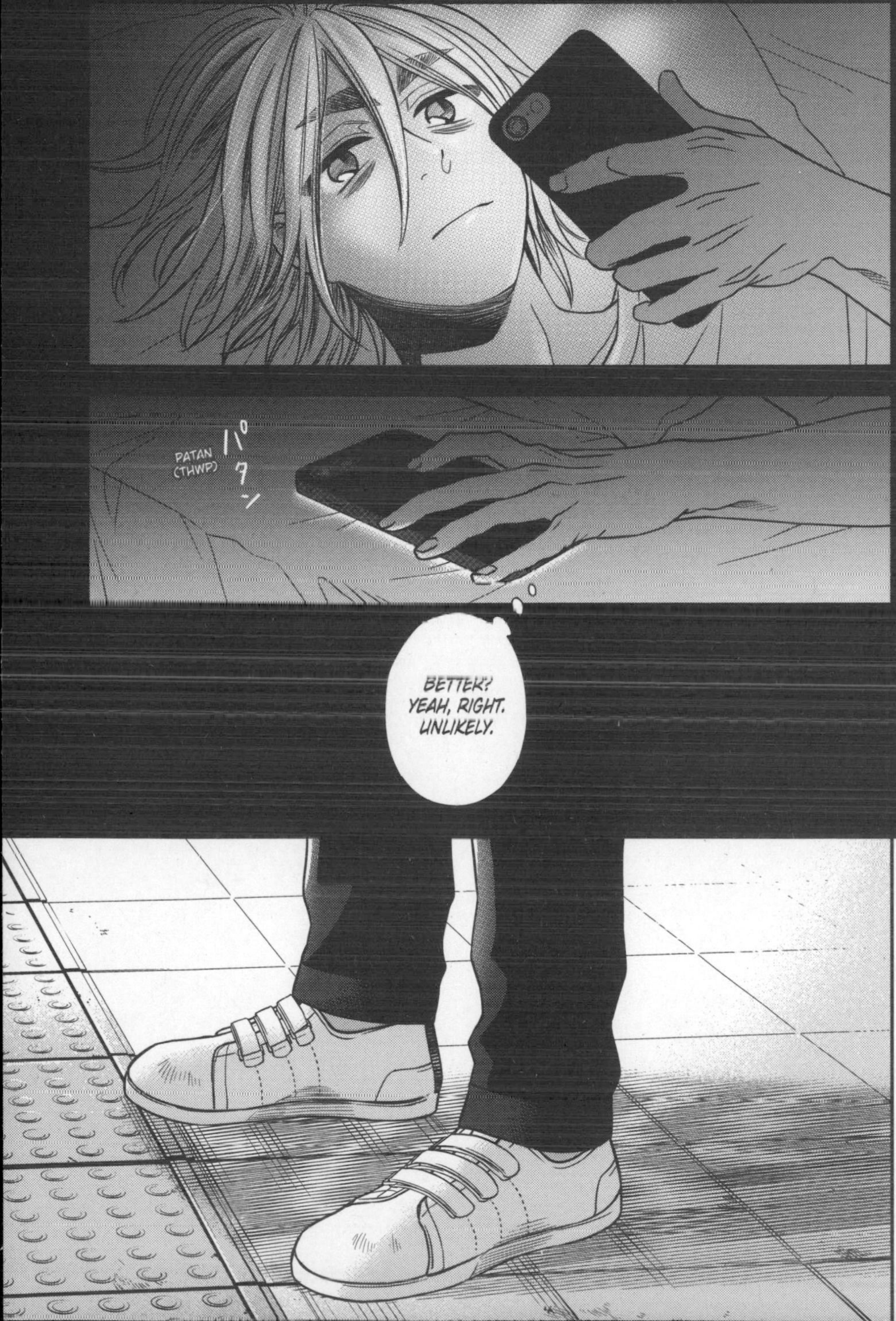
パタン
PATAN (THWP)
BETTER? YEAH, RIGHT. UNLIKELY.

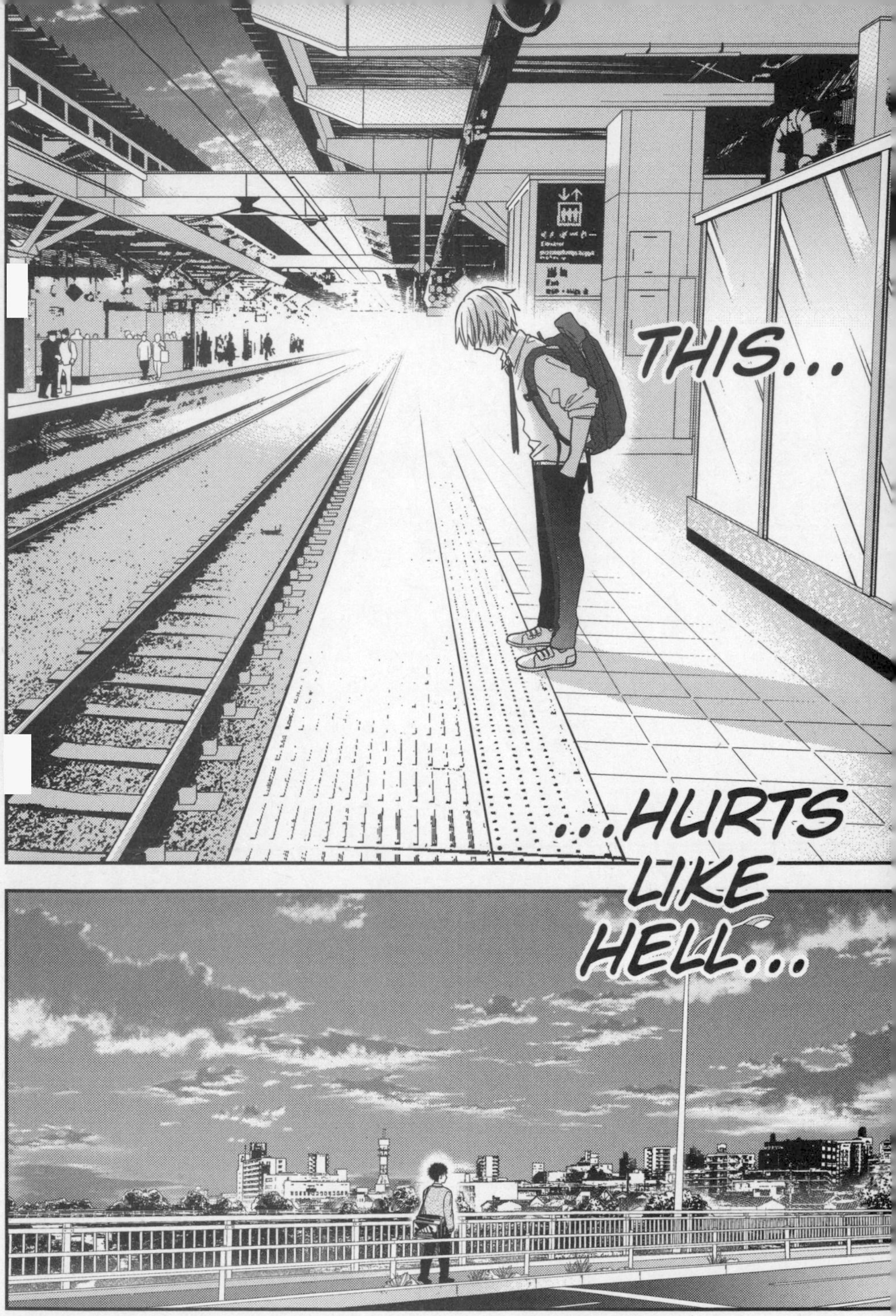
THIS...
...HURTS LIKE HELL...

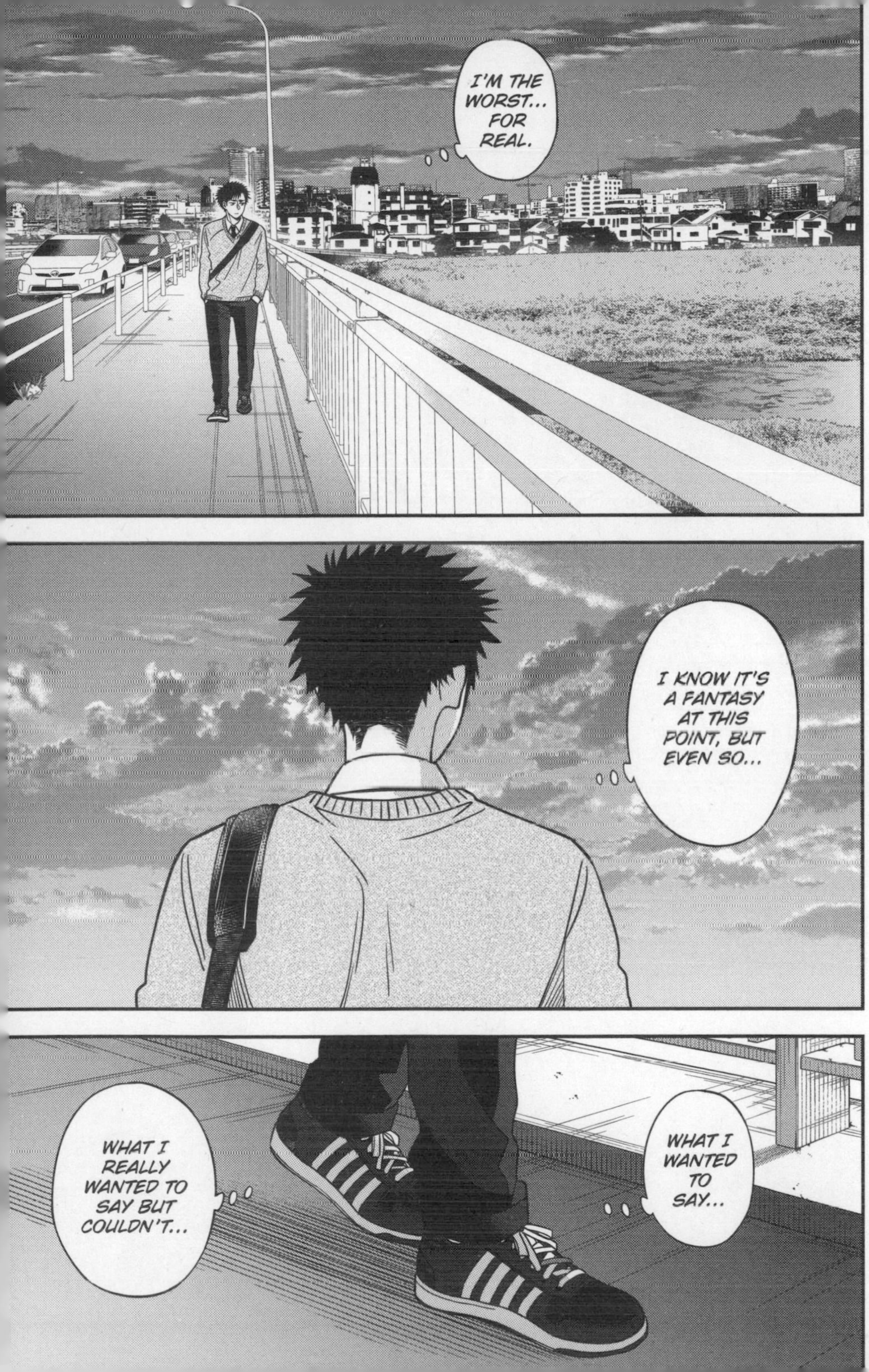
I'M THE WORST... FOR REAL.
I KNOW IT'S A FANTASY AT THIS POINT, BUT EVEN SO...
WHAT I WANTED TO SAY...
WHAT I REALLY WANTED TO SAY BUT COULDN'T...

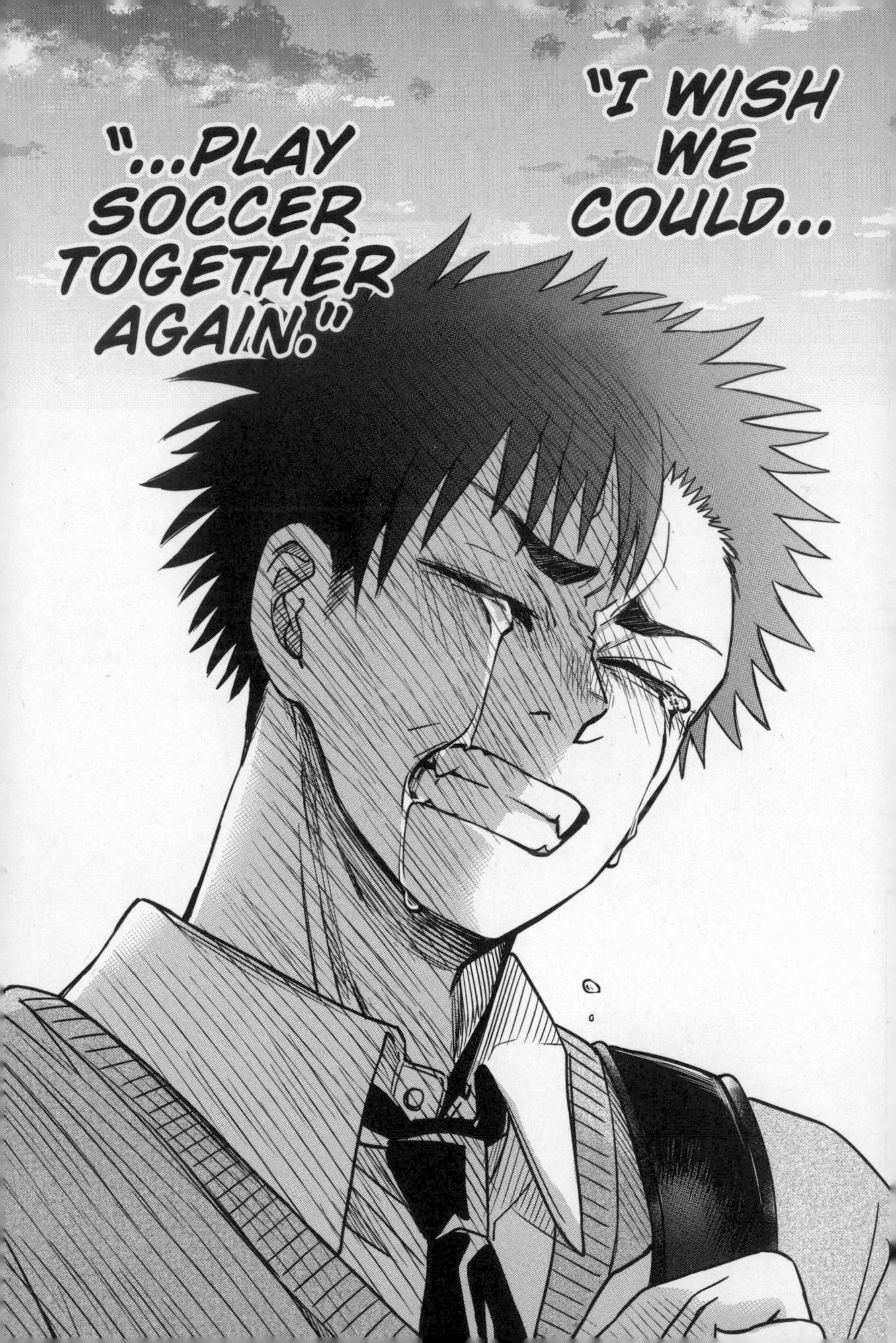
"I WISH WE COULD...
"...PLAY SOCCER TOGETHER AGAIN."

Chapter 19: To Cheer Him Up

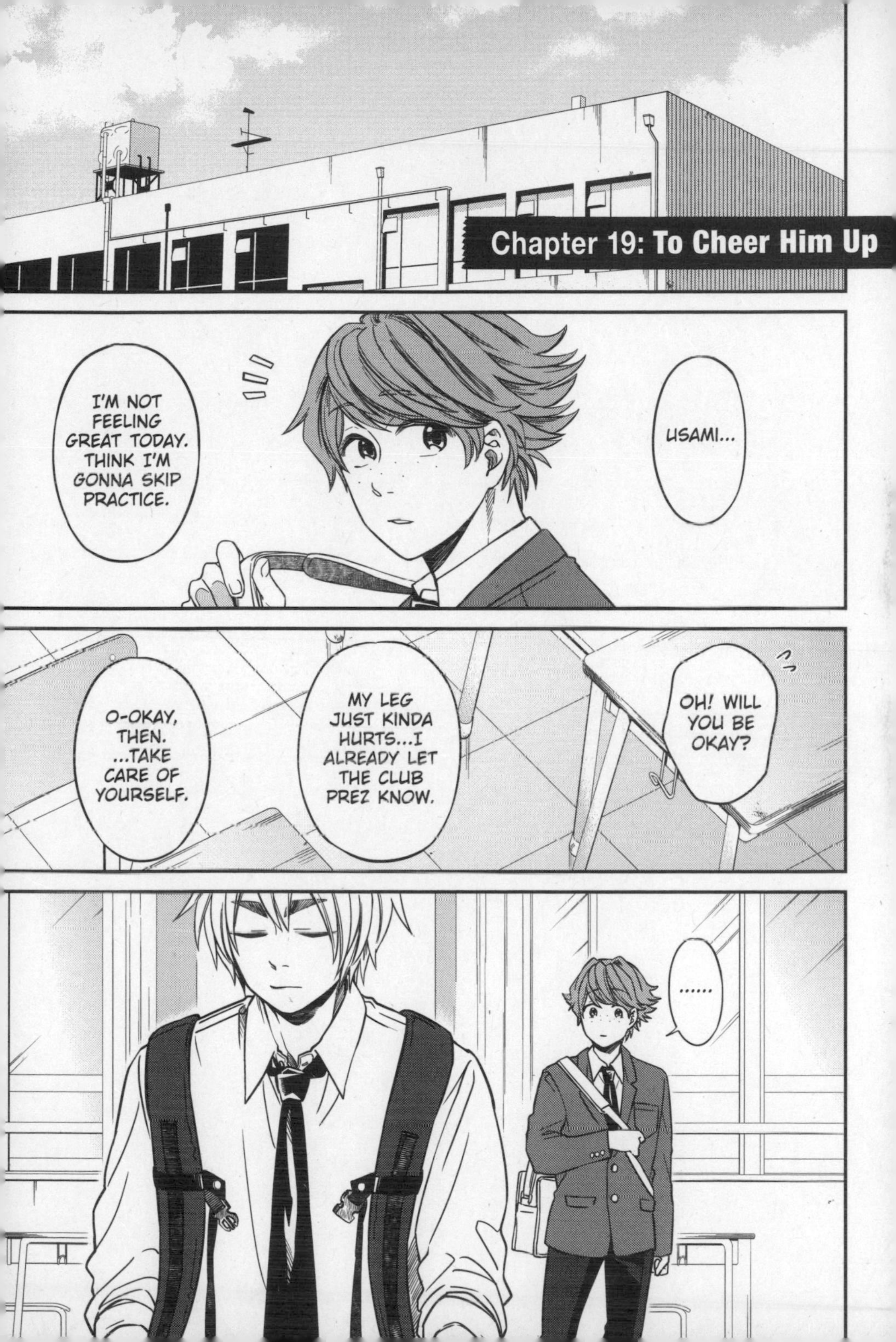
USAMI...
I'M NOT FEELING GREAT TODAY. THINK I'M GONNA SKIP PRACTICE.
OH! WILL YOU BE OKAY?
MY LEG JUST KINDA HURTS...I ALREADY LET THE CLUB PREZ KNOW.
O-OKAY, THEN. ...TAKE CARE OF YOURSELF.
......

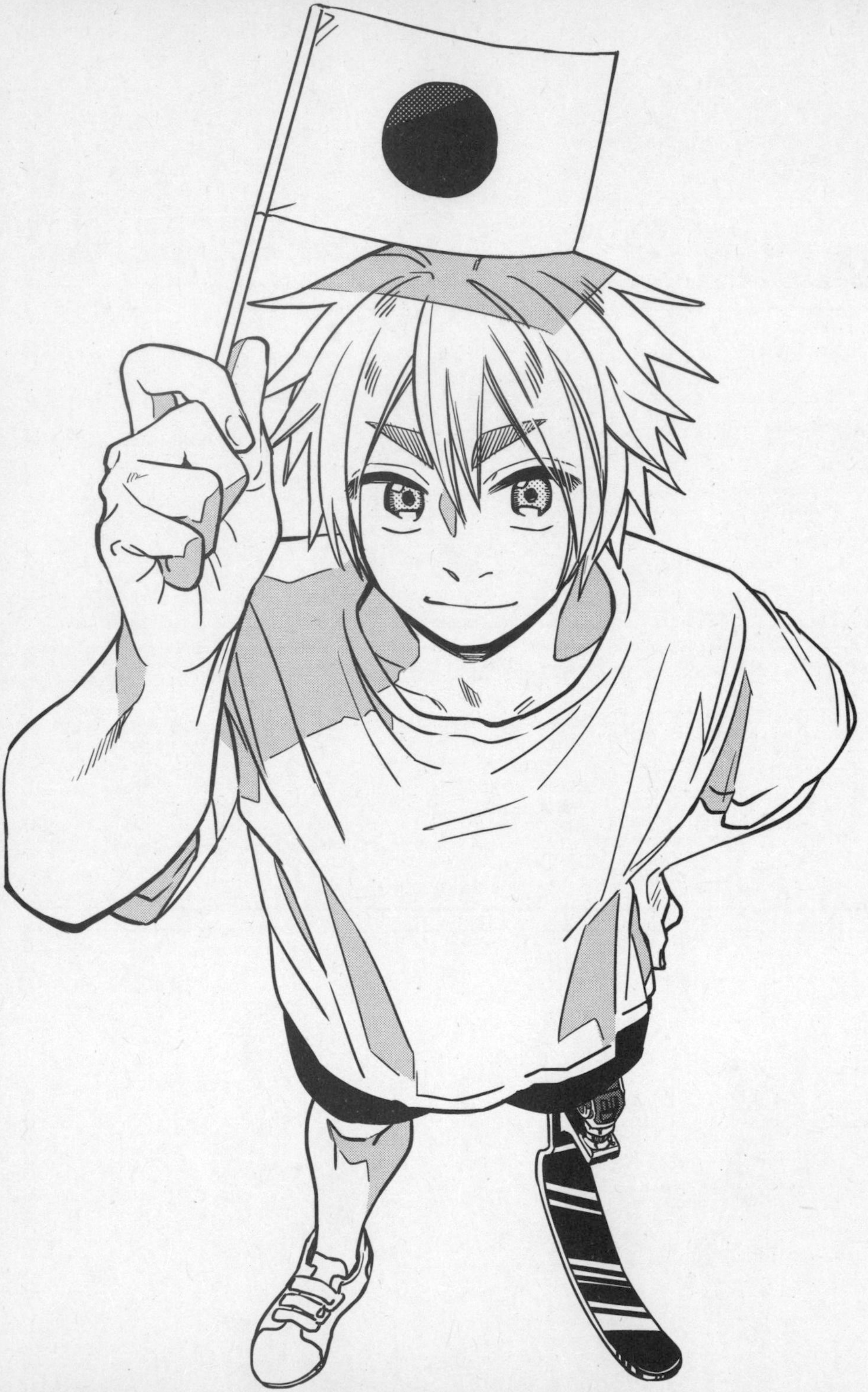

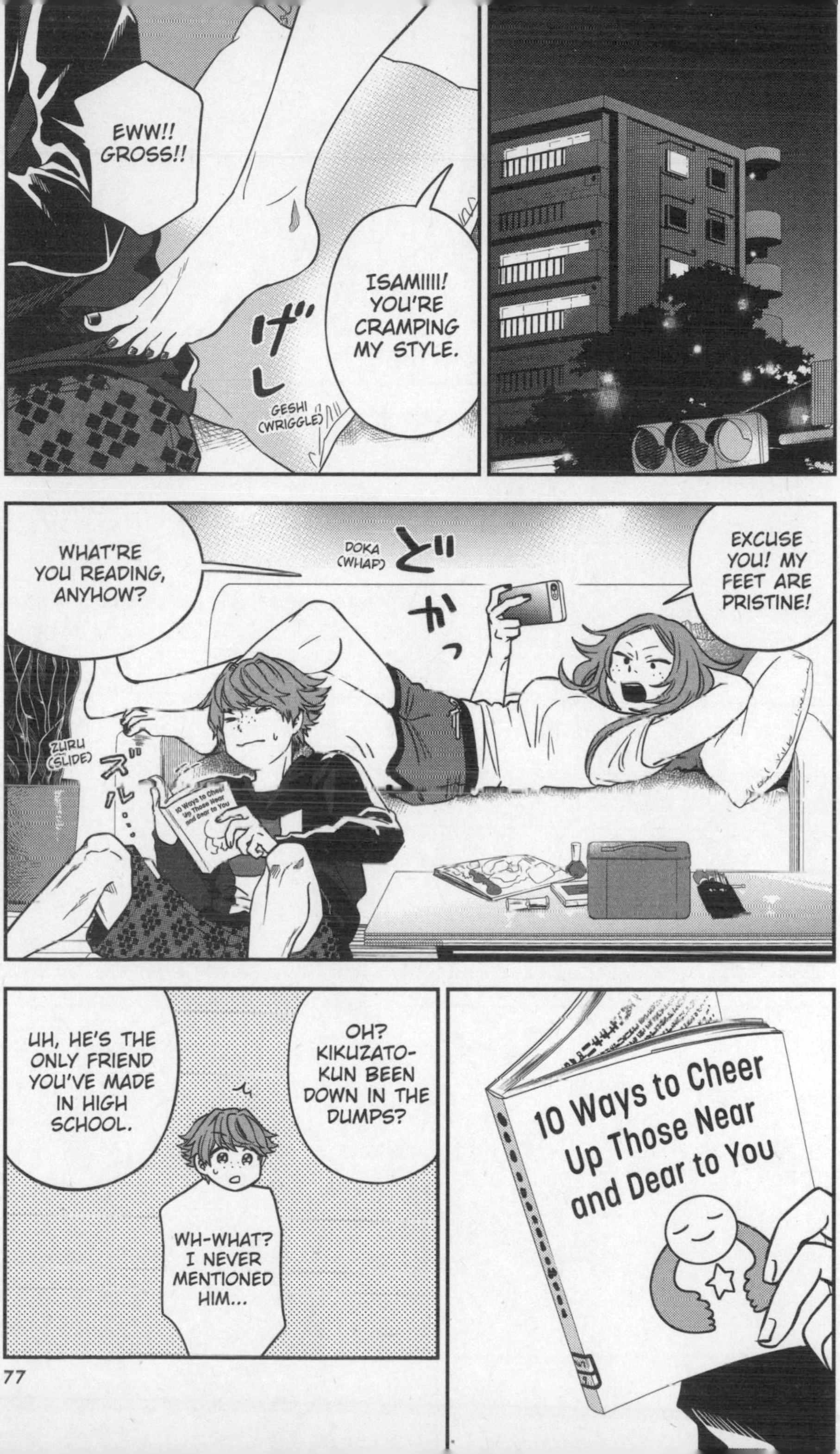

ISAMIIII! YOU'RE CRAMPING MY STYLE.
げし
GESHI (WRIGGLE)
EWW!! GROSS!!
EXCUSE YOU! MY FEET ARE PRISTINE!
どかっ
DOKA (WHAP)
WHAT'RE YOU READING, ANYHOW?
ズル
ZURU (SLIDE)
10 Ways to Cheer Up Those Near and Dear to You
10 Ways to Cheer Up Those Near and Dear to You
OH? KIKUZATO-KUN BEEN DOWN IN THE DUMPS?
UH, HE'S THE ONLY FRIEND YOU'VE MADE IN HIGH SCHOOL.
WH-WHAT? I NEVER MENTIONED HIM...

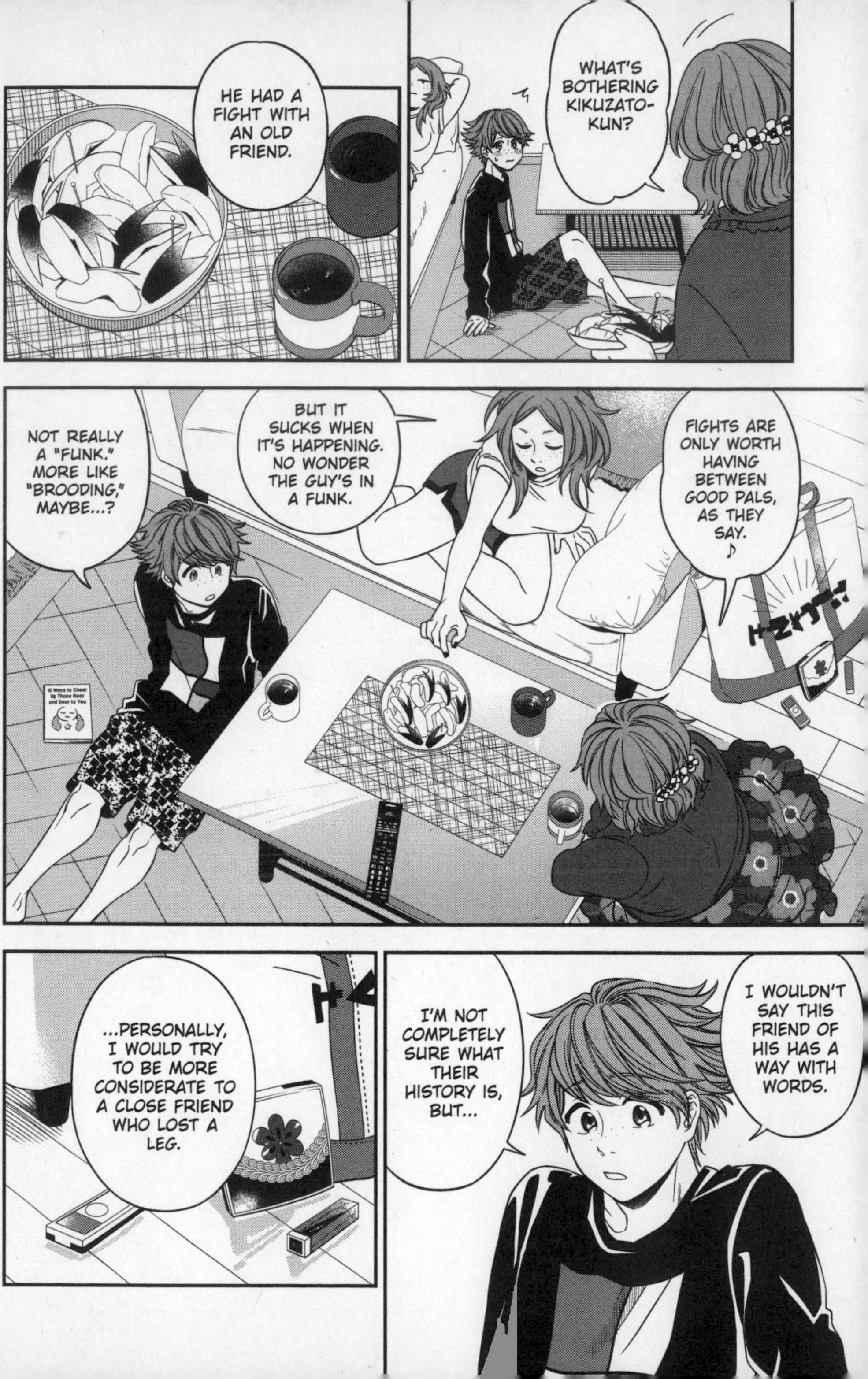
WHAT'S BOTHERING KIKUZATO-KUN?
HE HAD A FIGHT WITH AN OLD FRIEND.
FIGHTS ARE ONLY WORTH HAVING BETWEEN GOOD PALS, AS THEY SAY. ♪
BUT IT SUCKS WHEN IT'S HAPPENING. NO WONDER THE GUY'S IN A FUNK.
NOT REALLY A "FUNK." MORE LIKE "BROODING," MAYBE...?
10 Ways to Cheer Up Those Near and Dear to You
I WOULDN'T SAY THIS FRIEND OF HIS HAS A WAY WITH WORDS.
I'M NOT COMPLETELY SURE WHAT THEIR HISTORY IS, BUT...
...PERSONALLY, I WOULD TRY TO BE MORE CONSIDERATE TO A CLOSE FRIEND WHO LOST A LEG.

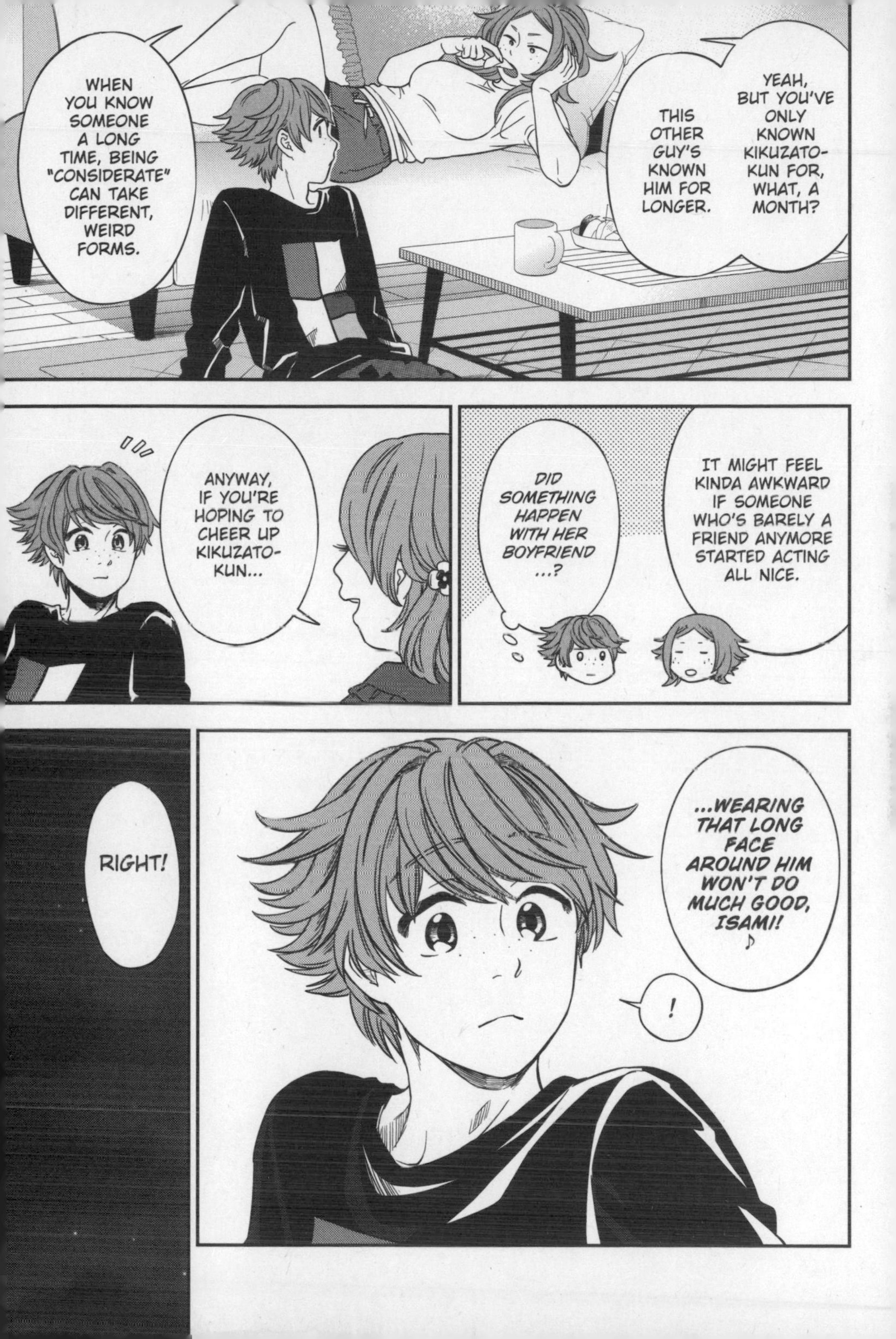
YEAH, BUT YOU'VE ONLY KNOWN KIKUZATO-KUN FOR, WHAT, A MONTH?
THIS OTHER GUY'S KNOWN HIM FOR LONGER.
WHEN YOU KNOW SOMEONE A LONG TIME, BEING "CONSIDERATE" CAN TAKE DIFFERENT, WEIRD FORMS.
IT MIGHT FEEL KINDA AWKWARD IF SOMEONE WHO'S BARELY A FRIEND ANYMORE STARTED ACTING ALL NICE.
DID SOMETHING HAPPEN WITH HER BOYFRIEND ...?
ANYWAY, IF YOU'RE HOPING TO CHEER UP KIKUZATO-KUN...
...WEARING THAT LONG FACE AROUND HIM WON'T DO MUCH GOOD, ISAMI! ♪
!
RIGHT!

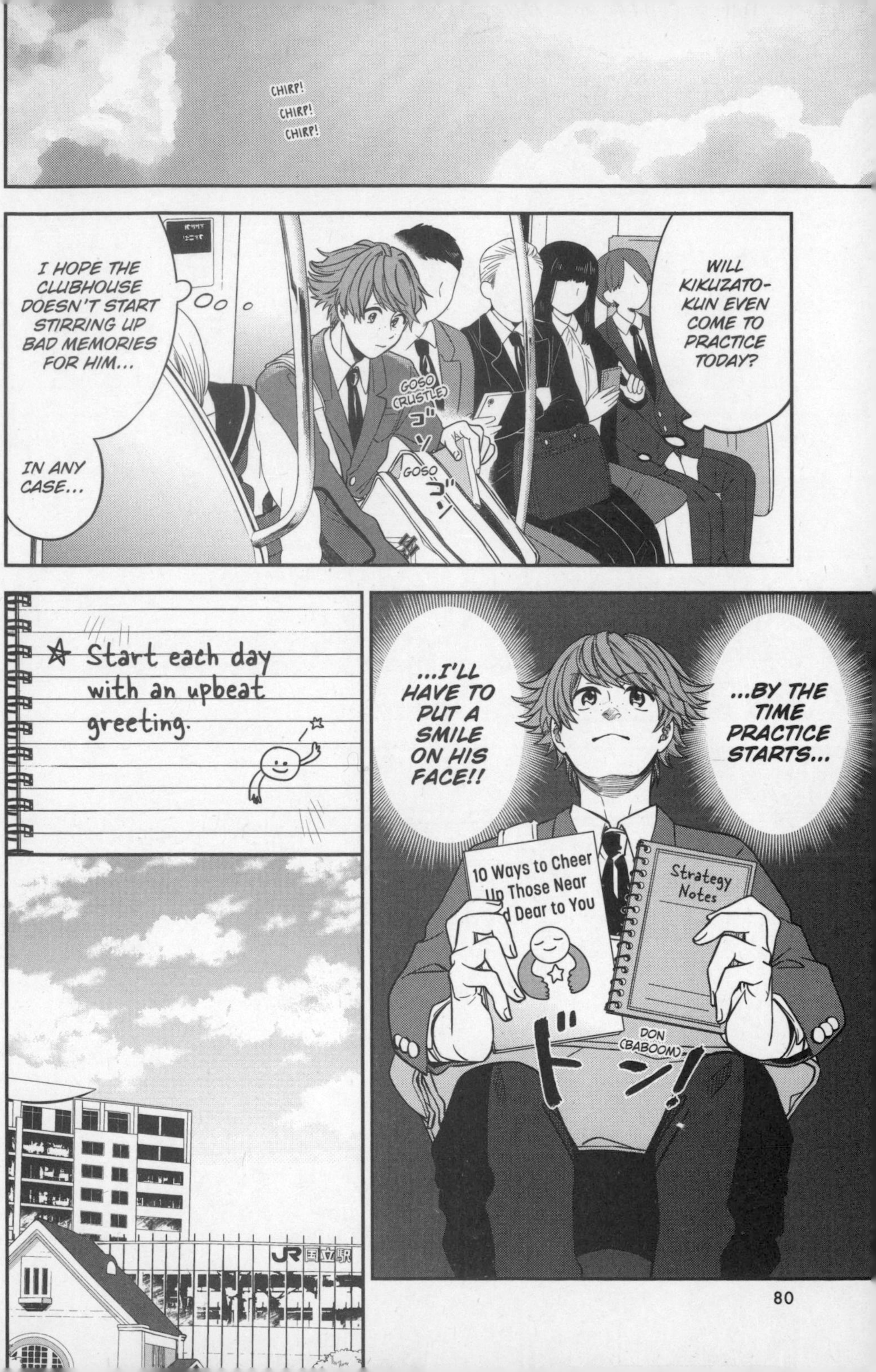

CHIRP!
CHIRP!
CHIRP!
WILL KIKUZATO-KUN EVEN COME TO PRACTICE TODAY?
I HOPE THE CLUBHOUSE DOESN'T START STIRRING UP BAD MEMORIES FOR HIM...
GOSO (RUSTLE)
GOSO
IN ANY CASE...
...BY THE TIME PRACTICE STARTS...
...I'LL HAVE TO PUT A SMILE ON HIS FACE!!
10 Ways to Cheer
Up Those Near
d Dear to You
Strategy Notes
DON (BABOOM)
☆ Start each day with an upbeat greeting.
JR 国立駅

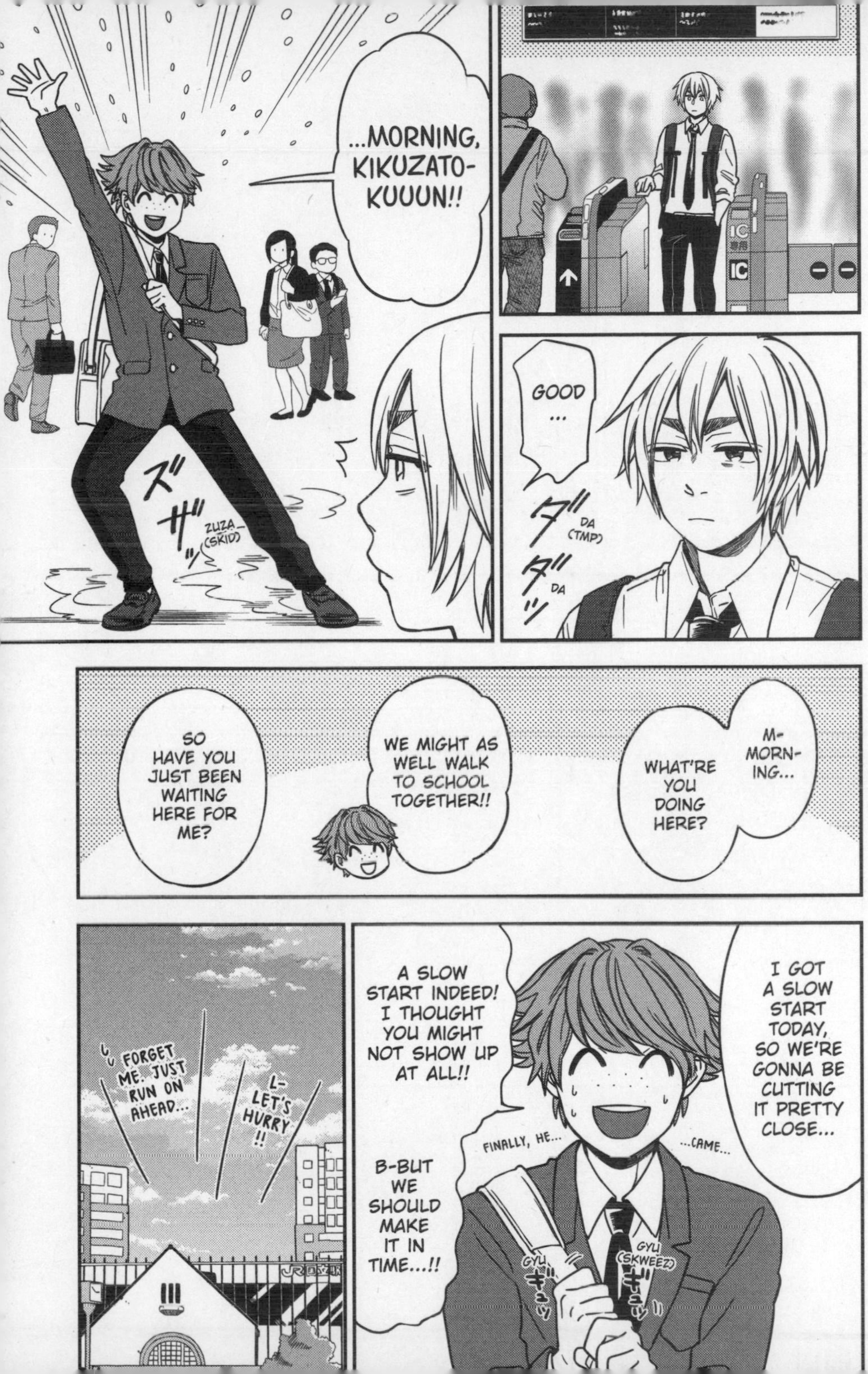
GOOD...
ダッ
DA (TMP)
ダッ
DA
...MORNING, KIKUZATO-KUUUN!!
ズザッ
ZUZA (SKID)
M-MORNING...
WHAT'RE YOU DOING HERE?
WE MIGHT AS WELL WALK TO SCHOOL TOGETHER!!
SO HAVE YOU JUST BEEN WAITING HERE FOR ME?
I GOT A SLOW START TODAY, SO WE'RE GONNA BE CUTTING IT PRETTY CLOSE...
...CAME...
A SLOW START INDEED! I THOUGHT YOU MIGHT NOT SHOW UP AT ALL!!
FINALLY, HE...
ギュッ
GYU (SKWEEZ)
B-BUT WE SHOULD MAKE IT IN TIME...!!
ギュッ
GYU
L-LET'S HURRY!!
FORGET ME. JUST RUN ON AHEAD...

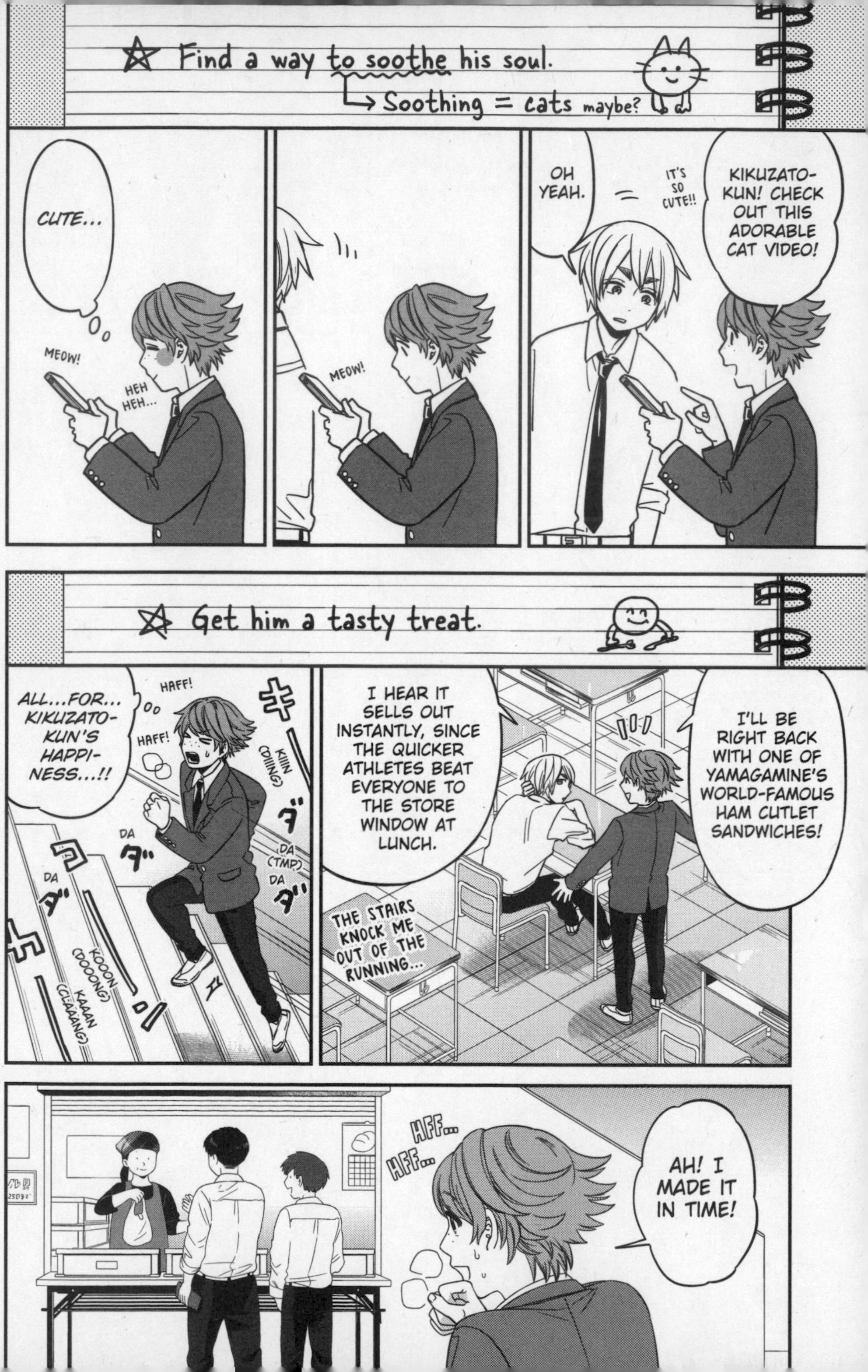

Find a way to soothe his soul.
Soothing = cats maybe?
KIKUZATO-KUN! CHECK OUT THIS ADORABLE CAT VIDEO!
IT'S SO CUTE!!
OH YEAH.
MEOW!
CUTE...
MEOW!
HEH HEH...
Get him a tasty treat.
I'LL BE RIGHT BACK WITH ONE OF YAMAGAMINE'S WORLD-FAMOUS HAM CUTLET SANDWICHES!
I HEAR IT SELLS OUT INSTANTLY, SINCE THE QUICKER ATHLETES BEAT EVERYONE TO THE STORE WINDOW AT LUNCH.
THE STAIRS KNOCK ME OUT OF THE RUNNING...
HAFF!
HAFF!
ALL...FOR... KIKUZATO-KUN'S HAPPI-NESS...!!
KIIN (DIIING)
DA (TMP)
DA
DA
DA
KOOON (DOOONG)
KAAAN (CLAAANG)
AH! I MADE IT IN TIME!
HFF... HFF...

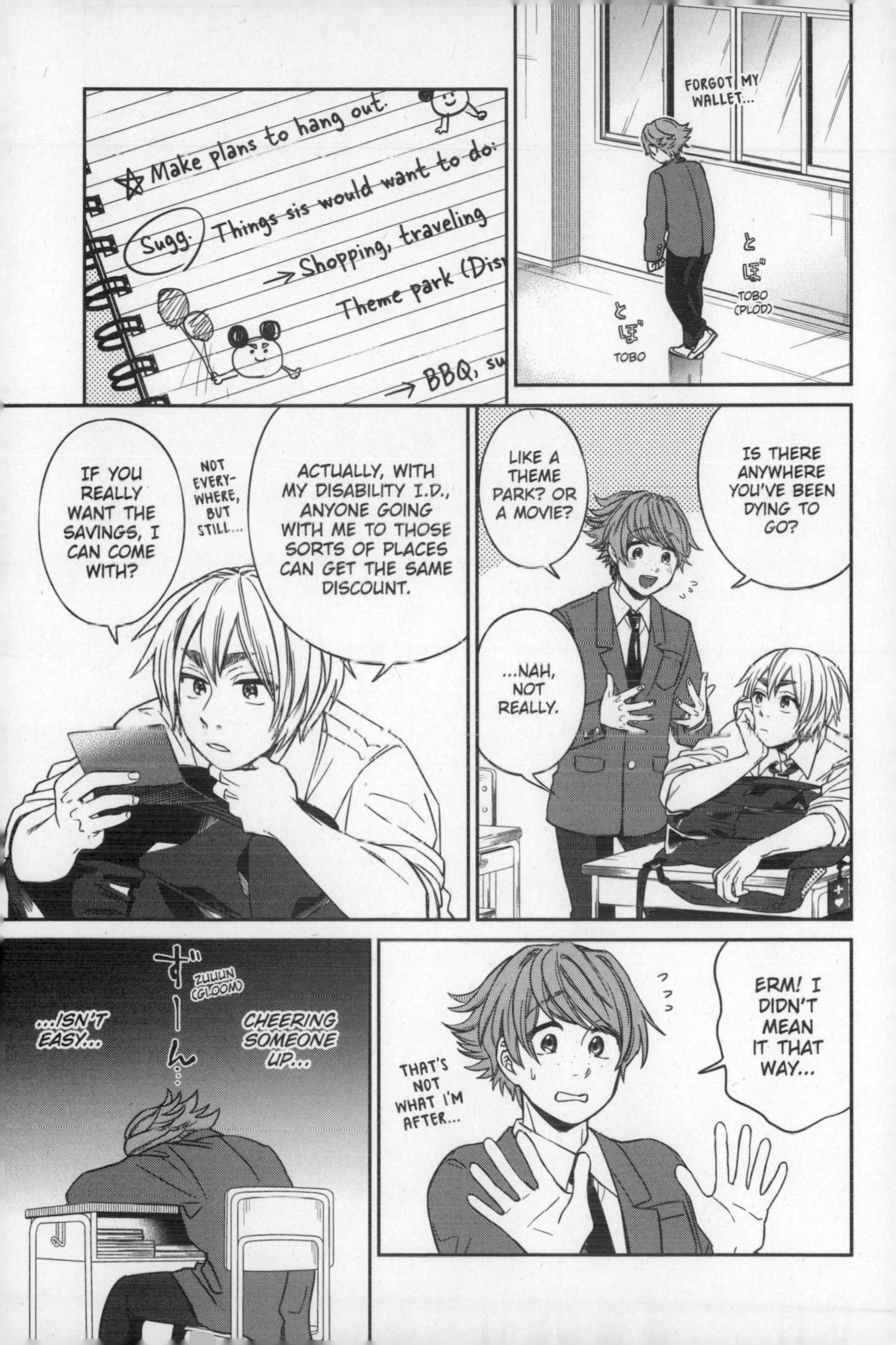
FORGOT MY WALLET...
とぼ
TOBO (PLOD)
とぼ
TOBO
☆ Make plans to hang out.
Sugg. Things sis would want to do:
→ Shopping, traveling
Theme park (Dis
→ BBQ, su
IS THERE ANYWHERE YOU'VE BEEN DYING TO GO?
LIKE A THEME PARK? OR A MOVIE?
...NAH, NOT REALLY.
ACTUALLY, WITH MY DISABILITY I.D., ANYONE GOING WITH ME TO THOSE SORTS OF PLACES CAN GET THE SAME DISCOUNT.
NOT EVERY-WHERE, BUT STILL...
IF YOU REALLY WANT THE SAVINGS, I CAN COME WITH?
ERM! I DIDN'T MEAN IT THAT WAY...
THAT'S NOT WHAT I'M AFTER...
ずーん...
ZUUUN (GLOOM)
CHEERING SOMEONE UP...
...ISN'T EASY...

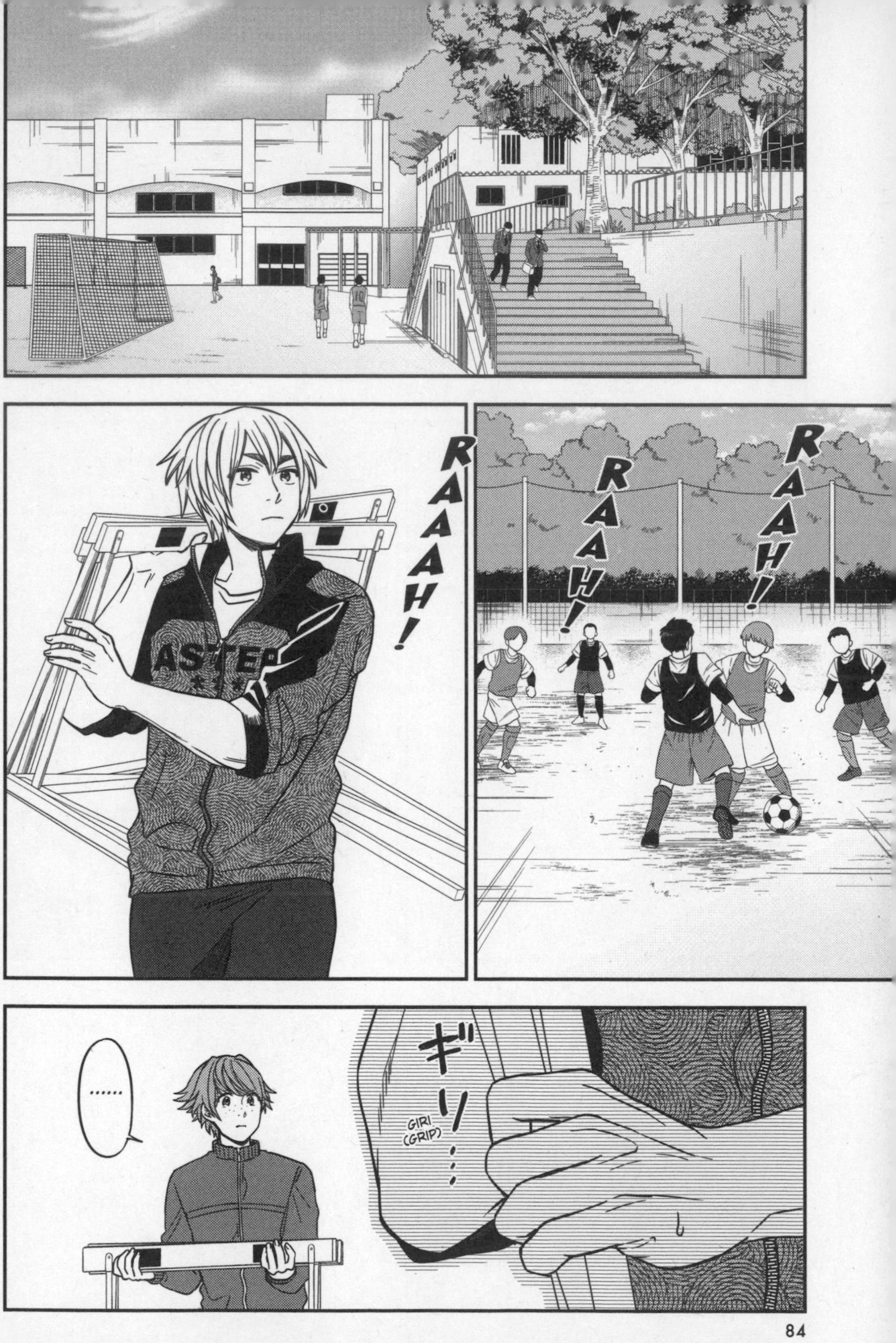
RAAH!
RAAH!
RAAAH!
ギリ…
GIRI (GRIP)
......

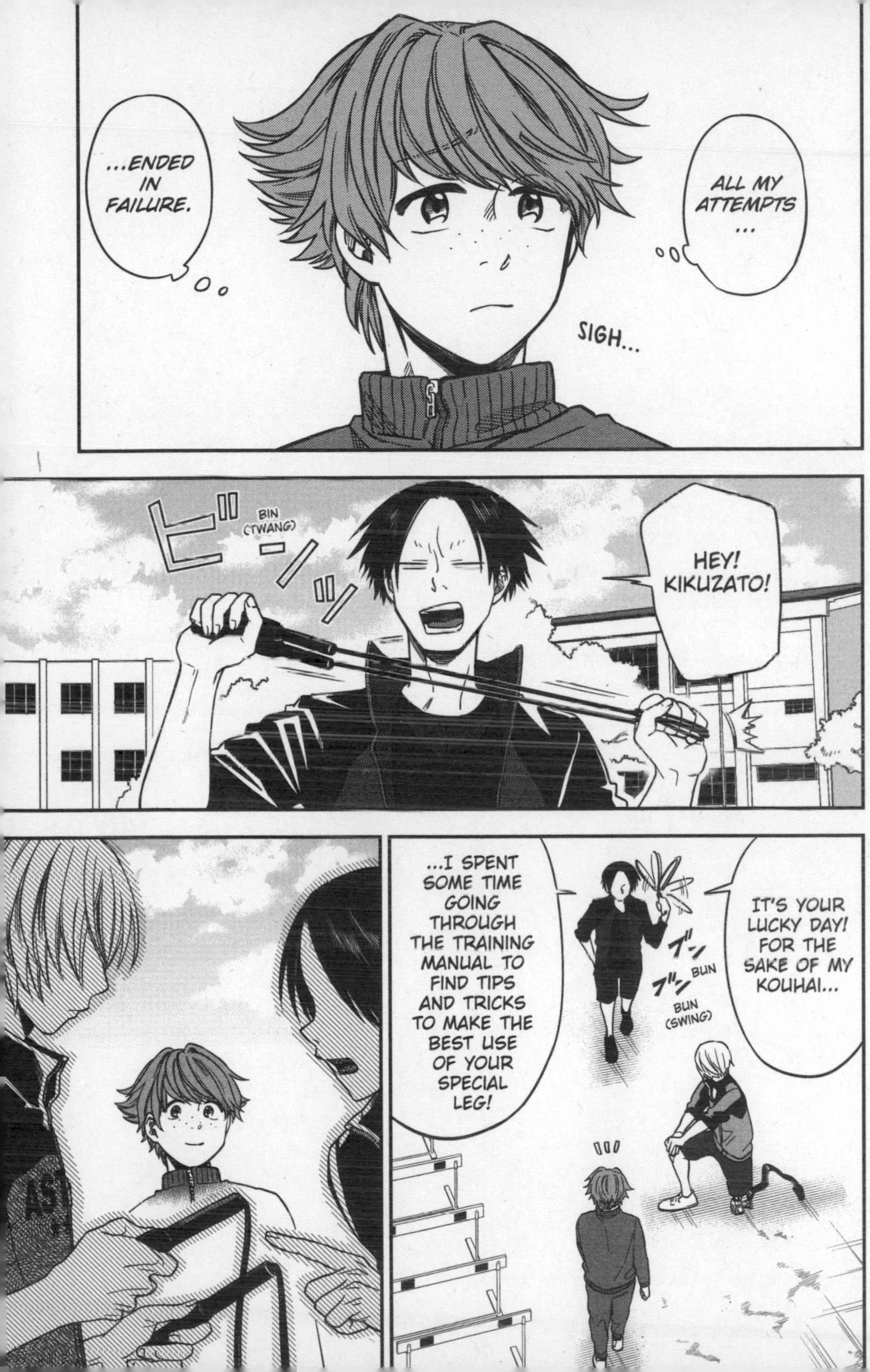
ALL MY ATTEMPTS ...
SIGH...
...ENDED IN FAILURE.
BIN (TWANG)
HEY! KIKUZATO!
IT'S YOUR LUCKY DAY! FOR THE SAKE OF MY KOUHAI...
BUN BUN (SWING)
...I SPENT SOME TIME GOING THROUGH THE TRAINING MANUAL TO FIND TIPS AND TRICKS TO MAKE THE BEST USE OF YOUR SPECIAL LEG!

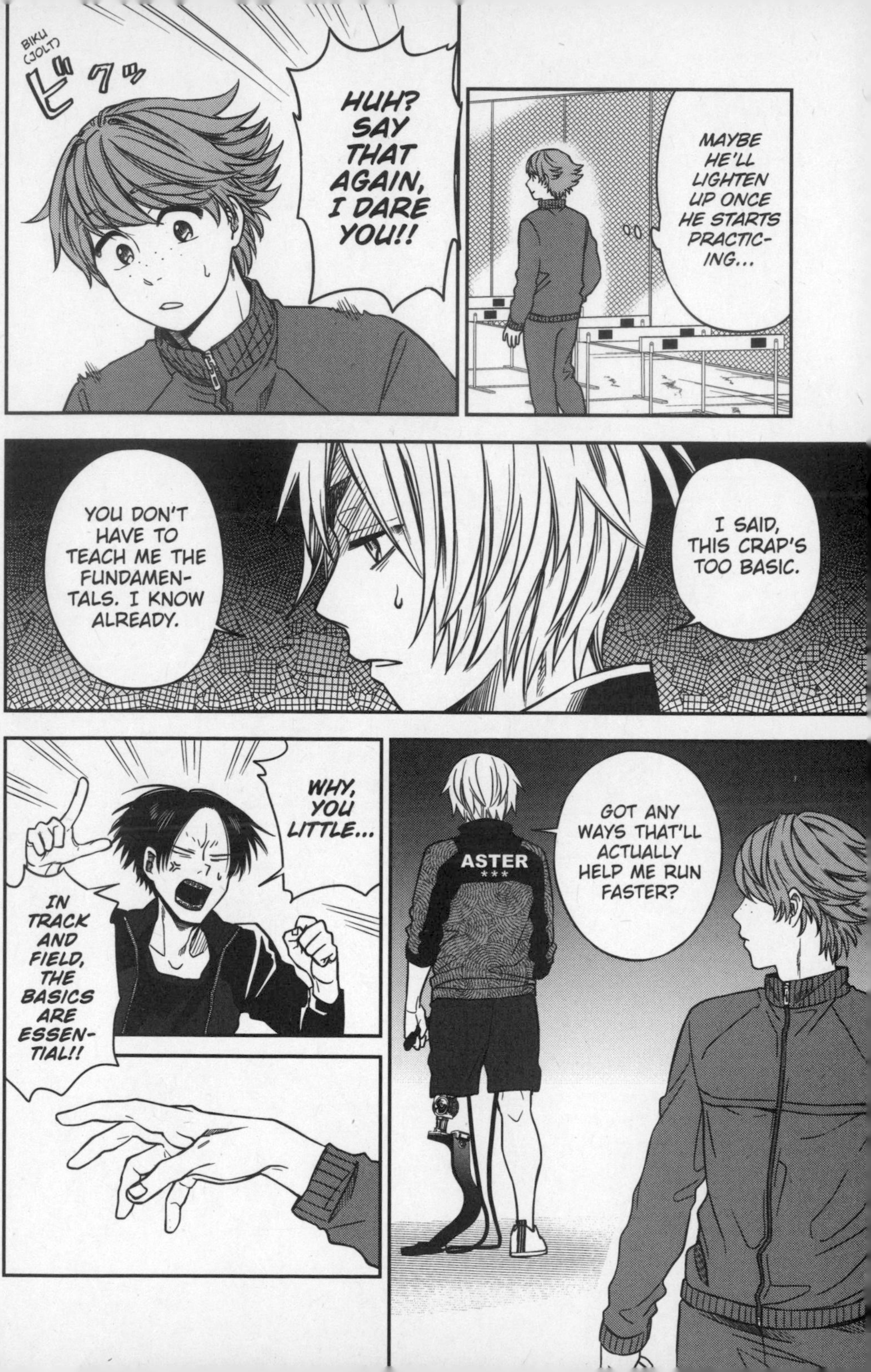
MAYBE HE'LL LIGHTEN UP ONCE HE STARTS PRACTIC-ING...
HUH? SAY THAT AGAIN, I DARE YOU!!
BIKU (JOLT)
ビクッ
I SAID, THIS CRAP'S TOO BASIC.
YOU DON'T HAVE TO TEACH ME THE FUNDAMEN-TALS. I KNOW ALREADY.
ASTER
GOT ANY WAYS THAT'LL ACTUALLY HELP ME RUN FASTER?
WHY, YOU LITTLE...
IN TRACK AND FIELD, THE BASICS ARE ESSEN-TIAL!!

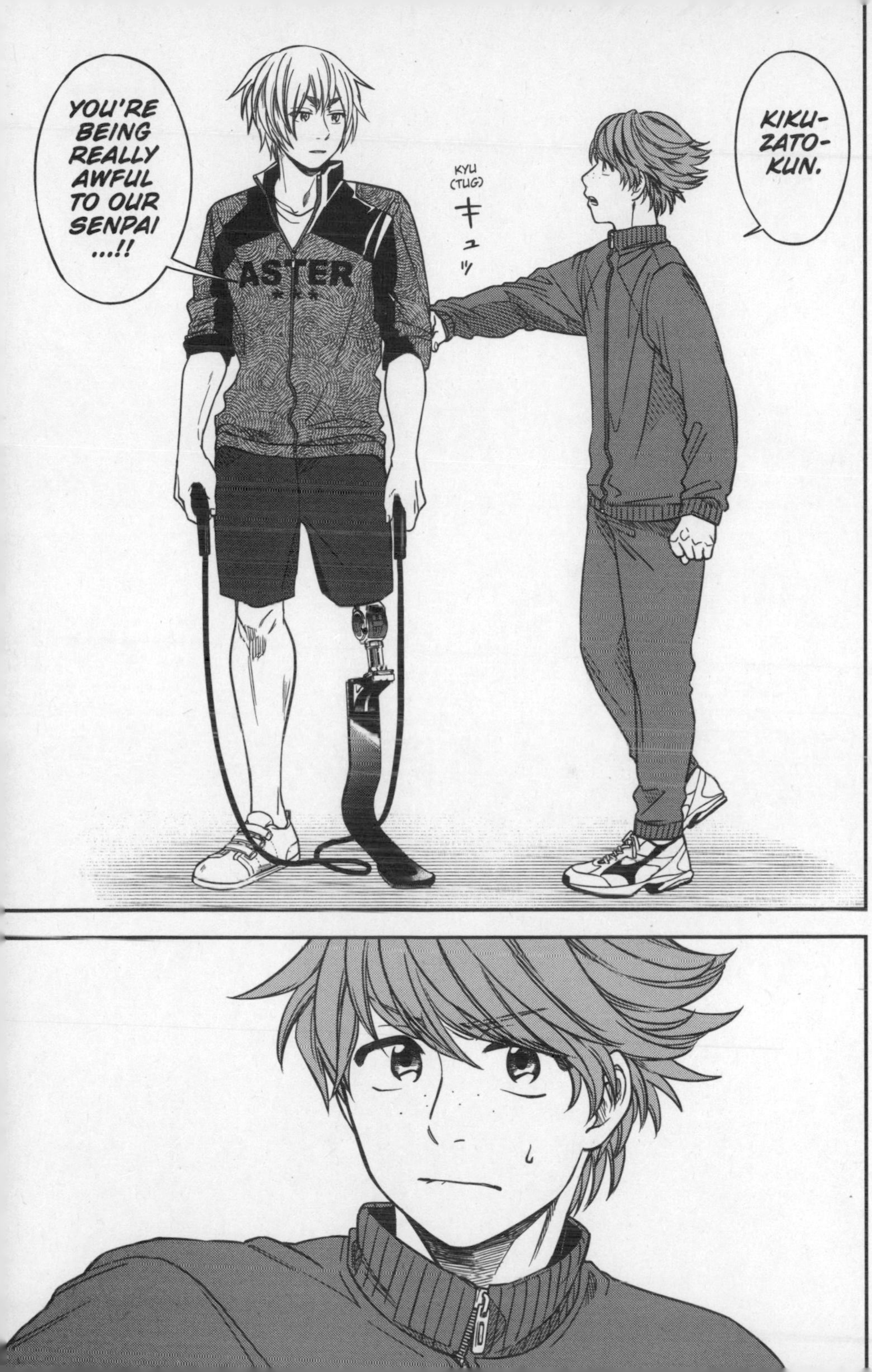
KIKU-ZATO-KUN.
KYU (TUG)
キュッ
YOU'RE BEING REALLY AWFUL TO OUR SENPAI ...!!

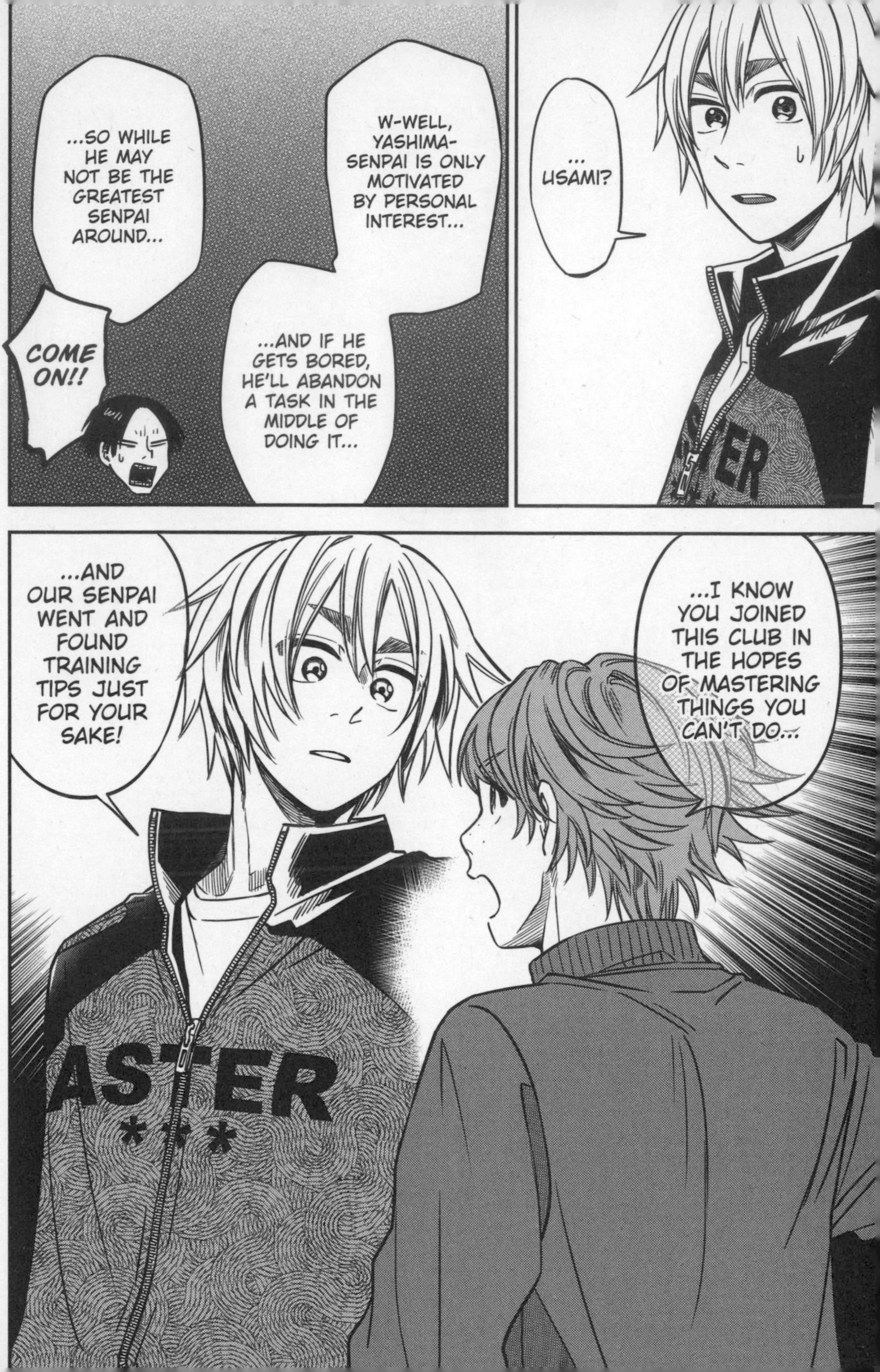
...USAMI?
W-WELL, YASHIMA-SENPAI IS ONLY MOTIVATED BY PERSONAL INTEREST...
...SO WHILE HE MAY NOT BE THE GREATEST SENPAI AROUND...
...AND IF HE GETS BORED, HE'LL ABANDON A TASK IN THE MIDDLE OF DOING IT...
COME ON!!
...I KNOW YOU JOINED THIS CLUB IN THE HOPES OF MASTERING THINGS YOU CAN'T DO...
...AND OUR SENPAI WENT AND FOUND TRAINING TIPS JUST FOR YOUR SAKE!
ASTER

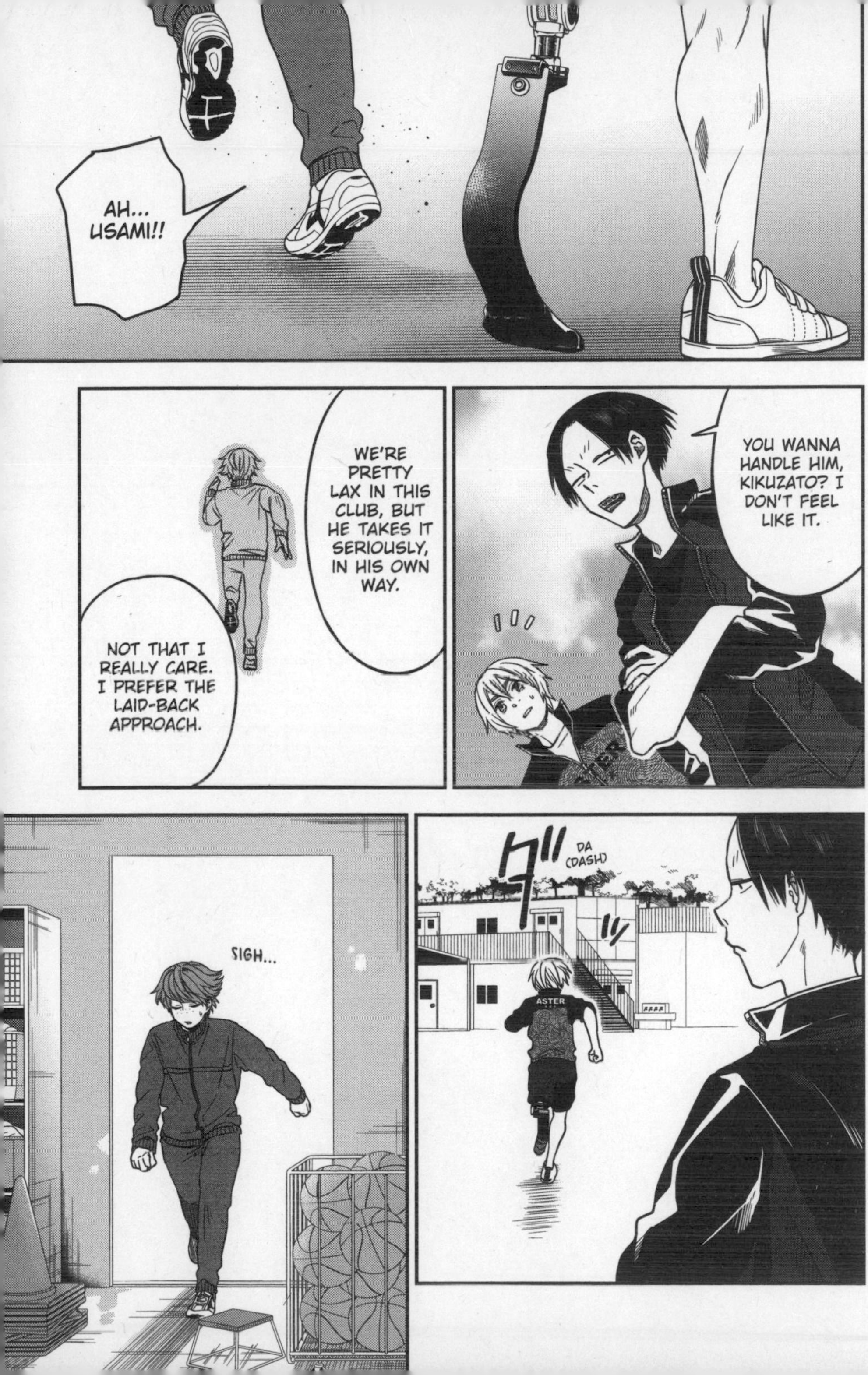
AH... USAMI!!
YOU WANNA HANDLE HIM, KIKUZATO? I DON'T FEEL LIKE IT.
WE'RE PRETTY LAX IN THIS CLUB, BUT HE TAKES IT SERIOUSLY, IN HIS OWN WAY.
NOT THAT I REALLY CARE. I PREFER THE LAID-BACK APPROACH.
DA (DASH)
ASTER
SIGH...

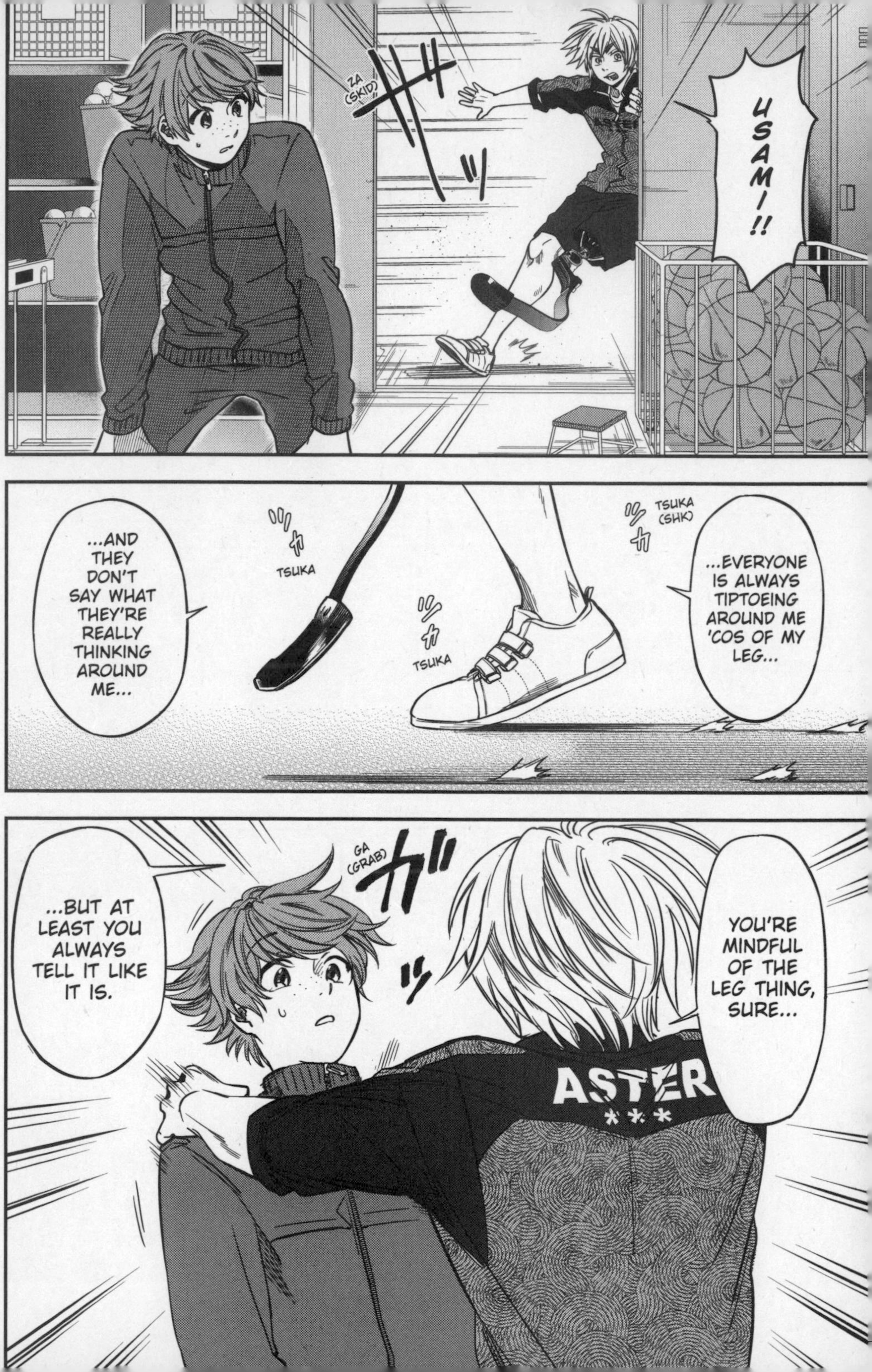
USAMI!!
ZA (SKID)
...EVERYONE IS ALWAYS TIPTOEING AROUND ME 'COS OF MY LEG...
TSUKA (SHK)
TSUKA
TSUKA
...AND THEY DON'T SAY WHAT THEY'RE REALLY THINKING AROUND ME...
YOU'RE MINDFUL OF THE LEG THING, SURE...
GA (GRAB)
...BUT AT LEAST YOU ALWAYS TELL IT LIKE IT IS.
ASTER

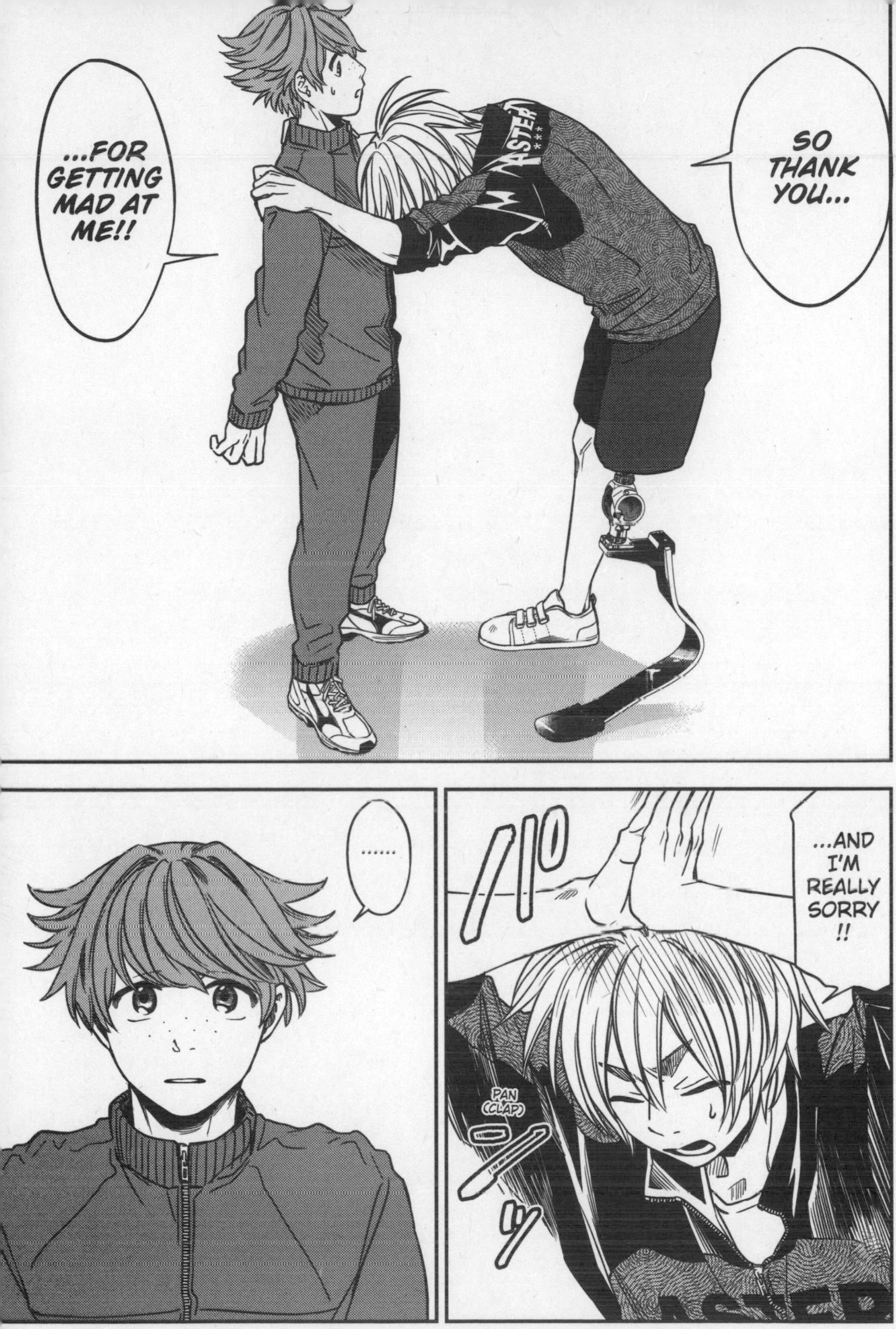
SO THANK YOU...
...FOR GETTING MAD AT ME!!
...AND I'M REALLY SORRY !!
PAN (CLAP)
......

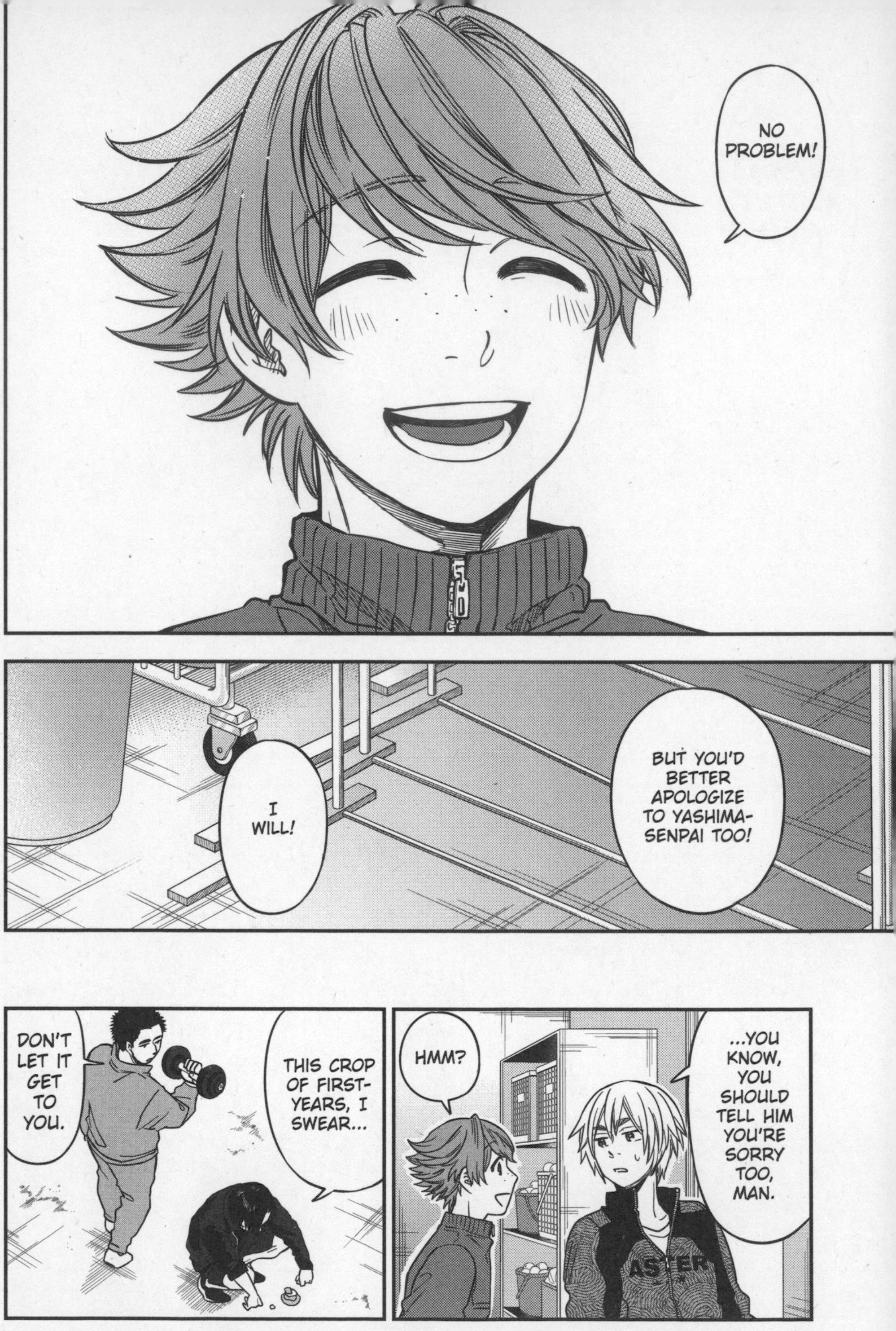
NO PROBLEM!
BUT YOU'D BETTER APOLOGIZE TO YASHIMA-SENPAI TOO!
I WILL!
...YOU KNOW, YOU SHOULD TELL HIM YOU'RE SORRY TOO, MAN.
HMM?
THIS CROP OF FIRST-YEARS, I SWEAR...
DON'T LET IT GET TO YOU.

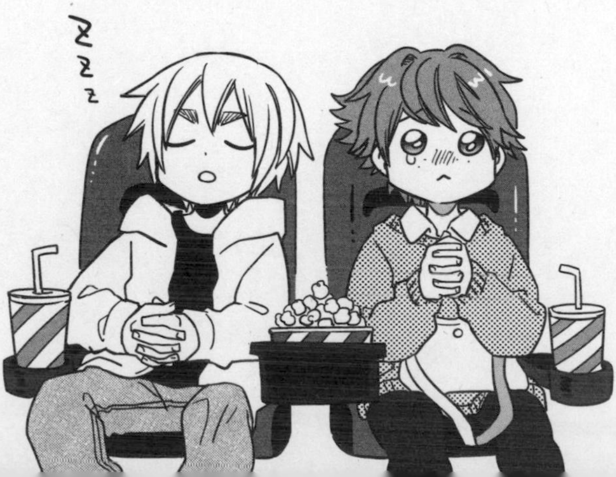
Z
Z
Z

RUN ON YOUR NEW LEGS

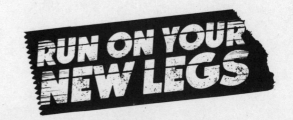

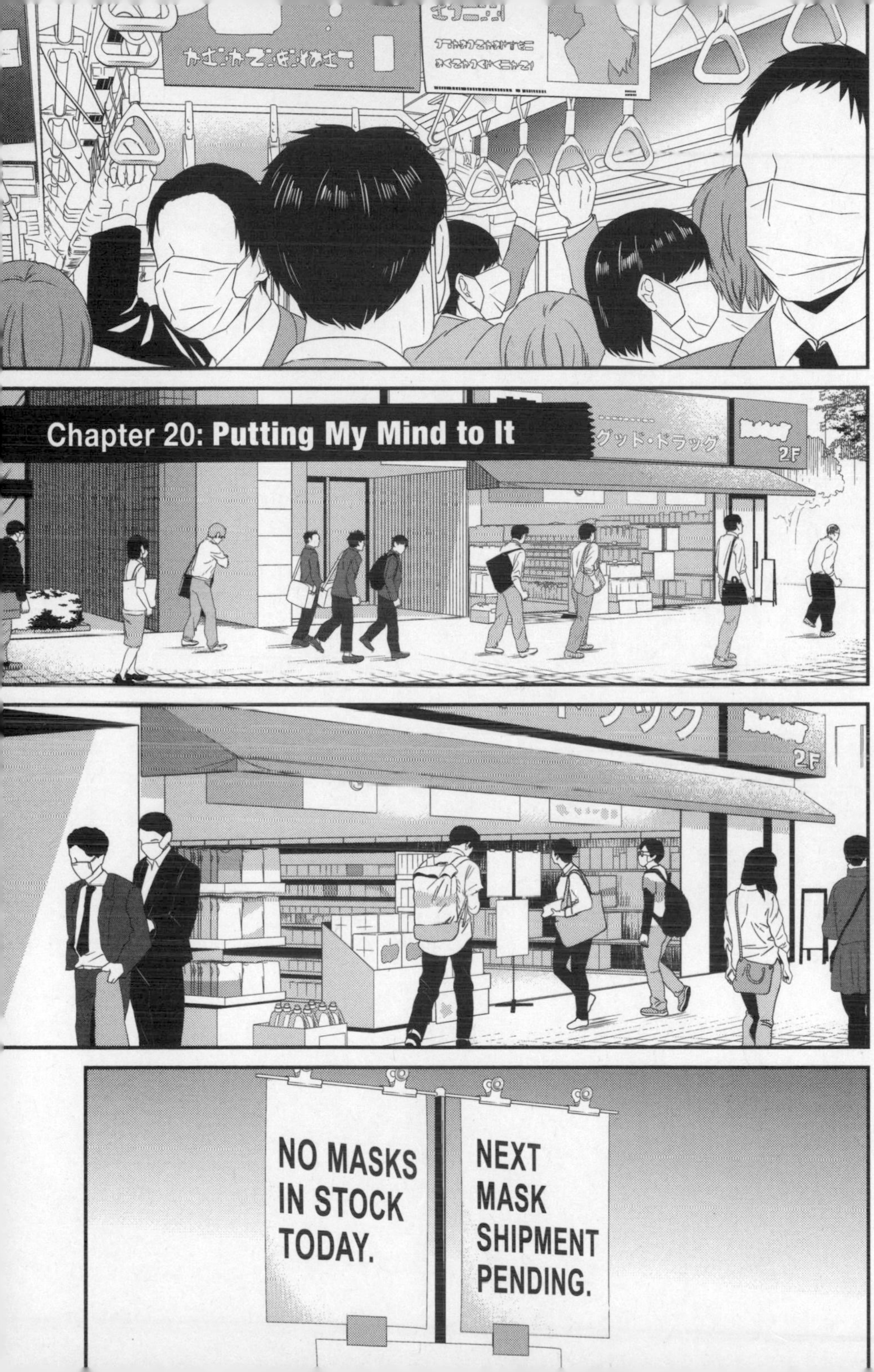
Chapter 20: Putting My Mind to It
グッド・ドラッグ
2F
2F
NO MASKS IN STOCK TODAY.
NEXT MASK SHIPMENT PENDING.

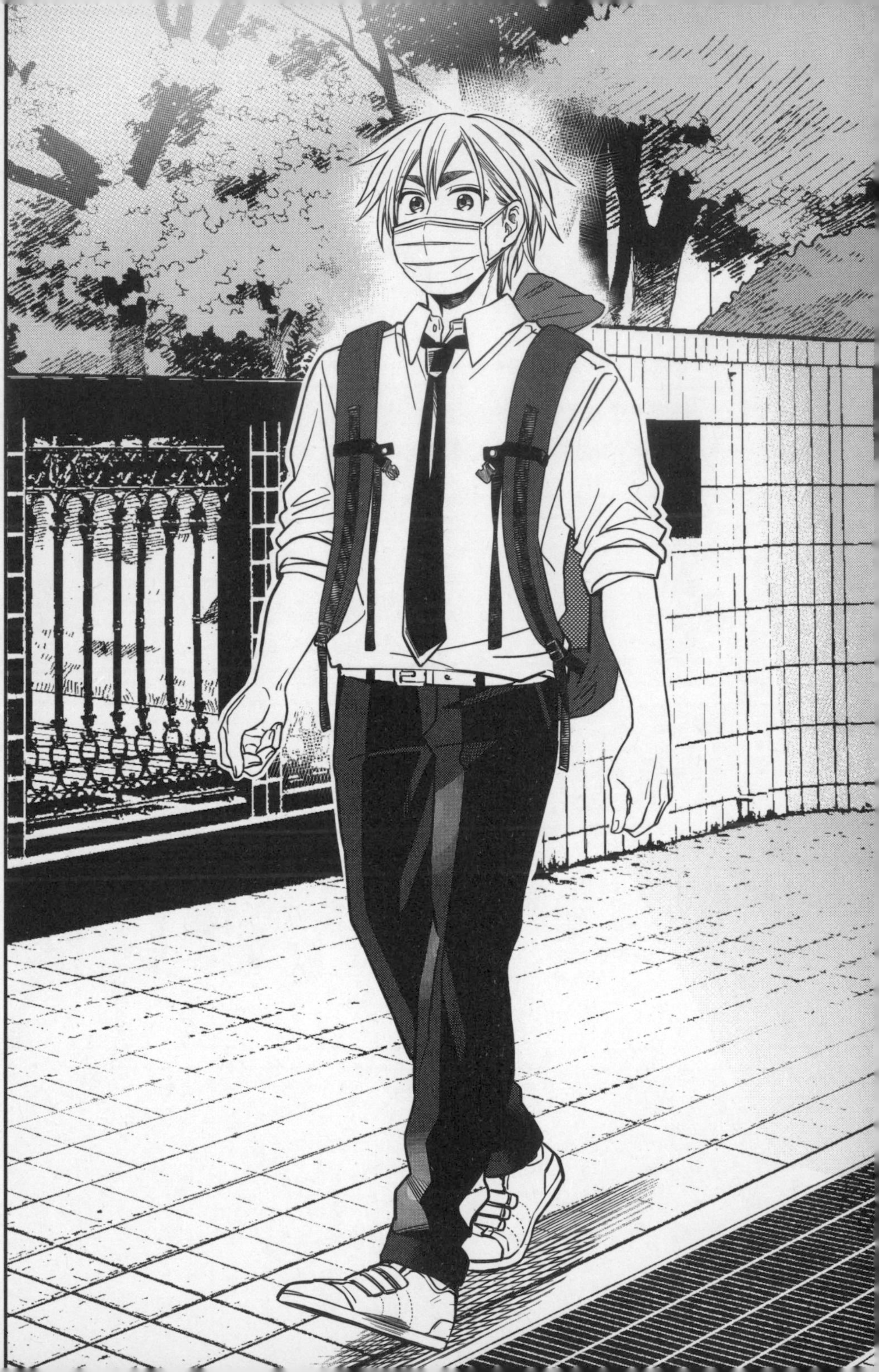

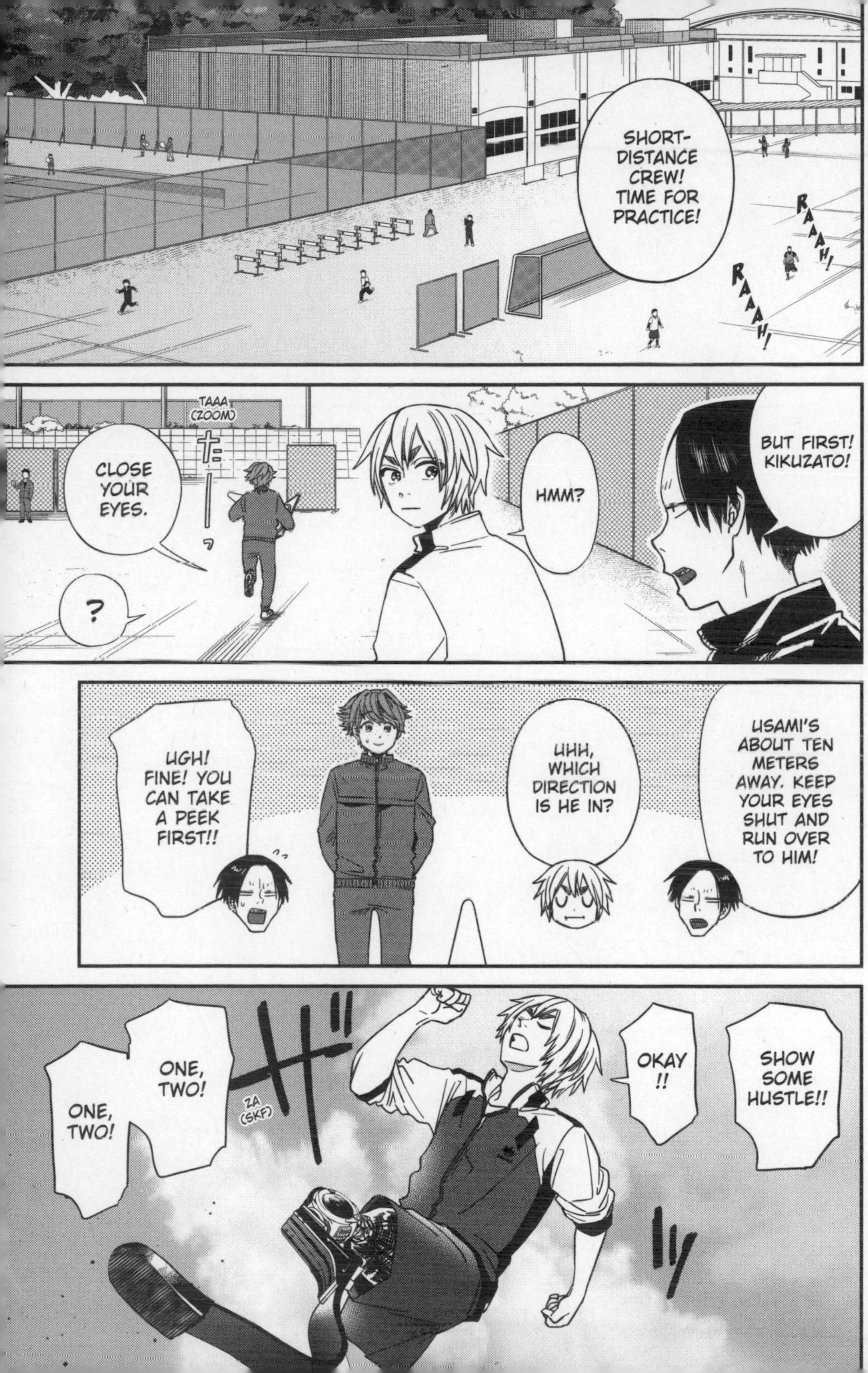

SHORT-DISTANCE CREW! TIME FOR PRACTICE!
RAAAH!
RAAAH!
BUT FIRST! KIKUZATO!
HMM?
TAAA (ZOOM)
CLOSE YOUR EYES.
?
USAMI'S ABOUT TEN METERS AWAY. KEEP YOUR EYES SHUT AND RUN OVER TO HIM!
UHH, WHICH DIRECTION IS HE IN?
UGH! FINE! YOU CAN TAKE A PEEK FIRST!!
SHOW SOME HUSTLE!!
OKAY!!
ZA (SKF)
ONE, TWO!
ONE, TWO!

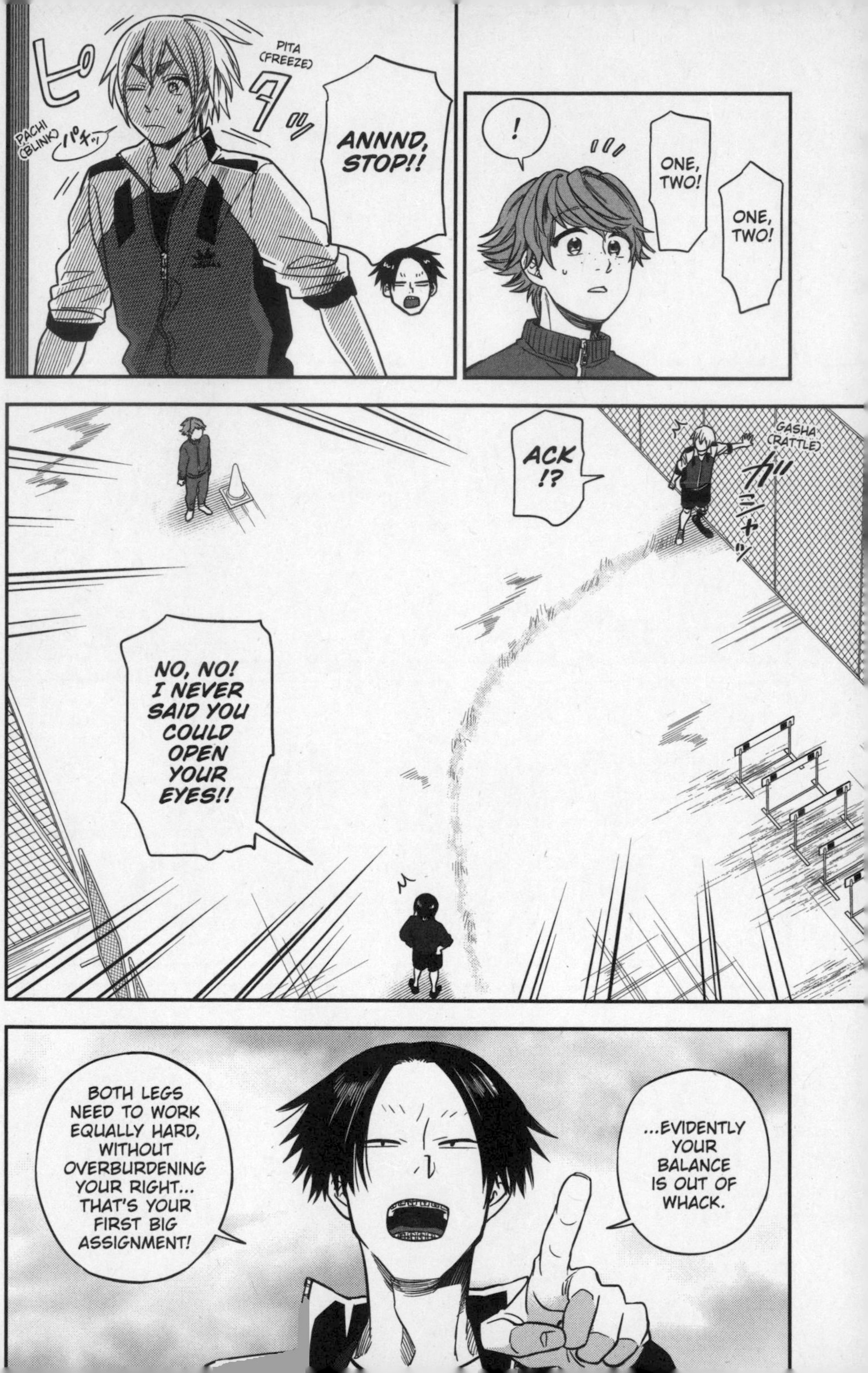
ONE, TWO!
ONE, TWO!
!
PITA (FREEZE)
ANNND, STOP!!
PACHI (BLINK)
GASHA (RATTLE)
ACK !?
NO, NO! I NEVER SAID YOU COULD OPEN YOUR EYES!!
...EVIDENTLY YOUR BALANCE IS OUT OF WHACK.
BOTH LEGS NEED TO WORK EQUALLY HARD, WITHOUT OVERBURDENING YOUR RIGHT... THAT'S YOUR FIRST BIG ASSIGNMENT!

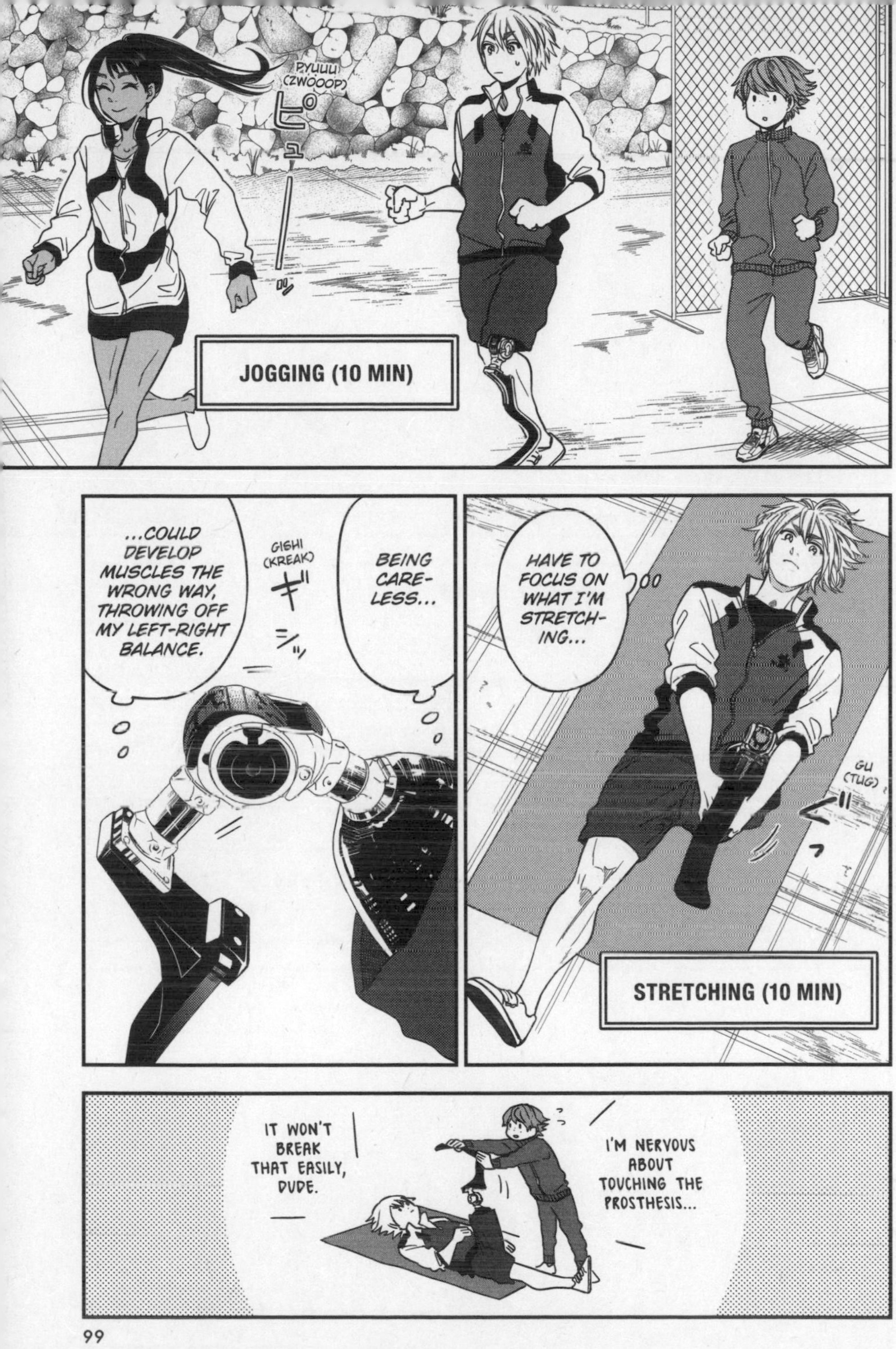
PYUUU (ZWOOOP)
ピューッ
JOGGING (10 MIN)
HAVE TO FOCUS ON WHAT I'M STRETCHING-ING...
GU (TUG)
STRETCHING (10 MIN)
BEING CARE-LESS...
GISHI (KREAK)
...COULD DEVELOP MUSCLES THE WRONG WAY, THROWING OFF MY LEFT-RIGHT BALANCE.
I'M NERVOUS ABOUT TOUCHING THE PROSTHESIS...
IT WON'T BREAK THAT EASILY, DUDE.

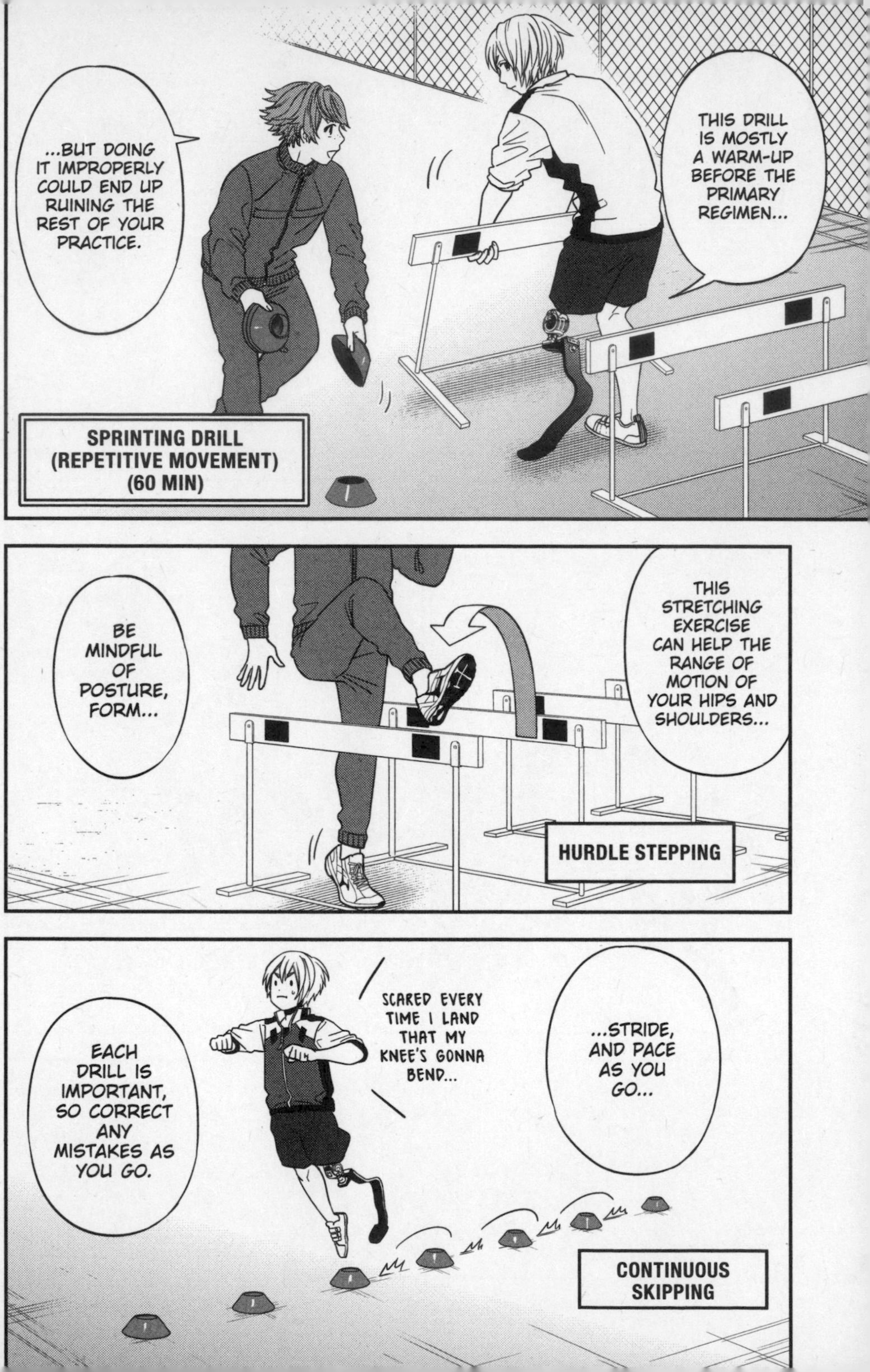
THIS DRILL IS MOSTLY A WARM-UP BEFORE THE PRIMARY REGIMEN...
...BUT DOING IT IMPROPERLY COULD END UP RUINING THE REST OF YOUR PRACTICE.
SPRINTING DRILL (REPETITIVE MOVEMENT) (60 MIN)
THIS STRETCHING EXERCISE CAN HELP THE RANGE OF MOTION OF YOUR HIPS AND SHOULDERS...
BE MINDFUL OF POSTURE, FORM...
HURDLE STEPPING
...STRIDE, AND PACE AS YOU GO...
SCARED EVERY TIME I LAND THAT MY KNEE'S GONNA BEND...
EACH DRILL IS IMPORTANT, SO CORRECT ANY MISTAKES AS YOU GO.
CONTINUOUS SKIPPING

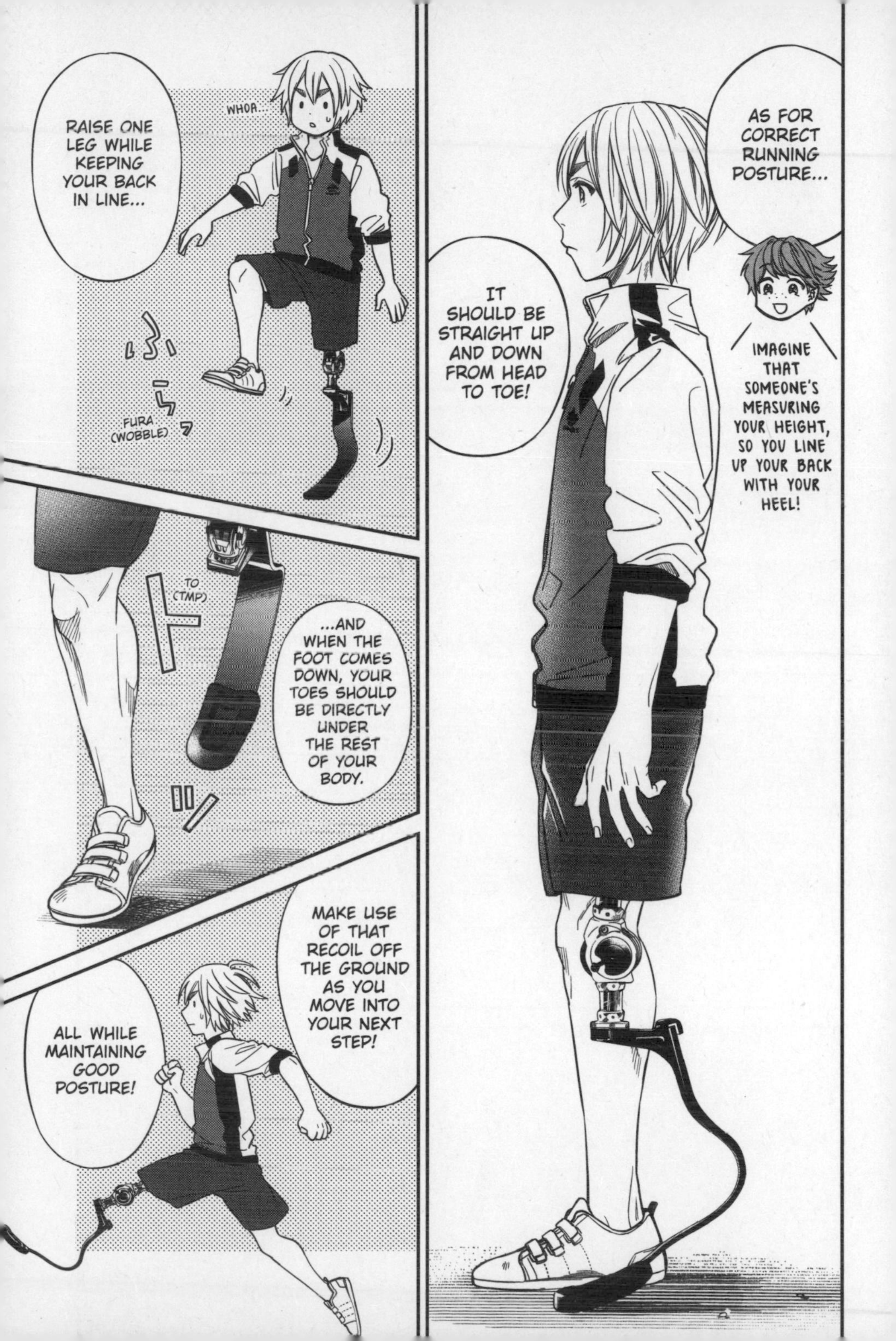
AS FOR CORRECT RUNNING POSTURE...
IT SHOULD BE STRAIGHT UP AND DOWN FROM HEAD TO TOE!
IMAGINE THAT SOMEONE'S MEASURING YOUR HEIGHT, SO YOU LINE UP YOUR BACK WITH YOUR HEEL!
RAISE ONE LEG WHILE KEEPING YOUR BACK IN LINE...
WHOA...
FURA (WOBBLE)
TO (TMP)
...AND WHEN THE FOOT COMES DOWN, YOUR TOES SHOULD BE DIRECTLY UNDER THE REST OF YOUR BODY.
MAKE USE OF THAT RECOIL OFF THE GROUND AS YOU MOVE INTO YOUR NEXT STEP!
ALL WHILE MAINTAINING GOOD POSTURE!

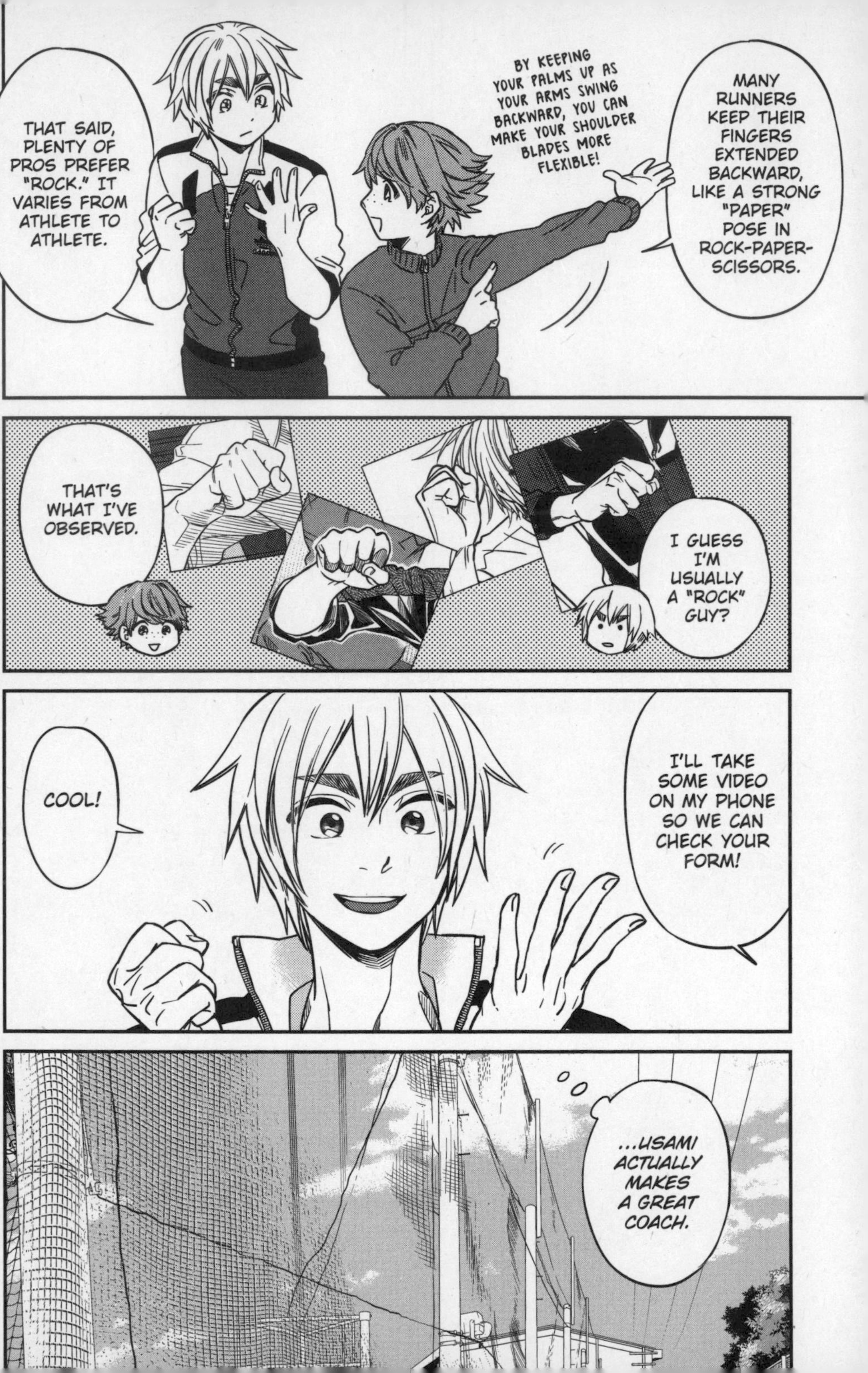
MANY RUNNERS KEEP THEIR FINGERS EXTENDED BACKWARD, LIKE A STRONG "PAPER" POSE IN ROCK-PAPER-SCISSORS.
BY KEEPING YOUR PALMS UP AS YOUR ARMS SWING BACKWARD, YOU CAN MAKE YOUR SHOULDER BLADES MORE FLEXIBLE!
THAT SAID, PLENTY OF PROS PREFER "ROCK." IT VARIES FROM ATHLETE TO ATHLETE.
I GUESS I'M USUALLY A "ROCK" GUY?
THAT'S WHAT I'VE OBSERVED.
I'LL TAKE SOME VIDEO ON MY PHONE SO WE CAN CHECK YOUR FORM!
COOL!
...USAMI ACTUALLY MAKES A GREAT COACH.

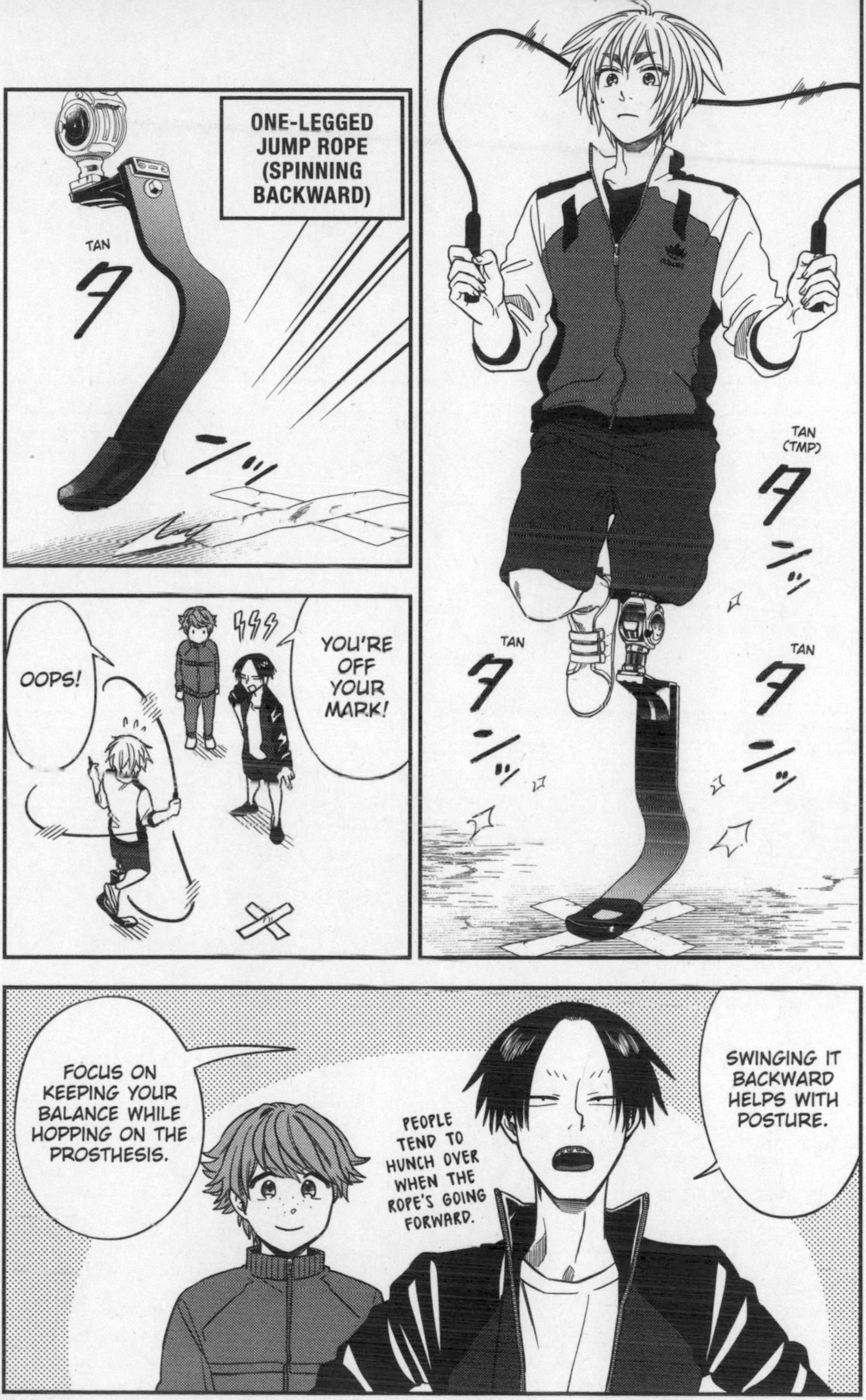
TAN (TMP)
タンッ
TAN
タンッ
TAN
タンッ
ONE-LEGGED JUMP ROPE (SPINNING BACKWARD)
TAN
タンッ
YOU'RE OFF YOUR MARK!
OOPS!
SWINGING IT BACKWARD HELPS WITH POSTURE.
PEOPLE TEND TO HUNCH OVER WHEN THE ROPE'S GOING FORWARD.
FOCUS ON KEEPING YOUR BALANCE WHILE HOPPING ON THE PROSTHESIS.

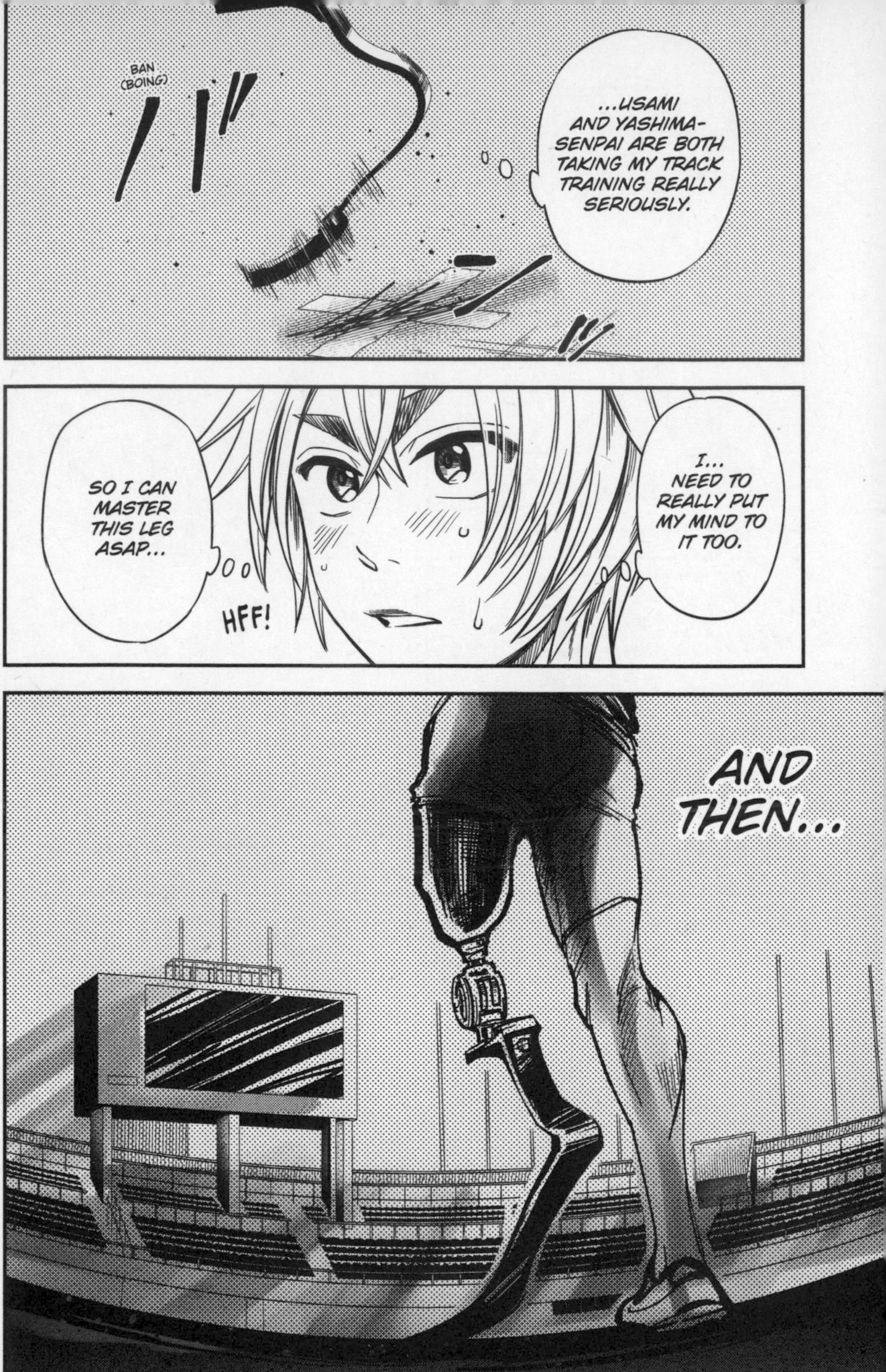
...USAMI AND YASHIMA-SENPAI ARE BOTH TAKING MY TRACK TRAINING REALLY SERIOUSLY.
BAN (BOING)
I... NEED TO REALLY PUT MY MIND TO IT TOO.
SO I CAN MASTER THIS LEG ASAP...
HFF!
AND THEN...

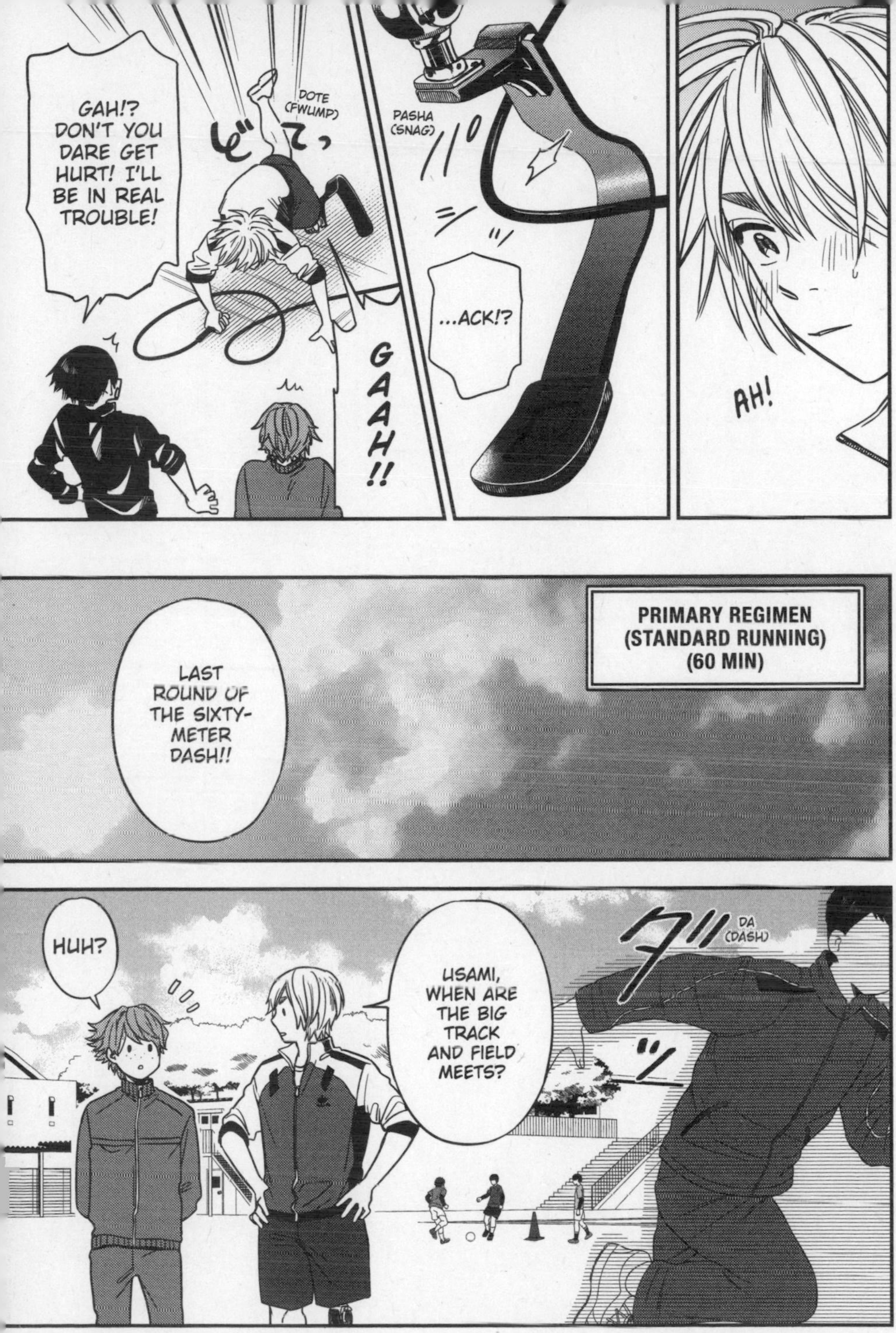
AH!
PASHA (SNAG)
...ACK!?
DOTE (FWUMP)
GAH!? DON'T YOU DARE GET HURT! I'LL BE IN REAL TROUBLE!
GAAH!!
PRIMARY REGIMEN (STANDARD RUNNING) (60 MIN)
LAST ROUND OF THE SIXTY-METER DASH!!
DA (DASH)
USAMI, WHEN ARE THE BIG TRACK AND FIELD MEETS?
HUH?

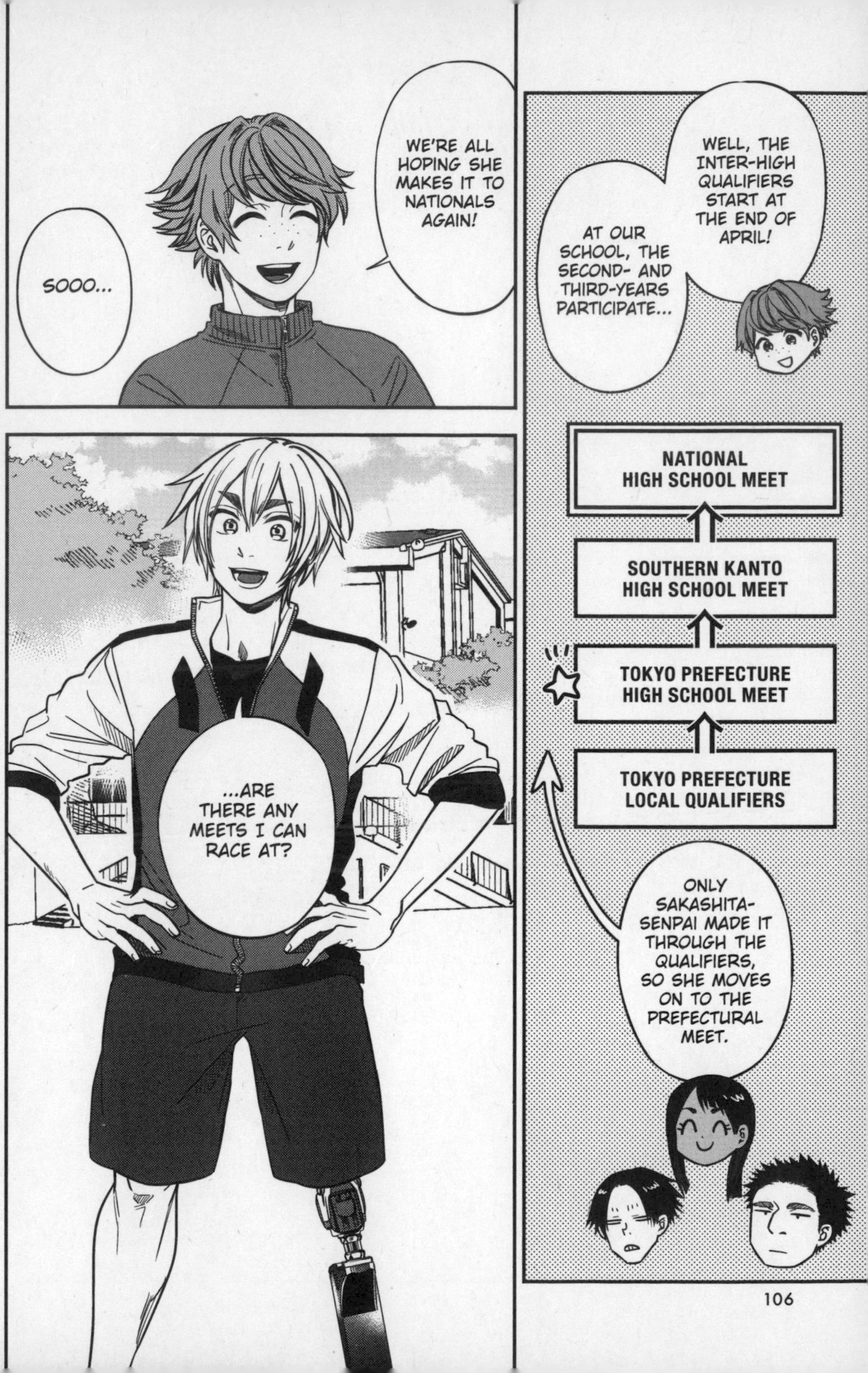

WELL, THE INTER-HIGH QUALIFIERS START AT THE END OF APRIL!
AT OUR SCHOOL, THE SECOND- AND THIRD-YEARS PARTICIPATE...
NATIONAL HIGH SCHOOL MEET
SOUTHERN KANTO HIGH SCHOOL MEET
TOKYO PREFECTURE HIGH SCHOOL MEET
TOKYO PREFECTURE LOCAL QUALIFIERS
ONLY SAKASHITA-SENPAI MADE IT THROUGH THE QUALIFIERS, SO SHE MOVES ON TO THE PREFECTURAL MEET.
WE'RE ALL HOPING SHE MAKES IT TO NATIONALS AGAIN!
SOOO...
...ARE THERE ANY MEETS I CAN RACE AT?

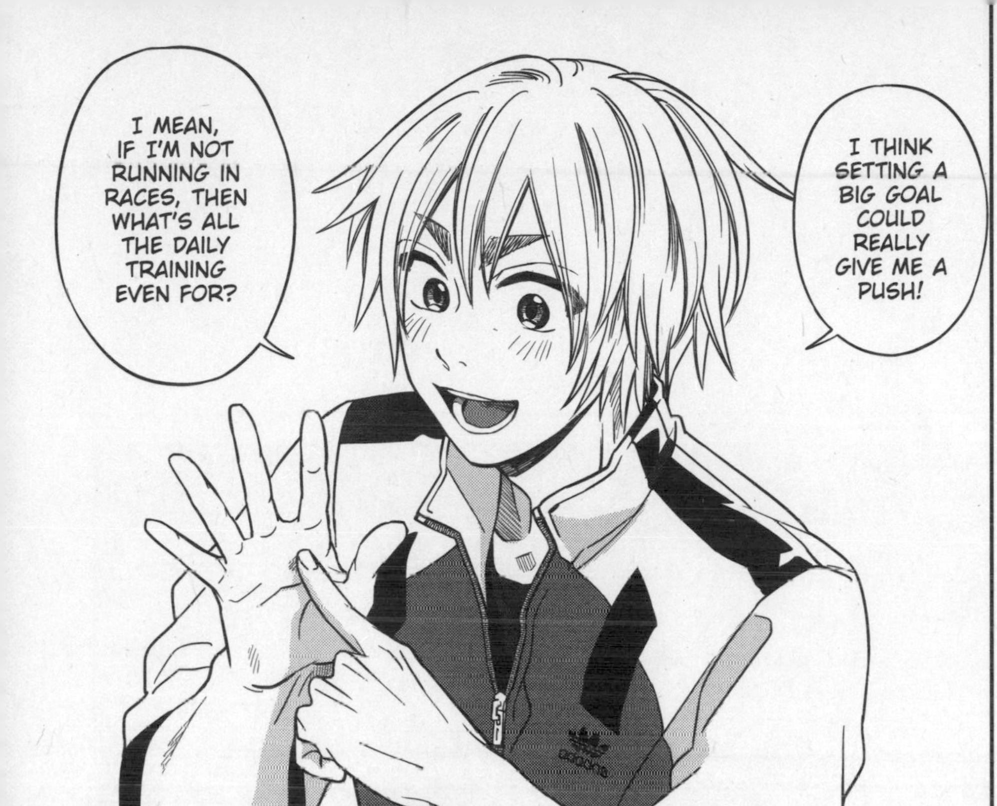
I THINK SETTING A BIG GOAL COULD REALLY GIVE ME A PUSH!
I MEAN, IF I'M NOT RUNNING IN RACES, THEN WHAT'S ALL THE DAILY TRAINING EVEN FOR?
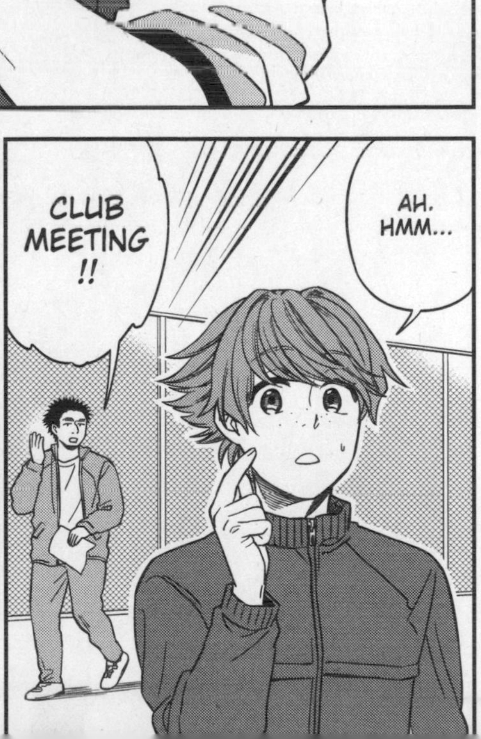
AH. HMM...
CLUB MEETING !!
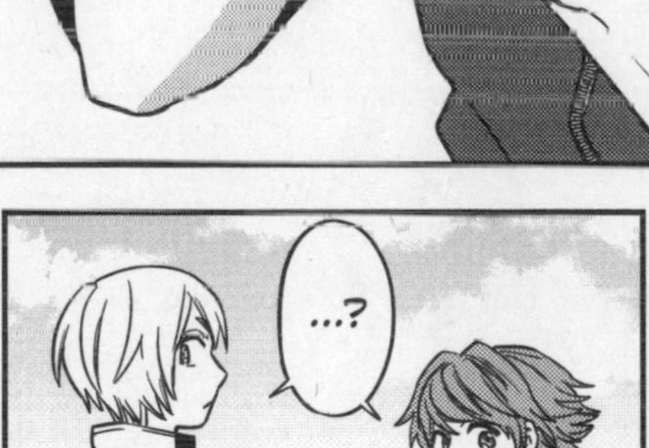
...?

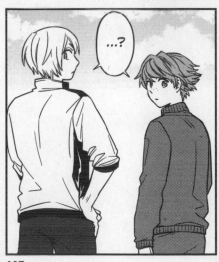

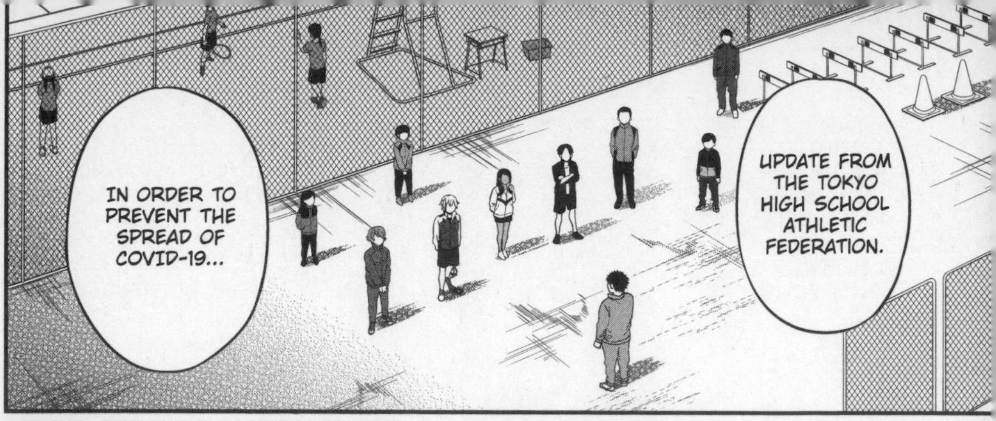
UPDATE FROM THE TOKYO HIGH SCHOOL ATHLETIC FEDERATION.
IN ORDER TO PREVENT THE SPREAD OF COVID-19...

NOTE: THIS UPDATE CAME AT THE START OF APRIL 2020.

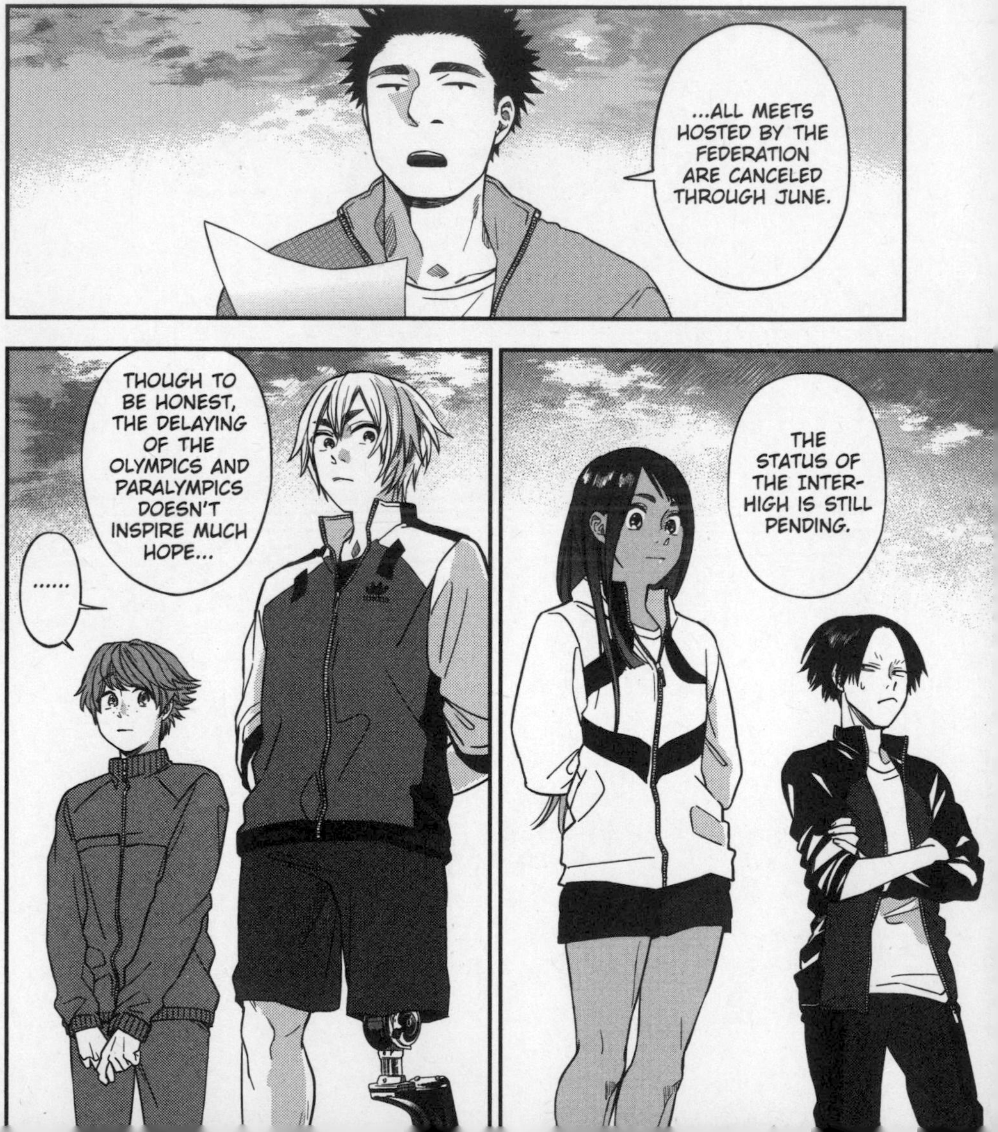
...ALL MEETS HOSTED BY THE FEDERATION ARE CANCELED THROUGH JUNE.
THE STATUS OF THE INTER-HIGH IS STILL PENDING.
THOUGH TO BE HONEST, THE DELAYING OF THE OLYMPICS AND PARALYMPICS DOESN'T INSPIRE MUCH HOPE...
......

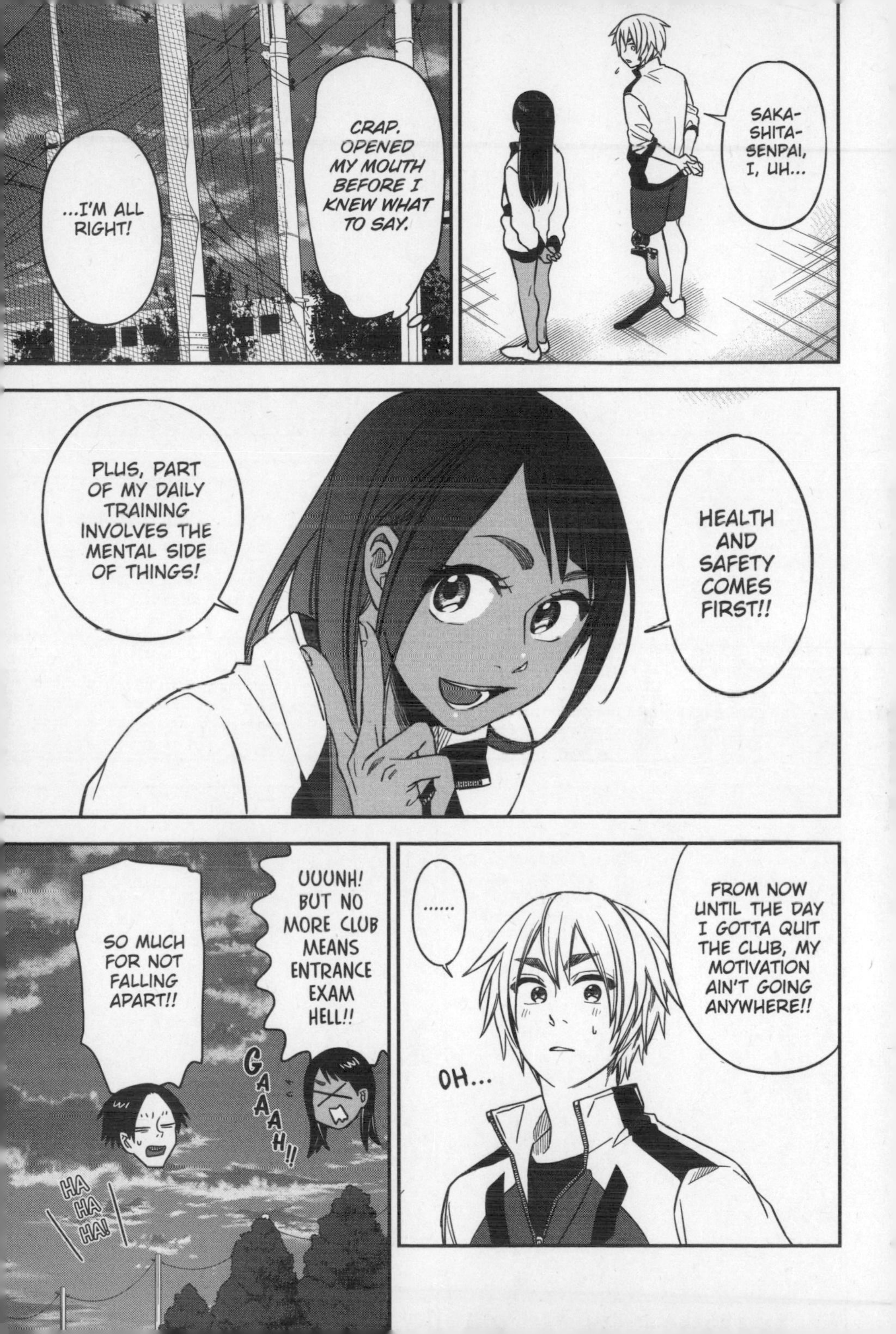
SAKA-SHITA-SENPAI, I, UH...
CRAP. OPENED MY MOUTH BEFORE I KNEW WHAT TO SAY.
...I'M ALL RIGHT!
HEALTH AND SAFETY COMES FIRST!!
PLUS, PART OF MY DAILY TRAINING INVOLVES THE MENTAL SIDE OF THINGS!
FROM NOW UNTIL THE DAY I GOTTA QUIT THE CLUB, MY MOTIVATION AIN'T GOING ANYWHERE!!
......
OH...
UUUNH! BUT NO MORE CLUB MEANS ENTRANCE EXAM HELL!!
GAAAH!!
SO MUCH FOR NOT FALLING APART!!
HA HA HA!

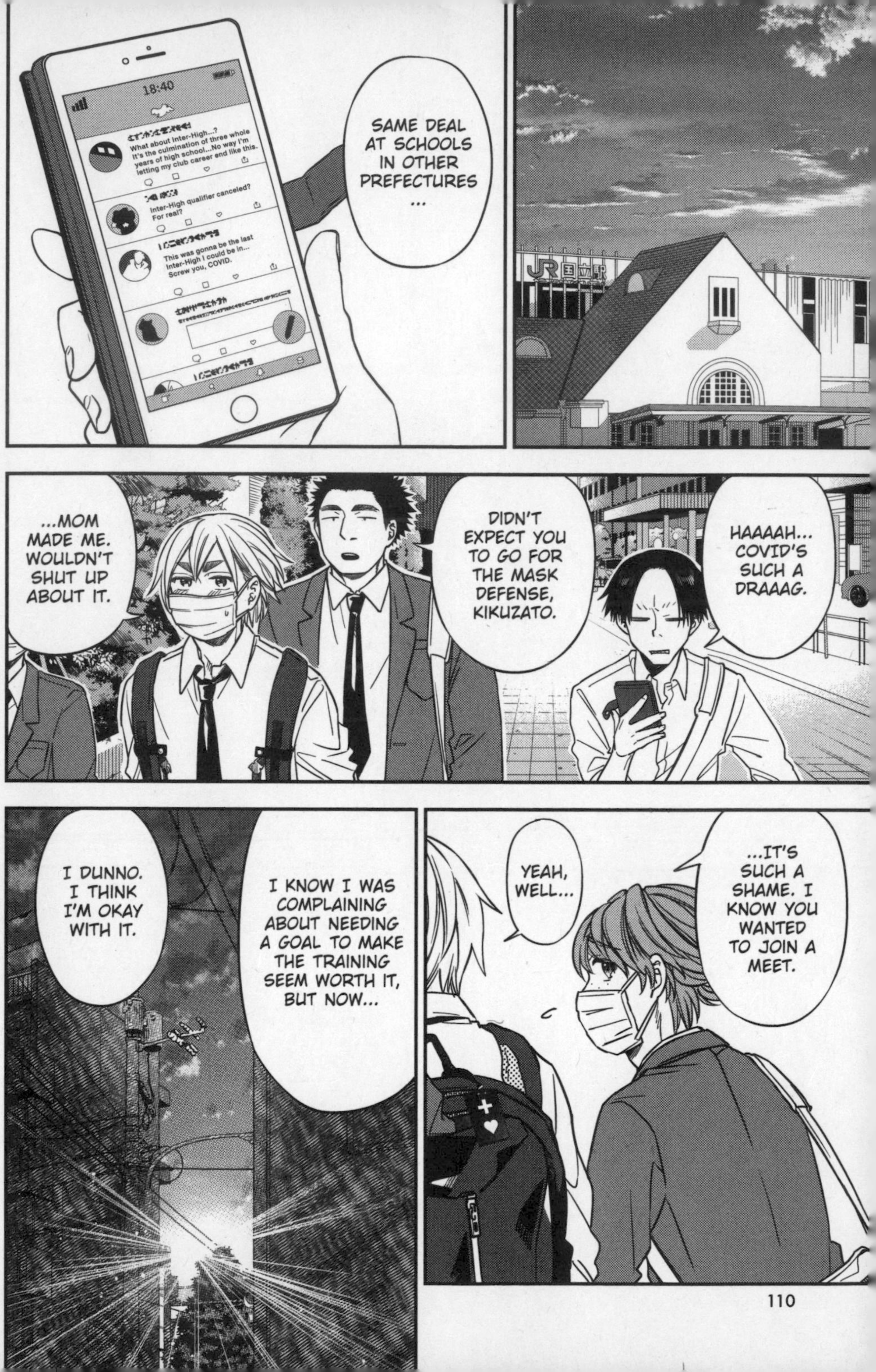

18:40
What about Inter-High...? It's the culmination of three whole years of high school...No way I'm letting my club career end like this.
Inter-High qualifier canceled? For real?
This was gonna be the last Inter-High I could be in... Screw you, COVID.
SAME DEAL AT SCHOOLS IN OTHER PREFECTURES ...
HAAAAH... COVID'S SUCH A DRAAAG.
DIDN'T EXPECT YOU TO GO FOR THE MASK DEFENSE, KIKUZATO.
...MOM MADE ME. WOULDN'T SHUT UP ABOUT IT.
...IT'S SUCH A SHAME. I KNOW YOU WANTED TO JOIN A MEET.
YEAH, WELL...
I KNOW I WAS COMPLAINING ABOUT NEEDING A GOAL TO MAKE THE TRAINING SEEM WORTH IT, BUT NOW...
I DUNNO. I THINK I'M OKAY WITH IT.

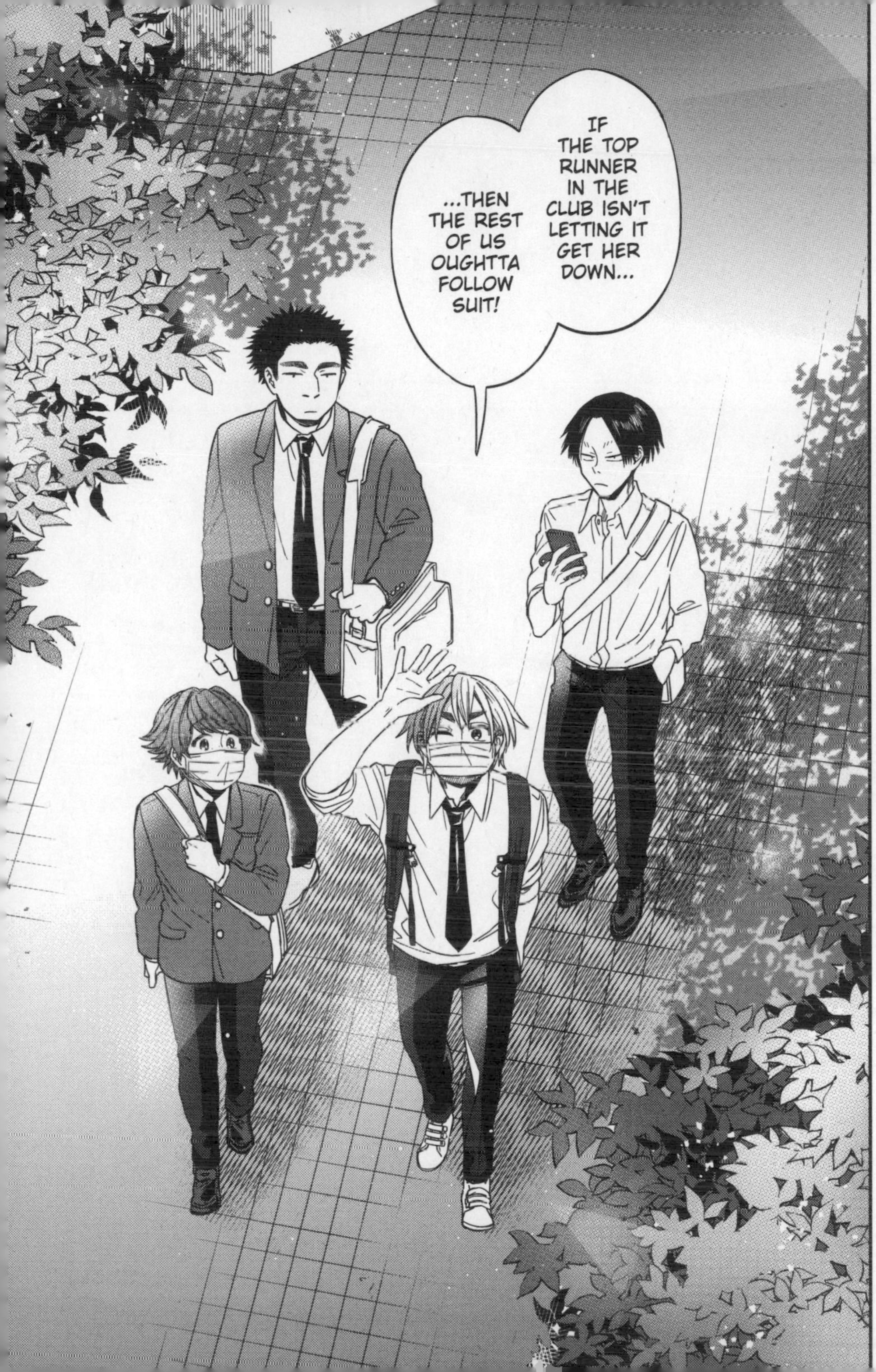
IF THE TOP RUNNER IN THE CLUB ISN'T LETTING IT GET HER DOWN...
...THEN THE REST OF US OUGHTTA FOLLOW SUIT!

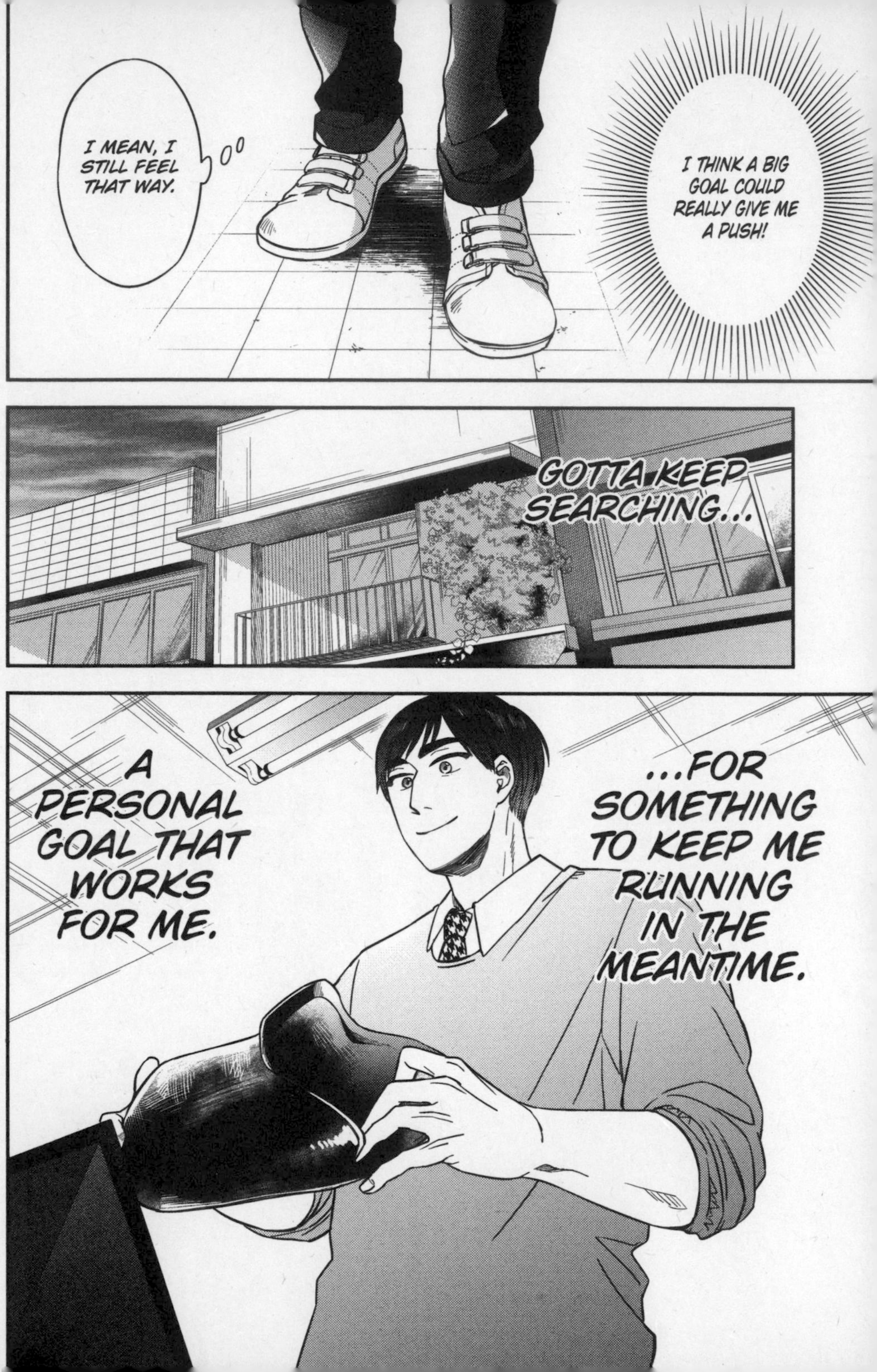
I THINK A BIG GOAL COULD REALLY GIVE ME A PUSH!
I MEAN, I STILL FEEL THAT WAY.
GOTTA KEEP SEARCHING...
...FOR SOMETHING TO KEEP ME RUNNING IN THE MEANTIME.
A PERSONAL GOAL THAT WORKS FOR ME.

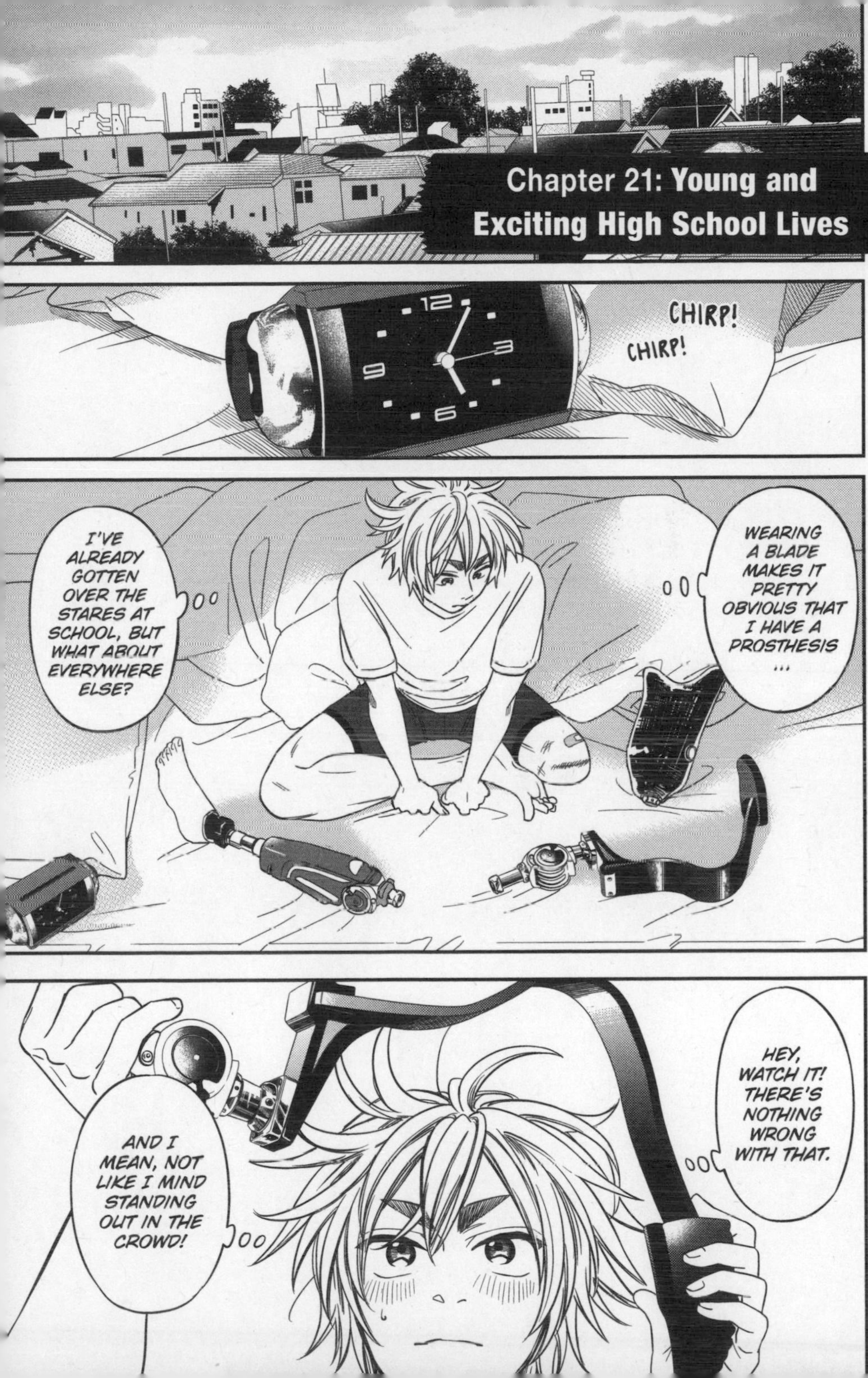
Chapter 21: Young and Exciting High School Lives
CHIRP!
CHIRP!
WEARING A BLADE MAKES IT PRETTY OBVIOUS THAT I HAVE A PROSTHESIS...
I'VE ALREADY GOTTEN OVER THE STARES AT SCHOOL, BUT WHAT ABOUT EVERYWHERE ELSE?
HEY, WATCH IT! THERE'S NOTHING WRONG WITH THAT.
AND I MEAN, NOT LIKE I MIND STANDING OUT IN THE CROWD!

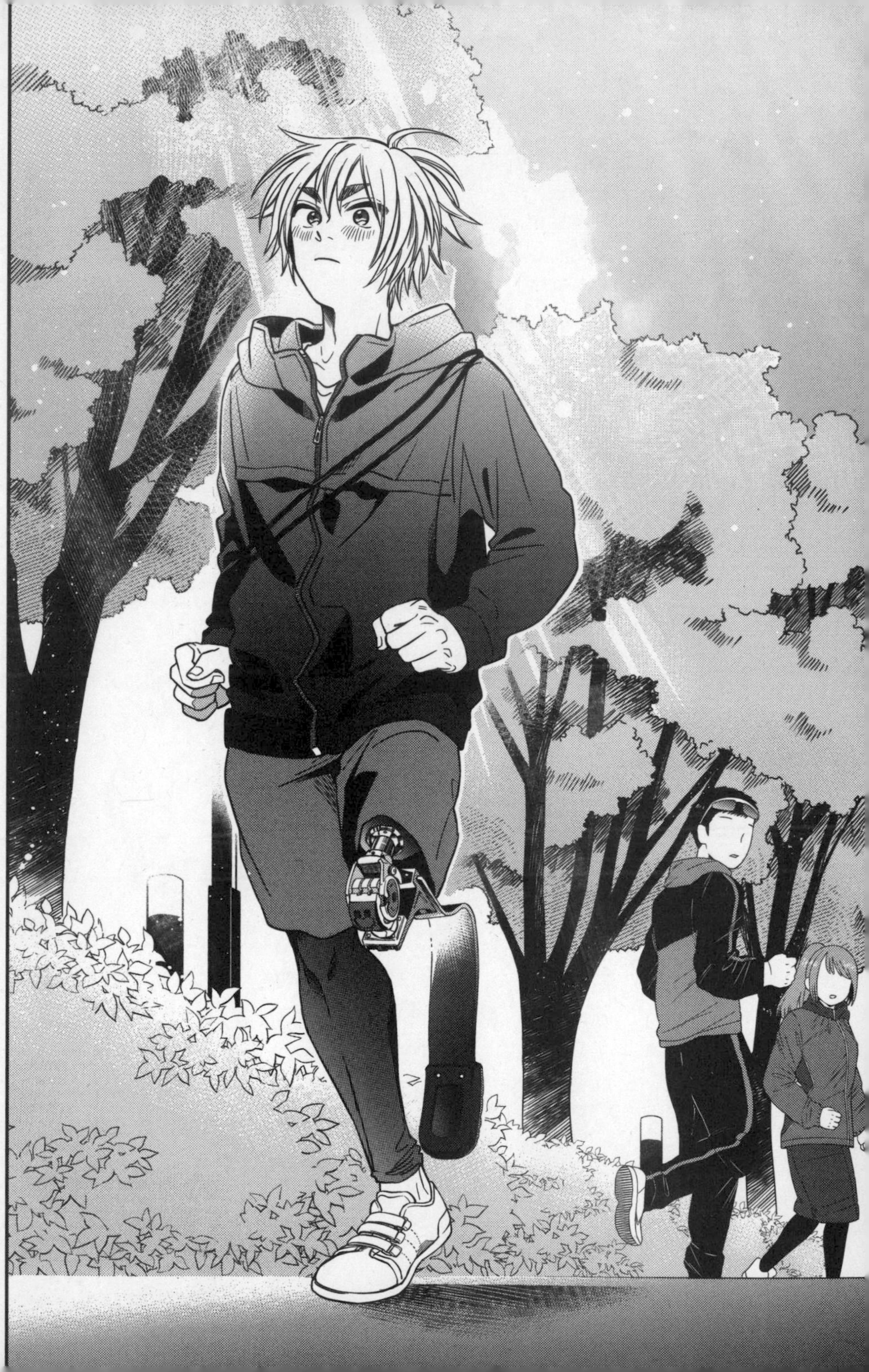

...OKAY. MANAGED TO GO FOR A RUN.

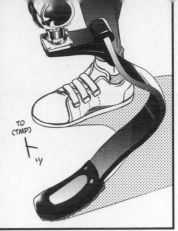

TO (TMP)

!

GACHA (KCHK)

I SHOULD HAVE TIME TO SWAP OUT THE BLADE AND EAT BREAKFAST, PROBABLY.

...HUH?

YAAAWN...

...DAD?

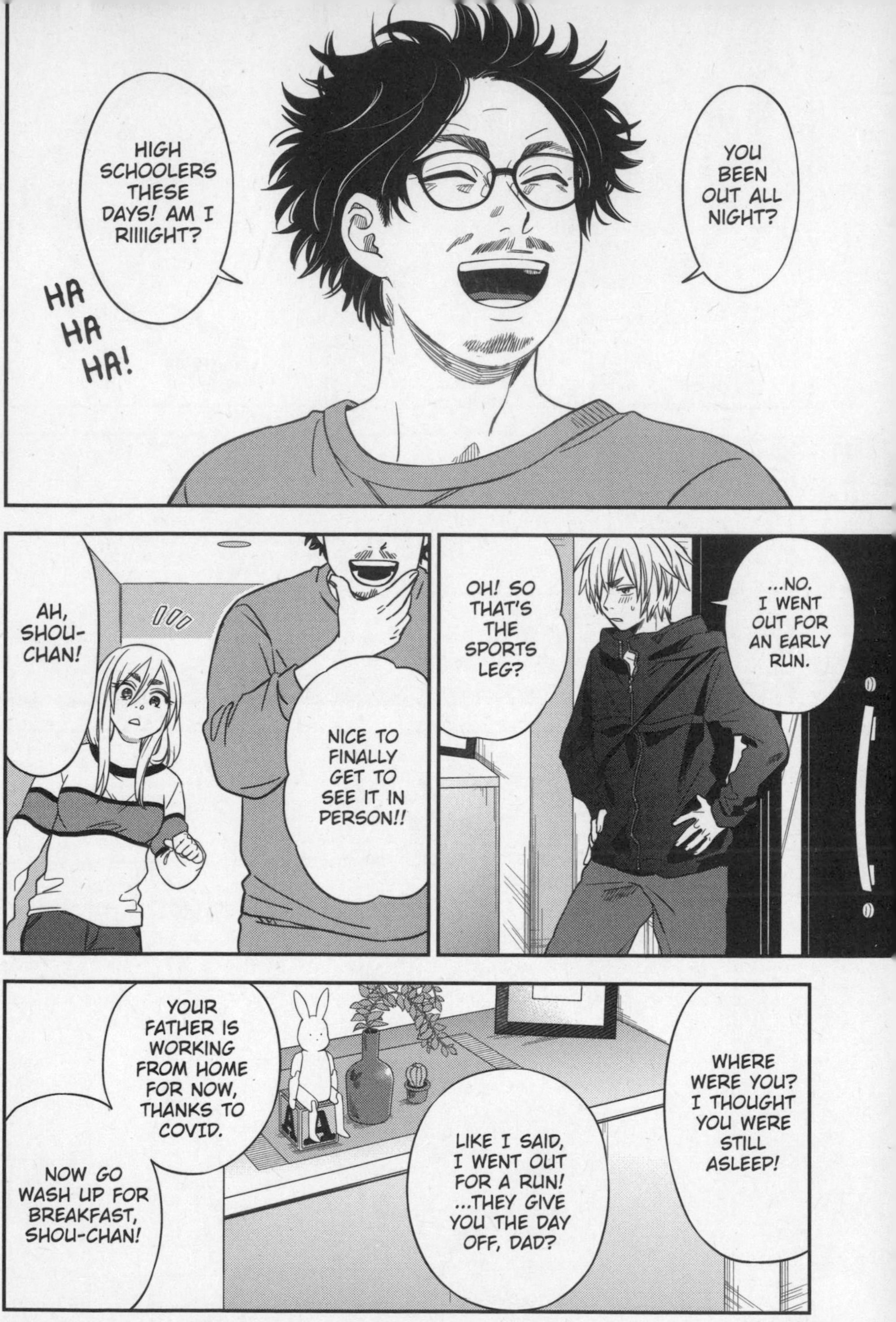
YOU BEEN OUT ALL NIGHT?
HIGH SCHOOLERS THESE DAYS! AM I RIIIIGHT?
HA HA HA!
...NO. I WENT OUT FOR AN EARLY RUN.
OH! SO THAT'S THE SPORTS LEG?
NICE TO FINALLY GET TO SEE IT IN PERSON!!
AH, SHOU-CHAN!
WHERE WERE YOU? I THOUGHT YOU WERE STILL ASLEEP!
LIKE I SAID, I WENT OUT FOR A RUN! ...THEY GIVE YOU THE DAY OFF, DAD?
YOUR FATHER IS WORKING FROM HOME FOR NOW, THANKS TO COVID.
NOW GO WASH UP FOR BREAKFAST, SHOU-CHAN!

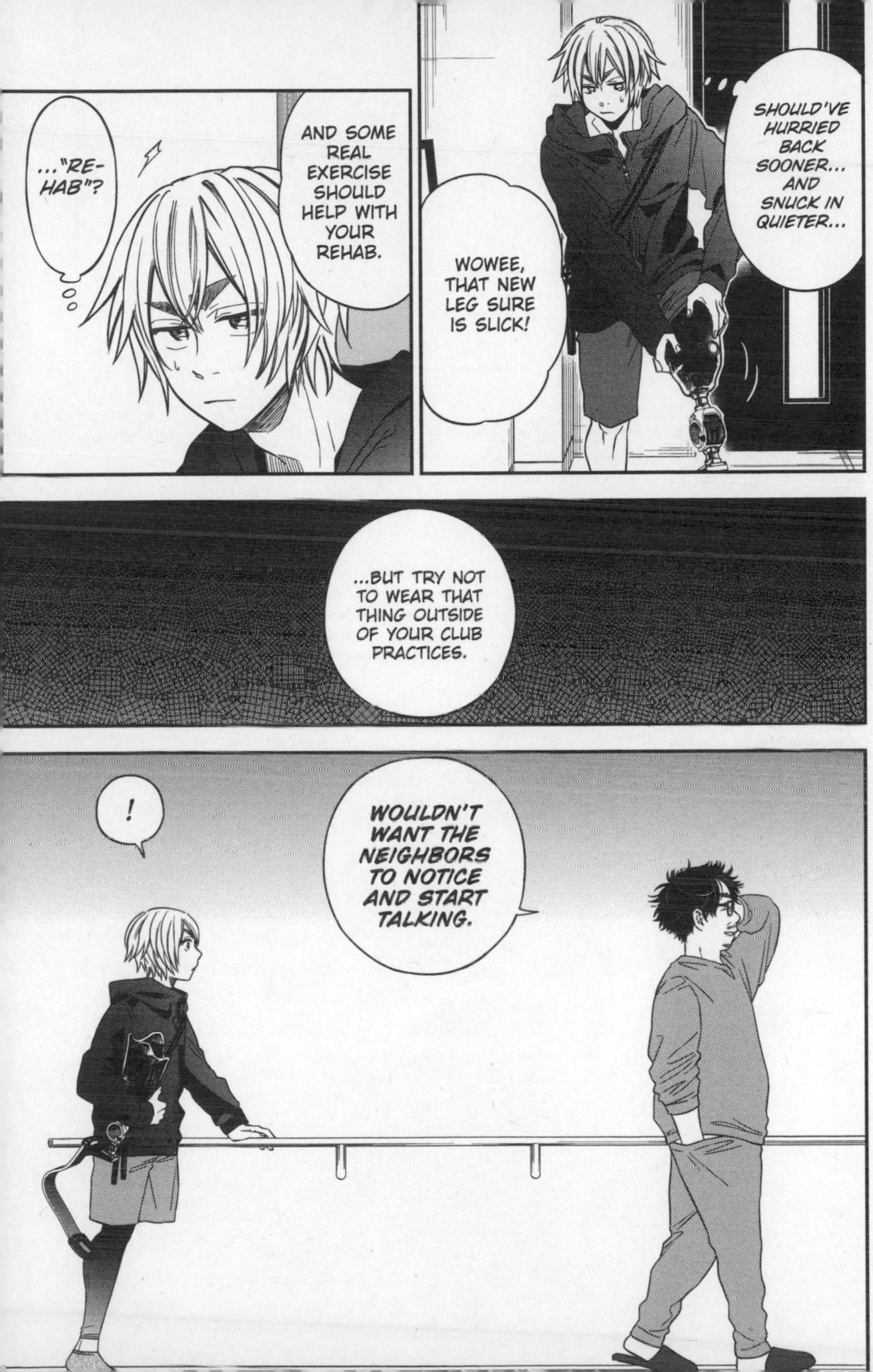
SHOULD'VE HURRIED BACK SOONER... AND SNUCK IN QUIETER...
WOWEE, THAT NEW LEG SURE IS SLICK!
AND SOME REAL EXERCISE SHOULD HELP WITH YOUR REHAB.
..."RE-HAB"?
...BUT TRY NOT TO WEAR THAT THING OUTSIDE OF YOUR CLUB PRACTICES.
WOULDN'T WANT THE NEIGHBORS TO NOTICE AND START TALKING.
!

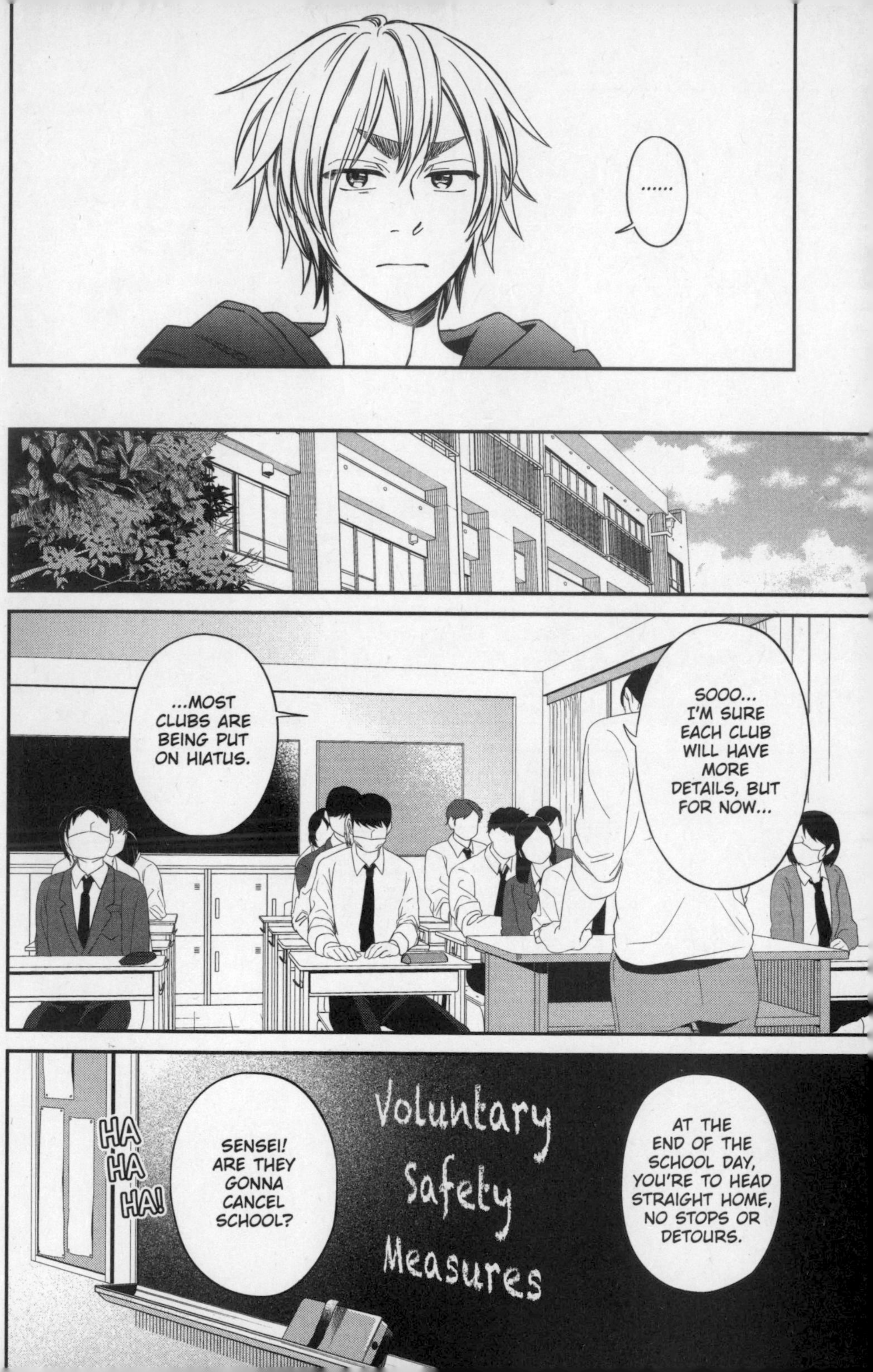
......
SOOO... I'M SURE EACH CLUB WILL HAVE MORE DETAILS, BUT FOR NOW...
...MOST CLUBS ARE BEING PUT ON HIATUS.
AT THE END OF THE SCHOOL DAY, YOU'RE TO HEAD STRAIGHT HOME, NO STOPS OR DETOURS.
Voluntary Safety Measures
SENSEI! ARE THEY GONNA CANCEL SCHOOL?
HA HA HA!

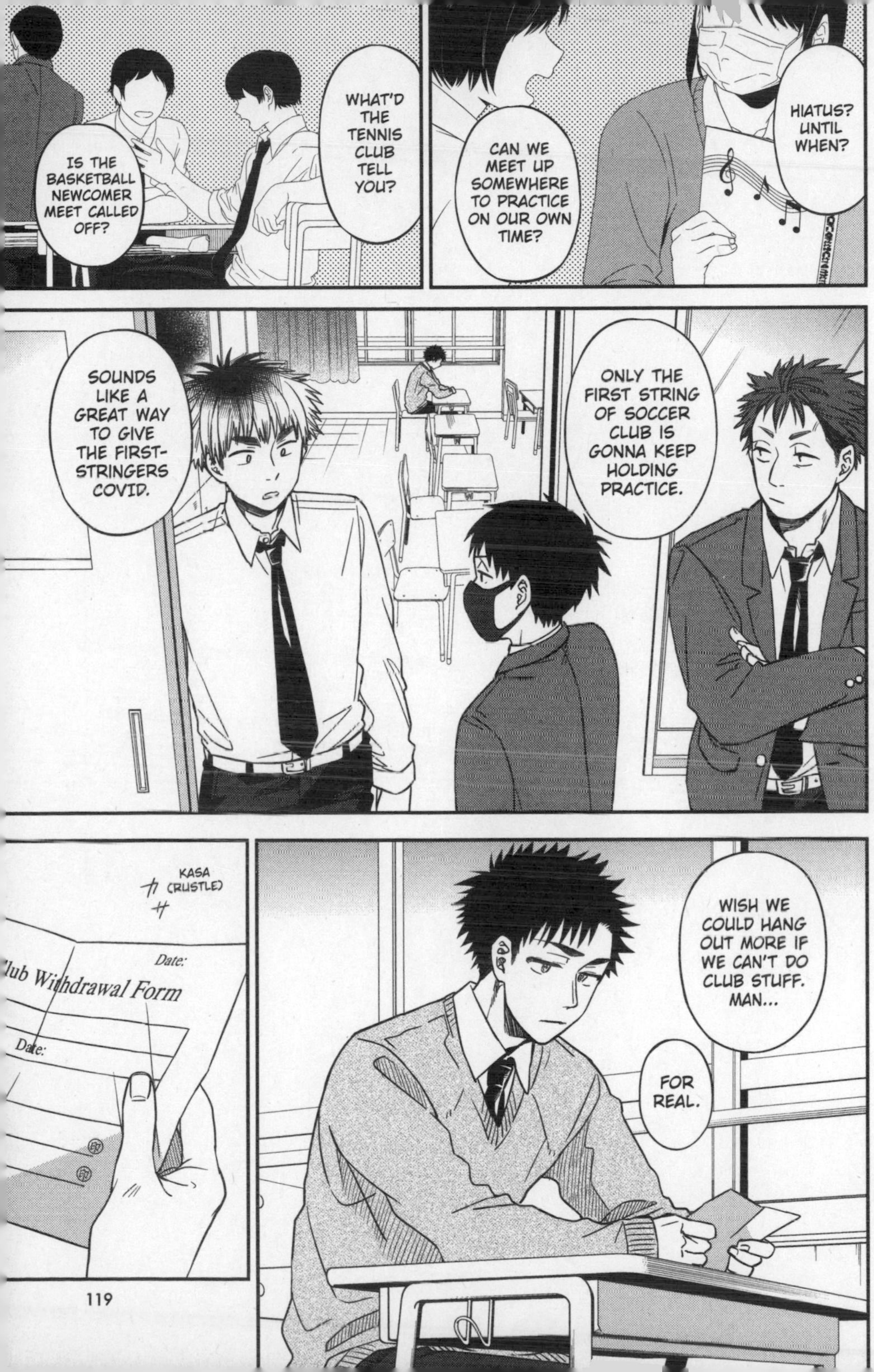

HIATUS? UNTIL WHEN?
CAN WE MEET UP SOMEWHERE TO PRACTICE ON OUR OWN TIME?
WHAT'D THE TENNIS CLUB TELL YOU?
IS THE BASKETBALL NEWCOMER MEET CALLED OFF?
ONLY THE FIRST STRING OF SOCCER CLUB IS GONNA KEEP HOLDING PRACTICE.
SOUNDS LIKE A GREAT WAY TO GIVE THE FIRST-STRINGERS COVID.
WISH WE COULD HANG OUT MORE IF WE CAN'T DO CLUB STUFF. MAN...
FOR REAL.
カサ
KASA (RUSTLE)
Date:
lub Withdrawal Form
Date:

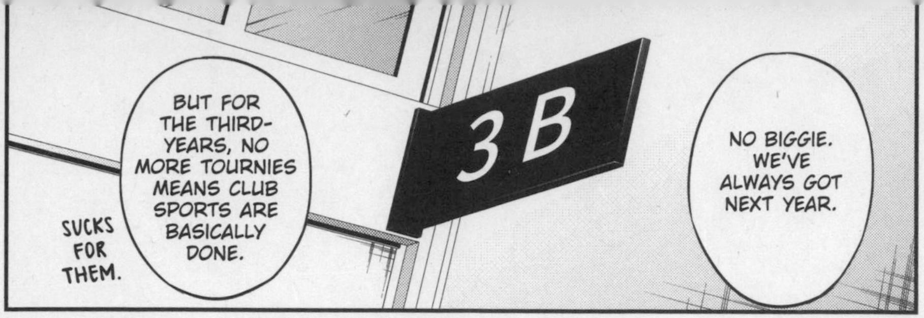
NO BIGGIE. WE'VE ALWAYS GOT NEXT YEAR.
3 B
BUT FOR THE THIRD-YEARS, NO MORE TOURNIES MEANS CLUB SPORTS ARE BASICALLY DONE.
SUCKS FOR THEM.
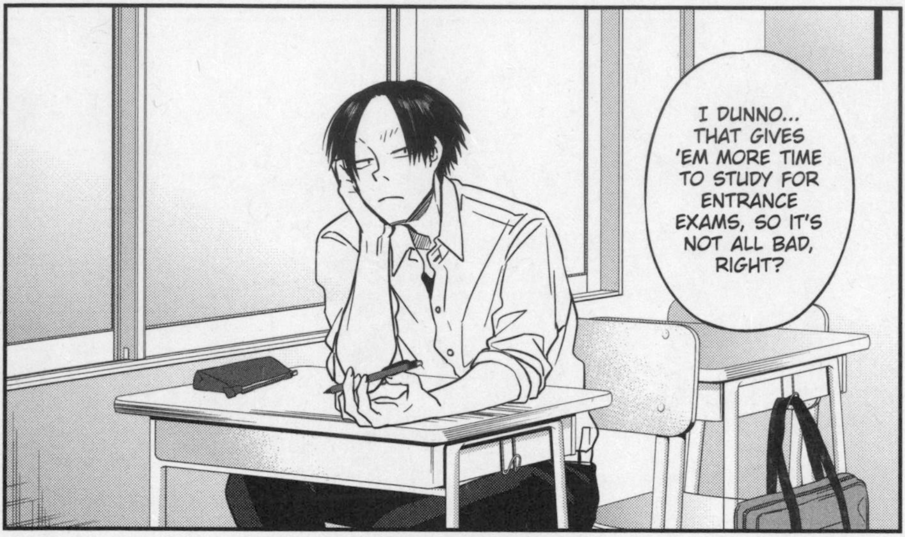
I DUNNO... THAT GIVES 'EM MORE TIME TO STUDY FOR ENTRANCE EXAMS, SO IT'S NOT ALL BAD, RIGHT?
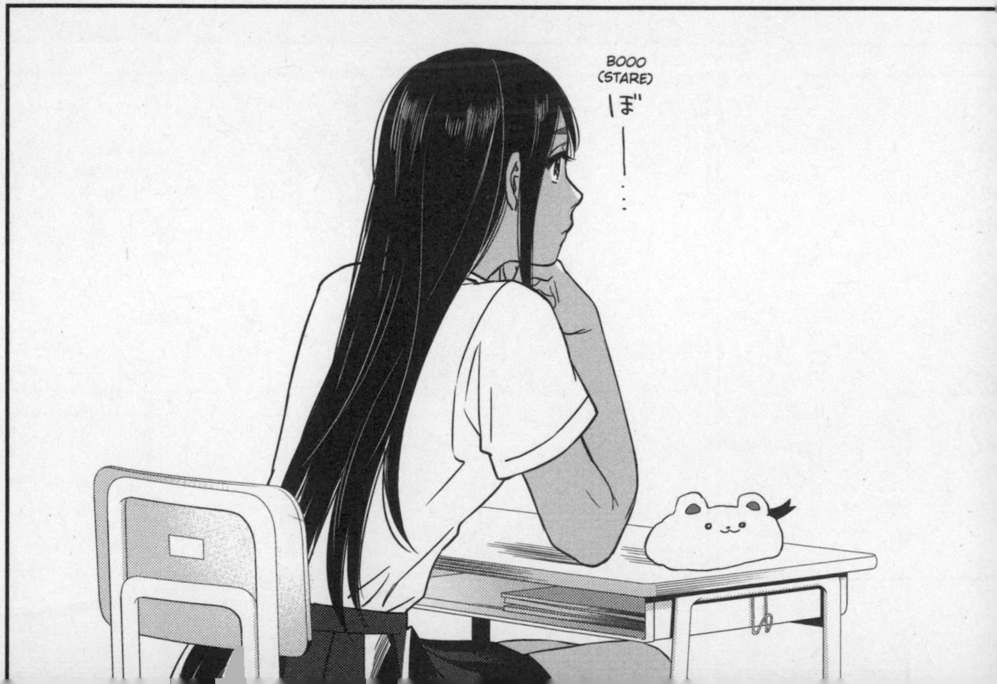
BOOO (STARE)
ぼ――…

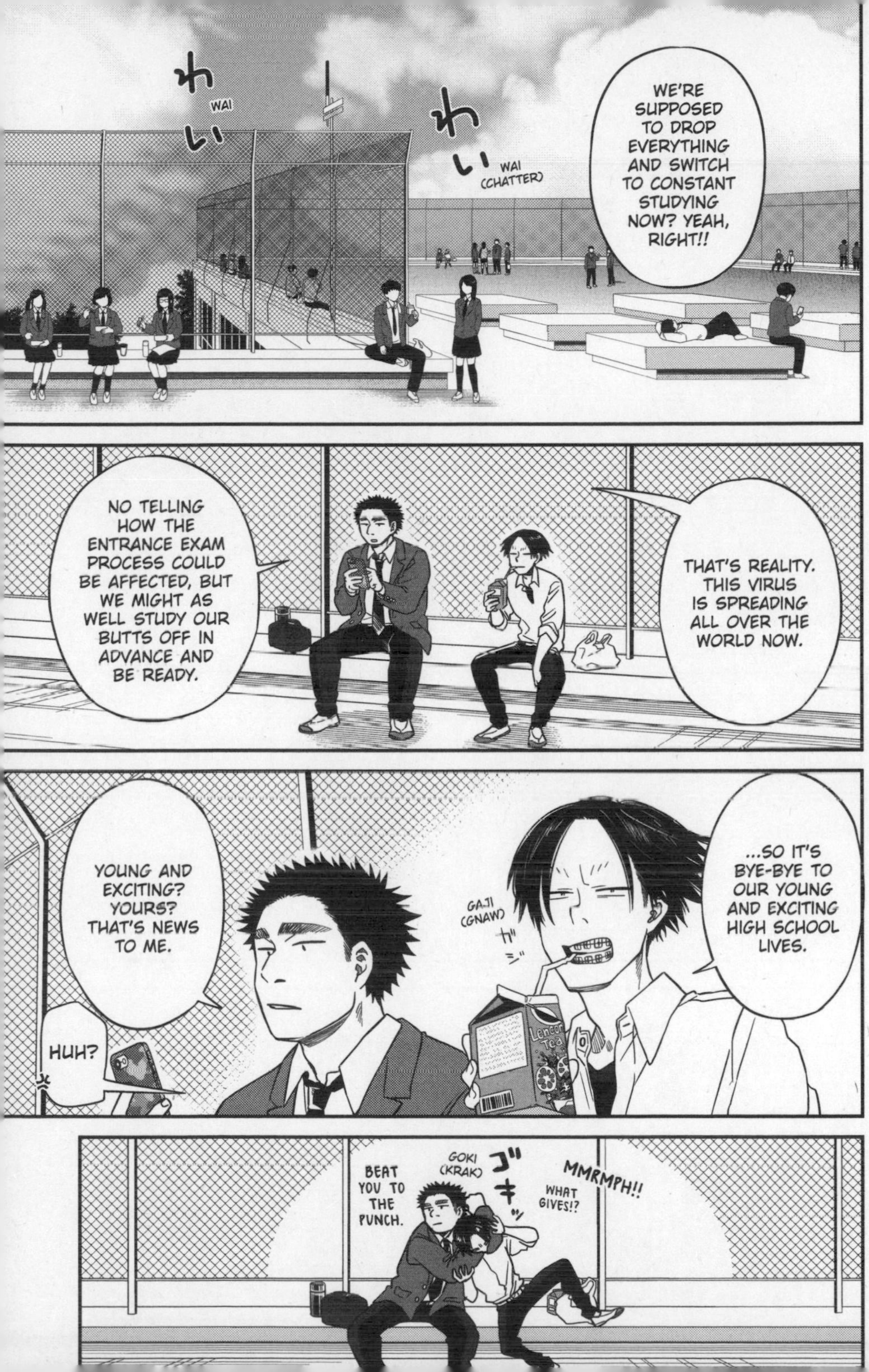
WE'RE SUPPOSED TO DROP EVERYTHING AND SWITCH TO CONSTANT STUDYING NOW? YEAH, RIGHT!!
わい
WAI (CHATTER)
わい
WAI
THAT'S REALITY. THIS VIRUS IS SPREADING ALL OVER THE WORLD NOW.
NO TELLING HOW THE ENTRANCE EXAM PROCESS COULD BE AFFECTED, BUT WE MIGHT AS WELL STUDY OUR BUTTS OFF IN ADVANCE AND BE READY.
...SO IT'S BYE-BYE TO OUR YOUNG AND EXCITING HIGH SCHOOL LIVES.
ガジ
GAJI (GNAW)
YOUNG AND EXCITING? YOURS? THAT'S NEWS TO ME.
HUH?
MMRMPH!!
WHAT GIVES!?
ゴキッ
GOKI (KRAK)
BEAT YOU TO THE PUNCH.

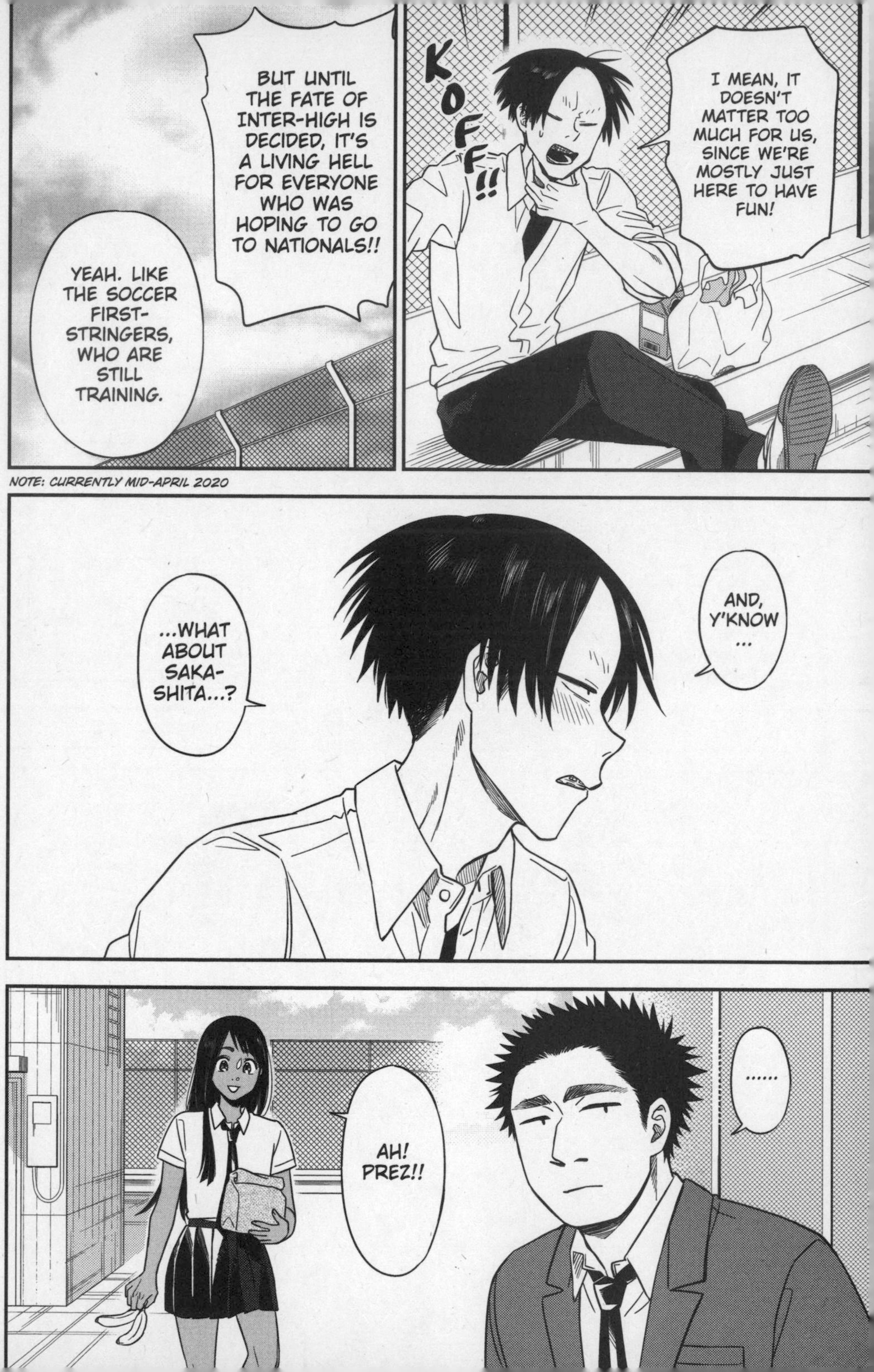
KOFF!!
I MEAN, IT DOESN'T MATTER TOO MUCH FOR US, SINCE WE'RE MOSTLY JUST HERE TO HAVE FUN!
BUT UNTIL THE FATE OF INTER-HIGH IS DECIDED, IT'S A LIVING HELL FOR EVERYONE WHO WAS HOPING TO GO TO NATIONALS!!
YEAH. LIKE THE SOCCER FIRST-STRINGERS, WHO ARE STILL TRAINING.
NOTE: CURRENTLY MID-APRIL 2020
AND, Y'KNOW ...
...WHAT ABOUT SAKA-SHITA...?
......
AH! PREZ!!

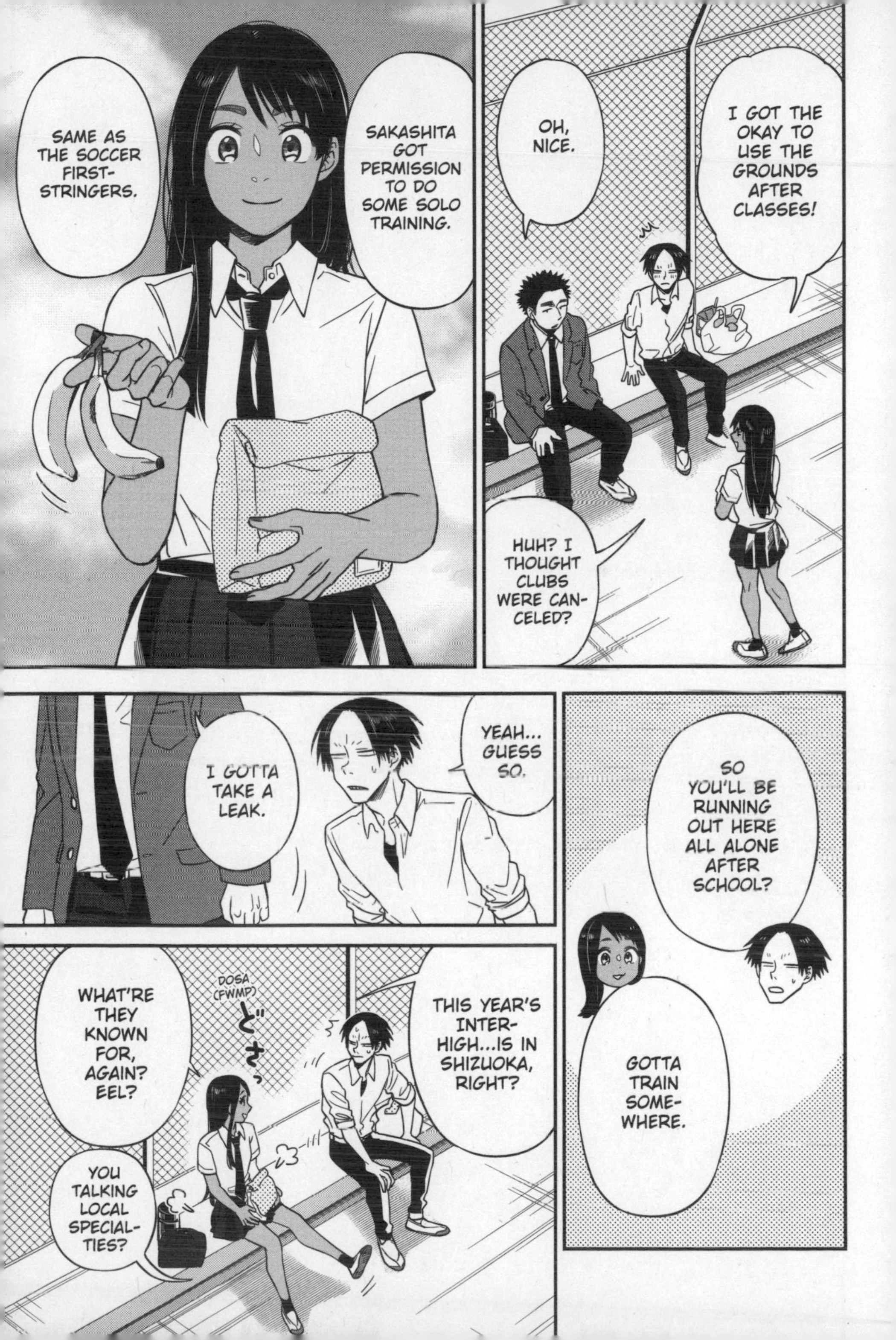

I GOT THE OKAY TO USE THE GROUNDS AFTER CLASSES!
OH, NICE.
HUH? I THOUGHT CLUBS WERE CANCELED?
SAKASHITA GOT PERMISSION TO DO SOME SOLO TRAINING.
SAME AS THE SOCCER FIRST-STRINGERS.
SO YOU'LL BE RUNNING OUT HERE ALL ALONE AFTER SCHOOL?
GOTTA TRAIN SOMEWHERE.
YEAH... GUESS SO.
I GOTTA TAKE A LEAK.
THIS YEAR'S INTER-HIGH...IS IN SHIZUOKA, RIGHT?
DOSA (FWMP) どさっ
WHAT'RE THEY KNOWN FOR, AGAIN? EEL?
YOU TALKING LOCAL SPECIALTIES?

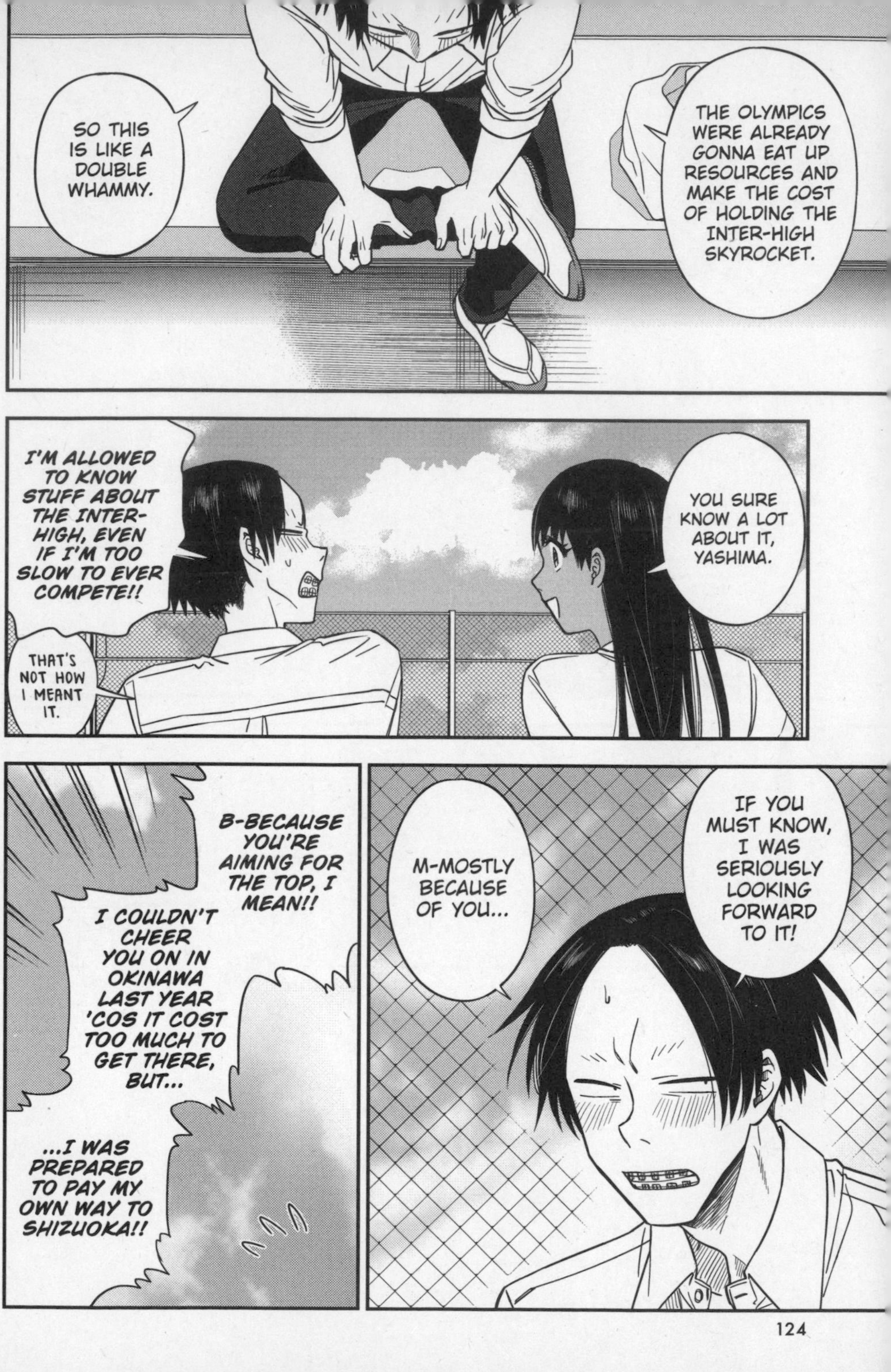
THE OLYMPICS WERE ALREADY GONNA EAT UP RESOURCES AND MAKE THE COST OF HOLDING THE INTER-HIGH SKYROCKET.
SO THIS IS LIKE A DOUBLE WHAMMY.
YOU SURE KNOW A LOT ABOUT IT, YASHIMA.
I'M ALLOWED TO KNOW STUFF ABOUT THE INTER-HIGH, EVEN IF I'M TOO SLOW TO EVER COMPETE!!
THAT'S NOT HOW I MEANT IT.
IF YOU MUST KNOW, I WAS SERIOUSLY LOOKING FORWARD TO IT!
M-MOSTLY BECAUSE OF YOU...
B-BECAUSE YOU'RE AIMING FOR THE TOP, I MEAN!!
I COULDN'T CHEER YOU ON IN OKINAWA LAST YEAR 'COS IT COST TOO MUCH TO GET THERE, BUT...
...I WAS PREPARED TO PAY MY OWN WAY TO SHIZUOKA!!

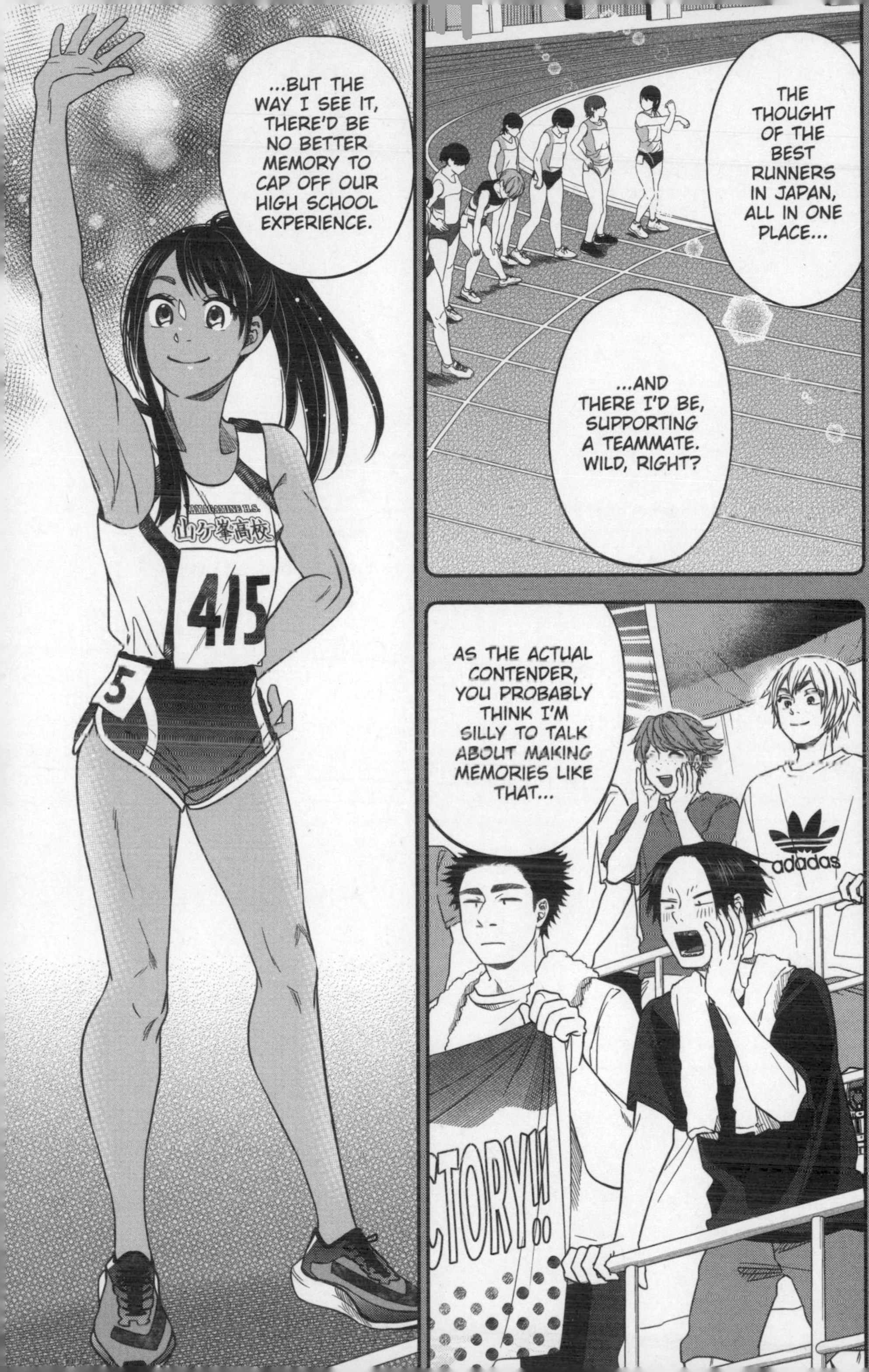
THE THOUGHT OF THE BEST RUNNERS IN JAPAN, ALL IN ONE PLACE...
...AND THERE I'D BE, SUPPORTING A TEAMMATE. WILD, RIGHT?
AS THE ACTUAL CONTENDER, YOU PROBABLY THINK I'M SILLY TO TALK ABOUT MAKING MEMORIES LIKE THAT...
adadas
CTORY!!
...BUT THE WAY I SEE IT, THERE'D BE NO BETTER MEMORY TO CAP OFF OUR HIGH SCHOOL EXPERIENCE.
山ケ峯高校
415
5

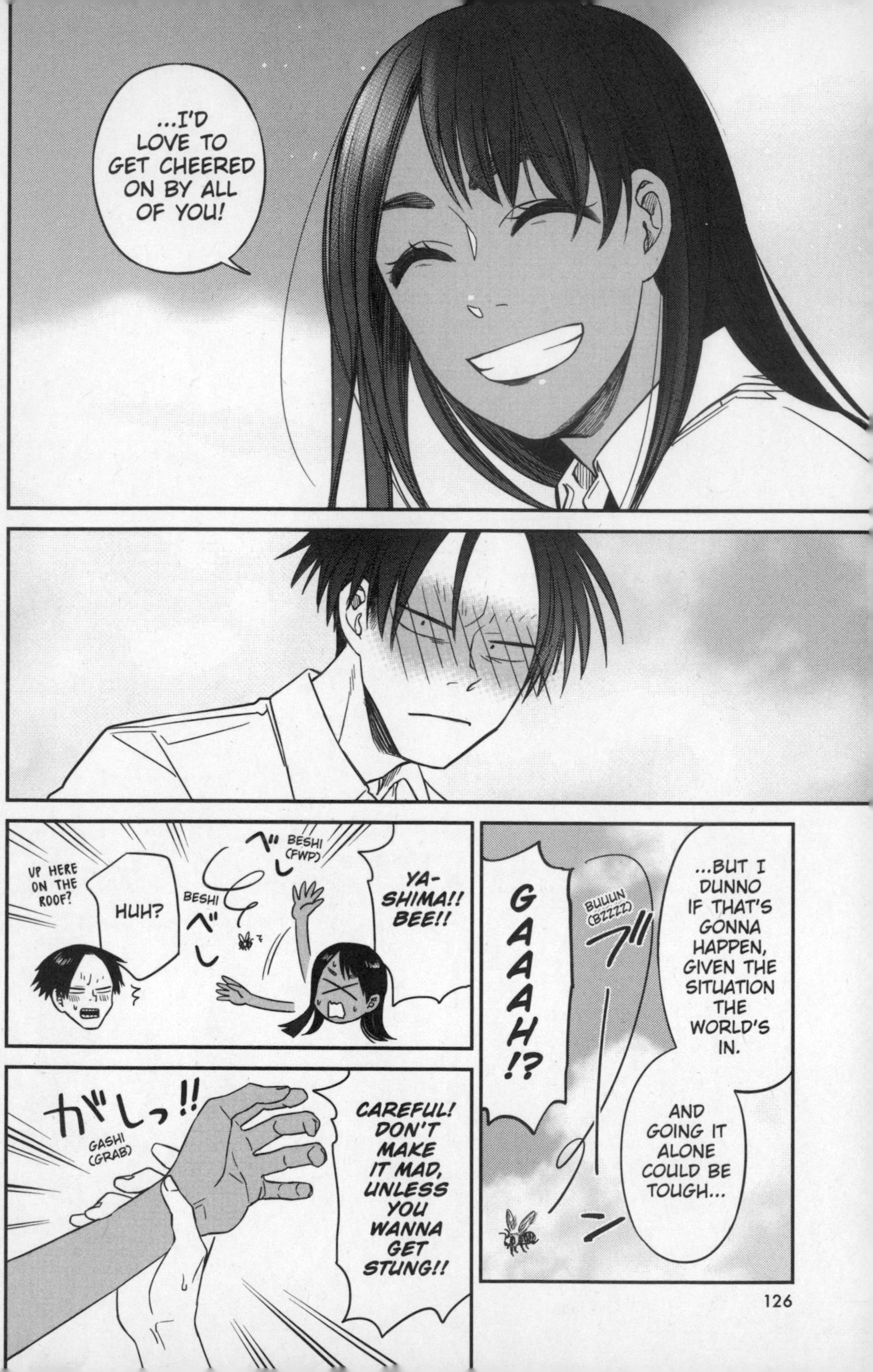
...I'D LOVE TO GET CHEERED ON BY ALL OF YOU!
...BUT I DUNNO IF THAT'S GONNA HAPPEN, GIVEN THE SITUATION THE WORLD'S IN.
AND GOING IT ALONE COULD BE TOUGH...
GAAAAH!?
ブーン
BUUUN (BZZZZ)
YA-SHIMA!! BEE!!
べし
BESHI (FWP)
べし
BESHI
HUH?
UP HERE ON THE ROOF?
CAREFUL! DON'T MAKE IT MAD, UNLESS YOU WANNA GET STUNG!!
がしっ!!
GASHI (GRAB)

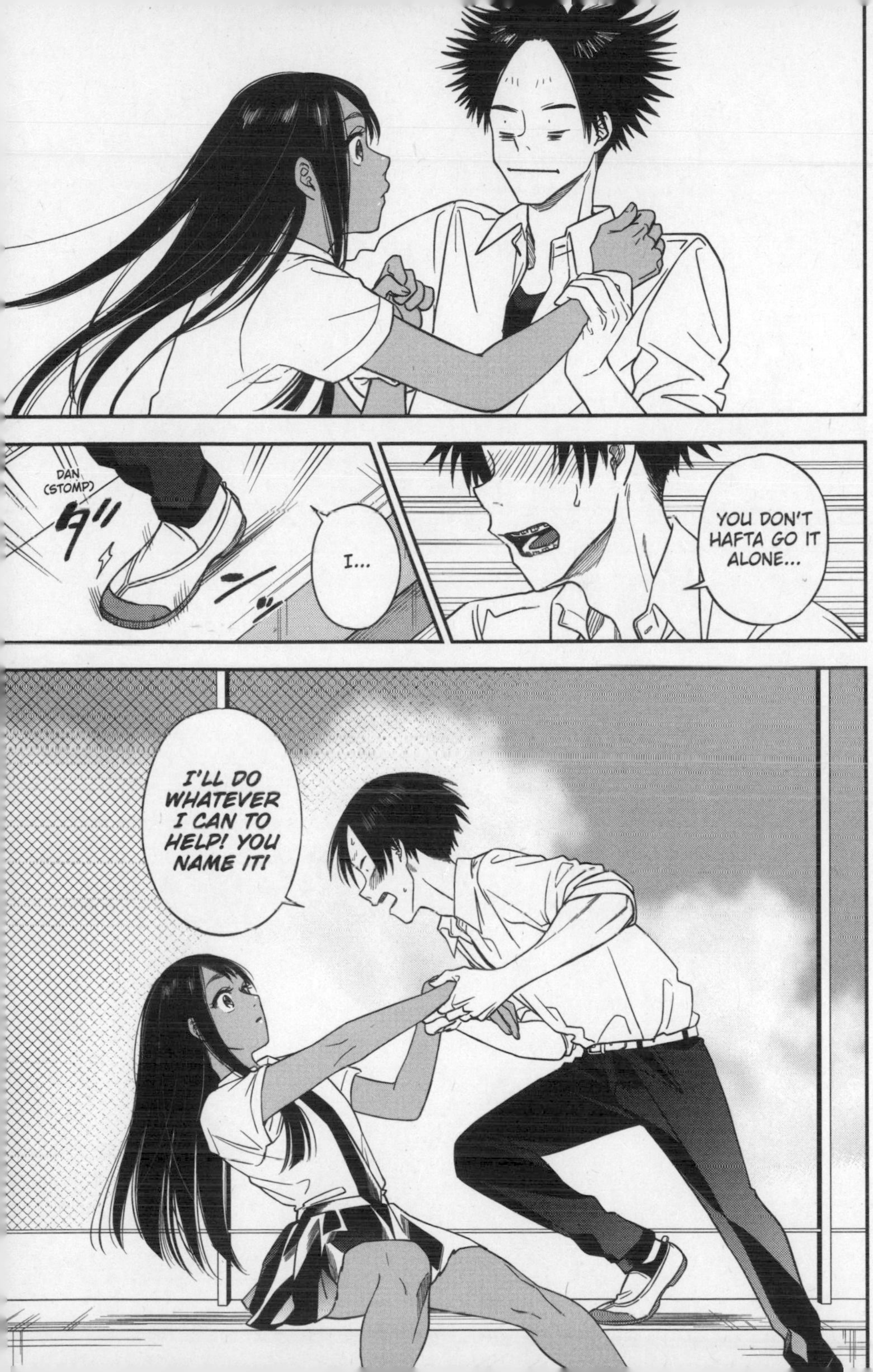
YOU DON'T HAFTA GO IT ALONE...
I...
ダッ
DAN (STOMP)
I'LL DO WHATEVER I CAN TO HELP! YOU NAME IT!

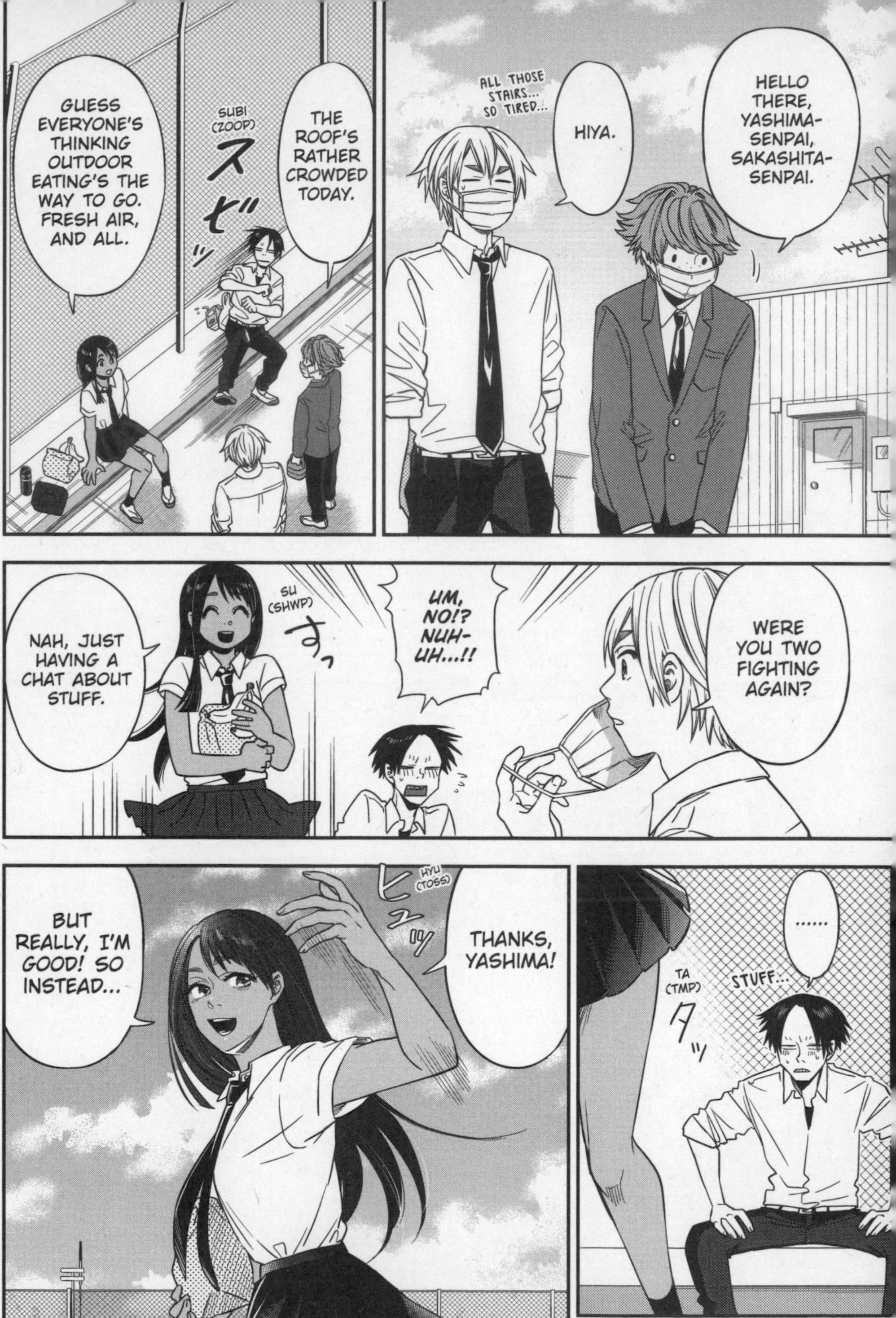
HELLO THERE, YASHIMA-SENPAI, SAKASHITA-SENPAI.
HIYA.
ALL THOSE STAIRS... SO TIRED...
THE ROOF'S RATHER CROWDED TODAY.
SUBI (ZOOP)
GUESS EVERYONE'S THINKING OUTDOOR EATING'S THE WAY TO GO. FRESH AIR, AND ALL.
WERE YOU TWO FIGHTING AGAIN?
UM, NO!? NUH-UH...!!
SU (SHWP)
NAH, JUST HAVING A CHAT ABOUT STUFF.
......
STUFF...
TA (TMP)
THANKS, YASHIMA!
HYU (TOSS)
BUT REALLY, I'M GOOD! SO INSTEAD...

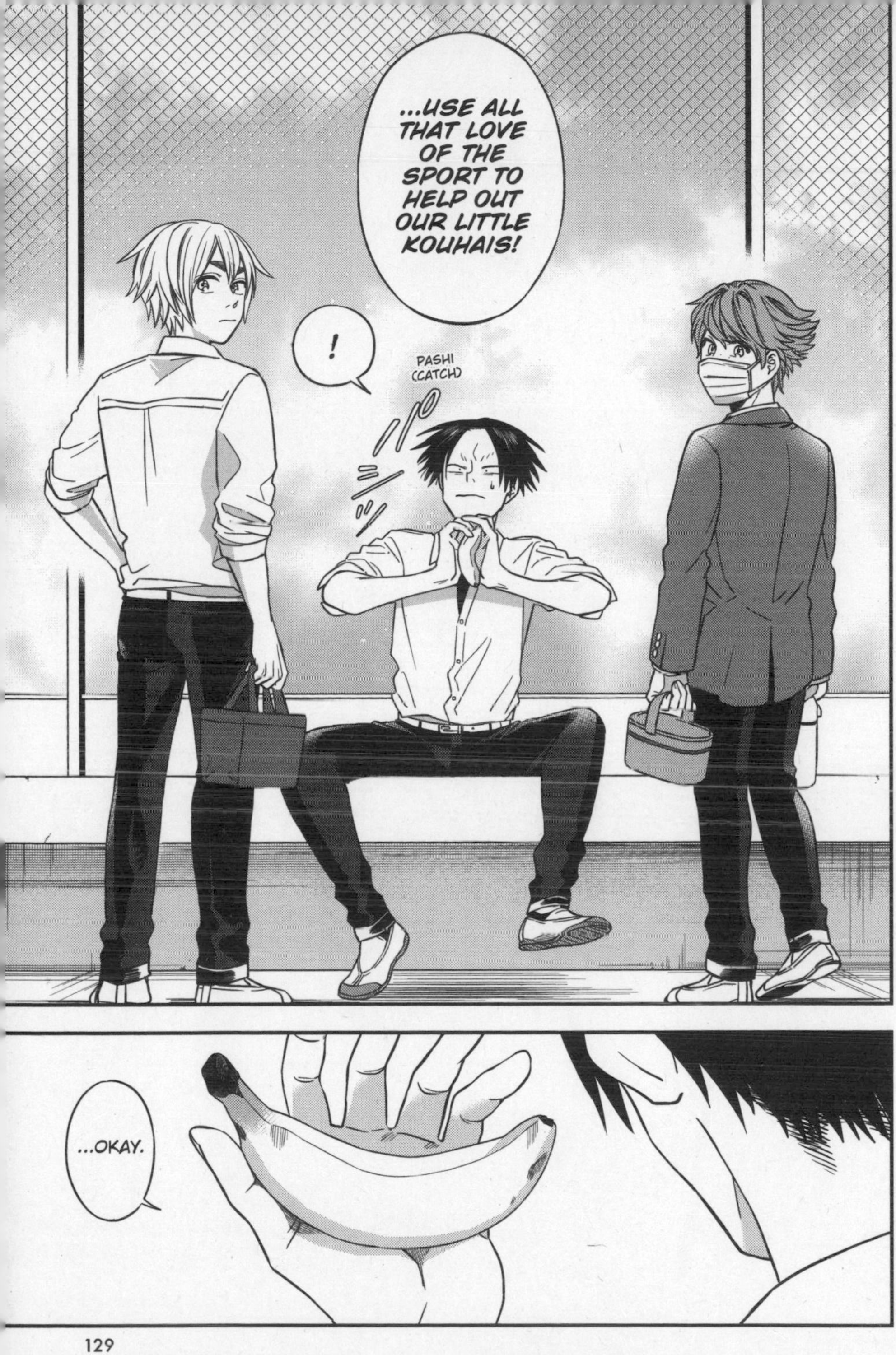
...USE ALL THAT LOVE OF THE SPORT TO HELP OUT OUR LITTLE KOUHAIS!
PASHI (CATCH)
!
...OKAY.

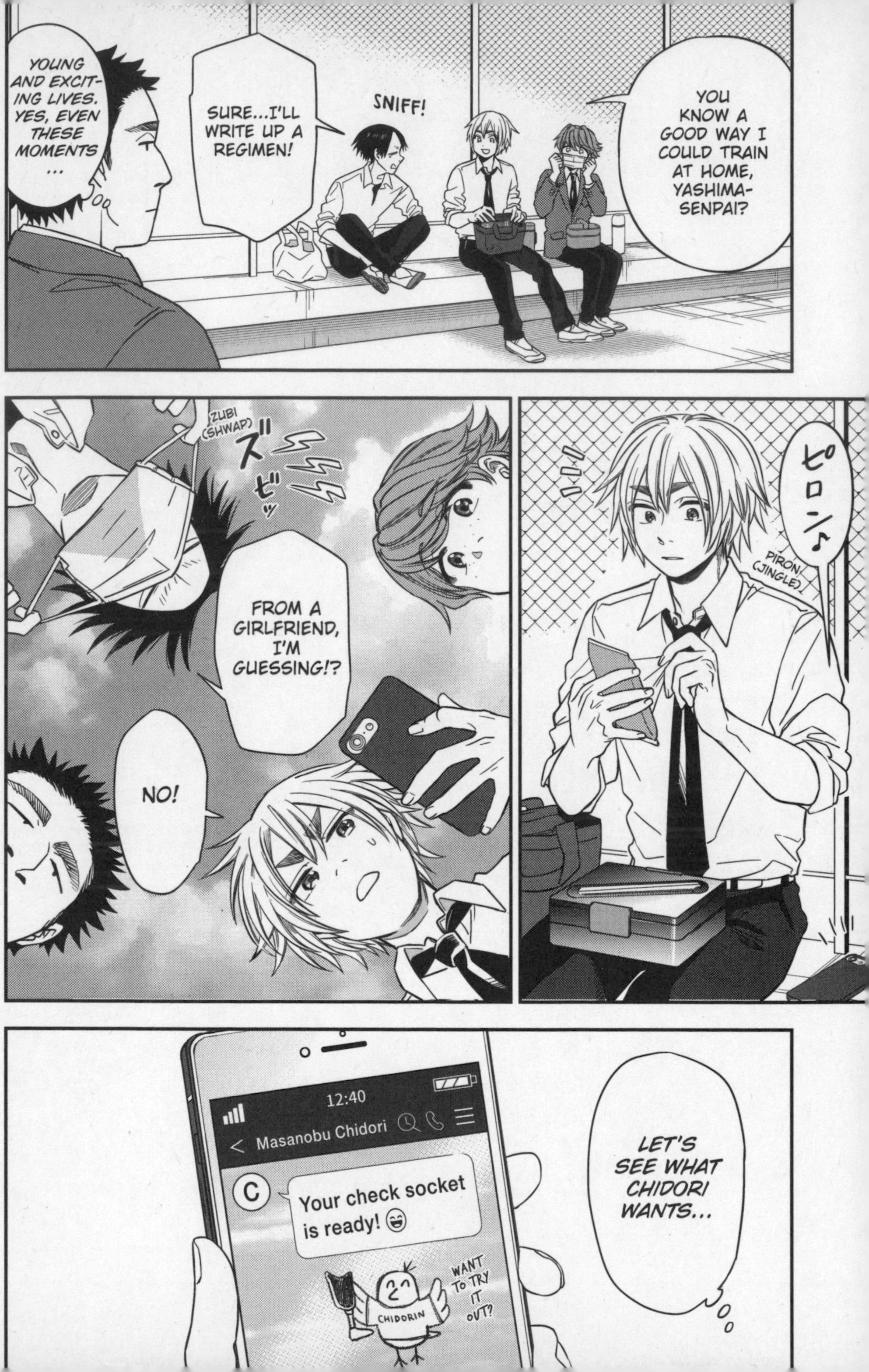
YOU KNOW A GOOD WAY I COULD TRAIN AT HOME, YASHIMA-SENPAI?
SNIFF!
SURE...I'LL WRITE UP A REGIMEN!
YOUNG AND EXCIT-ING LIVES. YES, EVEN THESE MOMENTS...
ピロン♪
PIRON (JINGLE)
ズビッ
ZUBI (SHWAP)
FROM A GIRLFRIEND, I'M GUESSING!?
NO!
LET'S SEE WHAT CHIDORI WANTS...
12:40
Masanobu Chidori
Your check socket is ready!
WANT TO TRY IT OUT?
CHIDORIN

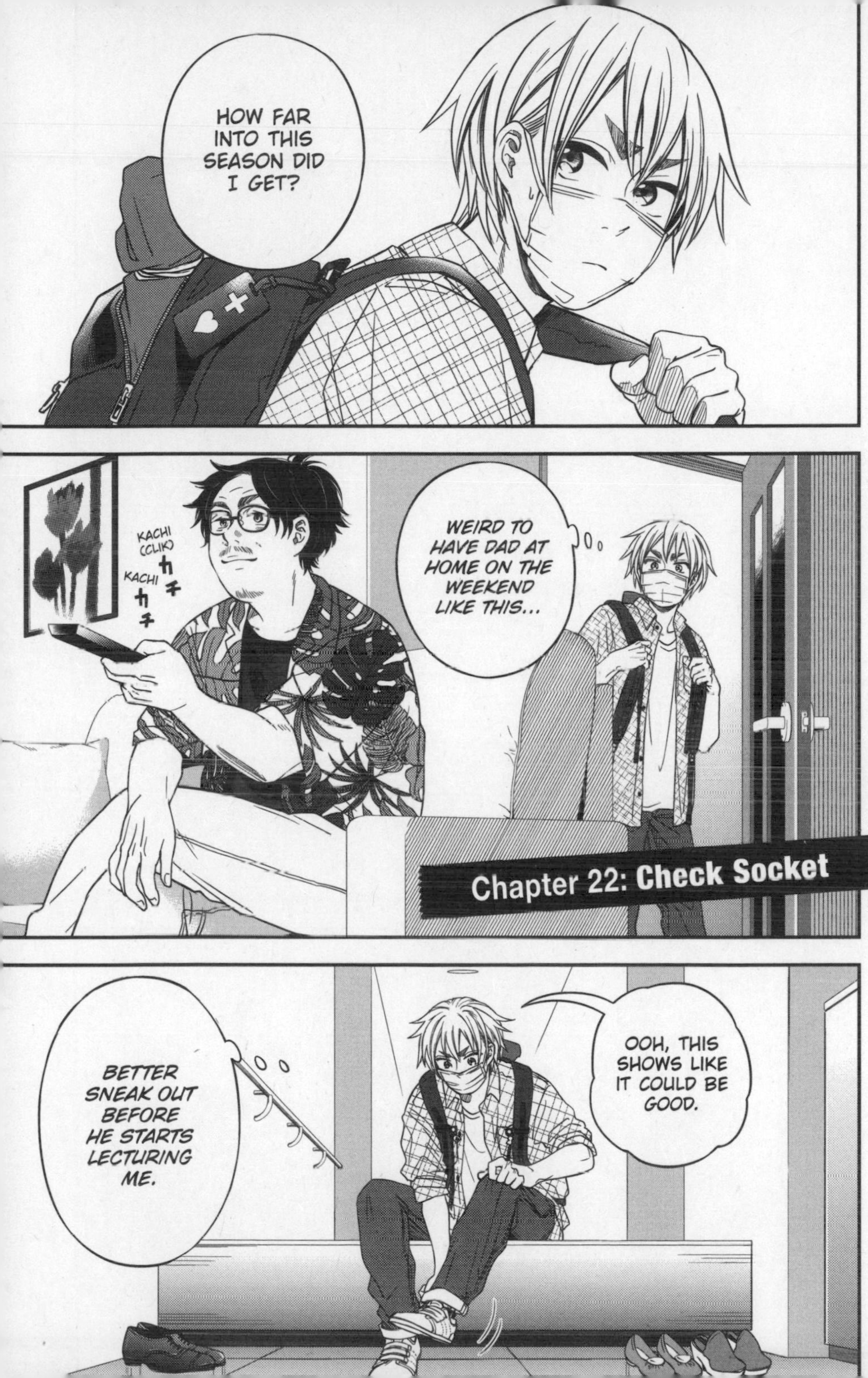
HOW FAR INTO THIS SEASON DID I GET?
WEIRD TO HAVE DAD AT HOME ON THE WEEKEND LIKE THIS...
KACHI (CLIK) カチ
KACHI カチ
Chapter 22: Check Socket
OOH, THIS SHOWS LIKE IT COULD BE GOOD.
BETTER SNEAK OUT BEFORE HE STARTS LECTURING ME.

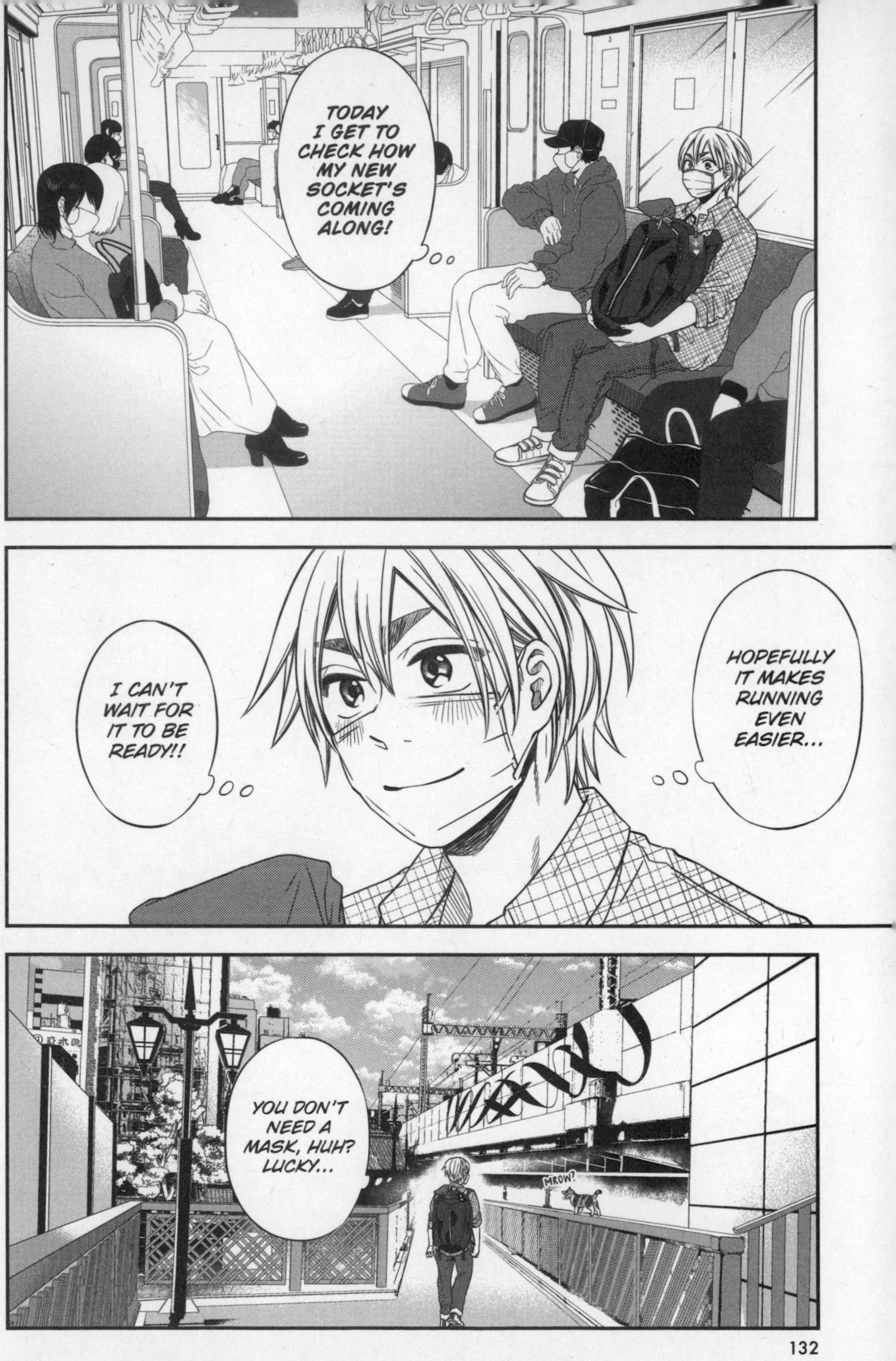
TODAY I GET TO CHECK HOW MY NEW SOCKET'S COMING ALONG!
HOPEFULLY IT MAKES RUNNING EVEN EASIER...
I CAN'T WAIT FOR IT TO BE READY!!
YOU DON'T NEED A MASK, HUH? LUCKY...
MROW?

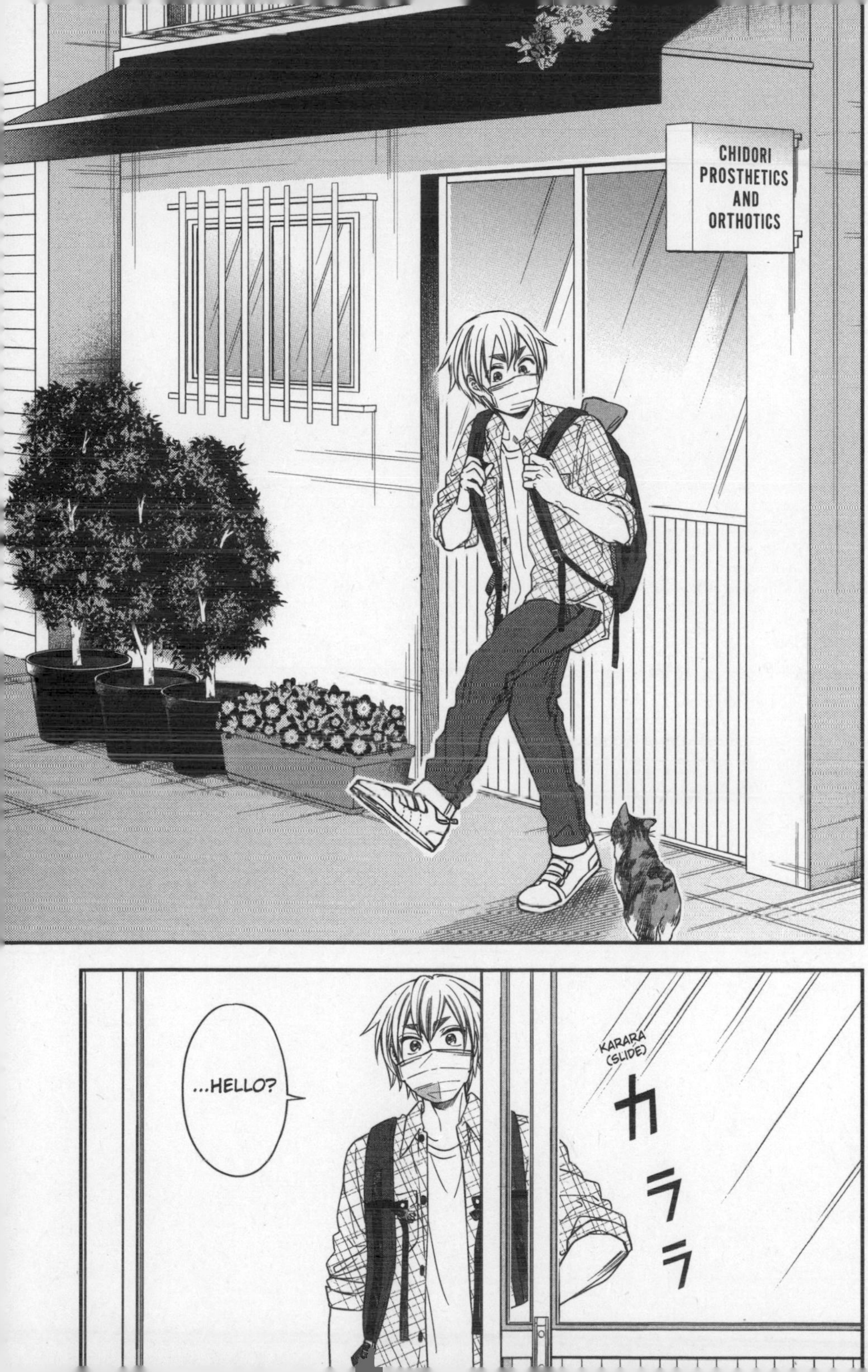
CHIDORI PROSTHETICS AND ORTHOTICS
KARARA (SLIDE)
カララ
...HELLO?

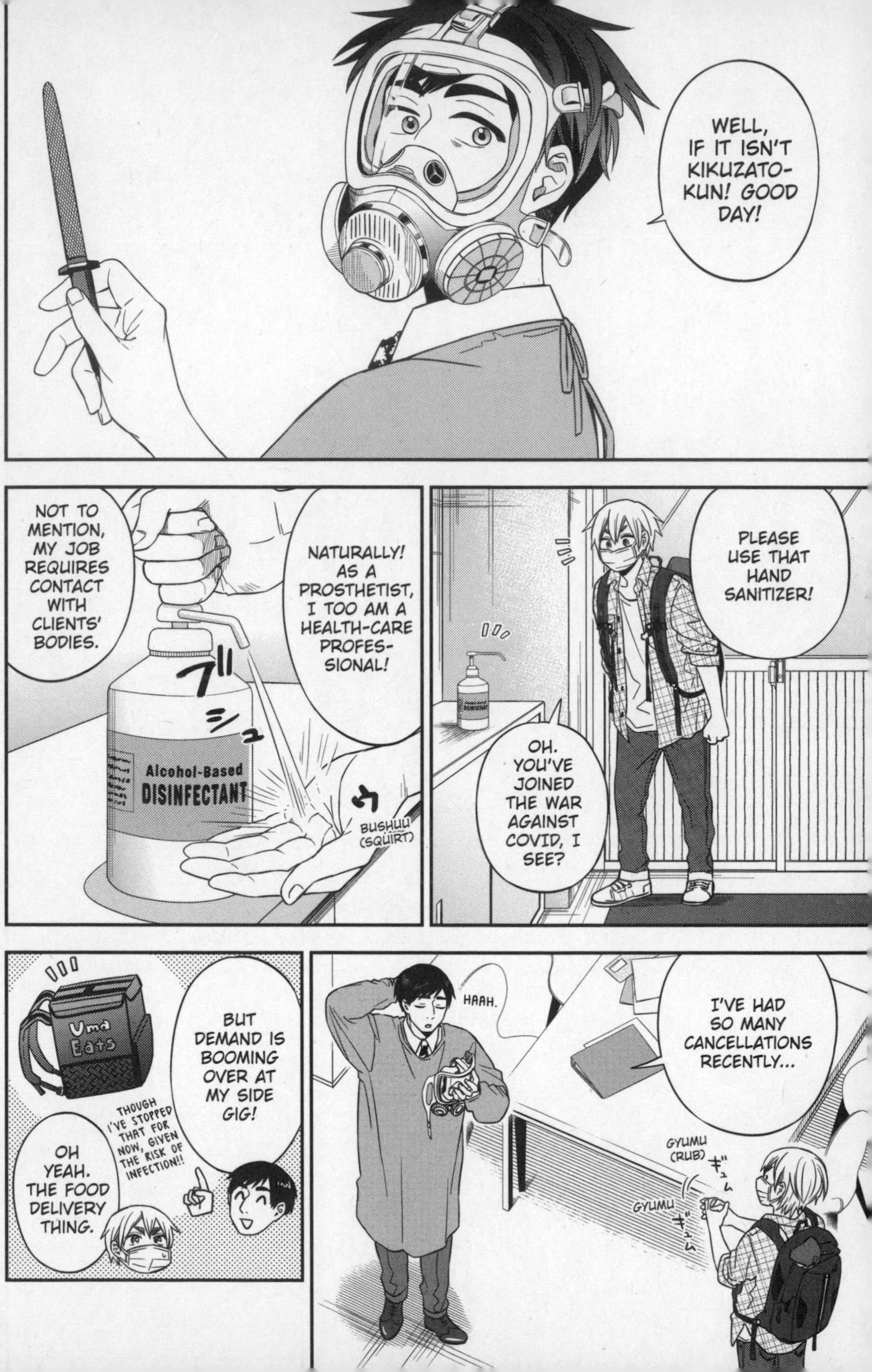
WELL, IF IT ISN'T KIKUZATO-KUN! GOOD DAY!
PLEASE USE THAT HAND SANITIZER!
OH. YOU'VE JOINED THE WAR AGAINST COVID, I SEE?
NATURALLY! AS A PROSTHETIST, I TOO AM A HEALTH-CARE PROFES-SIONAL!
NOT TO MENTION, MY JOB REQUIRES CONTACT WITH CLIENTS' BODIES.
Alcohol-Based DISINFECTANT
ブシュ
BUSHUU (SQUIRT)
HAAH.
I'VE HAD SO MANY CANCELLATIONS RECENTLY...
GYUMU (RUB)
GYUMU
BUT DEMAND IS BOOMING OVER AT MY SIDE GIG!
Uma Eats
THOUGH I'VE STOPPED THAT FOR NOW, GIVEN THE RISK OF INFECTION!!
OH YEAH. THE FOOD DELIVERY THING.

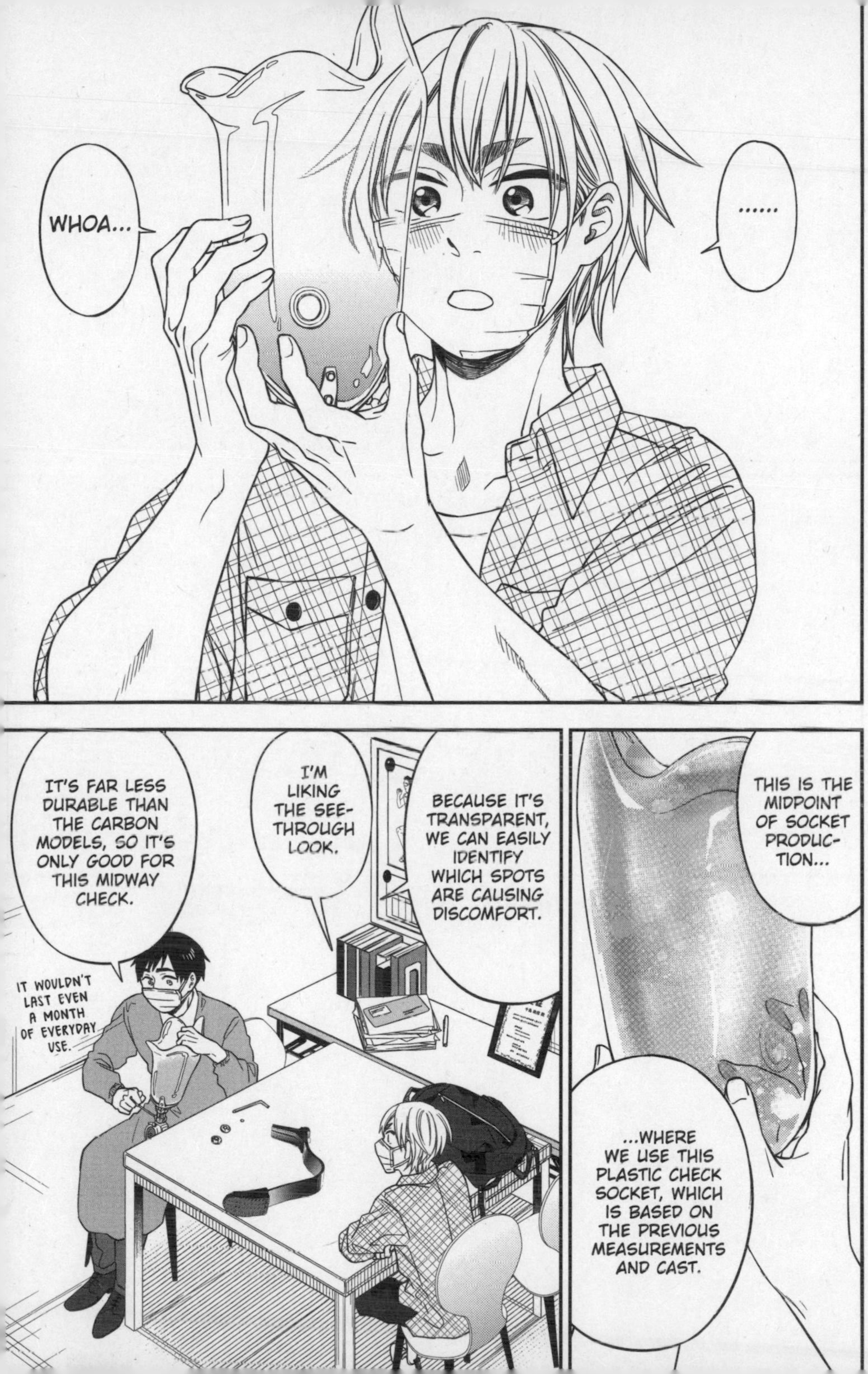
......
WHOA...
THIS IS THE MIDPOINT OF SOCKET PRODUCTION...
...WHERE WE USE THIS PLASTIC CHECK SOCKET, WHICH IS BASED ON THE PREVIOUS MEASUREMENTS AND CAST.
BECAUSE IT'S TRANSPARENT, WE CAN EASILY IDENTIFY WHICH SPOTS ARE CAUSING DISCOMFORT.
I'M LIKING THE SEE-THROUGH LOOK.
IT'S FAR LESS DURABLE THAN THE CARBON MODELS, SO IT'S ONLY GOOD FOR THIS MIDWAY CHECK.
IT WOULDN'T LAST EVEN A MONTH OF EVERYDAY USE.

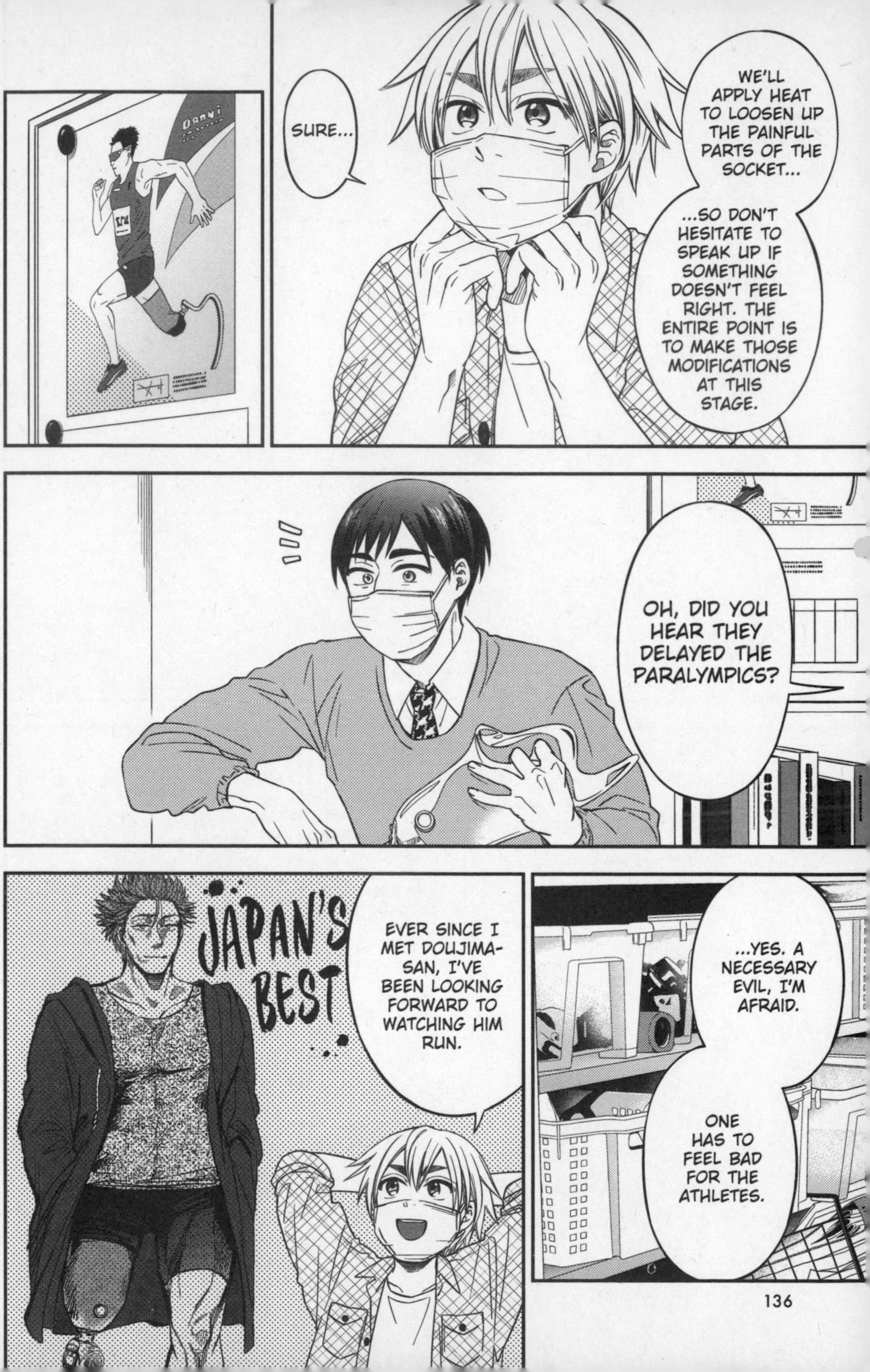
WE'LL APPLY HEAT TO LOOSEN UP THE PAINFUL PARTS OF THE SOCKET...
...SO DON'T HESITATE TO SPEAK UP IF SOMETHING DOESN'T FEEL RIGHT. THE ENTIRE POINT IS TO MAKE THOSE MODIFICATIONS AT THIS STAGE.
SURE...
OH, DID YOU HEAR THEY DELAYED THE PARALYMPICS?
...YES. A NECESSARY EVIL, I'M AFRAID.
ONE HAS TO FEEL BAD FOR THE ATHLETES.
EVER SINCE I MET DOUJIMA-SAN, I'VE BEEN LOOKING FORWARD TO WATCHING HIM RUN.
JAPAN'S BEST

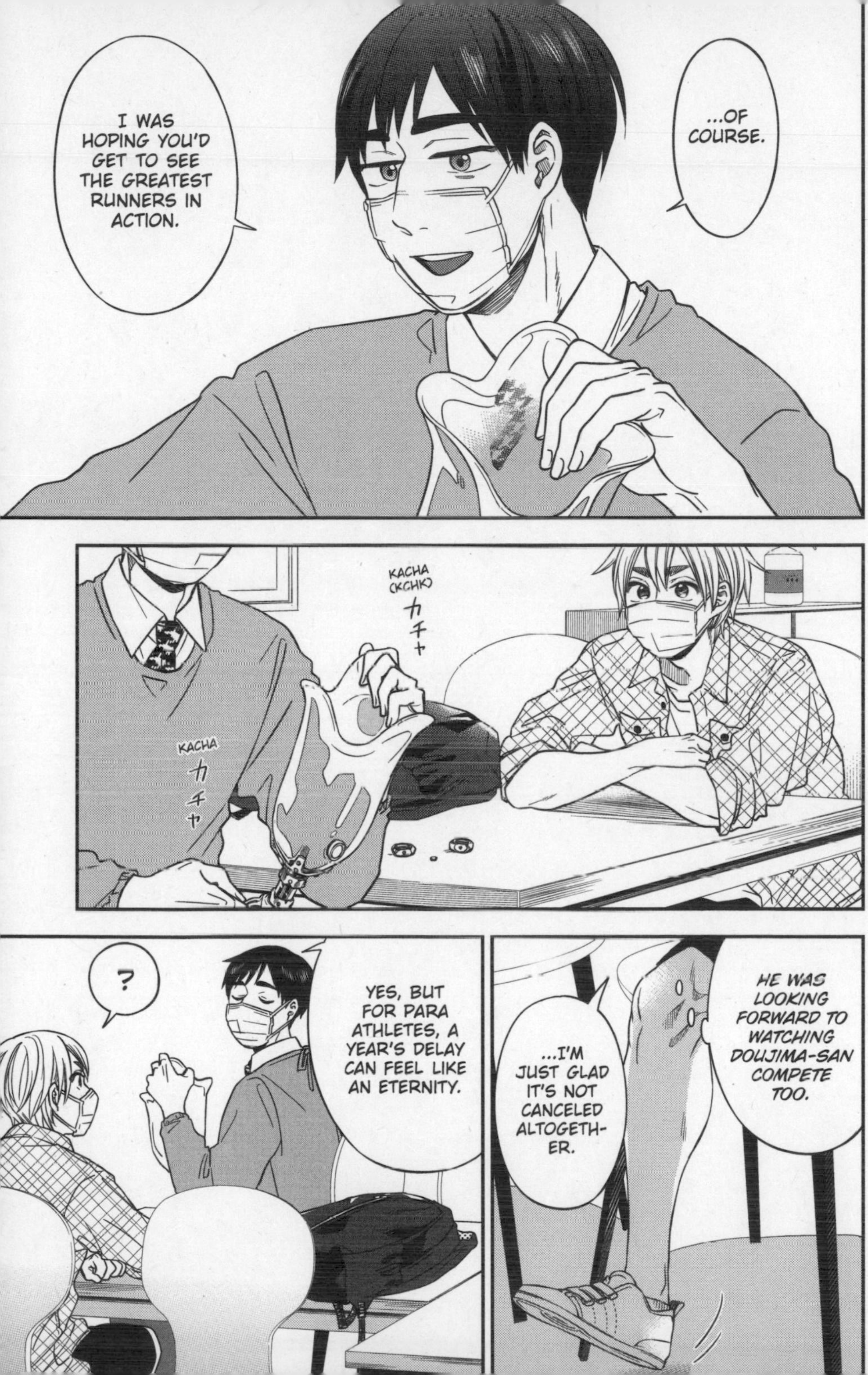
...OF COURSE.
I WAS HOPING YOU'D GET TO SEE THE GREATEST RUNNERS IN ACTION.
KACHA (KCHK)
カチャ
KACHA
カチャ
HE WAS LOOKING FORWARD TO WATCHING DOUJIMA-SAN COMPETE TOO.
...I'M JUST GLAD IT'S NOT CANCELED ALTOGETH-ER.
YES, BUT FOR PARA ATHLETES, A YEAR'S DELAY CAN FEEL LIKE AN ETERNITY.
?

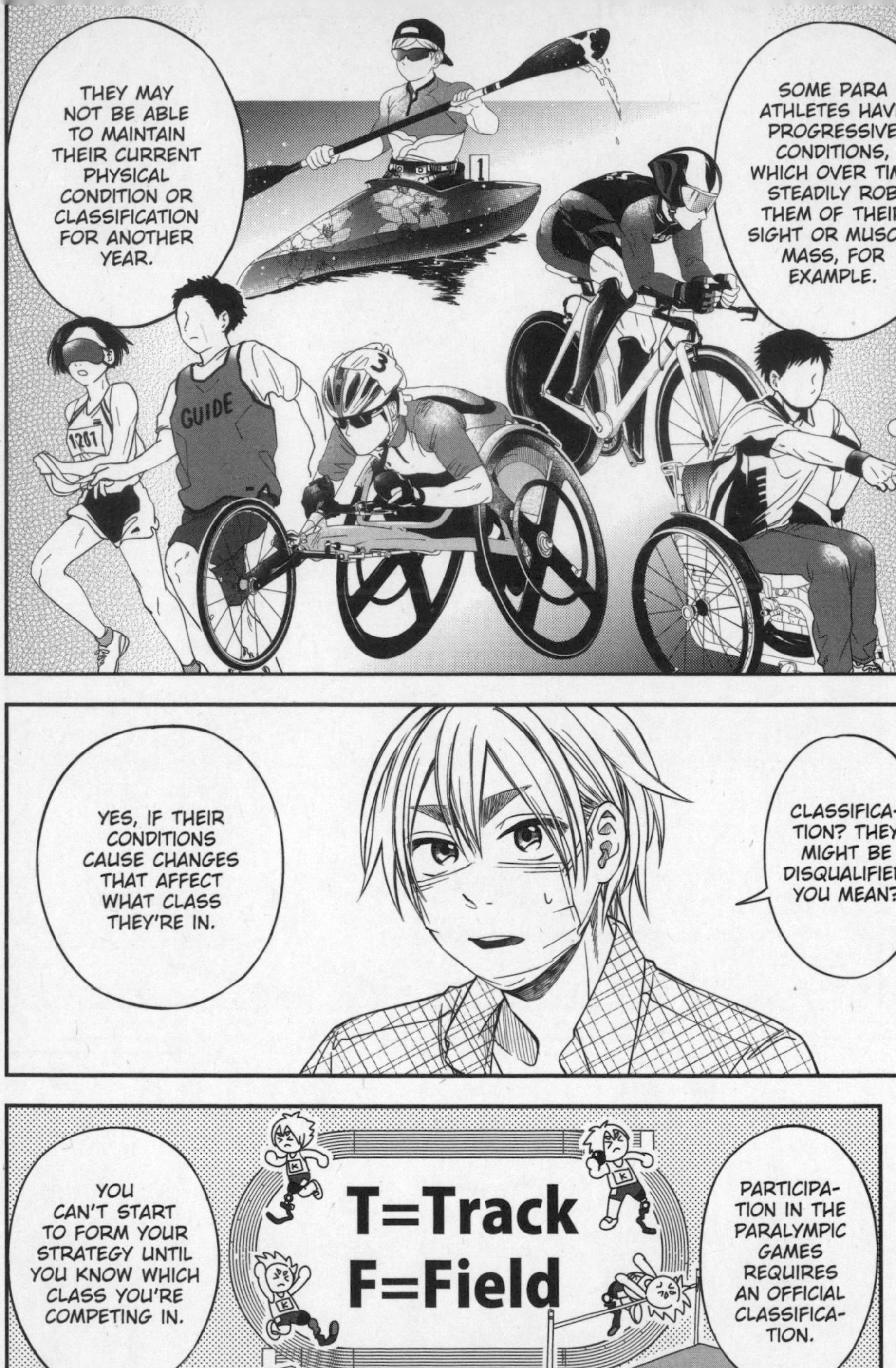
SOME PARA ATHLETES HAVE PROGRESSIVE CONDITIONS, WHICH OVER TIME STEADILY ROB THEM OF THEIR SIGHT OR MUSCLE MASS, FOR EXAMPLE.
THEY MAY NOT BE ABLE TO MAINTAIN THEIR CURRENT PHYSICAL CONDITION OR CLASSIFICATION FOR ANOTHER YEAR.
GUIDE
1207
CLASSIFICA-TION? THEY MIGHT BE DISQUALIFIED, YOU MEAN?
YES, IF THEIR CONDITIONS CAUSE CHANGES THAT AFFECT WHAT CLASS THEY'RE IN.
PARTICIPA-TION IN THE PARALYMPIC GAMES REQUIRES AN OFFICIAL CLASSIFICA-TION.
T=Track
F=Field
YOU CAN'T START TO FORM YOUR STRATEGY UNTIL YOU KNOW WHICH CLASS YOU'RE COMPETING IN.

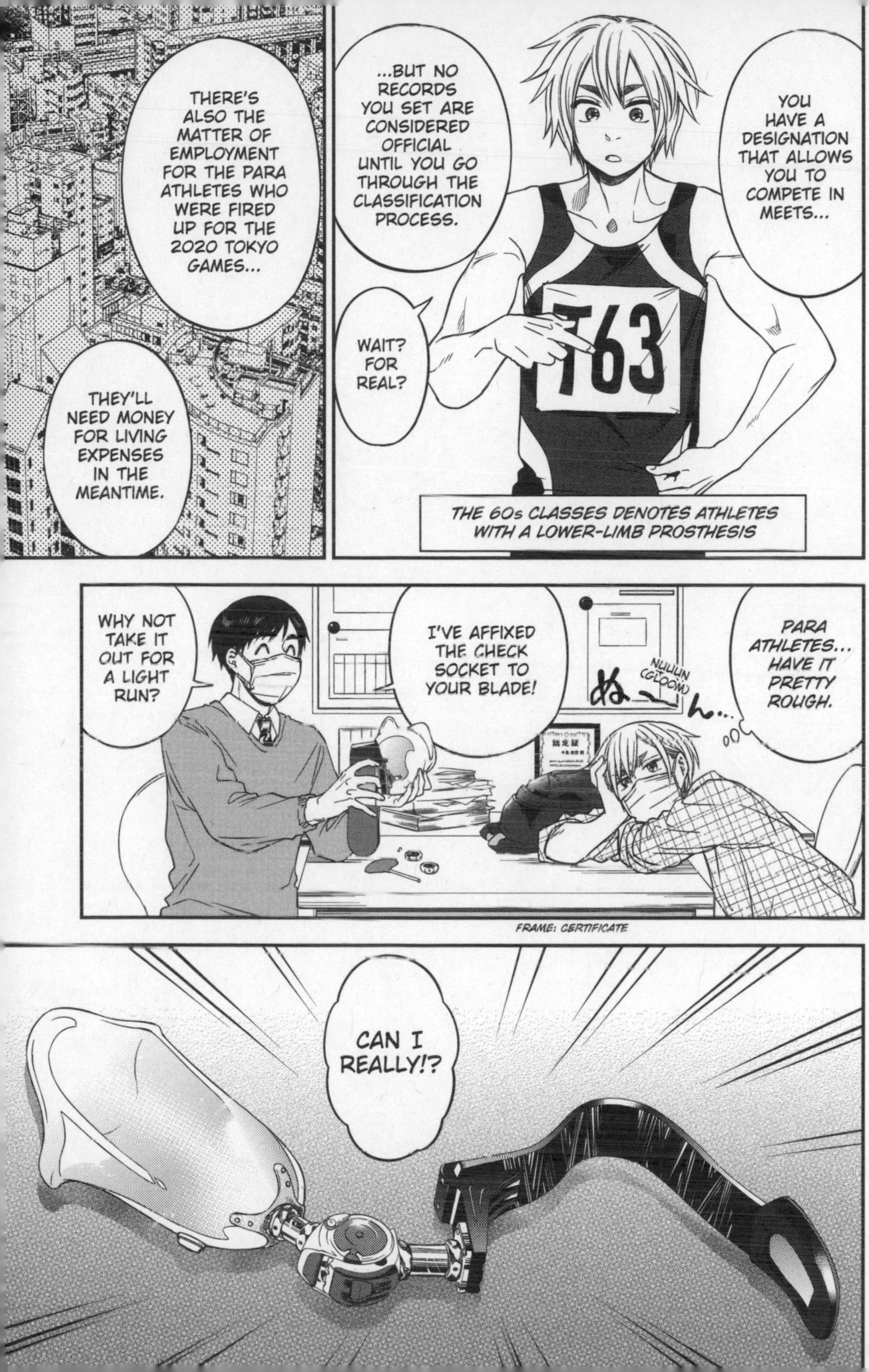
YOU HAVE A DESIGNATION THAT ALLOWS YOU TO COMPETE IN MEETS...
...BUT NO RECORDS YOU SET ARE CONSIDERED OFFICIAL UNTIL YOU GO THROUGH THE CLASSIFICATION PROCESS.
T63
WAIT? FOR REAL?
THE 60s CLASSES DENOTES ATHLETES WITH A LOWER-LIMB PROSTHESIS
THERE'S ALSO THE MATTER OF EMPLOYMENT FOR THE PARA ATHLETES WHO WERE FIRED UP FOR THE 2020 TOKYO GAMES...
THEY'LL NEED MONEY FOR LIVING EXPENSES IN THE MEANTIME.
PARA ATHLETES... HAVE IT PRETTY ROUGH.
ぬ～ん...
NUUUN (GLOOM)
I'VE AFFIXED THE CHECK SOCKET TO YOUR BLADE!
WHY NOT TAKE IT OUT FOR A LIGHT RUN?
FRAME: CERTIFICATE
CAN I REALLY!?

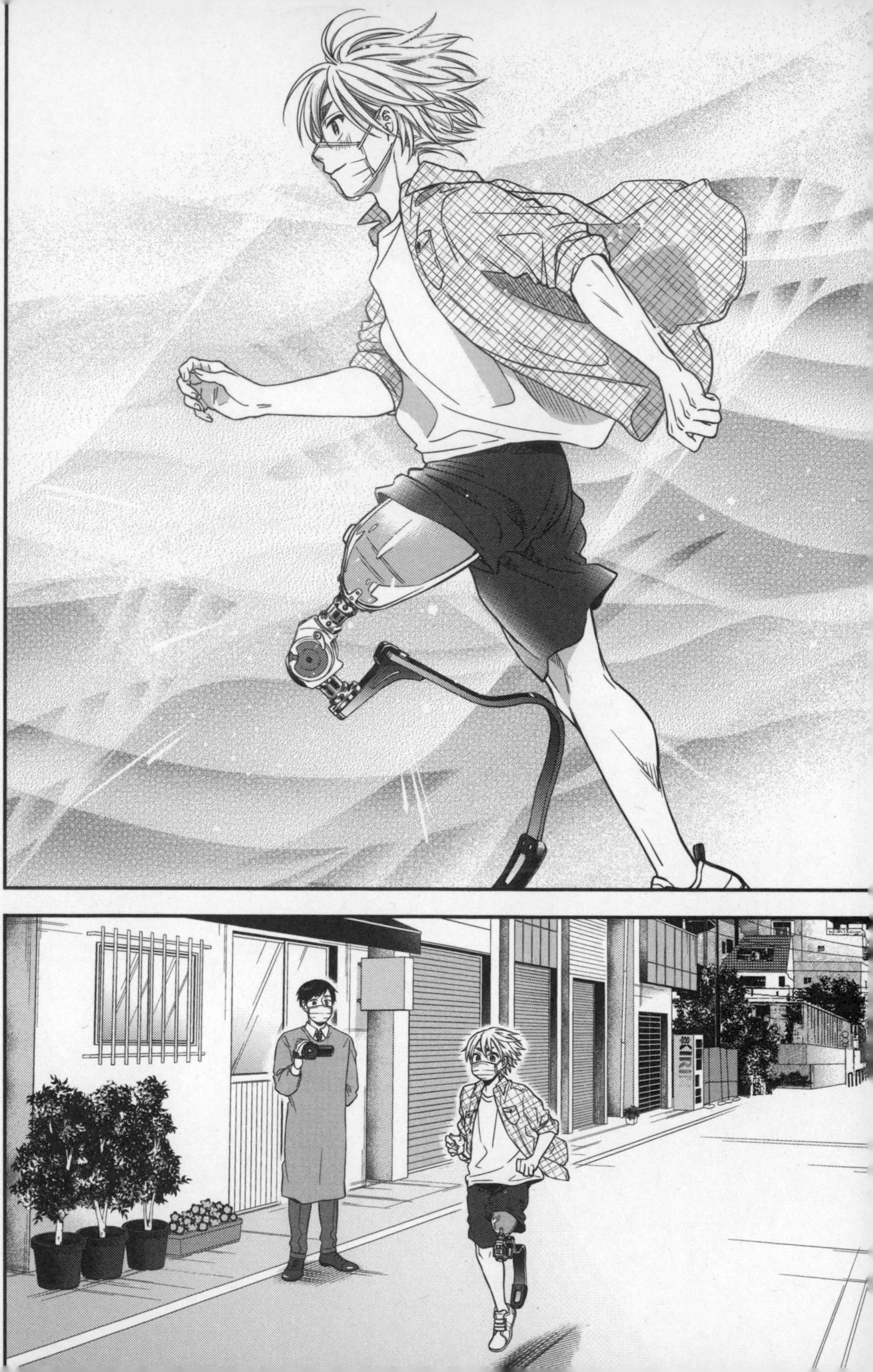

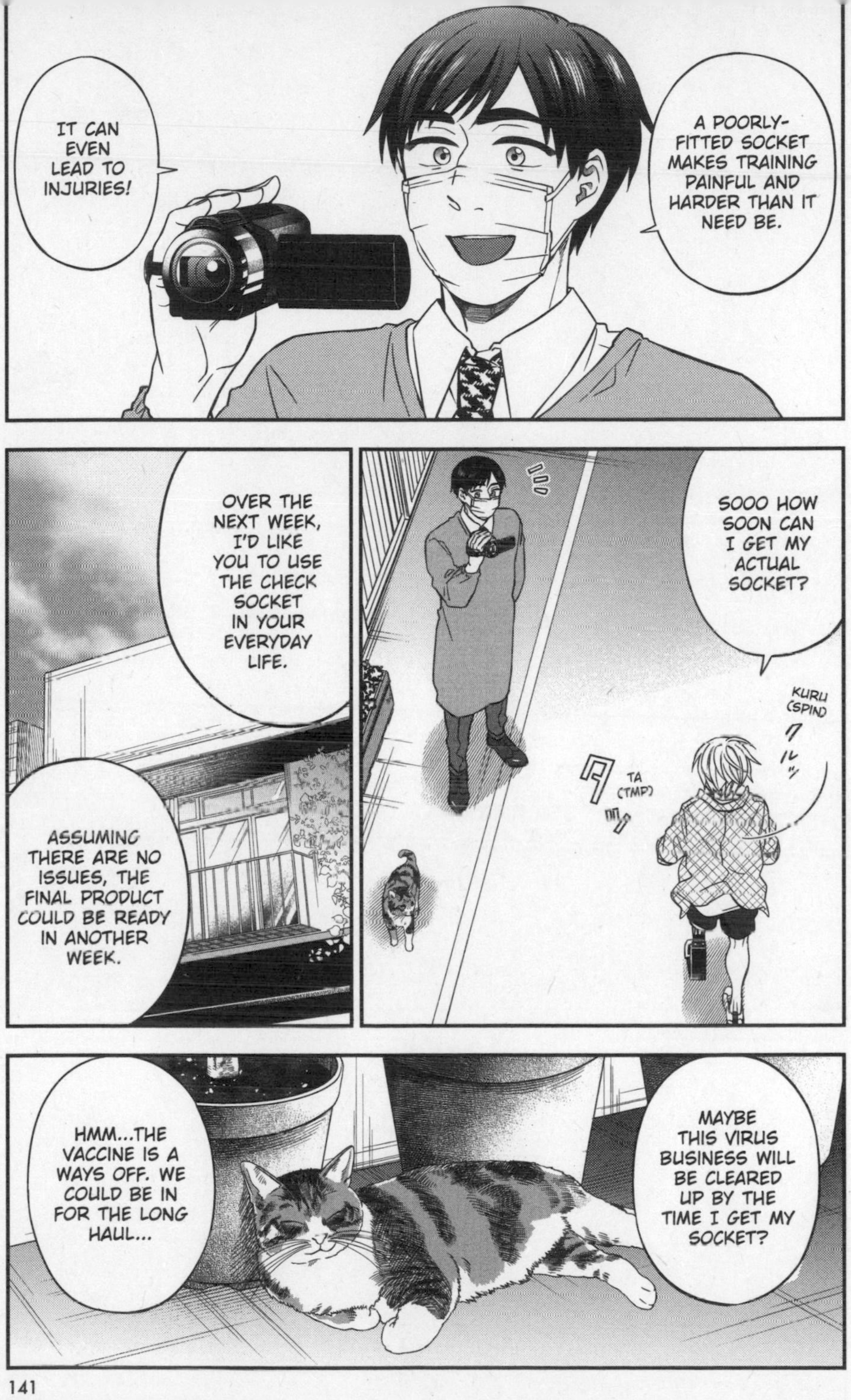

A POORLY-FITTED SOCKET MAKES TRAINING PAINFUL AND HARDER THAN IT NEED BE.
IT CAN EVEN LEAD TO INJURIES!
SOOO HOW SOON CAN I GET MY ACTUAL SOCKET?
KURU (SPIN)
TA (TMP)
OVER THE NEXT WEEK, I'D LIKE YOU TO USE THE CHECK SOCKET IN YOUR EVERYDAY LIFE.
ASSUMING THERE ARE NO ISSUES, THE FINAL PRODUCT COULD BE READY IN ANOTHER WEEK.
MAYBE THIS VIRUS BUSINESS WILL BE CLEARED UP BY THE TIME I GET MY SOCKET?
HMM...THE VACCINE IS A WAYS OFF. WE COULD BE IN FOR THE LONG HAUL...

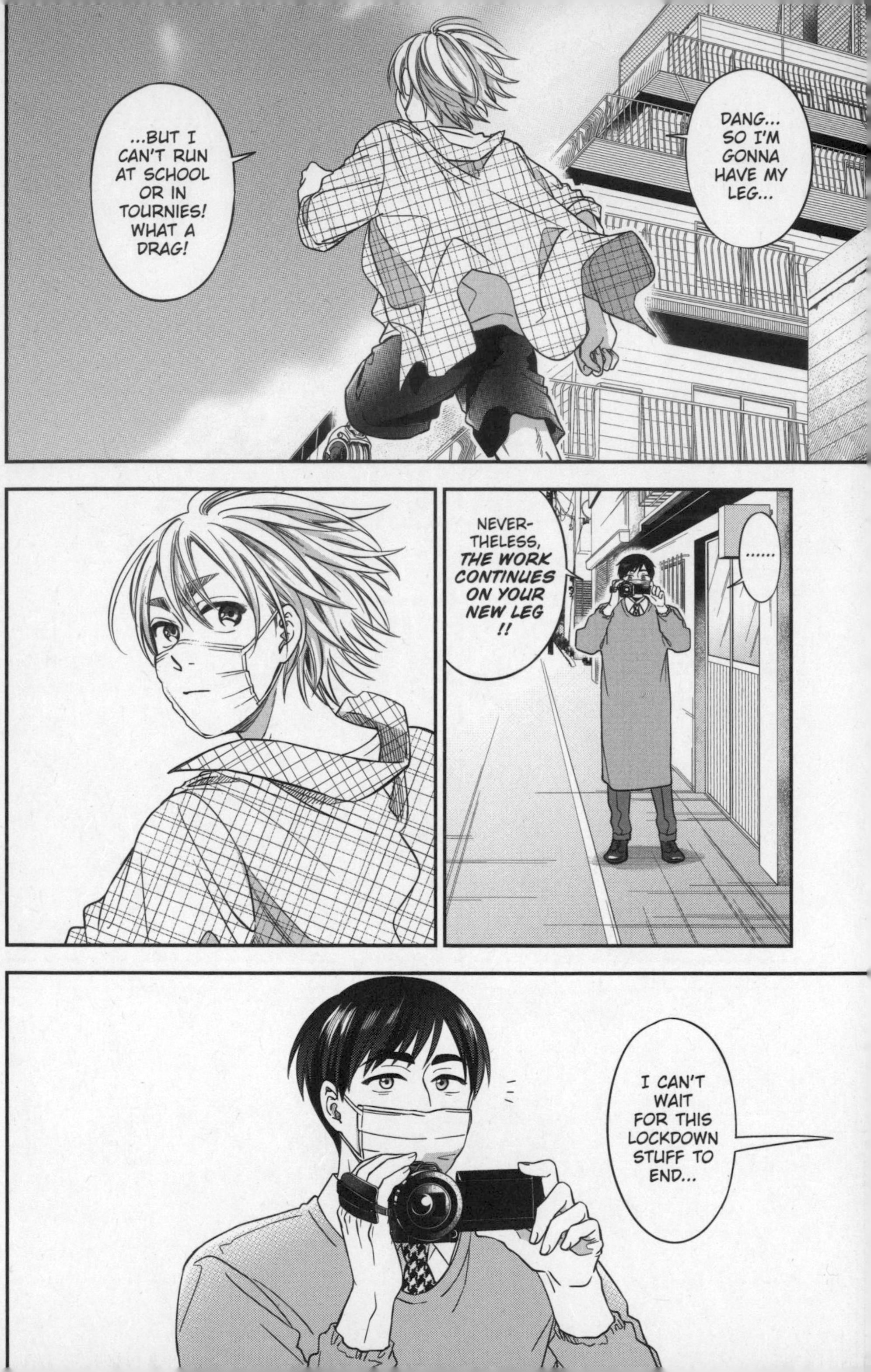
DANG... SO I'M GONNA HAVE MY LEG...
...BUT I CAN'T RUN AT SCHOOL OR IN TOURNIES! WHAT A DRAG!
......
NEVER-THELESS, *THE WORK CONTINUES ON YOUR NEW LEG* !!
I CAN'T WAIT FOR THIS LOCKDOWN STUFF TO END...

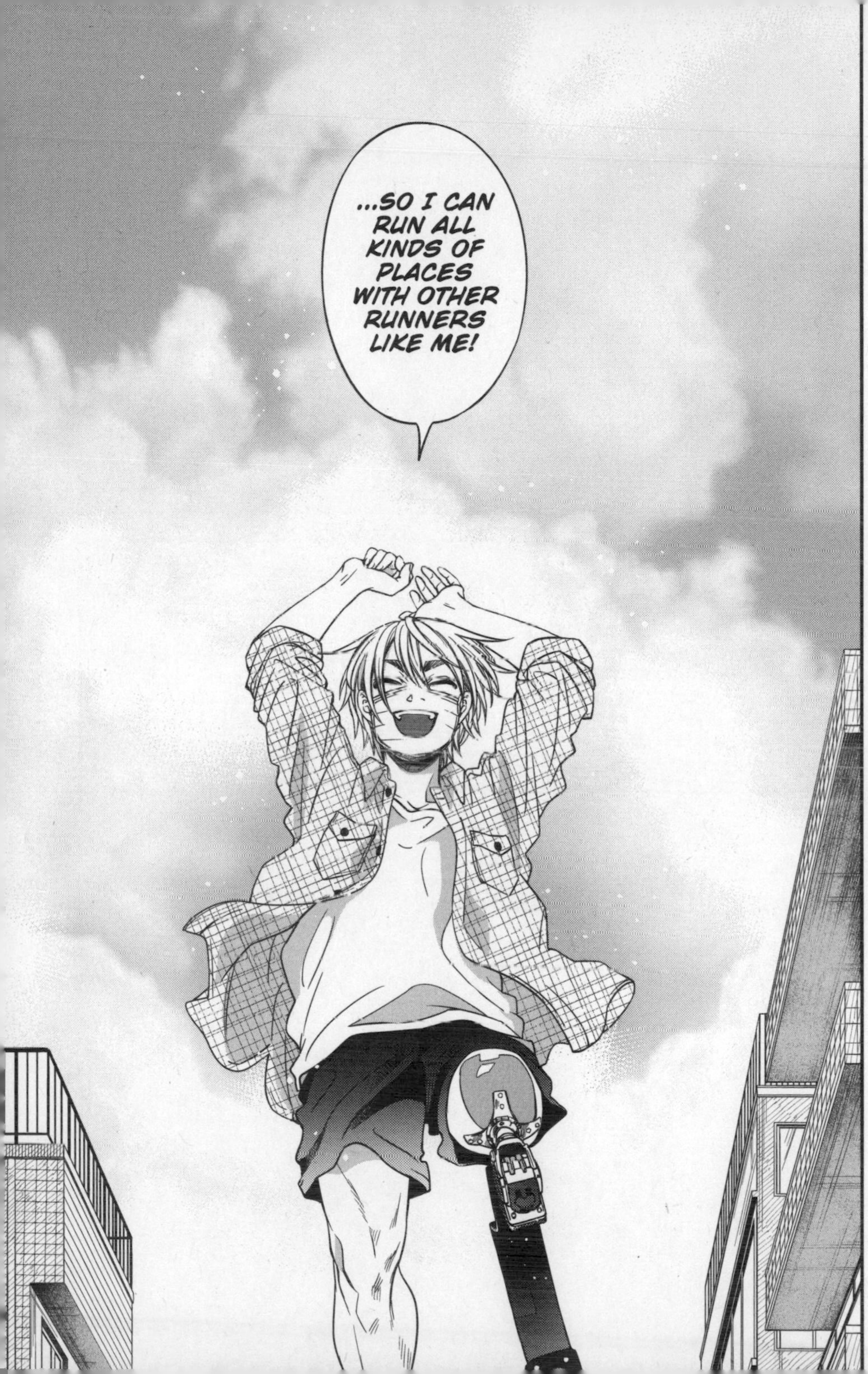
...SO I CAN RUN ALL KINDS OF PLACES WITH OTHER RUNNERS LIKE ME!

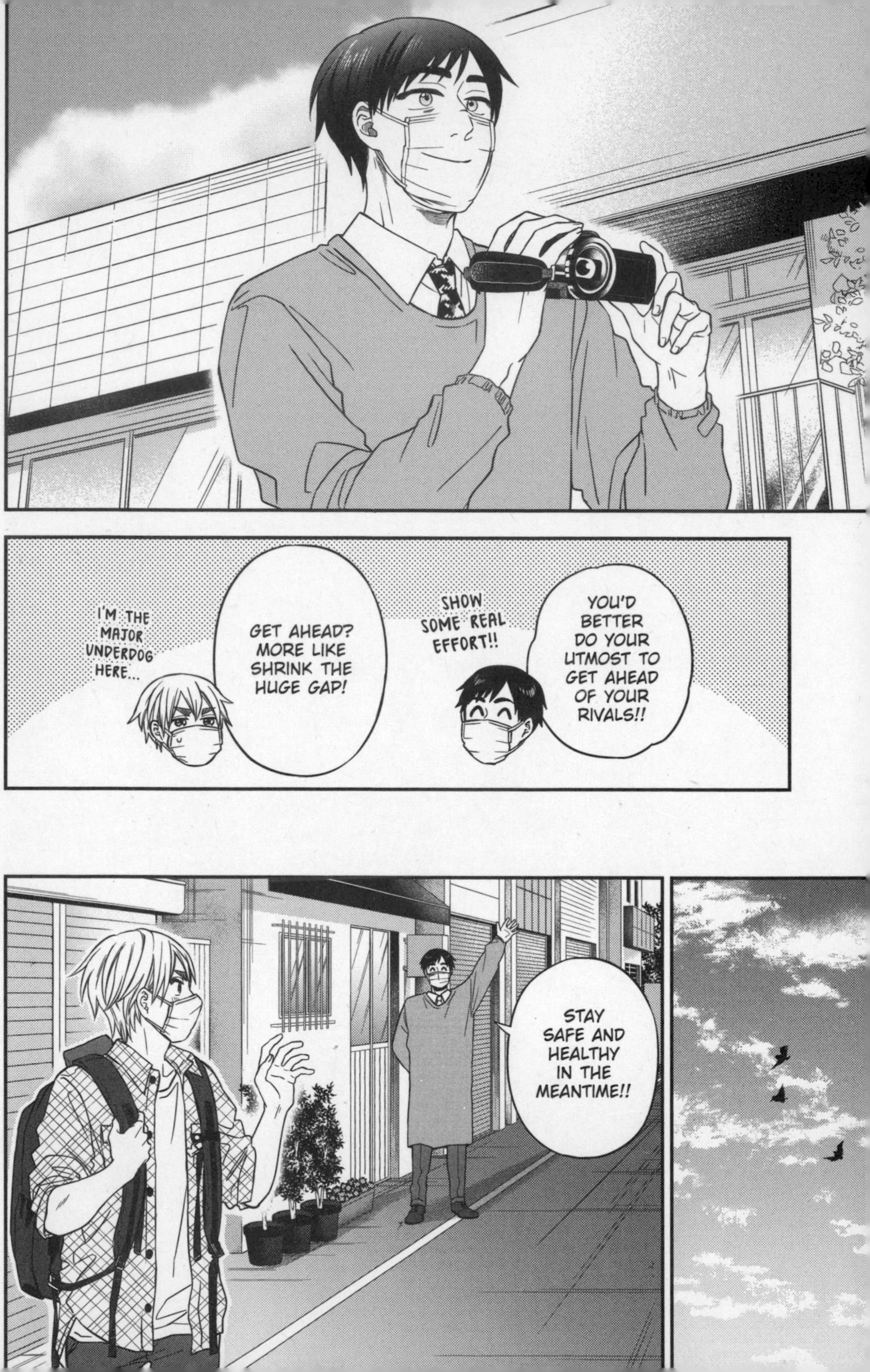
YOU'D BETTER DO YOUR UTMOST TO GET AHEAD OF YOUR RIVALS!!
SHOW SOME REAL EFFORT!!
GET AHEAD? MORE LIKE SHRINK THE HUGE GAP!
I'M THE MAJOR UNDERDOG HERE...
STAY SAFE AND HEALTHY IN THE MEANTIME!!

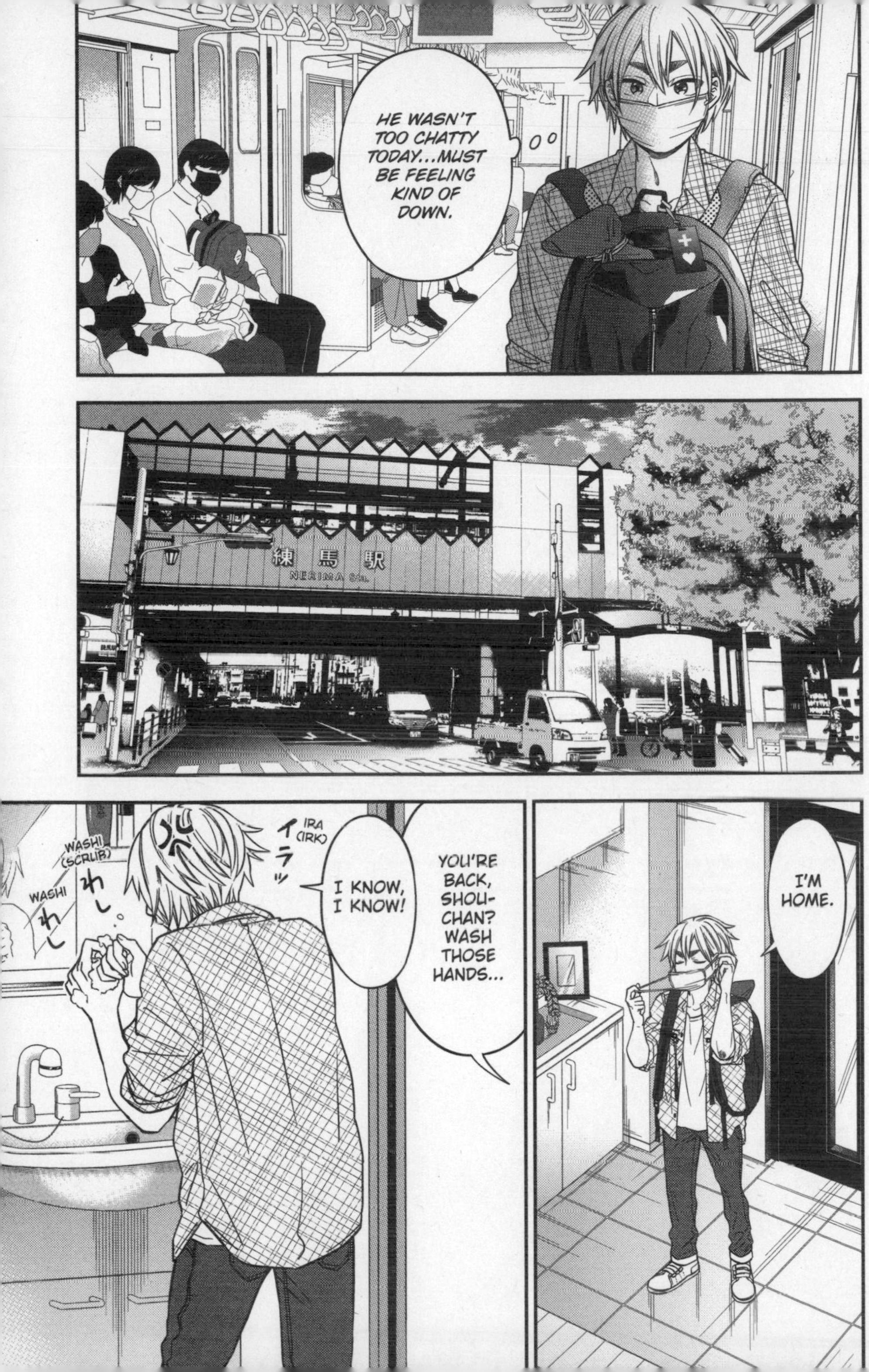
HE WASN'T TOO CHATTY TODAY...MUST BE FEELING KIND OF DOWN.
練馬駅
NERIMA Sta.
I'M HOME.
YOU'RE BACK, SHOU-CHAN? WASH THOSE HANDS...
I KNOW, I KNOW!
IRA (IRK)
イラッ
WASHI (SCRUB)
わし
WASHI
わし

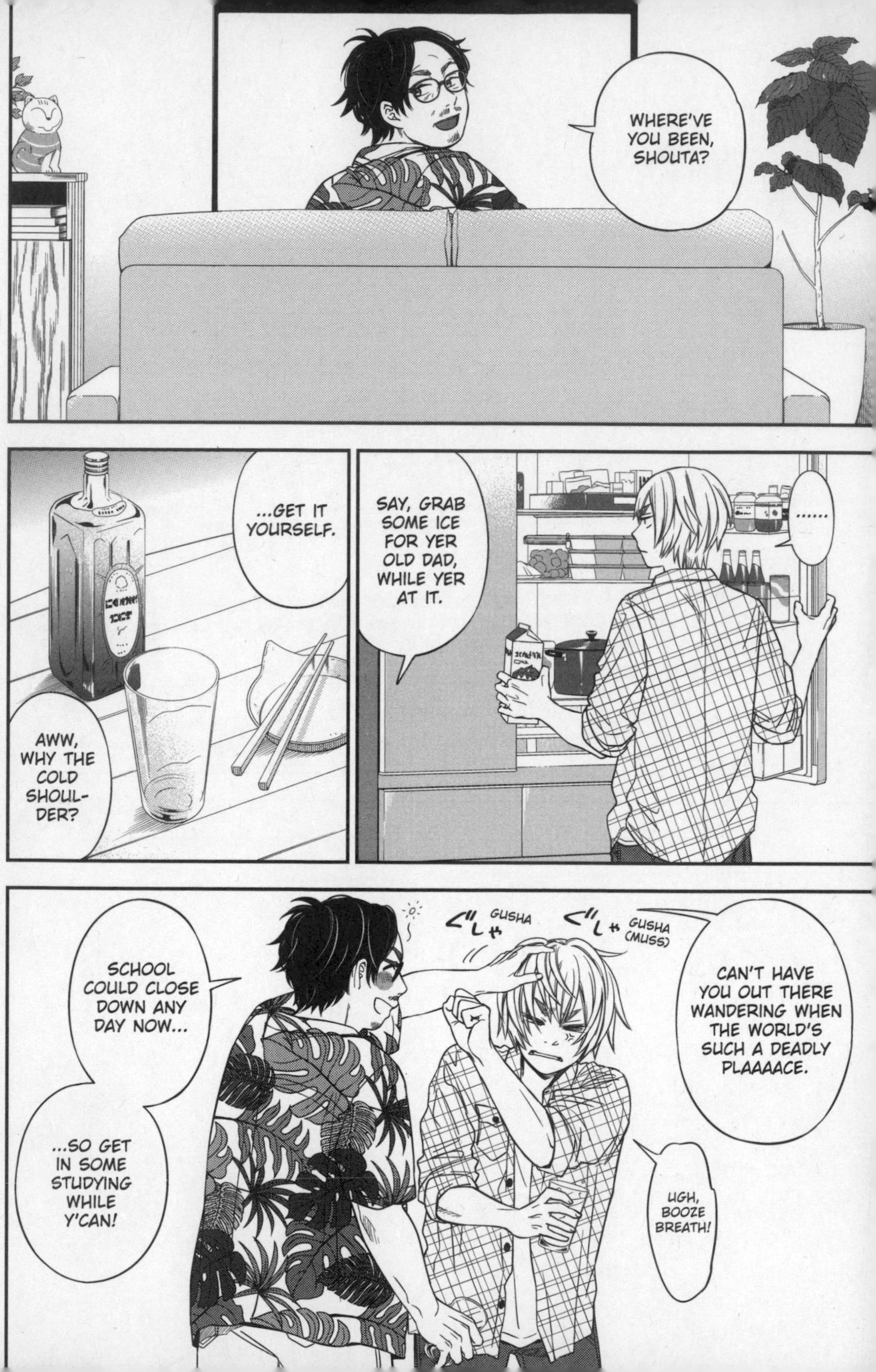
WHERE'VE YOU BEEN, SHOUTA?
......
SAY, GRAB SOME ICE FOR YER OLD DAD, WHILE YER AT IT.
...GET IT YOURSELF.
AWW, WHY THE COLD SHOUL-DER?
CAN'T HAVE YOU OUT THERE WANDERING WHEN THE WORLD'S SUCH A DEADLY PLAAAACE.
ぐしゃ GUSHA (MUSS)
ぐしゃ GUSHA
SCHOOL COULD CLOSE DOWN ANY DAY NOW...
UGH, BOOZE BREATH!
...SO GET IN SOME STUDYING WHILE Y'CAN!

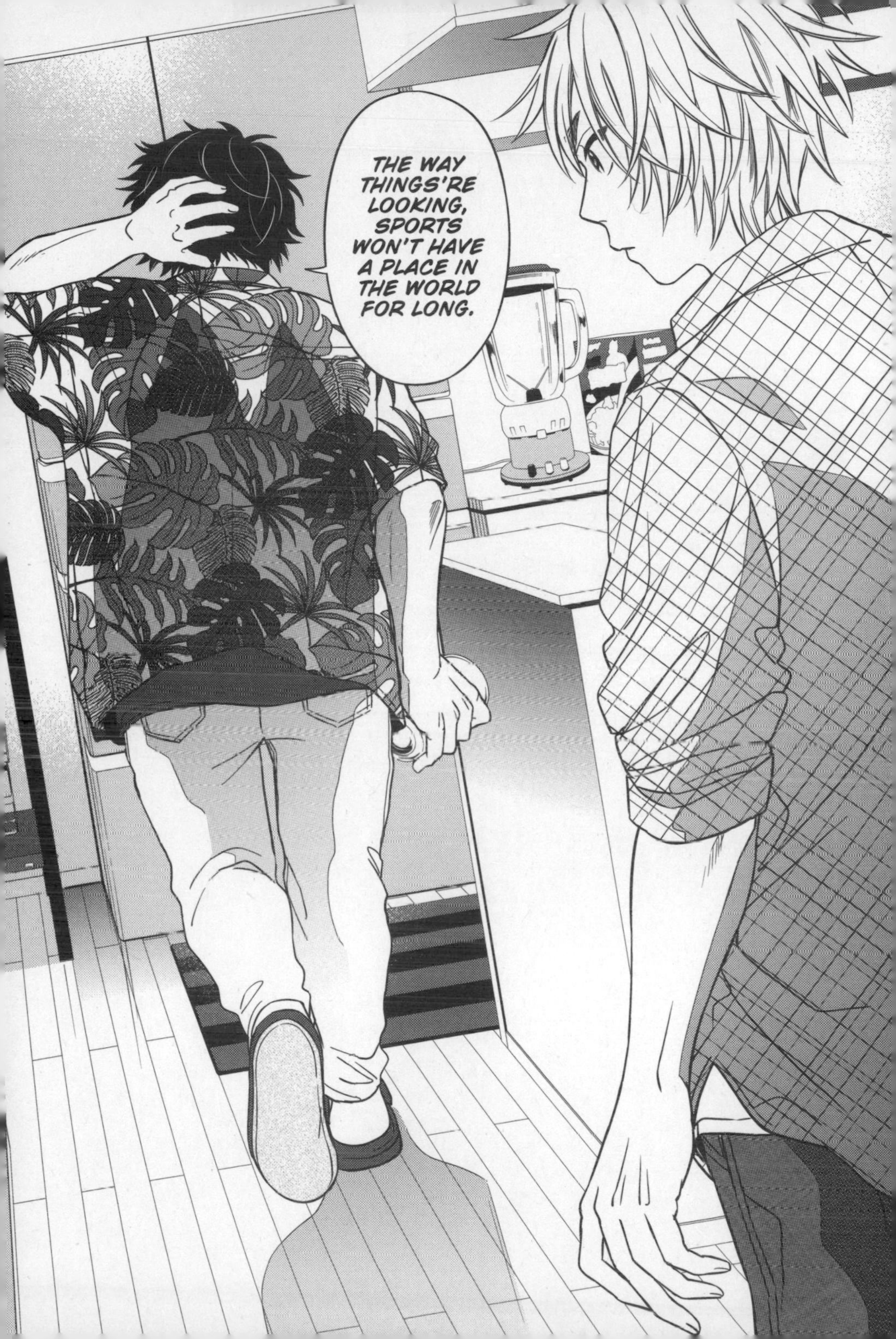
THE WAY THINGS'RE LOOKING, SPORTS WON'T HAVE A PLACE IN THE WORLD FOR LONG.

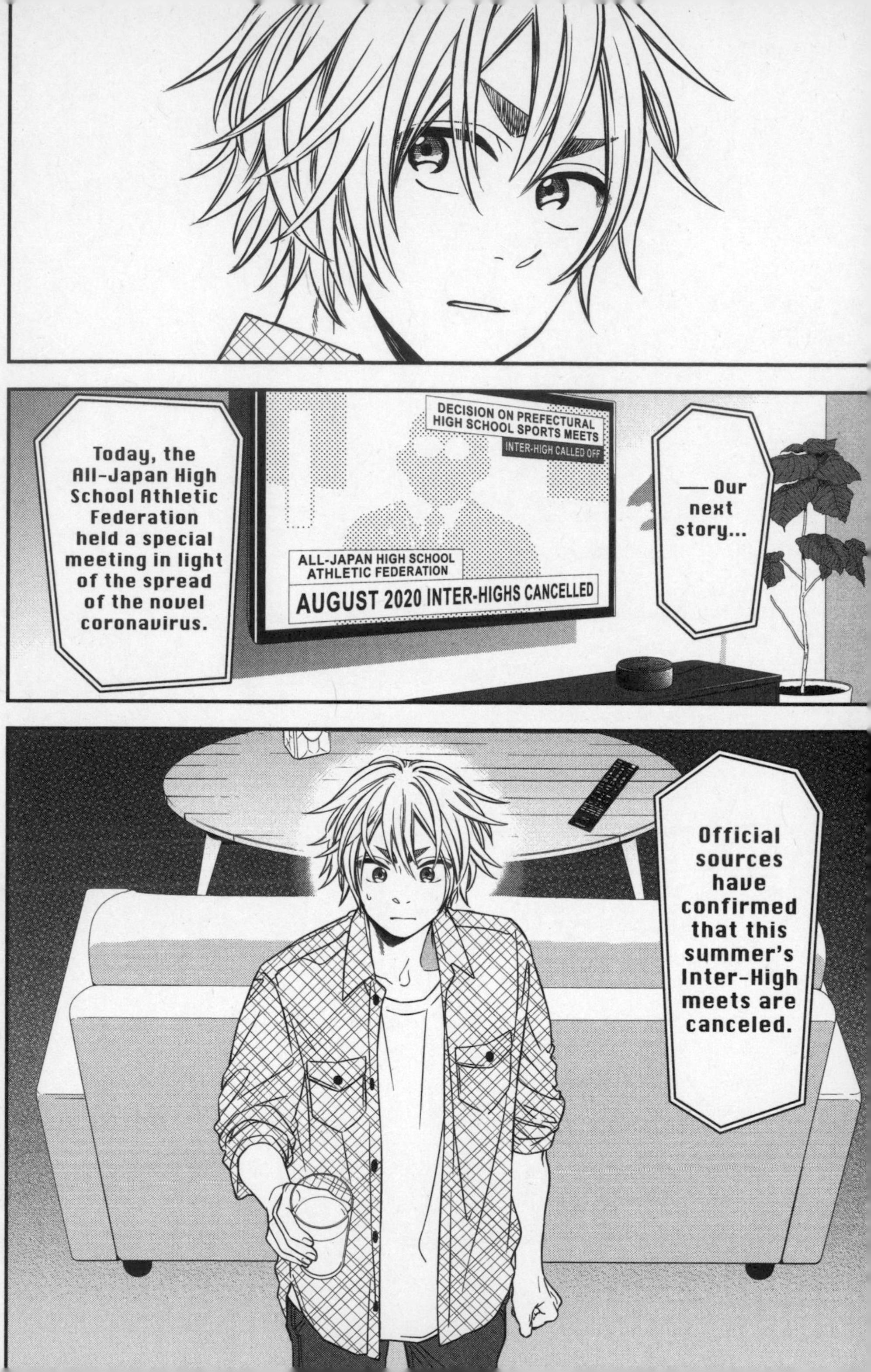

— Our next story...
DECISION ON PREFECTURAL HIGH SCHOOL SPORTS MEETS
INTER-HIGH CALLED OFF
ALL-JAPAN HIGH SCHOOL ATHLETIC FEDERATION
AUGUST 2020 INTER-HIGHS CANCELLED
Today, the All-Japan High School Athletic Federation held a special meeting in light of the spread of the novel coronavirus.
Official sources have confirmed that this summer's Inter-High meets are canceled.

Run on Your New Legs, Vol. 3 : END

RUN ON YOUR NEW LEGS

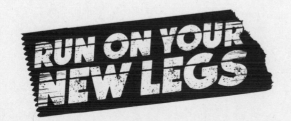

Special thanks
to all my consultants

Atsushi Yamamoto (Shin Nihon Jusetsu)
Junta Kosuda (Open House)
Mikio Ikeda (Digital Advertising Consortium)
Tomoki Yoshida

Xiborg
Otto Bock Japan
Okino Sports Prosthetics & Orthotics (Atsuo Okino)
D'ACTION (Shuji Miyake)
Naoto Yoshida (Writer)

Thank you to everyone else who contributed to this book!

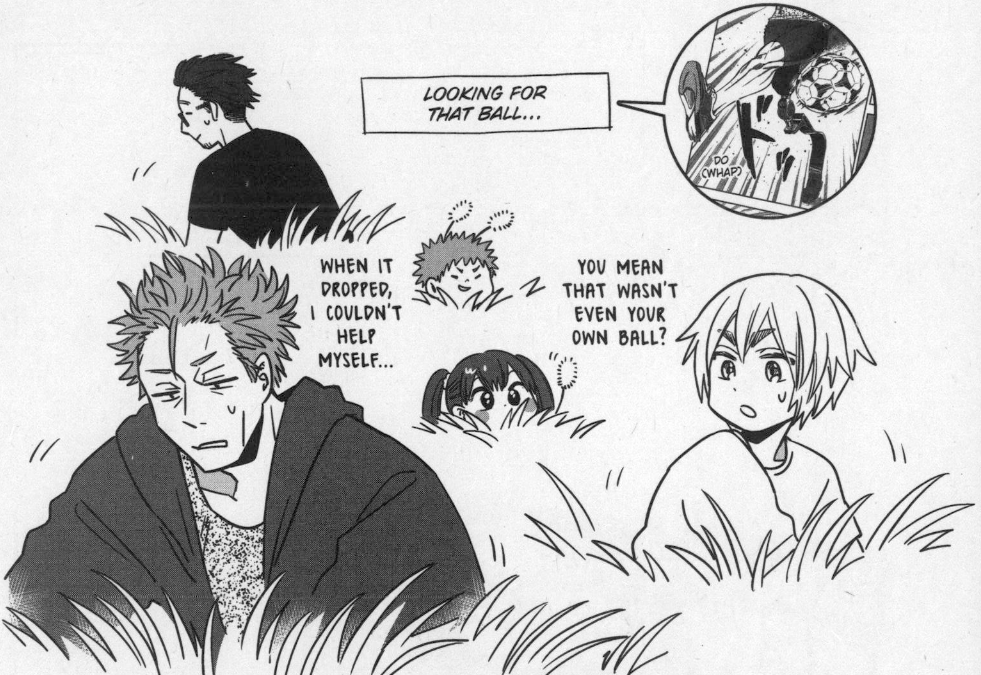
ドッ
DO (WHAP)
LOOKING FOR THAT BALL...
YOU MEAN THAT WASN'T EVEN YOUR OWN BALL?
WHEN IT DROPPED, I COULDN'T HELP MYSELF...

BONUS

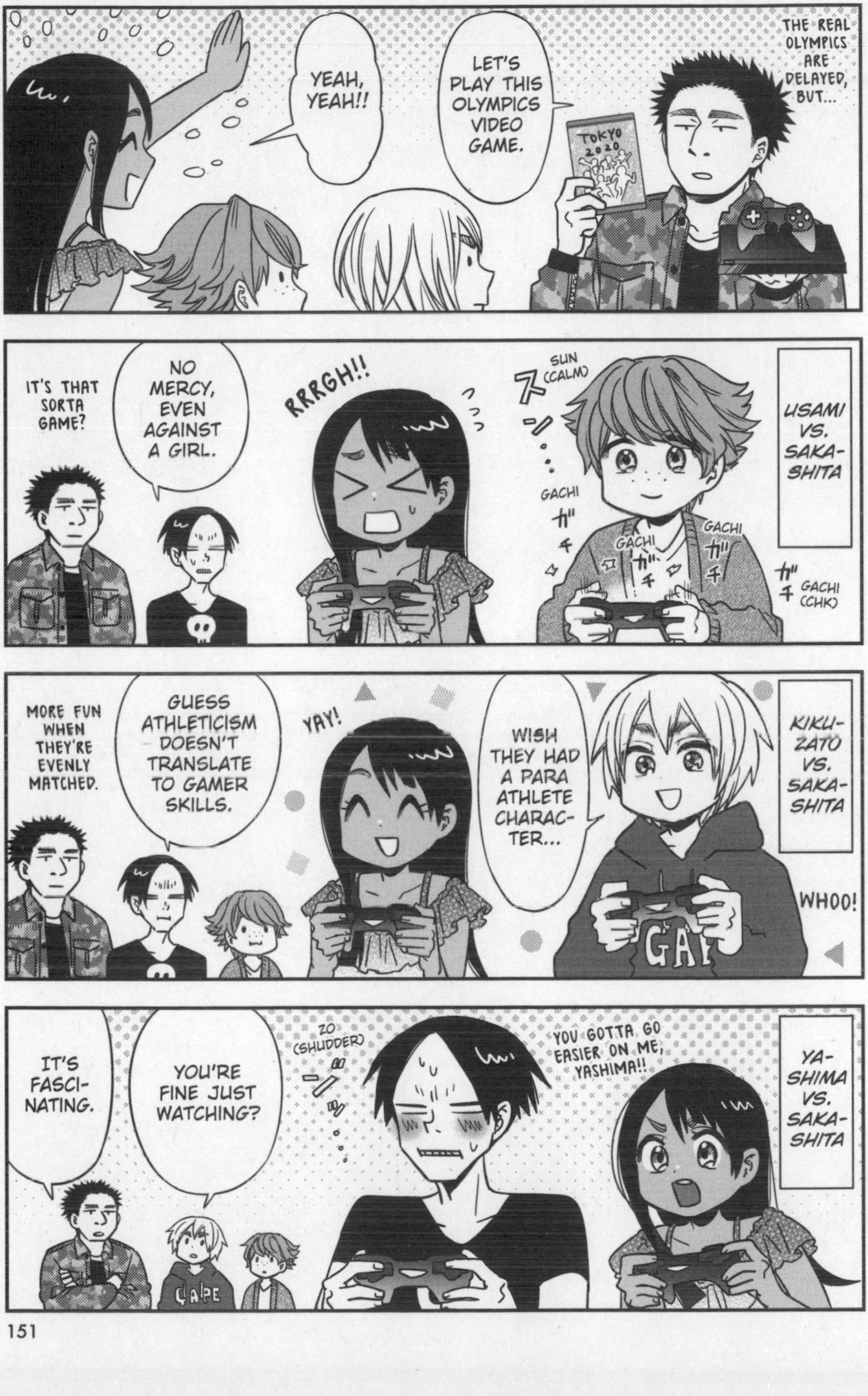

THE REAL OLYMPICS ARE DELAYED, BUT...
LET'S PLAY THIS OLYMPICS VIDEO GAME.
TOKYO 2020
YEAH, YEAH!!
USAMI VS. SAKASHITA
SUN (CALM)
GACHI
GACHI
GACHI
GACHI (CHK)
RRRGH!!
NO MERCY, EVEN AGAINST A GIRL.
IT'S THAT SORTA GAME?
KIKUZATO VS. SAKASHITA
WHOO!
WISH THEY HAD A PARA ATHLETE CHARACTER...
YAY!
GUESS ATHLETICISM DOESN'T TRANSLATE TO GAMER SKILLS.
MORE FUN WHEN THEY'RE EVENLY MATCHED.
YASHIMA VS. SAKASHITA
YOU GOTTA GO EASIER ON ME, YASHIMA!!
ZO (SHUDDER)
YOU'RE FINE JUST WATCHING?
IT'S FASCINATING.

STORYBOARD BY: ART BY: NAKAJIMA-SAN (ASSISTANT)

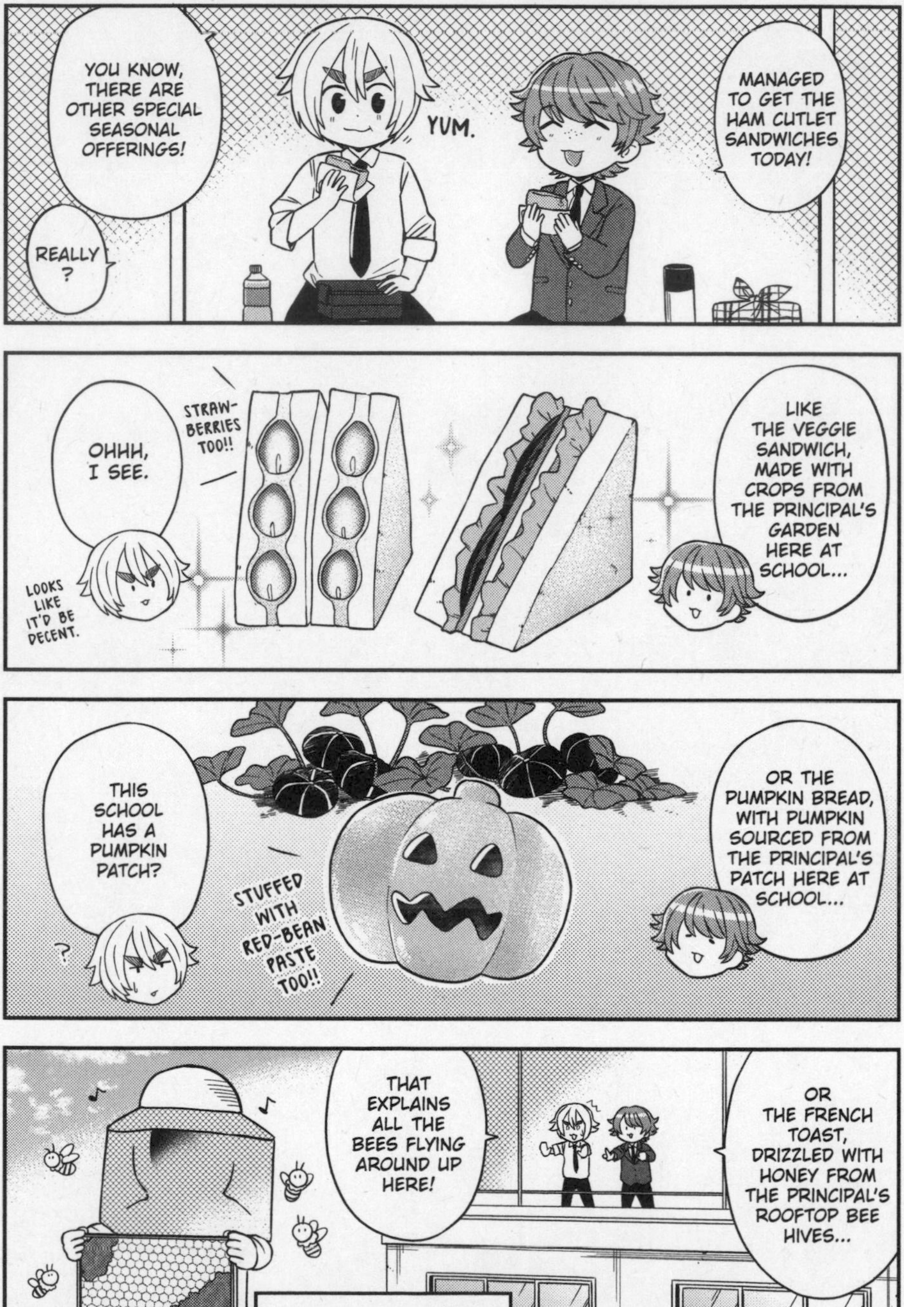
MANAGED TO GET THE HAM CUTLET SANDWICHES TODAY!
YUM.
YOU KNOW, THERE ARE OTHER SPECIAL SEASONAL OFFERINGS!
REALLY ?
LIKE THE VEGGIE SANDWICH, MADE WITH CROPS FROM THE PRINCIPAL'S GARDEN HERE AT SCHOOL...
STRAW-BERRIES TOO!!
OHHH, I SEE.
LOOKS LIKE IT'D BE DECENT.
OR THE PUMPKIN BREAD, WITH PUMPKIN SOURCED FROM THE PRINCIPAL'S PATCH HERE AT SCHOOL...
STUFFED WITH RED-BEAN PASTE TOO!!
THIS SCHOOL HAS A PUMPKIN PATCH?
?
OR THE FRENCH TOAST, DRIZZLED WITH HONEY FROM THE PRINCIPAL'S ROOFTOP BEE HIVES...
THAT EXPLAINS ALL THE BEES FLYING AROUND UP HERE!
NO STUDENT ACCESS

STORYBOARD BY: ART BY: MORUNGA-SAN (ASSISTANT)

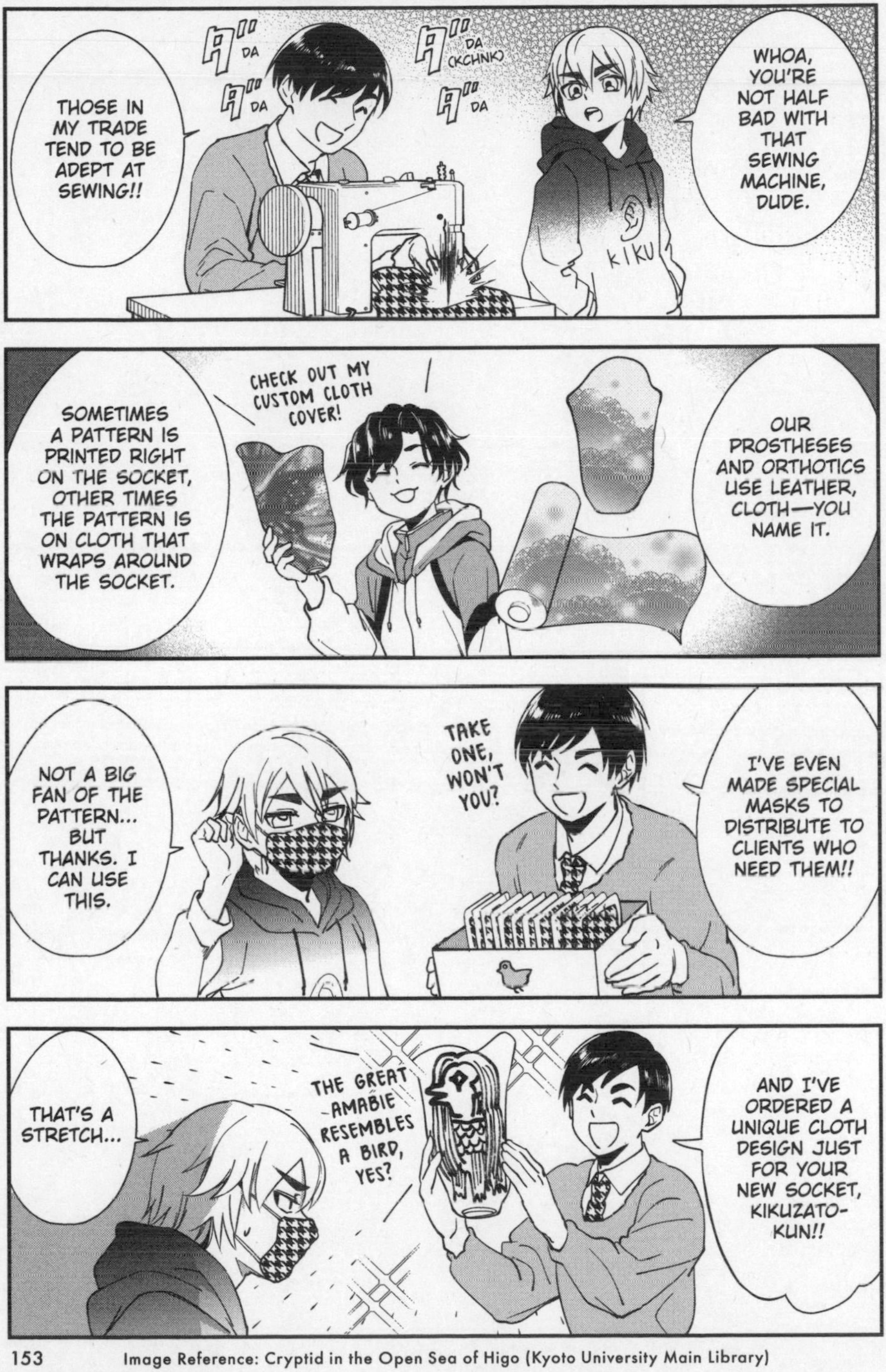
WHOA, YOU'RE NOT HALF BAD WITH THAT SEWING MACHINE, DUDE.
KIKU
DA (KCHNK)
DA
DA
DA
THOSE IN MY TRADE TEND TO BE ADEPT AT SEWING!!
OUR PROSTHESES AND ORTHOTICS USE LEATHER, CLOTH—YOU NAME IT.
CHECK OUT MY CUSTOM CLOTH COVER!
SOMETIMES A PATTERN IS PRINTED RIGHT ON THE SOCKET, OTHER TIMES THE PATTERN IS ON CLOTH THAT WRAPS AROUND THE SOCKET.
I'VE EVEN MADE SPECIAL MASKS TO DISTRIBUTE TO CLIENTS WHO NEED THEM!!
TAKE ONE, WON'T YOU?
NOT A BIG FAN OF THE PATTERN... BUT THANKS. I CAN USE THIS.
AND I'VE ORDERED A UNIQUE CLOTH DESIGN JUST FOR YOUR NEW SOCKET, KIKUZATO-KUN!!
THE GREAT AMABIE RESEMBLES A BIRD, YES?
THAT'S A STRETCH...

 Image Reference: Cryptid in the Open Sea of Higo (Kyoto University Main Library)

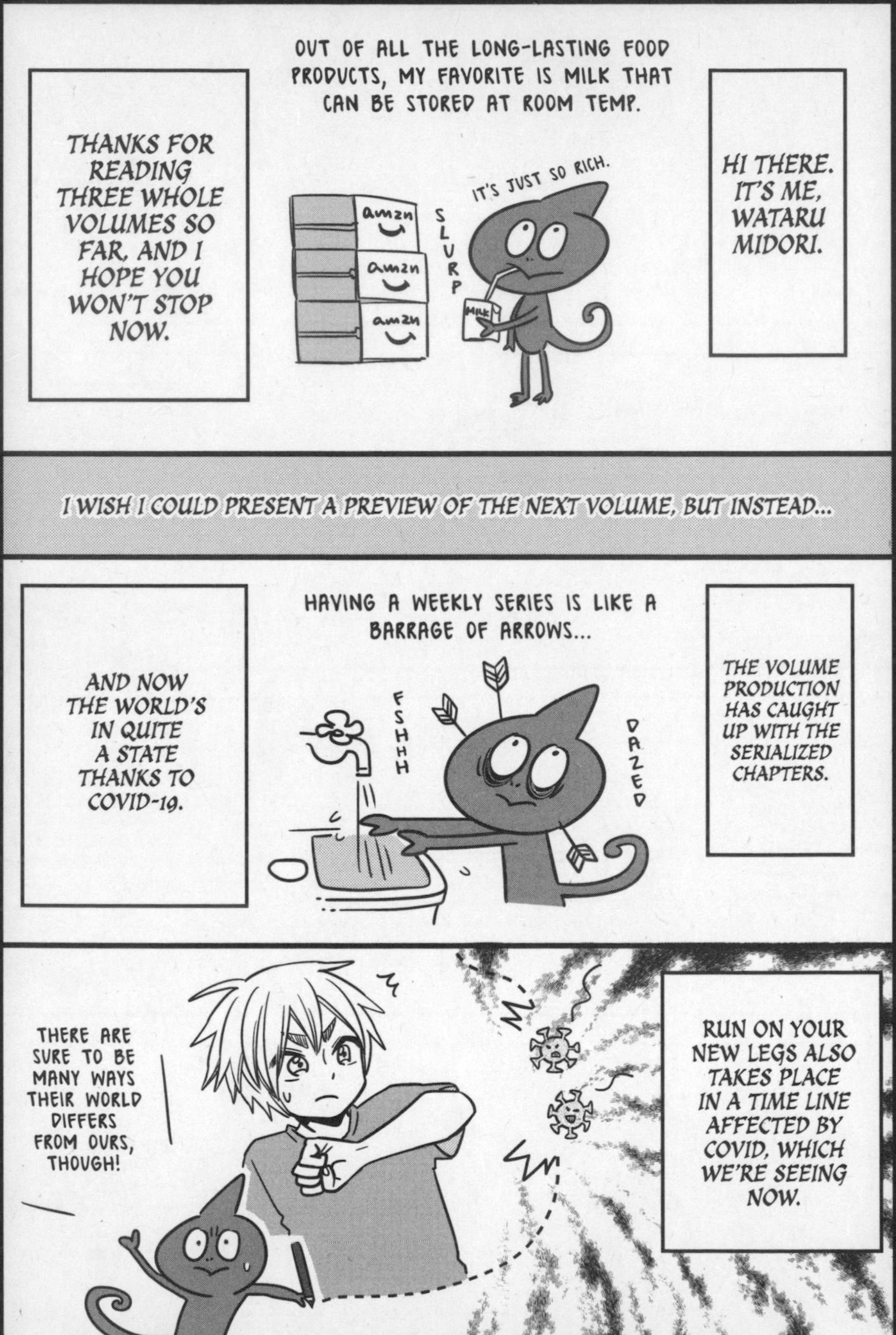
HI THERE. IT'S ME, WATARU MIDORI.
OUT OF ALL THE LONG-LASTING FOOD PRODUCTS, MY FAVORITE IS MILK THAT CAN BE STORED AT ROOM TEMP.
IT'S JUST SO RICH.
SLURP
MILK
amzn
amzn
amzn
THANKS FOR READING THREE WHOLE VOLUMES SO FAR, AND I HOPE YOU WON'T STOP NOW.
I WISH I COULD PRESENT A PREVIEW OF THE NEXT VOLUME, BUT INSTEAD...
THE VOLUME PRODUCTION HAS CAUGHT UP WITH THE SERIALIZED CHAPTERS.
HAVING A WEEKLY SERIES IS LIKE A BARRAGE OF ARROWS...
DAZED
FSHHH
AND NOW THE WORLD'S IN QUITE A STATE THANKS TO COVID-19.
RUN ON YOUR NEW LEGS ALSO TAKES PLACE IN A TIME LINE AFFECTED BY COVID, WHICH WE'RE SEEING NOW.
THERE ARE SURE TO BE MANY WAYS THEIR WORLD DIFFERS FROM OURS, THOUGH!

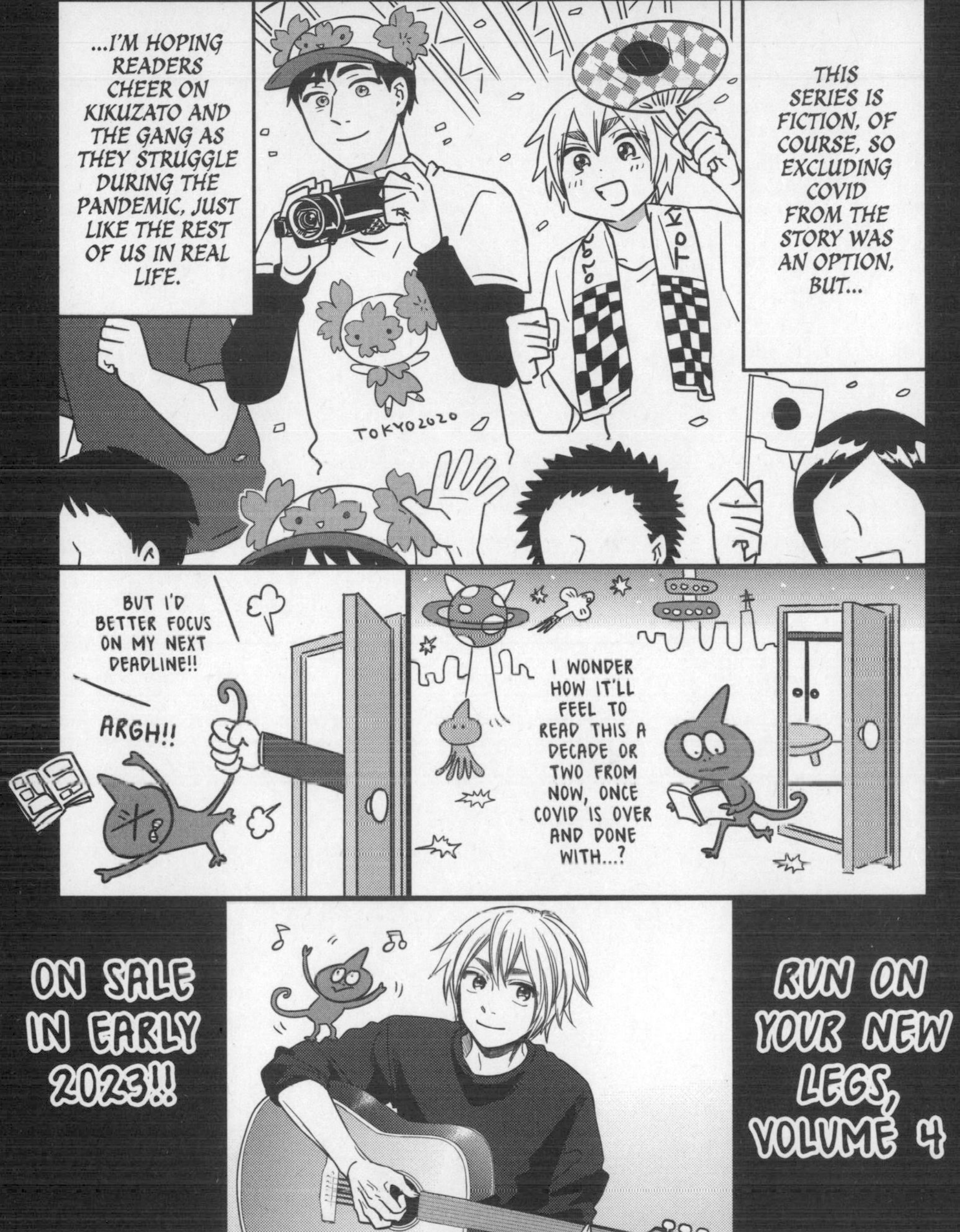
THIS SERIES IS FICTION, OF COURSE, SO EXCLUDING COVID FROM THE STORY WAS AN OPTION, BUT...
...I'M HOPING READERS CHEER ON KIKUZATO AND THE GANG AS THEY STRUGGLE DURING THE PANDEMIC, JUST LIKE THE REST OF US IN REAL LIFE.
TOKYO2020
I WONDER HOW IT'LL FEEL TO READ THIS A DECADE OR TWO FROM NOW, ONCE COVID IS OVER AND DONE WITH...?
BUT I'D BETTER FOCUS ON MY NEXT DEADLINE!!
ARGH!!
RUN ON YOUR NEW LEGS, VOLUME 4
ON SALE IN EARLY 2023!!

RUN ON YOUR NEW LEGS

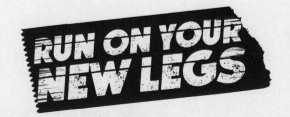

TRANSLATION NOTES

COMMON HONORIFICS

no honorific: Indicates familiarity or closeness; if used without permission or reason, addressing someone in this manner would constitute an insult.

-*san*: The Japanese equivalent of Mr./Mrs./Ms. This is the fail-safe honorific if politeness is required.

-*kun*: Used most often when referring to boys, this honorific indicates affection or familiarity. Occasionally used by older men among their peers, but it may also be used by anyone referring to a person of lower standing.

-*chan*: Affectionate honorific indicating familiarity used mostly in reference to girls; also used in reference to cute persons or animals of any gender.

-*senpai*: A suffix used when addressing upperclassmen or more senior coworkers.

-*sensei*: A respectful term for teachers, artists, or high-level professionals.

-*sama*: An honorific conveying great respect.

CURRENCY CONVERSION

While exchange rates fluctuate daily, a good approximation is ¥100 to 1 USD.

Page 32: On the day of graduation, it's a common Japanese custom for boys to give away their **school uniform buttons** to friends, crushes, etc. Each button may carry a different meaning, depending on the era and the region.

Page 85: The term *kouhai* is used for underclassmen or junior coworkers.

Page 124: Yashima couldn't afford the trip to the Inter-High meet in **Okinawa** because getting there from Japan's mainland involves either a flight or a very long boat ride to the southern island chain. However, **Shizuoka** is only a few prefectures away from Tokyo, so he could have afforded the relatively short train trip there if the 2020 Inter-High hadn't been canceled.

Page 153: The Japanese term for the **houndstooth pattern** is *chidori goushi* (literally, "thousand-bird lattice"), which explains why Chidori has chosen that pattern for his necktie and face masks.

Page 153: Amabie is a mythical Japanese mermaid with long hair and a birdlike face that is said to emerge from the sea to warn of coming pandemics. Making art in its image supposedly defends against sickness, which is why it saw renewed popularity during the COVID-19 pandemic. Chidori clearly appreciates the bird connection he shares with Amabie.

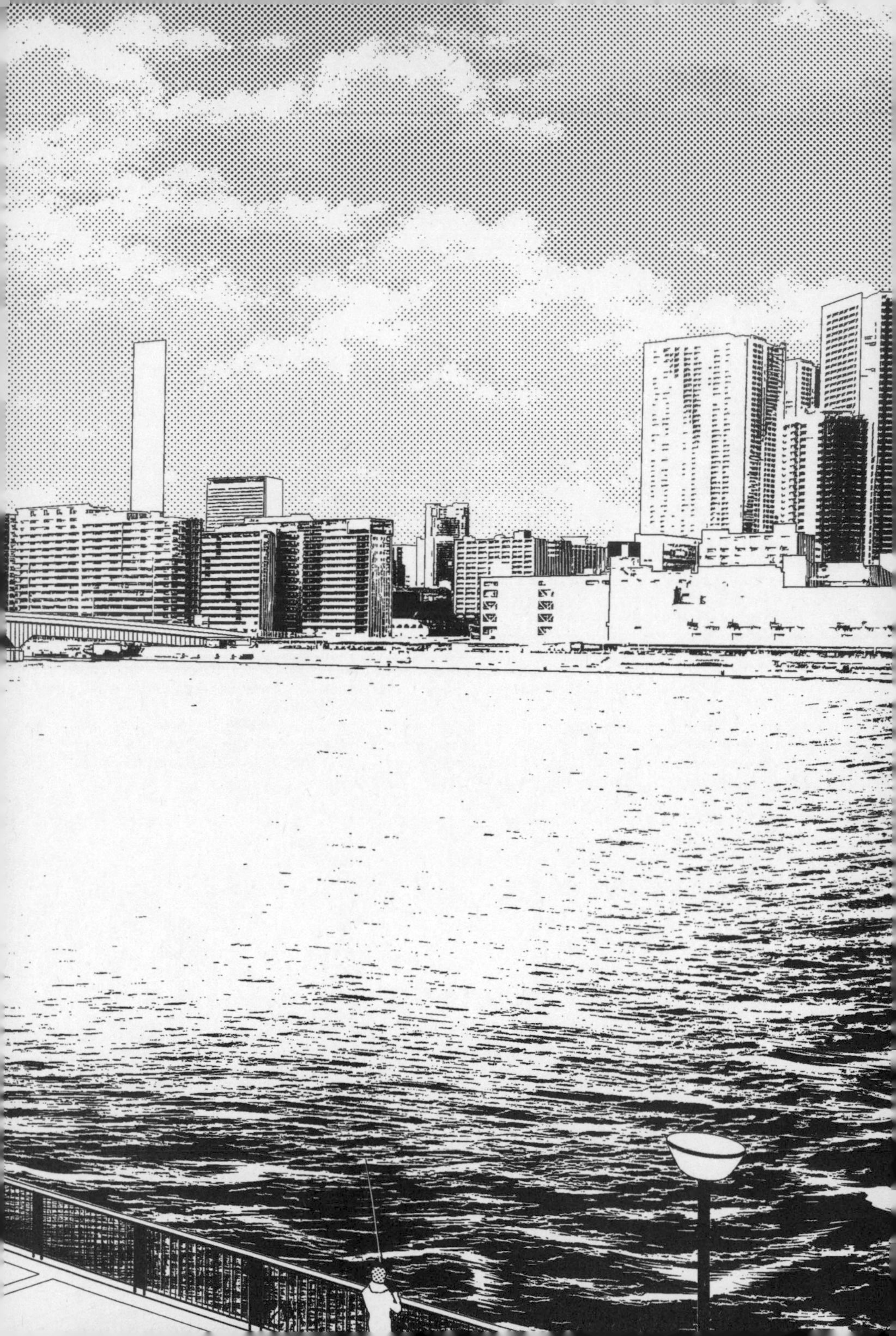

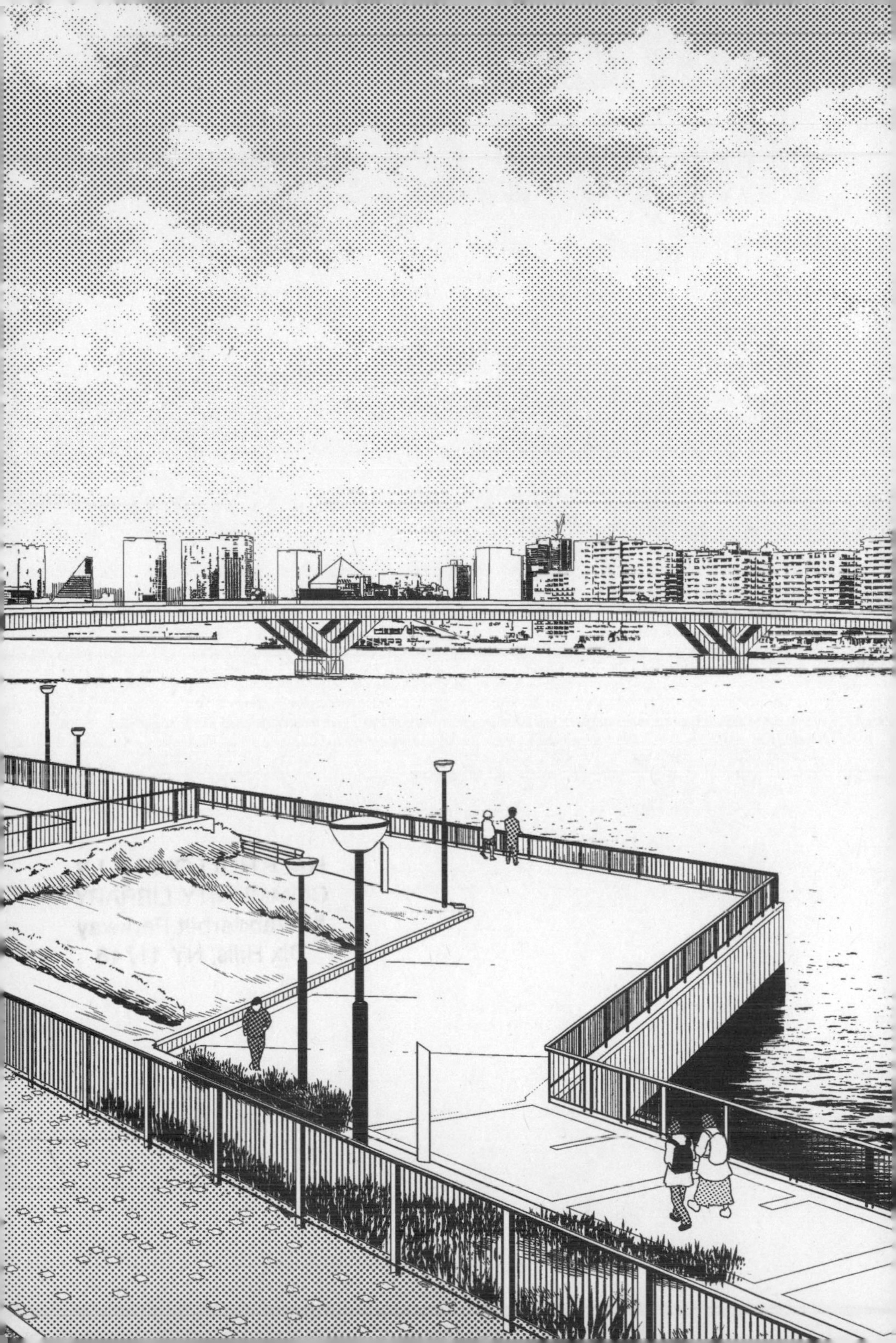

RUN ON YOUR NEW LEGS 3

WATARU MIDORI

TRANSLATION: Caleb Cook • **LETTERING:** Abigail Blackman

ATARASHII ASHI DE KAKENUKERO. Vol. 3
by Wataru MIDORI
© 2020 Wataru MIDORI
All rights reserved.
Original Japanese edition published by SHOGAKUKAN.
English translation rights in the United States of America, Canada, the United Kingdom, Ireland, Australia and New Zealand arranged with SHOGAKUKAN through Tuttle-Mori Agency, Inc.

Original Cover Design: Yoko AKUTA

English translation © 2022 by Yen Press, LLC

Yen Press
150 West 30th Street, 19th Floor
New York, NY 10001

Visit us at yenpress.com
facebook.com/yenpress
twitter.com/yenpress
yenpress.tumblr.com
instagram.com/yenpress

First Yen Press Edition: December 2022
Edited by Abigail Blackman & Yen Press Editorial: Carl Li
Designed by Yen Press Design: Liz Parlett, Wendy Chan

Yen Press is an imprint of Yen Press, LLC.
The Yen Press name and logo are trademarks of Yen Press, LLC.

The publisher is not responsible for websites (or their content) that are not owned by the publisher.

Library of Congress Control Number: 2021951359

ISBNs: 978-1-9753-3902-9 (paperback)
       978-1-9753-4571-6 (ebook)

10 9 8 7 6 5 4 3 2 1

WOR

Printed in the United States of America